CONTEMPORARY
CONTINENTAL
PHILOSOPHY

Dimensions of Philosophy Series
Norman Daniels and Keith Lehrer, Editors

CONTEMPORARY CONTINENTAL PHILOSOPHY

Robert D'Amico

UNIVERSITY OF FLORIDA, GAINESVILLE

Westview Press
A Member of the Perseus Books Group

Dimensions of Philosophy

Copyright © 1999 by Westview Press, A Member of the Perseus Books Group

Published in 1999 in the United States of America by Westview Press, 5500 Central Avenue, Boulder, Colorado 80301-2877, and in the United Kingdom by Westview Press, 12 Hid's Copse Road, Cumnor Hill, Oxford OX2 9JJ

Library of Congress Cataloging-in-Publication Data
D'Amico, Robert.
    Contemporary continental philosophy / Robert D'Amico.
       p.   cm. — (Dimensions of philosophy series)
    Includes bibliographical references and index.
    ISBN 0-8133-3221-4 (hc.) — ISBN 0-8133-3222-2 (pbk.)
    1. Philosophy, Modern—20th century.   2. Philosophy,
European—20th century.   I. Title.   II. Series.
B804.D28   1999
190'.9'04—dc21   98-37834
                                                                        CIP

The paper used in this publication meets the requirements of the American National Standard for Permanence of Paper for Printed Library Materials Z39.48-1984.

10   9   8   7   6   5   4   3   2   1

CONTENTS

INTRODUCTION

In 1949 Gilbert Ryle published *The Concept of Mind,* a work that defined for the postwar generation the very idea of analytic philosophy. Some twenty years earlier Ryle had reviewed Martin Heidegger's *Being and Time,* which defined the future of continental philosophy for its audience, and noted in his review some agreement with Heidegger over how a latent "Cartesianism" in philosophy led to the so-called mind-body problem.[1] Ryle's review predates, therefore, the notion that there are two distinct and incommensurate philosophical traditions in the twentieth century.

I begin with this comment not only to recognize Ryle's breadth of philosophical interests, all too rare these days, but to introduce the topic of this book by stressing, now in contrast with him, how very different were these two philosophical works, even given some common aims; it is as though an era, not twenty years, separated them.

Ryle's book begins with an "official doctrine" about minds, prevalent among theorists and laypersons alike, whose central principles Ryle aims to challenge:

> Such in outline is the official theory. I shall often speak of it, with deliberate abusiveness, as "the dogma of the Ghost in the machine." I hope to prove that it is entirely false, and false not in detail but in principle. It is not merely an assemblage of particular mistakes. It is one big mistake and a mistake of a special kind. It is, namely, a category-mistake. . . .The dogma is therefore a philosopher's myth. In attempting to explode the myth I shall probably be taken to be denying well-known facts about . . . mental life . . . and my plea that I aim at doing nothing more than rectify the logic of mental-conduct concepts will probably be disallowed as mere subterfuge.[2]

Heidegger also begins challenging a prejudice:

> The question to be *formulated* is about the meaning of being . . . the average, vague understanding of being can be permeated by traditional theories and opinions about being in such a way that these theories, as the sources of the prevailing understanding, remain hidden. What is sought in the question of being is not completely unfamiliar, although it is at first totally ungraspable. What is *asked about* in the question to be elaborated is being, that which de-

termines beings as beings, that in terms of which beings have already been understood no matter how they are discussed. The being of beings "is" itself not
a being. . . . Hence, what is to be *ascertained,* the meaning of being, will require its own conceptualization, which again is essentially distinct from the
concepts in which beings receive their determination of meaning.[3]

The contrast between these passages is not just stylistic, though they exemplify British humor versus Germanic solemnity. Behind these words, behind even some agreement about whom to criticize and why, there lie
deeply different understandings of the discipline of philosophy, its central
concerns, and its very purpose.

This book details how the continental philosophical tradition developed
in the twentieth century in such a philosophically distinct manner. It is neither a purely historical study, however, nor a partisan defense or attack. I
will not document how this tradition emerged from various critical reactions to nineteenth-century philosophy. Even where I briefly discuss influ-
ences, my aim is thematic, not synoptic. I wish to focus on the central
philosophical ideas, specifically the core issues in epistemology and ontology, that constitute this tradition or approach as distinct. Concerns of
length and emphasis preclude discussing ethics, political philosophy, or aesthetics. Before clarifying what I mean by writing a nonpartisan study, I
want to emphasize how I understand this study's focus by mentioning two
philosophers I exclude.

Nicolai Hartmann was a major German philosopher of his day and remained so even after Edmund Husserl's work eclipsed philosophical discussion in Europe. Further, Hartmann's defense of the study of ontology and
philosophical realism relates to themes discussed in this book. But, as often
happens in the history of philosophy, he is virtually unread today (except
by specialists) and simply does not speak to any contemporary understanding of these issues. Thus when I say this study is not a historical survey, I
mean that though some of those I discuss were familiar with Hartmann's
work, Hartmann is not part of the core conception of continental philosophy as a distinct tradition. I do not think Hartmann belongs to what
philosophers, in either tradition today, consider the procedures or tasks of
philosophy. Whether philosophers are right to ignore him and whether his
status might someday change is not my concern here.

In contrast with the lack of interest in Hartmann, there have been a number of recent studies of the French philosopher and theologian Emmanuel
Levinas. Until these appeared, he would have been considered a relatively
minor commentator on Martin Heidegger. Jacques Derrida, a figure who
does enter this study, proclaimed Levinas's importance in a 1964 essay.
Subsequently, and likely due to Derrida's growing influence far beyond philosophy, Levinas has been treated as overlooked and significant. I confess

that I cannot see the innovative aspects of his work as found by others and, even if I could, Levinas's theology and ethics (even given the very broad conception he favors) fall outside the compass of this study. Whatever the continental philosophical tradition is today and whether it constitutes a distinct philosophical tradition with a future does not depend, in my view, on understanding Levinas; at least it does not depend on it in the same way that it does on understanding Husserl.

I am aware that such judgments, with the passing of time, may be found wanting in both detail and emphasis. It will be apparent, for instance, that Jean-Paul Sartre, who would have loomed especially large in a book such as this one some twenty or thirty years ago, shrinks quite considerably in my study. But I can only carry out such a project as I see it, making whatever case I can for these decisions. In the end, however, such judgments fall where they may.

That comment brings me to clarifying why I say my aim is not to produce a partisan account either for or against this tradition as philosophy. I do not mean that by being nonpartisan all I aim at is one of those endless expository productions in which positions are moved on and off stage for their allotted summaries (though I cannot say I wholly avoid that grueling and tiresome effect). As I hope will quickly emerge, this study is meant to be a critical discussion of these philosophical ideas. Summaries of philosophical issues die on the page, at least in my experience, if they are not animated by some effort to explore their defenses and problems beyond what amounts to simply paraphrasing the original. I also believe that a reader, even if the reader is finally led to reject my questions, objections, or comments as misdirected, arrives at a surer grasp of the issues in virtue of thinking through these criticisms or doubts.

What I do mean by being nonpartisan is that I neither defend this tradition's philosophical superiority over analytic philosophy nor find it wanting in comparison.[4] (Neither of these labels is, of course, very precise, but I use them in roughly the same way everybody else does. I do, however, avoid the even more misleading "Anglo-American philosophy.") Though I consider the similarities in philosophical strategies and problems between them, comparative judgments are, in effect, suspended for much of the book. In my expositions I appeal to philosophers from either tradition if I think their views help focus the discussion, but my use is explicative, not comparative. In the conclusion to this study I will assess these traditions as competitors, albeit very briefly, and discuss my view of the future of continental philosophy. But I am confident that the critical expositions, which are the book's aim and, I hope, main contribution, are independent of those specific conclusions.

I had a final motivation for attempting such a book. Many of the figures and ideas discussed in this book have become, oddly enough, more widely read and even familiar to nonacademic audiences than their analytic counterparts. I do not want to speculate on the reasons for this state of affairs, though I think it simply is related to the increasingly technical character of some analytic philosophy along with the increasingly literary veneer of some continental philosophy. I call it odd because continental philosophers are, on the whole, forbidding and extremely difficult to read or understand. As can be noted from the comparison that begins this introduction, it is a tradition that favors a kind of "high," obscure diction, if I may put it that way, unwelcoming to outsiders—often intentionally so, I believe.

The coincidence of a growing interest in these writers by those in many disciplines, some only distantly related to philosophy, and the kind of philosophy produced in this tradition has resulted in confusing and extremely contentious interpretations and debates. A book such as this one provides readers with at least some tools for both debating and critically assessing the many contending and adventuresome accounts of these ideas that flourish in the secondary literature. I believe that this pedagogic aim is not unrelated to my overriding conception, repeated in the conclusion, that there is more to the continental tradition in its core conception of philosophy and in its contributions than the many popular and partisan accounts serve to make clear.

The structure of the book allows chapters to be read separately from each other, though there are interconnected themes, and I often refer readers to discussions in other chapters. The central themes of the book are in Chapters 1 and 2, covering Edmund Husserl and Martin Heidegger, respectively. Jean-Paul Sartre and Maurice Merleau-Ponty are also discussed in those two chapters, but only within the compass of the central figures in this tradition, Husserl and Heidegger. Chapters 3, 4, and 5 are, in contrast, more thematically organized, and I have chosen what I consider the central or more philosophically relevant representatives. The Conclusion lifts the suspended judgment about the continental tradition in the twentieth century and considers it in comparison with analytic philosophy and in terms of its future as a philosophical tradition. For readers' convenience, at the end of each chapter is a list of the main works cited in that chapter with their title abbreviations. In lieu of providing a complete bibliography, which would neither be practical nor suit the nature of this study, each chapter ends with Suggested Readings.[5]

Notes

1. Gilbert Ryle, "Heidegger's *Sein und Zeit*," in *Collected Papers,* vol. 1 (London: Hutchinson, 1971), pp. 197–214. "Heidegger imposes on himself the hard task of coining, and on us the alarming task of understanding, a completely new vo-

cabulary of terms—mostly many-barreled compounds of everyday 'nursery' words and phrases—made to denote roots and stems of Meaning more primitive than those in which Plato, Aristotle, and subsequent scientists and philosophers have so taught us to talk and think, that we, by the strong force of habit, have come to regard as ultimate and pivotal ideas which are in fact composite and derivative" (p. 206).

2. Gilbert Ryle, *The Concept of Mind* (New York: Barnes & Noble, 1949), p. 13.

3. Martin Heidegger, *Being and Time*, trans. Joan Stambaugh (Albany: State University of New York Press, 1996), pp. 4–5.

4. Bertrand Russell and Edmund Husserl, to mention two unquestionably major philosophers of the early twentieth century and the originators of what are now claimed to be distinct traditions, knew each other's work and would have thought it odd to be identified in geographically and thematically separate traditions. Therefore this book raises the question, as we come to the end of the twentieth century, why philosophers came to have the conception of their discipline that they now do and whether it will survive into the next century.

5. I remain uncertain, even now, that a century of philosophical activity can be captured in this manner. But the result, however limited, would not exist at all if Spencer Carr, former editor at Westview Press, had not convinced me, and I am still not sure exactly how, that such a book could and should be written. During its preparation Barry Smith and Georgia Warnke generously gave their time reading earlier drafts and making valuable suggestions. Sarah Warner saw the project through the editorial process, and Ann Moru provided me with invaluable assistance in editing its final version. Anne Glasgow patiently saw me through all of the above.

1

PHENOMENOLOGY

Edmund Husserl came to intellectual maturity at a time when philosophy was coming to be viewed with considerable disdain and suspicion. This discredit extended not only to the way philosophy had been traditionally written and discussed, especially in the worst of its "Romantic excess" (as Husserl called it) among the German idealists, but to the very purpose of philosophy as a subject matter, whatever its style. Husserl's generation had begun to think of philosophers as failed scientists at best and charlatans at worst. In the late nineteenth and early twentieth centuries, the fields of psychology, logic, and mathematics reached levels of development that were assumed to eclipse any claim by philosophy to universal inquiry. For example, Franz Brentano, Husserl's teacher, debunked the philosophical tradition in his 1889 lecture "On the Concept of Truth":

> I consider Kant's entire philosophy a confusion, and one which gave rise to even greater mistakes, and which, finally, led to complete philosophical chaos. I do believe that I learned a great deal from Kant; I learned, however, not what he wanted to teach me, but, above all, how seductive for the philosophical public, and how deceptive, is the fame which the history of philosophy has tied to names. Every man who has made history must have had a powerful personality; but in any particular case the question will remain whether the influence of the personality was beneficial or disastrous, and whether we do well to make him our ideal and our master.[1]

Though Husserl would come to think more highly of Kant than did Brentano, this passage emphasizes the kind of break with the authority of the philosophical tradition that was no doubt liberating for a young, ambitious scholar such as Husserl. Husserl's later reformatory project for philosophy was predicated on the dismal failure of the philosophical tradition to solve, let alone clearly state, its basic problems. The endless debates and ever shifting vocabularies of both eighteenth- and nineteenth-century philosophy struck Husserl as symptomatic of deep confusions and unexamined assumptions that were eroding what he continued to consider, in spite of his teacher's doubts, an irreplaceable and important discipline. He saw the perpetuation of this state of confusion as not only weakening philosophy, but encouraging dogmatism in the sciences, a development Husserl feared would ultimately halt scientific progress and foster irrationalism.[2] These fears were especially strong toward the end of his life when he warned that "specialized science" and the "fashionable degenerations of philosophy into irrationalistic busy-work" would fully discredit the idea of "philosophy as the ultimately grounding and universal science" (Crisis 197).

Husserl sought to conserve the "inextinguishable idea of philosophy" while accepting, in large part, contemporary criticisms of traditional philosophy. To preserve philosophy in this way without repeating traditional failure, Husserl pursued two aims. First, he proposed a methodology for philosophical research, which he called alternatively phenomenology, the phenomenological reduction, or transcendental phenomenology, capable of reaching agreement on and resolving long-standing philosophical disputes. In his view, a strict methodology was the key to rescuing philosophy from endless clashes of speculative systems, rhetorical flourishes, and the appeal to unexamined prejudices and assumptions. Lacking methodological reform, philosophical debate remains sterile and pointless. If there were no agreed upon procedures for settling philosophical disputes, philosophers would continue to follow their mere whims.

Second, Husserl held, now clashing with the mood of his contemporaries, that philosophical questions could *not* be replaced by further scientific inquiry. Specifically, philosophy could not be eliminated by any future science of psychology. Husserl thus found it necessary to defend what he considered the essential task of philosophy (though not of course as traditionally pursued) and in addition, as his thinking matured, philosophical idealism.

Though Husserl's dense, jargon-laden prose makes it difficult, it is important to keep the following topics distinct when critically examining his views. First, much of Husserl's writing is preparatory to philosophical inquiry and is explicitly neutral between competing philosophical views.[3] Second, Husserl often mounts a defense of the entire enterprise of philosophy against what he calls "naturalism," his general term for efforts to replace philosophy by scientific explanation. But the argument that philosophical problems persist in spite of scientific successes, or that naturalism fails to understand its own philosophical underpinnings, does not immediately suggest which philosophical position one ought to defend.

Finally, there are those writings in which Husserl defends a version of transcendental idealism, a view he contrasts with past and present philosophies. Though these arguments are partisan, unlike the preparatory discussions, Husserl does not present transcendental idealism as challenging the empirical claims of either common sense or the sciences.

If the different intent of these three contexts is not kept in view, especially with regard to the relation between philosophy and science, Husserl's already complex effort becomes hopelessly muddled and confused. For example, Husserl is not, in any literal sense, a critic of the sciences, an antirationalist, or an idealist in the traditional sense of that term.[4] Husserl's methodological strategy, which I will discuss at length below, is meant to uncover philosophical assumptions in the way science has been understood, but not to compete with or replace the sciences; nor does he propose, as he has been widely misread, a new scientific method; nor are his criticisms of naturalism support for some religious, mystical, or moral conception of nature. Husserl is a critic of naturalism because of its implied philosophy of science, not because he believes science is either dangerous or inadequate to the task of comprehending the natural world. Selective or elliptical quotations, however, contribute to such misinterpretations, which are reinforced, unfortunately, by Husserl's tendency toward careless and confusing presentations of his main ideas.

In this chapter I begin with Husserl's general defense of philosophy, a position I think has relevance for current philosophy, even among those unaware of Husserl's work. The second part of this chapter concerns Husserl's method and his excessively technical vocabulary. In the third part I discuss what he means by transcendental idealism. I characterize Husserl as an epistemological "internalist," a current term for characterizing an approach to the theory of knowledge since Descartes. The philosophical project of pure, internal inquiry is one Husserl embraces and attempts to defend against its critics.[5]

Husserl's idealism came under sustained criticism by many of his followers. The chapter concludes with these criticisms, focusing primarily on Maurice Merleau-Ponty. A discussion of Husserl's critical reaction to cultural and historical relativism, including comments on his late writings, are found in the fourth part.

The Inextinguishable Task

Husserl defended a strict distinction between philosophical questions and empirical questions about the natural world. He argued that confusing philosophical with scientific questions generated "naive" (the adjective Husserl favored) philosophical positions. The failure to understand the autonomy of philosophy and the attempt to seek its elimination by science were symptoms of what Husserl called an intellectual and cultural crisis.

The basic distinction between empirical and philosophical questions has been a leitmotif of twentieth-century philosophy. Echoes of it, with diverse implications, can be heard in such major thinkers of Husserl's generation as Bertrand Russell, Rudolf Carnap, G. E. Moore, Ludwig Wittgenstein, and William James. This distinction, it has been argued, rests upon a more basic distinction between analytic and synthetic claims, or upon the a posteriori/a priori distinction. This entire network of distinctions has, however, been under sustained attack in much of current philosophy.[6] Weakening the distinction between analytic and empirical claims is often credited with weakening confidence in the entire idea of an autonomous philosophical subject matter and thereby supporting some form of naturalism.

Husserl never doubted the clarity of this central distinction and upon it he proclaimed the "dream" of philosophy becoming a "rigorous science."[7] A robust and straightforward statement of this distinction, unusual for Husserl, occurs in his programmatic essay "Philosophy as a Rigorous Science." Husserl argues there that the failure to distinguish clearly between what is empirical and what is a matter of a priori necessity concerning knowledge is at the root of both cultural and theoretical confusions, confusions a properly understood philosophy would dispel.

Husserl, using the language of Kant, states the distinction as that between what can be known as a contingent matter of fact about the world—what is synthetic, a posteriori, or experiential—and that which can be known necessarily, purely as a matter of the concepts involved—what is analytic, a priori, or "pure," the last a term he often uses. These essential aspects of experience discovered by philosophical reflection constrain any possible empirical inquiries, and therefore, like mathematics, philosophy precedes factual inquiry. Philosophical topics concern a priori necessities of experience and thus stand apart from disputes about contingent matters of fact.[8]

Husserl was aware of how seductive it was to run roughshod over this distinction. In his earliest major publication, *The Philosophy of Arithmetic*, he had entertained the possibility of a type of empirical, psychological inquiry into the formal structures of mathematics and arithmetic. Though precisely what Husserl claimed in that early work about psychology is beyond the scope of this discussion, he came to see his early efforts as implicitly collapsing the formal necessity of arithmetic relations into whatever were contingent features of how our minds operate and function.

Husserl quickly abandoned this early project, though he did not entirely abandon some results of that work and its overall aim, and concluded that no possible discovery in psychology would result in a situation in which what were previously thought to be problems in arithmetic suddenly revealed themselves as those of experimental psychology. Mathematics does not await breakthroughs in cognitive psychology. In flirting with that possibility, even if he did not exhibit the crude errors of a Millian psychologist on this topic, Husserl had fallen prey to confusions, betraying thereby an early philosophical "naïveté."

The "absurdities" Husserl warns of arise because the a priori/a posteriori distinction preserves what he considers an irreducible difference in the type of knowledge involved. The certainty and indubitability of mathematics is due to its truths depending only on what Husserl calls "pure" relations of meaning. Whatever knowledge is gained of psychology or human neurophysiology is, in contrast, contingent and empirical. Even if these discoveries concern regularities, they do not concern whatever *must* be the case, as in the pure, essential necessities, but whatever as a matter of fact happens to be the case, given the contingent features of the natural world.

The facts of the natural world cannot be converted into the foundation of formal or conceptual necessity. That insight may have been Husserl's most important intellectual breakthrough. To speak of the formal or conceptual necessity as though it were a species of causation, for instance, is a prime example of what he dismisses as an "absurd" confusion.

Husserl will furthermore hold, as discussed below, that these conceptual or meaningful necessities extend to how the world is presented phenomenally in any mental experience whatsoever. Hence, by the phrase "mental experience" Husserl is not restricting himself to neurological and psychological facts about human experience. There is rather a pure form of any possible experience, and with regard to the term "phenomena" he asserts: "To attribute a nature to phenomena, to investigate their component parts, their causal connections—that is pure absurdity, no better than if one wanted to ask about the causal properties, connections, etc., of numbers. It is the absurdity of naturalizing something whose essence excludes the kind of being that nature has" (PRS 106).

Whether philosophy could be subsumed under or replaced by inquiry in the sciences resolves, for Husserl, into the question of whether reason can be naturalized.[9] What does that additional question mean? Husserl uses the term "naturalism" as a characterization of the underlying conceptions of the sciences and the "common sense conception of the world" (or perhaps, more accurately, the idea of common sense as shaped by the modern scientific revolution). The natural attitude views the world as a collection of objects and physical processes whose properties, dispositions, and regularities can be captured by scientific laws (and thus partly explained, controlled, and predicted). This physicalist picture extends, in principle, to psychology and sociology, in which psychophysical beings and complex social or institutional objects also exhibit lawlike regularities. In that sense, naturalism is a summary of the results of a long history of empirical inquiry. It is also not itself a philosophical claim about the world.

Husserl, however, also uses the term "naturalism" to refer to the protophilosophical views that emerge within this general picture of the natural world. Such views range from those held implicitly within untutored common sense (as in the spontaneous opinions of laypersons or scientists) to explicit philosophical positions such as logical positivism (which Husserl calls "sensation-monism") and pragmatism. All these diverse accounts of science and its supremacy over competitors share, in Husserl's opinion, the key philosophical assumption that consciousness, and thus reason itself, can be studied in the same manner as any other natural object and thereby explained as processes falling under ideal scientific laws. These otherwise diverse positions then agree in treating philosophical inquiry as obsolete and converting the above empirical results into some prototype of a scientific study of epistemology and reason.

This discussion requires a brief warning or digression before I proceed with Husserl's explicit arguments against the project of naturalizing reason and consciousness. It would be wrong to leap to the conclusion that Husserl, by virtue of his opposition to the above, believes that consciousness, and whatever it is that physically makes it possible for humans to reason, *cannot* be studied by the natural sciences or that consciousness is *not* a natural phenomena. In fact, Husserl makes clear in numerous passages that he considers human beings natural, psychophysical beings whose psychological states are caused by or realized in their neurophysiological states. Human behavior and its dispositions, like any natural objects, are subsumable under scientific laws in his view, and thus consciousness, in that sense, can be an object of scientific study like any other object.

But when Husserl asks whether reason can be naturalized, he is not asking whether psychological studies of reasoning are possible. Husserl's question is epistemological, not empirical. The possibility of naturalizing reason concerns, then, a philosophical position with regard to reason. He views the persistent effort to dismiss the difference between these two questions as the root of naturalism's illusory escape from philosophical quandaries.

In unintentionally reinforcing this illusion, some readers of Husserl have mistaken his discussion of this philosophical problem for a dispute about the scientific status of psychology, as though Husserl were arguing that a science of human behavior was impossible. But taking a stance on the future of psychology or inventing a new method for psychology is as alien to Husserl's intent as it would be to think he intends to reinvent physics as a result of the same philosophical inadequacies of naturalism. This misreading of Husserl is simply a failure to make the distinctions he laboriously defends.

> Precisely in the energy with which naturalism seeks to realize the principle of scientific rigor in all the spheres of natural and spirit, in theory and practice, and in the energy with which naturalism seeks to solve the philosophical problems of being and value ... *lies its merit and the major part of its strength in our era* [emphasis added]. There is, perhaps, in all modern life no more powerfully, more irresistibly progressing idea than that of science. *Nothing will hinder its victorious advance* [emphasis added] ... there belong

in the domain of strict science all the theoretical, axiological, and practical ideals that naturalism, by giving them a new empirical meaning, at the same time falsifies. (PRS 83)

What this passage stresses is a distinction between scientific naturalism per se and naturalism as a philosophy of science. He holds that the success, extension, respect for, and influence of the sciences are proper. The problem lies in naturalism's philosophical account of this scientific success and influence, a problem Husserl locates with the notion of "empirical meaning."

Since Husserl's dispute is with philosophical naturalism (not with the sciences per se), it is not a dispute about matters of evidence, scientific method, or the possibility of lawlike regularities. Husserl challenges what he considers an unexamined or naive view of philosophy, not the results of the scientific method. Husserl can therefore praise the extension of science into psychology at the same time that he rejects "psychologism" as pseudo-epistemology.

What concerns Husserl is not the spread of scientific inquiry from the natural to the sociopsychological worlds, but the accompanying defense of empirical realism, a theory of knowledge masquerading as empirical science. Research into the nature of psychophysical being, as Husserl calls it, provides information and evidence concerning the natural world, as does all proper science. But it both raises and leaves unresolved, as do all sciences, philosophical problems, problems for which naturalism is either one among many philosophical responses, to be judged strictly on those terms, or a confusion of philosophical and scientific problems.

Husserl claims he has "decisive arguments to prove that physical natural science cannot be philosophy" (PRS 86). He admits that science, like philosophy, can be "critical" of experience by questioning evidence, rejecting isolated experiences, and demanding methodical support for knowledge claims. Also science, like philosophy, presupposes the grasp of fundamental concepts of truth, objectivity, and evidence. But the critical stance of science is not sufficiently "radical." Science cannot, as a discipline, question deep, fundamental assumptions concerning the possibility of knowledge. Husserl indicates the kind of questions he considers philosophical, genuinely radical, and outside the scope of science.

How can experience as consciousness give or contact an object? How can experiences be mutually legitimated or corrected by means of each other, and not merely replace each other or confirm each other subjectively? . . . How is natural science comprehensible in absolutely every case, to the extent that it pretends at every step to posit and to know a nature that is in itself—in itself in opposition to the subjective flow of consciousness? . . . It is well known that theory of knowledge is the discipline that wants to answer such questions, and

also that up to the present, despite all the thoughtfulness employed by the
greatest scholars in regard to these questions, this discipline has not answered
in a manner scientifically clear, unanimous, and decisive. (PRS 87–88)

These questions judge naturalism against traditional epistemology
(again, somewhat confusingly, Husserl employs the word "science" for
both the possible philosophical project and the empirical inquiries from
which he wishes to distinguish it). These questions are variations upon:
How is objective knowledge possible?

Husserl offers three arguments showing that philosophical questions cannot be replaced by scientific inquiry. First, Husserl claims that these "rid-
dles" about the principles of science cannot be solved by the principles of
science itself and that all attempts to investigate the theory of knowledge
through science itself lead to a vicious circle. Second, the theory of knowledge requires excluding all scientific and prescientific "existential positings." Epistemology should adopt a "veil of ignorance," to borrow John
Rawls's phrase, with regard to empirical evidence concerning the natural
world and even cognition itself, no matter how secure those results.

Third, the theory of knowledge studies mental states such as those of distinguishing, believing, classifying, picturing, and identifying. But epistemology is not concerned with the actual nature of these states or their inner
mechanisms and functions, only with their content or meaning as intentional states directed toward the world. What makes it possible, epistemologically, to represent the external world in such a way that the representation can be said to be objective or evidential is part of the meaning of these
mental activities, not a part of their contingent physical realization.

Husserl's first point is difficult to defend as stated. He does not show in the
article that a scientific investigation of the theory of knowledge (what contemporary philosophers now call "naturalized epistemology") is viciously
circular.[10] Naturalism appears no more circular than philosophy itself. Philosophy also raises questions about the objectivity and validity of knowledge
while using the concepts of validity and objectivity. If this procedure proves
limiting, it is limiting for philosophy as well as scientific naturalism.

The scientific method does adopt critical self-examination of knowledge
claims, as Husserl readily admits. Although debates within science presuppose concepts of evidence, for instance, he is not able to show, contrary to
his claim, that it would be countersensical or logically improper for the sciences to proceed by criticizing (or clarifying) these very concepts even while
using the scientific method.

Husserl's point about circularity may simply reflect his assumption of the
distinction between philosophical epistemology and scientific, empirical research. But that distinction is precisely what is at issue. We already saw
above that Husserl often argues circularly himself. He defends the auton-

omy of philosophy by, in effect, reiterating that philosophical and scientific questions are distinct. By merely assuming the distinction, however, Husserl has also neither shown that empirical studies of knowledge are viciously circular nor provided a "decisive reason" for the distinction in question.

The second argument concerns Husserl's methodological directive to suspend or bracket all ontological commitments before reflecting on epistemology. (This methodical device will be discussed in greater detail below.) Husserl does have an important strategic point here. Scientific research often treats its ontological commitments as obvious or uncontroversial, and such unexamined assumptions could very well contaminate the subsequent epistemological claim of objectivity or evidential support for it within naturalism.

Husserl, as pointed out, allows that the sciences are capable of suspending judgment about "existential positings." Scientific theories "bracket" such assumptions when treating themselves and any competitors as merely hypothetical accounts of phenomena. Such a device, similar in ways to Husserl's technique of reduction to be discussed below, allows for examining the implications of a theory, for instance, without simultaneously assuming the reality of the claims made within that theory. But even if he could show that the sciences were unable to examine all their ontological commitments in this way, he does not demonstrate how that failure is *necessarily* tied to the device of hypothetical reasoning or why it could not be carried through by the sciences, given sufficient care and attention.

With respect to the third point, Husserl makes his strongest argument, though he does not fully develop it in this essay. The natural world presupposed in scientific and prescientific inquiry is an empirically realistic world. It is a world of real, external objects given in experience. But for that world of objects to be given in experience, it is necessarily the case, for instance, that there be a distinction between the subjective state of recognition and the objectivity presented to it. To have an experience at all is necessarily, prior to and independent of that particular experience, to have this distinction between the experienced object and the act of experiencing it. For there to be a world of experience there must be, not factually but conceptually, a "directedness toward objects." This is a feature of experience Husserl calls "intentionality"; it will be the focus of the next section.

This feature of experience is what Husserl calls a matter of meaning for objectivity in general. Object-directedness is not, then, a contingent feature of some experience or even a hypothesis about the nature of experience in some future physiological psychology. Intentionality concerns what makes any form of experience possible, and its formal study occurs apart from determining whatever are the empirical facts about how experience is actually (but then contingently) realized psychologically and physiologically for the natural world such as it is.

The task of epistemology, in Husserl's language, is then to study the "form of all experience," a study alien to any particular science. What the sciences investigate and make evidential claims about presupposes (conceptually, or "formally" as Husserl prefers to state it) this "form of all experience." Thus whether judgments made concerning experience are objective or even meaningful, understood as independent of any and all facts concerning the nature of experience, is a wholly improper and even impossible problem for the sciences to raise. What science must presuppose is simply that the world is given in experience in this fashion. This assumption admits of clarification only by shifting to a separate and distinct mode of investigation.

> Every type of object that is to be the object of a rational proposition, of a prescientific and then a scientific cognition, must manifest itself in knowledge, thus in consciousness itself, and it must permit being brought to givenness, in accord with the sense of all knowledge. All types of consciousness, in the way they are, so to speak, teleologically ordered under the title of knowledge and, even more, in the way they are grouped according to the various object categories—considered as the groups of cognitive functions that especially correspond to these categories—must permit being studied in their essential connection and in their relation back to the forms of the consciousness of givenness belonging to them. The sense of the question concerning legitimacy, which is to be put to all cognitive acts, must admit of being understood, the essence of grounded legitimation and that of ideal groundableness or validity must admit of being fully clarified, in this manner—and with respect to all levels of cognition, including the highest, that of scientific cognition. (PRS 90)

Husserl agrees, then, with naturalism in its confidence that humans acquire knowledge through experience and that knowledge acquisition must require specific physiological mechanisms of some sort. But the task of epistemology is not one of ascertaining what the physical realization of such an ability actually is. The actual mechanism of intentionality is, for example, a possible and legitimate object of scientific inquiry, but results from it would not affect the study of the meaning of intentional objects, as psychology is irrelevant to the study of arithmetic. The mechanism of intentionality, whatever it is, remains then irrelevant to epistemology. As Husserl puts it, even a godlike control over the natural world would provide no deeper access to determining the meaning of experience as evidential: "Even an absolute God cannot create a 'feeling of evidence' that absolutely guarantees the being of Nature—or, in a better formulation, a self-contained process of external experience that, no matter how different it might conceivably be from 'our' sensuous experience, would give something—itself apodictically and adequately" (FTL 284).

Hence, empirical naturalism is not, as it presents itself, the abolition of philosophical speculation; it *is* philosophical speculation, and it rests upon a significant assumption concerning the naturalization of meaning.

Such a defense of science ultimately betrays the aim of science, and once its presuppositions are made explicit, the spell of naturalism will be finally broken.

Against Born Dogmatists

I now turn to what Husserl considered his major contribution to the future of philosophy.[11] Husserl's claim to have crafted a philosophical method should be approached first by discussing the concept of intentionality, already introduced above. Intentionality is not only the central theme in Husserl's return to philosophy after his flirtation with psychology, but it has become a central theme in twentieth-century philosophy. He inherited the concept from Franz Brentano.

Though Husserl always called Brentano his only real teacher, he came to reject Brentano's conception upon reaching philosophical independence. Late in his life he wrote to Marvin Farber, "Even though I began in my youth as an enthusiastic admirer of Brentano, I must admit I deluded myself, for too long, and in a way hard to understand now, into believing that I was a co-worker on his philosophy ... though his psychology is nothing less than a science of intentionality, *the proper problems of intentionality never dawned upon him.*"[12] Husserl's reexamination of the concept of intentionality is, in my view, one of his major contributions to the philosophy of mind and language.

Intentionality, Brentano claimed, was the intrinsic feature of all mental life and thus the exclusive subject matter of psychology, the "mark of the mental" as it has come to be called. He coined the term to name the property of referring to or standing for something in the external world or having in the mind a thought about some state of affairs in the world. Brentano thought that the feature of intentionality differentiated the mind from the rest of the physical world and, correlatively, psychology from the natural sciences.

> Every mental phenomenon is characterized by what the Scholastics of the Middle Ages called the intentional (or mental) inexistence of an object, and what we might call, though not wholly unambiguously, reference to a content, direction toward an object (which is not to be understood here as meaning a thing), or immanent objectivity. Every mental phenomenon includes something as object within itself, although they do not all do so in the same way. In presentation, something is presented, in judgement something is affirmed or denied, in love loved, in hate hated, in desire desired and so on. This intentional inexistence is characteristic exclusively of mental phenomena. No physical phenomenon exhibits anything like it. We can, therefore, define mental phenomena by saying that they are those phenomena which contain an object intentionally within themselves.[13]

Psychology studies this property of reference, aboutness, or content as present internally within consciousness.

> The unity of consciousness, as we know with evidence through inner perception, consists in the fact that all mental phenomena which occur within us simultaneously such as seeing and hearing, thinking, judging and reasoning, loving and hating, desiring and shunning, etc., no matter how different they may be, all belong to one unitary reality only if they are inwardly perceived as existing together. They constitute phenomenal parts of a mental phenomenon, the elements of which are neither distinct things nor parts of distinct things but belong to a real unity. This is the necessary condition for the unity of consciousness, and no further conditions are required.[14]

As already mentioned, Brentano conceived of this intentional psychology as resolving some traditional philosophical disputes. However, Brentano does not envisage a science of psychology in the current sense of experimental psychology, nor does his conception of psychology countenance physiological explanations. It is, in his sense, purely descriptive.

The significant problems raised by Brentano's account of intentionality can only be briefly outlined and thus somewhat simplified here. First, as already cited, Brentano is an "internalist" about psychology, ignoring, for instance, any inquiry into causal relations or the physiological realization of these mental phenomena. His aim is descriptive—hence the use of the term "empirical"—and he treats his focus on intentionality as a return to the "facts themselves" about mental phenomena rather than speculation in psychology or philosophy. What makes intentionality the proper object with respect to this phenomenology of the mind is that it functions as it does whether what it represents actually exists or not.[15]

Brentano's discussion of these inexistent intentional objects of thought suggests a two-place relation between the mind and intentional objects (excluding in this way the real, extrinsic objects). Though this approach to the mind was meant to capture the "mark of the mental," Brentano also wanted to retain the commonsense view that the object of thought is the extrinsic object in the world that is being thought about. To meet both of these aims, however, seems to require that the intentional object, which is wholly internal, have some sort of entity-like existence (or "inexistence," as he somewhat confusingly stated it) in the mind standing in that two-place relation characterizing the nature of mental phenomena, whether there is an extrinsic object, as in normal perception, or no extrinsic object, as in the case of a hallucination or an imaginary entity.

The idea of intentionality or directedness toward an object was then forced to accommodate at least the following two features of mental life. It must allow for the possibility of thinking about things that do not exist—such as centaurs—and it must allow for representing the same state of affairs in the world in very different ways. Thus intentionality must capture the difference between perceiving and then remembering the very same state of affairs. Accounts inspired by Brentano often switch back and forth ambiguously between whether the intentional object being discussed is the actual external object of some mental act or this internal, inexistent intentional object.

For example, in a hallucination there is an intentional object, which is what the act of seeing is directed at, but obviously no external object. However, a hallucination is, by definition, a mental act of seeing not an "imaginary bloody dagger," but an actual bloody dagger; if one saw the dagger as imaginary, there would be no hallucination. Given the internalist stance that Brentano defends, an empirical psychology would study the nonexistent intentional objects of such hallucinatory mental acts. The analysis of the mental act is not, it would then appear, clarified by the concept of intentionality, because hallucinations and perceptions are in fact distinct kinds of acts, even though they may each claim to have as their intentional nonexistent object a real bloody dagger. Given that Brentano disavows any resort to speculative causal and physiological explanations of mental life, the introduction of intentionality seems, in the end, both beside the point and obscure.

Husserl concluded that these complex demands were not being met because Brentano misunderstood the fundamental notion of intentionality, even as he introduced it into both philosophy and psychology. If intentionality simply consisted of a two-place relation between a mental act and some kind of object of that mental state, then intentional analysis would be burdened with the following difficulties. When there are different representations of the same object, such as perceiving and remembering the same object, there are, given the simplest reading of Brentano's above account, distinct intentional objects for each intentional state. This account, then, makes problematic the common act of representing, in different ways, the same state of affairs in the world.

Equally worrisome, if every mental phenomenon is characterized by a distinct intentional object, then states of hallucination concerning bloody daggers, for instance, or imaginary centaurs or golden mountains, would each likewise have inexistent objects. Psychology would then require a rather extravagant ontology of inexistent intentional objects.

But this growing ontological extravagance leads to a final and most difficult problem. Even were Brentano's inexistent objects admitted as a necessary evil, it would appear that the analysis extends, in the same fashion, to the perception of the extrinsic real objects of everyday life, which Brentano began wanting to preserve against doubt. Given the above picture, then, to perceive objects is not to see the object itself, but the intentional object of a perceptual mental act. Husserl believes that the price of making Brentano's account of normal and hallucinatory experiences consistent is shadowy intentional objects doubling for real objects of normal perception.

Brentano complained bitterly of being misunderstood on these points and resisted, wisely, the notion that the intentional object was a shadowy representation of the real object. But he was nevertheless unable to carry out analyses, given the constraints on his conception of psychology, in which intentional inexistent objects and real, extrinsic objects did not become confused or irrelevant, at least in view of almost all of his followers. Many of them struggled to accommodate these difficulties while retaining what I am calling the two-place model of intentionality and therefore the idea of the intentional object's "inexistent" status.

Husserl dramatically cut through this tangled knot in such a way that he could retain the notion of intentionality while eliminating the need to posit inexistent entities. Husserl also thought his solution freed a new domain of philosophical inquiry distinct from that of psychology or any other empirical science.[16] Husserl, like Brentano, begins as a realist.

> For everyone except confused philosophers it is absolutely without question that the thing perceived in perception *is the physical thing itself*, in its own factual being, and that, when perceptions are deceptive, that signifies that they are in conflict with new perceptions, which show with certainty what is actual *in the place of* the illusory. Whatever further questions should be asked here must, in any case, be directed to the experiences concerned; by an intentional analysis of them, we can gain an (essentially universal) understanding of how an experience can, in itself, give an existent itself as experienced, and yet this existent can become cancelled. (FTL 281)

In Husserl's account, however, the intentional object is not itself in such a relation with the mind; it is, rather, the way of presenting or a way of referring to objects or states of affairs in the world. What is intrinsic and thus an essential aspect of presentation is that mental acts have a meaning or sense. (Husserl uses the term "ideal meaning" to indicate that although these senses are not physical entities or even causal features of the world, they are independent of their being expressed or thought about; they are not psychological phenomena. Husserl decided in later writings to replace the idea of an independent, nonnaturalistic meaning with the single term "noema.") "As content we take the 'sense,' of which we say that in or through it consciousness relates to something objective as 'its' something objective. ... Each noema has a '*content*,' that is to say, its 'sense,' and is related through it to 'its' *object*" (Ideas 309).

The ability to refer to or pick out some specific object is possible by virtue of the meaning, sense, content, or noema of the mental act. Therefore, this conception of intentionality, in which directedness is preserved by sense or meaning rather than by the actual or the inexistent object, is

Husserl's device for allowing intentionality to capture the two features of mental experience discussed above, avoid the dilemmas outlined in Brentano's initial approach, and serve as the foundation of Husserl's philosophical project; he thus speaks of how "the great *problems of reason*, the clarification of which within the realm of phenomenology . . . will become our aim" (Ideas 308).

Since what preserves the directedness of all of these intentional states, in Husserl's reformulation, is the noematic meaning or content, not whether there really are these objects of thought, ontological disputes do not become entangled with intentional analyses. Intentional analysis is pure conceptual analysis; it is not a prototype causal explanation, nor does it posit a mysterious "third realm" of entities somewhere between physical objects and mental states. Yet as a priori analysis, this analysis holds for all possible experience no matter what the physiological or psychological facts are.

In this way, it simply falls out of Husserl's account that intentionality holds for imaginary or hallucinatory experiences as well as normal experience. In such a case the meaning or sense is what allows for something to be referred to, presented to the mind, or even "seen" and it neither depends upon nor requires that there be an actual object being referred to. More important for Husserl, intentionality is independent of and does not simply presuppose the kind of realism he reaffirmed in the above quotation against "confused philosophers." Rather than presupposing such realism, as Brentano had conceived it, intentional analysis would, Husserl hoped, serve in the epistemological justification of knowledge.

Husserl's choice of the term "ideal object," as noted above, may have been an unnecessarily mysterious way to put his point that these senses or meanings are abstract, conceptual contents, rather than physical features of the world or the mind. It would certainly be wrong to attribute to Husserl the view that meanings are pseudo-entities. Husserl's distinction between noemata (ideal objects) and real objects echoes his more fundamental distinction, for purposes of preserving the inextinguishable task of philosophy, between empirical, causal inquiry and a priori, conceptual analysis. "The tree simpliciter can burn up, be resolved in its chemical elements, etc. But the sense—the sense *of this* perception, something belonging essentially to its essence—cannot burn up; it has no chemical elements, no forces, no real properties" (Ideas 216).

The most important point to stress for my purposes is how Husserl's introduction of the noematic content of intentional analysis leads to the "phenomenological reduction."[17] The reduction, which I will discuss next, is a way of directing our attention to only the noema of experience, not the external object; it directs analysis to experience as experience and to its purely notional content, not to any matters of fact concerning that experience.

The phenomenological reduction is possible because of the noematic correlates, as Husserl calls them, of all mental experience. They emerge in their full appearance, in their essential structure, whenever judgments are suspended concerning the nature of the extrinsic object of intentional acts. But suspending this external question about experience is not the same thing as doubting the existence of these referred objects or removing them from existence into a state of inexistence. The complete complexity of experience remains and nothing new is added. All that happens is attention shifts exclusively to meaning and content purely and without introducing any other assumption concerning the nature of the mental act.

> As phenomenologists we abstain from all such positing. But on that account we do not reject them by not "taking them as our basis," by not "joining in" them. They are indeed there, they also essentially belong to the phenomenon. Rather we contemplate them; instead of joining in them, we make them Objects, take them as component parts of the phenomenon—the positing pertaining to perception as well as its components.
> And, keeping these excludings in their clear sense, we therefore ask quite universally, then, about what is evidentially "inherent" in the whole "reduced" phenomenon. Now, inherent too precisely in perception is this: that it has its noematic sense, its "perceived as perceived," "this blooming tree there, in space"—understood with inverted commas—precisely the *correlate* belonging to the essence of phenomenologically reduced perception. Figuratively stated: the "parenthesis" undergone by perception prevents any judgement about perceived actuality. . . . But it does not prevent the judgement about the fact that perception is consciousness *of* an actuality . . . ; and it does not prevent any description of this perceptually appearing actuality as appearing with the particular ways in which it is here untended to. (Ideas 220)

The phenomenological reduction, which Husserl also often refers to with the Greek term *epochē*, is his central methodological device. Husserl has some useful, figurative language meant to capture the aim of this methodological device. He speaks of "doffing the empirical-objective robe . . . that remains unnoticed in the course of naive experience" and he uses the verb "to bracket," or as often translated "put into parentheses," to capture what happens to ordinary ontological commitments during the reduction.[18]

It is important not to be confused about Husserl's choice of the word "reduction" in view of how that term is now commonly used by philosophers. By "reduction" Husserl does not mean translating sentences that use mental predicates into sentences that use only physical predicates. The effort to purge philosophy of mentalistic language would be considered by Husserl an illicit introduction of ontological, naturalistic assumptions into the issue (namely, the naturalistic assumption that all states of the world are physical states). Nor does Husserl adopt the even more familiar usage of the term "reduction" as describing the type of dependence found in physics in which higher-level phenomena rest upon or disappear into lower-level physical states in such a way that, for example, a macroproperty such as solidity is said to reduce to its microphysical realization in a molecular structure. Husserl's reduction is neither a philosophical nor a scientific conclusion. It is a device, not a claim about the fundamental nature of the world.

The method accomplishes two aims. First, it prevents empirical, commonsense assumptions from surreptitiously influencing epistemological reflection on the nature of evidence, objectivity, or truth. Second, it forces attention, by a careful procedure, to senses, meanings, or noemata, that is, the essential structure of intentionality. Husserl often worries about the "unnaturalness" of this exercise and how readers may be misled by its similarity to, but in his view significant difference from, the epistemological strategies of Descartes, Hume, and Kant, the three philosophers Husserl read most carefully and to whose work he continually refers.

For example, though Husserl often related his procedure to what Descartes and Hume had attempted (and even named one introduction to phenomenology *Cartesian Meditations*), it would be a misunderstanding, as he continually repeats, to read him as raising skeptical doubts about the existence of the external world or reducing the external world to the subjective experience of that world, reducing its existence to that of our private *qualia*.[19] Skepticism, after all, is precisely what Husserl neutralizes or suspends, and subjectivity, if that term is used to name a characteristic of having sensations, is not Husserl's concern. Simply put, the reduction passes no judgments on the world. "I am not negating this 'world' as though I were a sophist; I am not *doubting its factual being* as though I were a skeptic; rather I am exercising the 'phenomenological *epochē*' which also *completely shuts me off from any judgement about spatiotemporal factual being*" (Ideas 61).[20]

Husserl believed this method would produce philosophical agreement because in foregoing theoretical claims, hypothetical explanations, or philosophical special pleading, it would ultimately adjudicate philosophical disputes. Husserl pictured the procedure as resolving philosophical debates in much the way that strictly empirical evidence resolves scientific disputes; phenomenology directs attention to what must at the end of the day constrain philosophizing, namely, the essential structure of any possible experience.

Although Husserl did emphasize that meanings and essential structures of intentionality are "seen" once reflective attention is directed to them, any naturalistic sense of "seeing" should not continue to attach to his comment. Husserl is not claiming that essences are seen in either the physiological or psychological sense normally associated with perception. These essences are abstract matters of conceptual and logical necessity and are "seen" as part of such reflection only when the naturalistic "cloak" of perception has been "doffed."[21]

The abstention toward existence required by the reduction thereby extends as much to psychology and the human physiology of consciousness as it does to the account of the natural world. The nature of consciousness itself is subject to the reduction, and that is why Husserl's methodical device blocks, as he often emphasizes, traditional phenomenalism. In other words, Husserl is not basing his device on a claim that a subject knows something about his or her mind or the world merely by reflecting upon it. The reflection made possible by the phenomenological reduction provides neither explanations nor privileged experiences of the world. Husserl warns his careless reader not to take what is left to reflection by the correct exercise of the reduction as the subject matter of psychology. "I with my mental life remain untouched in my existential status, regardless of whether or not the world exists. . . . This ego, with its ego-life . . . necessarily remains for me by virtue of such an *epochē*" (CM 25).

Paradoxically, then, although reference to the reality of the subject's mental states or acts is bracketed by the procedure, the procedure leaves the subject with only reference to his or her own mental acts and contents. But this result is not paradoxical at all. It is the content and meaning of the intentional state, the noematic correlates, that remain after reduction, not the psychological or physiological reality of anyone's particular mental life; what remains is neither particular, nor private, nor contingent, nor factual. What Husserl calls "ideal meaning" is autonomous from its contingent expression in any given thought or experience. Everything remains as before the reduction; nothing has been lost, nothing created. "The transcendent world enters its brackets . . . we exercise the *epochē.* . . . Yet we find everything remains as before. . . . The tree has not forfeited the least nuance of all the moments, qualities, or characteristics with which it appeared in this perception" (Ideas 260).

This reflective departure from the natural attitude results in what Husserl rather ponderously calls "transcendental subjectivity." By this Kantian term Husserl names the philosophical or epistemological stance made possible by critical reflection upon the meaning of intentional experience. Husserl's use of the term "transcendental" should not be taken as committing Husserl to any of Kant's philosophical conclusions. In most contexts Husserl uses "transcendental" as simply another way to say the phrase "suspension of the natural attitude." (In the next section I will discuss his use of "transcendental idealism" as a distinct philosophical position.) Once the complex pattern of beliefs and commitments underlying everyday and scientific worldviews is bracketed, a reflective, critical subjectivity emerges that is not to be confused with the particular or contingent subjectivity of anyone's experience.

For when I am not philosophizing, when I live naively . . . intentionality carries me along; it predelineates; it determines me practically in my whole procedure, including the procedure of my natural thinking, whether this yields being or illusion. The living intentionality does all that, even though, as actually functioning, it may be non-thematic, undisclosed, and thus beyond my ken. (FTL 235)

Reflective inquiry neither rejects nor deflates the complicated ontological claims in question; what changes is our *stance* toward these claims.

We do not give up the positing we effected, we do not in any respect alter our conviction which remains in itself as it is as long as we do not introduce new judgement-motives: precisely this is what we do not do. Nevertheless the positing undergoes a modification: while it in itself remains what it is *we, so to speak, "put it out of action," we "exclude it," we "parenthesize it."* It is still there, like the parenthesized in the parenthesis, like the excluded outside the context of inclusion. (Ideas 58–59)

The most important feature of the reduction is, however, its claimed neutrality. The phenomenological reduction, if it is as Husserl claims it is, does not presuppose any philosophical view; nor does its descriptive analyses alone constitute a philosophical position, though his aim is ultimately to judge philosophical positions by these analyses.[22] As I said above, the reduction is itself neither a commitment to skepticism nor idealism. Husserl can be faulted for some persistent confusion about this claimed neutrality, since he unfortunately uses the term "transcendental" for both the critical sense of subjectivity emerging after the reduction and for the type of idealism he ultimately defends. But I consider his philosophical position distinct from his phenomenological analyses. Thus, in my view, Husserl allows for the possibility of agreeing with his phenomenological descriptions while resisting his commitment to idealism.

I will now, as briefly as possible, summarize Husserl's lengthy defense of his method's neutrality in *Cartesian Meditations*. This discussion, though notoriously difficult to follow and in my opinion unnecessarily so, sets the stage for discussing Husserl's transcendental idealism in the following section. This discussion also provides an opportunity to introduce examples of the kind of a priori analyses Husserl claims for his method, and these are the analyses most often challenged by his critics.

In a rare sarcastic comment, Husserl challenges what he considers a common misunderstanding of his method:

But the "I am" is the primitive intentional basis, not only for "the" world, the one I consider real, but also for any "ideal world" that I accept. . . . For children in philosophy, this may be the dark corner haunted by the specters of solipsism and, perhaps, of psychologism, of relativism. The true philosopher, instead of running away, will prefer to fill the dark corner with light. (FTL 237)

The charge that Husserl is responding to above is that the phenomenological reduction is simply the equivalent of philosophical solipsism and thus amounts to a sort of skepticism about other minds. The reason this point is critical is that if any such ontological claim about the external world (in this case the nonexistence of other egos) escaped the phenomenological reduction, then the method would have dramatically failed in what it was designed to do.

How does Husserl answer this objection? First, Husserl clarifies what he means by describing the phenomenological reduction as "radical." He does not mean that it is an exercise in imagining the strangest possible world. If I simply think of the world existing apart from me and thus imagine myself as the only ego experiencing the world (if I imagine, for example, that a terrible plague leaves me the world's only human survivor), I have not carried through the phenomenological reduction. My thought experiment remains wholly naturalistic, in Husserl's sense of that term. I am continuing to assume the naturalistic sense of an external world while modifying the possible matters of fact within it.

The reduction is not concerned with actual or possible scenarios about the world's matters of fact. The transcendental stance of the ego as a result of the reduction is not that of any natural ego looking at the world. The aim is not varying matters of fact, but abstracting the ego's directedness toward the meaning from its normal directedness toward the world. If this procedure is pursued correctly, the features of experience that can neither be bracketed nor abstracted from, namely, the a priori, essential meaning of experience, are given intuitively as essences; they are in effect "seen." Whether some object does or does not exist is a question left aside by this procedure; phenomenological reflection examines only the noematic content of any and all experience.

Given Husserl's clarification, let me try to restate the objection that concerns him. Husserl's method can be challenged, as a more careful critic might now put it, because the method entails a metaphysical claim that only the existence of the transcendental ego escapes the reduction. The objection is not that the method establishes, as a matter of fact, that no other selves exist. The more careful critic stresses that the existence of other selves, along with all objects, has been put into parentheses. But why is the transcendental ego exempt from this bracketing? (A later section of this chapter discusses Jean-Paul Sartre's version of this criticism.)

Therefore, the more careful critic continues, the escape of the transcendental ego from the reduction amounts to a failure of the method. To achieve its appropriately radical level of subjectivity, the reduction already excludes, albeit at the transcendental level, the existence of other egos. Hence solipsistic idealism has been presupposed and Husserl's claim to neutrally adjudicate philosophical debates collapses.

Husserl's reply to this clarified objection, the kind of reply he makes it unnecessarily difficult to follow, begins by assuming the truth of the critic's charge. If transcendental solipsism were actually presupposed, Husserl argues, then intentional experience would be unintelligible. Husserl argues that it is necessarily the case that an appearance is an appearance for others; that result follows, I think, from his account of phenomena (and meaning) as objective and autonomous (but not physical). The coherence or synthesis of experience presupposes this form of objectivity. However, since reflection has suspended all existential claims, this condition is purely formal and involves no assertions concerning the reality of other egos. Since the phenomenological method examines intentional objects while suspending all prejudgments, transcendental solipsism could not have been presupposed.

Perhaps a clearer way to put Husserl's point, which in the text still reads as though he were presupposing the falsity of solipsism as a philosophical position, is that a philosophical debate about solipsism is constrained to agree on the essential structures of experience. Even were philosophical solipsism true, there must be, at the cost of a coherent account of experience, the intentional meaning of experience as objective for oneself and for others.

> Transcendental reduction restricts me to the stream of my pure conscious processes. . . . But what about other egos, who surely are not a mere intending and intended *in me,* merely synthetic unities of possible verification *in me,* but, according to their sense, precisely *others?* Have we not therefore done transcendental realism an injustice? . . . Before one decides in favor of . . . dialectical argumentations and self-styled "metaphysical" hypotheses (whose supposed possibility may turn out to be a complete absurdity), it might indeed be more fitting to undertake the *task of phenomenological explication* indicated in this connexion by the "alter ego" and carry it through in concrete work. We must, after all, obtain for ourselves insight into the explicit and implicit intentionality wherein the alter ego becomes evinced and verified in the realm of our transcendental ego. . . . These experiences and their work are facts belonging to my phenomenological sphere. How else than by examining them can I explicate the sense, existing others, in all its respects? (CM 89–90)[23]

The critic's objection arose in the first place because the critic noted that, within the reduction, the "interiority" of other egos cannot appear to the reflective ego. The reflective ego directs itself to the world as phenomenally presented, but then it is necessarily the case that other egos appear only as other objects. That insight correctly repeats Husserl's radical internalism; access to the immediacy of only one's own mental contents is the indubitable foundation of his method.

But Husserl argues after the above quotation that the critic has ignored how other egos are presented to the reflective ego as *conceptually* or noematically distinct (distinct in terms of their sense or meaning as experience) from how other objects appear. It is this phenomenal difference, his only concern at this point, that preserves the neutrality of the method with regard to solipsism.

The argument for this difference runs as follows. A physical object presents itself in a series of aspects. Husserl uses the verb "appresented" to capture the feature of physical objects always being presented partially from some particular perspective. Thus, any physical object presents itself fully to the observer only in time and fully only in principle. Another ego, since it appears as an object, is also given in perspectives. But there constitutes an important phenomenal difference between egos and objects. The presentation of the other ego cannot, even in principle, be fully accessible by these multiple perspectives. The interiority of the other ego cannot be experienced at all. The interiority of the other appears, reflectively, either as an object or as the reflective ego's own subjectivity. It is thus an essential feature of the meaning of appearances, not a physiological or psychological limit of human cognition, that other selves appear only as objects.

> I do not apperceive him as having, more particularly, the spatial modes of appearance that are mine from here; rather, as we find on close examination, I apperceive him as having spatial modes of appearance like those I should have if I should go over there and be where he is. . . . In this appresentation, therefore, the body in the mode *There,* which presents itself in *my* monadic sphere and is apperceived as another's live body (the animate organism of the alter ego)—that body indicates "the same" body in the mode *Here,* as the body experienced by the other ego in *his* monadic sphere. Moreover it indicates the "same" body concretely, with all the constitutive intentionality pertaining to this mode of givenness in the other's experience." (CM 117)

But our critic might still persist that Husserl has simply restated the objection. Other egos appear to the reflective ego as objects or as the transcendental ego's own interiority. But that is just to say that in reflection the reality of other egos is denied, while the objectivity or reality of the transcendental or reflective ego is simply assumed. The criticism is again that transcendental solipsism has been presupposed in the reduction. The existence of other selves is at best only being inferred from the appearance of objects, and in that way realism about these egos has been excluded by the phenomenological exercise, in opposition to Husserl's claims.

But now the more careful critic has misunderstood the conditions of the reduction and the point of Husserl's reply. It is illicit to shift from what can or cannot be conceived to what does or does not exist. Husserl is not, as the critic now assumes, replying to solipsism or skepticism about other minds with this methodical exercise. He is not declaring the existence or nonexistence of the objects of any of these appearances. Such a reply would require reintroducing presuppositions and removing the methodically maintained neutrality. Husserl's conclusion is much weaker. The phenomenological reduction does reveal a phenomenal difference, a difference with regard to the meaning of the intentional correlates, of other selves and other objects. There is, therefore, no a priori limit, then, on whether there is evidence for the existence of other egos. Whether there are or are not other egos is thus not a topic decided from within the limits of the reduction; nor then is solipsism presupposed.

All philosophical positions remain possible. But Husserl does believe that, given the clarification of these a priori constraints discovered by phenomenological reflection, constraints constituting the formal necessities for any experience at all, some philosophical positions will prove epistemologically idle.

Transcendental Interiority

Husserl's philosophical problem is: What makes objectivity possible? What must objectivity necessarily mean or conceptually depend on (apart from and independent of the relevant matters of fact) for any possible intentional experience? Thus, Husserl's questions include: How do events in the natural world come to be evidential? How does intentionality stand for or represent any object whatsoever? "How can a component part of the world, its human subjectivity, constitute the whole world, namely, constitute it as its intentional formation . . . ?" (Crisis 179).

> That I attain certainties, even compelling evidences, in my own domain of consciousness, in the nexus of motivation determining me, is understandable. But how can this business, going on wholly within the immanency of conscious life, acquire Objective significance? How can evidence . . . claim to be more than a characteristic of consciousness within me? (CM 82–83)

By turning objectivity notional, making it a matter of meaning "inside," Husserl reanimated a classic philosophical question. How can purely conceptual matters of the mind refer to matters of fact independent of those mental concepts? Husserl believes that this question can be satisfactorily answered by a type of transcendental idealism. Husserl chose to adopt this name for his philosophical view even though it obscures his rejection of the traditional philosophical distinction between realism and idealism. As I said above, I would prefer to call Husserl an epistemological "internalist," and he does occasionally identify his view as that of "transcendental interiority."[24]

Husserl thought that transcendental idealism properly answered skepticism and properly supported perceptual realism; "the thing perceived in perception *is the physical thing itself,* in its own factual being, . . . which show with certainty what is actual *in the place of* the illusory" (FTL 281). Baldly stated in this way, however, realism lacks a proper philosophical defense in Husserl's view. Specifically, it lacks the kind of defense that holds independently of scientific results concerning, for example, biological evolution, cognitive psychology, or physics. *"Thus I exclude all sciences relating to this natural world* no matter how firmly they stand there for me, no matter how much I admire them, no matter how little I think of making even the least objection to them; *I make absolutely no use of the things posited in them"* (Ideas 61).

Husserl's project is audacious since it is precisely this trick of converting first-person authority about internal mental states into support for claims about the external world that had eluded the philosophical tradition of epistemological "internalism" beginning with Descartes. The twist Husserl introduces is to claim that the phenomenological method serves to whittle down the types of criticisms of realism by setting as a minimal condition that such criticisms preserve the essential features of phenomenal experience, understood nonnaturalistically.

Husserl significantly broadened the application of the concept of meaning. Like the contemporary analytic philosopher John Searle, Husserl treats strictly linguistic meaning as a subcategory of the meaning of intentional content in general. To put it as Searle does, the philosophy of language rests upon the philosophy of mind.[25] The intentionality of the mind, specifically as found in perception, makes meaningful communication possible. In directing our attention to meanings, Husserl claimed that he could set conditions for how representation necessarily involves these meanings.

But even assuming Husserl were correct, given the claimed neutrality of his method, the following philosophical questions still arise: How does one know that in describing objects, even given evidential support, one captures the way the objects really are? How, trapped within subjectivity, does one determine that an account of the world, and the world admits of diverse meaningful accounts, matches or fits the world as it is, independent of mental life, that is, fits the world as it is and not just the world as it appears to us to be?

Though these are classical philosophical questions, Husserl thinks they are persistently misunderstood because the distinction between transcendental and naturalistic stances is forgotten. Thus, spontaneously, these questions are read as demands for some additional empirical evidence concerning either the world or the brain. But no amount of empirical evidence could answer these kind of questions, Husserl holds. What they demand is not more empirical evidence, but pure intuitions concerning the meaningful structure of evidential justification, whatever the evidence. The questions concern what makes it possible for there to be evidence with regard to any account of the nature of the world, and the worry is that nothing about justification holds independently of the facts of a private mental state. But Husserl believes the meaning structure of this experience, which is not private at all, provides the right kind of answer to these questions and the right kind of dismissal of the threat of this kind of global skepticism.

Husserl's choice of "transcendental idealism" to capture the philosophical version of his answer to these questions is unfortunate. When Immanuel Kant called himself a transcendental idealist, he set out a controversial type of compromise with the threat of skepticism. Kant protected empirical realism, needed for the defense of scientific objectivity, by taking the view that there was a domain of features about the world that are mind-dependent; hence his stance toward this domain was idealist. Kant thought the failure of philosophy in his day was due to its various attempts to secure a defense of empirical realism (i.e., the reality of the world as it appears to the senses) by securing access to what Kant called "things-in-themselves" as parallel to or providing the foundation for access to the empirical world.

But, in this sense, Kant's position is not at all what Husserl means by "transcendental idealism." Specifically, Husserl holds that objects given in perception are transcendent; they are what Kant misleadingly called "things-in-themselves." Or to put the point slightly differently, there is no realm of entities independent of all forms of experience in Husserl for which either the idealist or realist must provide a foundation. What there is a priori is meaning. Transcendental reflection, though distinct from empirical inquiry, is wholly within the same mundane world; transcendental reflection is also not a form of ontological inquiry.

Why, then, does Husserl insist on the phrase? First, it marks the reflective stance from which the analysis of the a priori constraints is carried out as distinct from the natural attitude; in reflection, thought is directed toward any possible experience. Second, he uses the term "idealism" to remind the reader of those meaning correlates (or the ideal objects, as he calls them) revealed as the essential feature of all intentional experience, the constraints, as I said above, within which any account of the world is possible and by which various challenges to realism are excluded.

After the reduction, to echo Ludwig Wittgenstein's similar insight, the world is as we found it. Husserl is neither competing with nor supplanting the painstaking search for evidence of the complex, ontic features of the world as that is carried on by the sciences, broadly understood, or by common sense. Rather, philosophy finally takes on its proper and culturally irreplaceable task of clarifying the meaning of evidence, truth, objectivity, and so on, through pure reflection on experience.

Within Husserl's strategy, Hume's empiricism, Locke's realism, even Leibniz's strange monadology and Descartes's flirtation with methodological solipsism in his defense of certainty in knowledge are not to be considered competitive hypotheses concerning the ultimate nature of the world, but protophenomenological analyses by past philosophers who spoke "prose," Husserl-style, without having realized it.

> Particularly in the case of the Objective world of realities . . . phenomenologi-
> cal explication does nothing but *explicate the sense this world has for us all,*
> *prior to any philosophizing,* and obviously gets solely from our experience—*a*
> *sense which philosophy can uncover but never alter,* and which, because of an
> essential necessity, not because of our weakness, entails (in the case of any ac-
> tual experience) horizons that need fundamental clarification. (CM 151)

Husserl's transcendental theory of knowledge carries out what traditional theory only grasped in a confused fashion. It is explicitly concerned
with only what makes it possible for an experience to be objective, evidential, or true. For example, it may be a psychological feature of the human
sensory apparatus that a strong "feeling" of certainty can be elicited under
such and such conditions, even while the facts preclude such justification.[26]
Epistemology can, however, ignore such a matter of fact. What makes it
possible for experience to be objective, to have that meaning as experience,
holds even where these psychological or physiological facts may differ; in
this way we can speak of objectivity for Martians. The naturalist, on the
other hand, confuses an objective account of the facts concerning experience with an account of objectivity.

> Natural science, then, simply follows consistently the sense of what the thing
> so to speak pretends to be as experienced, and calls this—vaguely enough—
> "elimination of secondary qualities," "elimination of the merely subjective in
> appearance," while "retaining what is left, the primary qualities." And that is
> more than an obscure expression; it is a bad theory regarding a good proce-
> dure. (PRS 106)

For naturalism, intentionality refers to the qualitative experience of mental life: what it is like for humans to have such and such an experience.
Husserl calls this treatment the reduction of intentionality to a "secondary
quality." This old and contentious philosophical distinction between primary and secondary qualities, a language Husserl has reintroduced to exemplify another naturalistic confusion, was drawn to distinguish how the
world appears from how the world is apart from any experience of it. In
this way of speaking, color, as experienced by humans, is a secondary quality since it does not, as qualitatively experienced, belong to the object,
which only appears to possess it. Color is thus an artifact of human sensation. The psychologist of mental life, Husserl suggests, attempts to treat intentionality in an identical fashion. Husserl's objection to this account is
that it is a "good procedure" because it directs attention to what it is about
experience that makes it capable of being a cognition (namely, its "directedness"), but a "bad theory" because this condition is immediately entangled
with unexamined ontological claims.

The same deep confusions recur. Intentionality is not a feature or property of any object in the world, including the brain. It concerns the condi-

tions that are necessarily the case for any mental experience to be a cognitive experience. The features of intentionality discovered by phenomenological reflection are neither causal nor physical features any more than numbers have causal, physical features that mathematicians, without realizing it, study. Naturalists have made a category mistake and it is an error of the merely "fact-minded."

The European Crisis

I have presented what I consider the "guts" of Husserl's ambitious project. The following is somewhat of a digression, since I do not think that the issues discussed in this section alter Husserl's basic project. Husserl, in his last work, a collection of essays called *The Crisis of European Sciences and Transcendental Phenomenology*, presented phenomenology through reflections upon the history of science and a new concept he called the "life-world." These writings, however, led some followers to conclude, against Husserl's intention, I believe, that he changed his view with regard to the relativism and historicism he vehemently rejected in his youth. Since these are important issues in the reception of Husserl in the continental tradition and since the revival of such a brand of relativism plays an important role in the final chapter of this book, I have decided to treat this topic in a separate section.

Wilhelm Dilthey, an exponent of Neo-Kantianism during Husserl's early career, popularized the treatment of philosophy as a mode of cultural expression comparable to literature and the arts.[27] Like Husserl, Dilthey hoped to account for the persistence of irresolvable conflict in the history of philosophy. But unlike Husserl's, Dilthey's answer to the persistence of such conflict depends largely on embracing the naturalist's dismissal of philosophy. Philosophical positions are not matters about which agreements can be reached; rather, they express and externalize the values and "worldview" of a culture or a historical period. The study of philosophy involves a purely historical or even aesthetic effort to reconstruct this expressive function for those values and presuppositions that have become alien or difficult to understand.

Dilthey claimed, in fact, that there was a typology of philosophical systems much as there was a typology of artistic styles. Also, in conformity with artistic styles, there was no point in judging these philosophical systems as one would the efforts of the sciences; specifically, the concepts of truth and objectivity were inapplicable. Philosophies, since they only express historical "worldviews," are not, contrary to their own self-conception, a kind of universal inquiry or "superscience." Those persistent disagreements in the history of philosophy are then hardly a matter for concern; such disagreements are necessarily the result of philosophy's relative and expressive function in relation to different historical "life forms." In much the same way, different artistic styles can be loosely said to "disagree," but such disagreement could not literally be resolved, nor does it constitute the point of artistic expression.

Husserl, from his earliest writings, argued that such historicism about philosophy can only remain consistent about the limits of philosophy by expanding into a deeper skepticism about the very possibility of knowledge, including the sciences; it would automatically extend, then, to the basic concepts of truth, validity, objectivity, and knowledge Dilthey must appeal to when distinguishing science from philosophy. Whatever Dilthey says about philosophy could equally be said about the natural sciences. Physics, for example, could be said to express the "worldview" of its period. Yet it remains possible to also ask whether a given scientific theory, in addition to having this expressive function, is supported by evidence or is true. To prevent the philosopher from making the same reply, the consistent historicist must extend "expressive relativism" to truth and objectivity itself. Once the position's skepticism extends beyond what was originally intended, it automatically includes the historical evidence of the expressive function. Historical skepticism proves in this way to be self-defeating.

Husserl holds additionally that the kind of historical evidence Dilthey collects, even if the above logical point were ignored, could not justify Dilthey's skepticism about philosophy. No matter how detailed our factual knowledge about some historical period or how slight the information, such evidence contributes to the sum total of matters of fact concerning that period. What Dilthey ignores is a discussion of what constitutes epistemological justification (a discussion, of course, that historicism condemns as merely expressive). Whether or not knowledge claims are justified is not simply a matter of empirical evidence; it is dispute concerning the logic of justification, whatever the evidence.

The skeptical historicist is then doubly confused. The historicist confuses factual historical claims with debates about the concepts of validity and objectivity. But, simultaneously, the historicist makes a philosophical claim without apparently realizing it. Historicism's confusion is the price of ignoring those basic distinctions Husserl continually reiterates.

It can as historical science in no way prove even the affirmation that up to the present there has been no scientific philosophy: it can do so only from other sources of knowledge, and they are clearly philosophical sources. For it is clear that philosophical criticism, too, is philosophy and that its sense implies the ideal possibility of a systematic philosophy as a strict science. The unconditional thought that any scientific philosophy is a chimaera, based on the argument that the alleged efforts of millennia make probable the intrinsic impossibility of such a philosophy, is erroneous not merely because to draw a conclusion regarding an unlimited future from a few millennia of higher culture would not be a good induction, but erroneous as an absolute absurdity, like 2 x 2 = 5. And this is for the indicated reason: if there is something there whose objective validity philosophical criticism can refute, then there is also an area within which something can be grounded as objectively valid. (PRS 127)

My simple task in the remainder of this section is to show that this line of criticism remains unaltered in his late writings.

In *Crisis* Husserl does present phenomenological reflection in a manner distinct from the versions given in *Ideas* and *Cartesian Meditations*. Husserl specifically criticizes his earlier efforts because they did not carry through the reduction carefully enough. Simply suspending the existential positings of the sciences leaves a background set of assumptions about the world that could play a decisive role in philosophical disputes. These deeper background assumptions must then be raised to the level of critical reflection and suspended along with the existential posits of the sciences that were his earlier focus.

Some commentators hold that Husserl was acquiescing in this way to Martin Heidegger's objection to an emphasis on scientific explanations and theories. But Husserl does continue to focus on the sciences. I believe the influence on Husserl's later writings was not Heidegger, but the French historian of science Alexander Koyré.[28] Koyré, who was a student of Husserl's, brought to his teacher's attention how the history of science shows that embedded commonsense assumptions had a considerable influence in the formation of the sciences. In the transition from the medieval to Renaissance conceptions of nature, for instance, Koyré claimed that these kinds of conceptual matters were far more critical than the extent of empirical evidence.

In *Crisis* scientific objectivity becomes part of a broader task of reflecting upon common sense.

Briefly reminding ourselves of our earlier discussion, let us recall the fact we have emphasized, namely, that science is a human spiritual accomplishment which presupposes as its point of departure, both historically and for each new student, the intuitive surrounding world of life, pregiven as existing for all in common. Furthermore, it is an accomplishment which, in being practiced and carried forward, continues to presuppose this surrounding world as it is given in its particularity to the scientist. For example, for the physicist it is the world in which he sees his measuring instruments, hears time-beats, estimates visible magnitudes, etc.—the world in which, furthermore, he knows himself to be included with all his activity and all his theoretical ideas. (Crisis 121)

Husserl describes the "life-world" as the "straight-forwardly intuited world." It is not to be confused with the objects of the sciences or even of those of common sense, which, of necessity, abstract from experience. The life-world is, therefore, the always presupposed background for the possibility of knowledge claims of any sort. Husserl speaks of this insight as "the most obvious of the obvious" and says that in the midst of life it is hardly worth noting. But what is "the most obvious of the obvious" has philosophical significance.

> Simply living in this manner, one does not need the word "pregiven"; there is no need to point out that the world is constantly actuality for us. All natural questions, all theoretical and practical goals taken as themes—as existing, as perhaps existing, as probable, as questionable, as valuable, as project, as action and result of action—have to do with something or other within the world-horizon. This is true even of illusion, nonactualities, since everything characterized through some modality of being is, after all, related to actual being. (Crisis 145–146)

Husserl then proceeds in a way wholly consistent with his previous work. He announces a new form of inquiry, in "opposition to all previously designed objective sciences," that would be a "science of the universal *how* of the pregivenness of the world, i.e., of what makes it a universal ground for any sort of objectivity" (Crisis 146). I offer, therefore, three possible misconceptions of "life-world" that I speculate might have led commentators to think that the conception of phenomenology and its philosophical aims had decisively altered and embraced relativism and historicism.

The first misconception involves treating the introduction of the notion of a "life-world" as a sociological, causal hypothesis explaining the emergence of the sciences by appeal to facts about their cultural context. This misreading is rather bald. Husserl repeats at length that claims about causality (scientific or practical) as well as other contingencies of fact and evidence are put into parentheses. Husserl clearly includes in this bracketing any possible sociological claims about science and culture. Sociology, like any science, presupposes the life-world in the above fashion. It would have been wildly inconsistent for Husserl to have adopted the concept of the life-world as prototype of some sociological or historical explanation of science.

The second misreading is due to the influence of Heidegger, and it claims that Husserl shifted his philosophical aim from that of epistemology to the new project of a fundamental ontology announced by Martin Heidegger's *Being and Time*. (I will discuss Heidegger's attack on Husserl's focus on the sciences and theoretical inquiry in Chapter 2.) First, Husserl still speaks of epistemology as the central philosophical problem. He treats ontological issues, as always, as derivative. He discusses science in terms of "the possibility of its objective accomplishments" and the need to "survey its theories and results" as "predicative thoughts and statements." There are numerous passages in which Husserl simply repeats his aim of investigating how the objective claims of science are made possible by "subjective elements which everywhere have a voice in what is taken for granted in advance" (Crisis 111). Husserl's approach is therefore indistinguishable on this point from what he says in *Ideas:*

> Is scientific knowledge as such not "objective" knowledge, aimed at a knowledge substratum which is valid for everyone with conditioned generality? And yet, paradoxically, we uphold our assertion and require that one not let the handed-down concept of objective science be substituted, because of the century-old tradition in which we have all been raised, for the concept of science in general. (Crisis 124)

As regards the claim that Heidegger's pursuit of fundamental ontology became Husserl's preoccupation, I offer the following explicit rejection of that shift. Husserl is clearly aware in the following quotation of Heidegger's different conception of the aim of philosophy as well as Heidegger's criticisms of Husserl's phenomenology; and the final phrase concerning "resurrected metaphysics" would leave no doubt for his philosophical readers where Husserl stood on the issue.

> Thus it could appear if one allows oneself to be carried along by the thoughtless naïveté of life even in the transition from the extralogical to the logical, to the objective-scientific praxis of thinking—that a separate investigation under the title of "life-world" is an intellectualistic enterprise born of a mania, peculiar to modern life, to theorize everything. But, on the other hand, it has at least become apparent that we cannot let the matter end with this naïveté. ... From here on this much is certain: that all problems of truth and of being, all methods, hypotheses, and results conceivable for these problems—whether for worlds of experience or for metaphysically higher worlds—can attain their ultimate clarity, their evident sense or the evidence of their nonsense, only through this supposedly intellectualistic hypertrophy. This will then include, certainly, all ultimate questions of legitimate sense and of nonsense in the busy routine of the "resurrected metaphysics" that has become so vocal and bewitching of late. (Crisis 132–133)

Finally, there is a third misreading that understands Husserl's discussion of the history of science as a form of skeptical historicism. Husserl does, under the influence of Koyré's historical studies (as I suggested), use the historical case study of Galileo arguing against medieval theories of physics to exemplify the philosophical confusion he labels "objectivism." He treats Galileo's error as characteristic of an epistemology found throughout science, traditional philosophy, and common sense.

> For the Galilean natural science, mathematical-physical nature is objective-true nature; it is this nature that is supposed to manifest itself in the merely subjective appearances. It is thus clear ... that nature, in exact natural science, is not the actually experienced nature, that of the life-world. It is an idea that

has arisen out of idealization and has been hypothetically substituted for actually intuited nature. (Crisis 221)

But this criticism is directed not at the sciences, since they cannot avoid such abstractions, but at the philosophy of science. Once again, Husserl is discussing naturalism or objectivism as a philosophical position concerning the nature of empirical evidence. The truth or falsity of the evidence and the subsequent sciences are thus bracketed during this reflection.

Suffice it to repeat, Husserl does not claim that scientific objectivity is historically or culturally conditioned, though the search for evidence stretches beyond any individual life and is properly a cultural task. The manner in which the life-world is presupposed is not that of making truth or objectivity relative to empirical facts about the world. Rather, reflection upon the life-world reveals what makes it possible for there to be truth and objectivity about the world, including truths about history and society. It is not Husserl's proposal that science be examined and then condemned for its ideological or functional role in society, though he believes it sometimes plays such a role. The crisis of the European sciences is a matter of a deep epistemological confusion, not a matter of feared technological evils or a Frankenstein-inspired revulsion against science's amorality. Therefore, the life-world is introduced into Husserl's account as the kind of presupposition that it is the task of a properly conceived epistemology to both clarify and ultimately justify. As such, it is presupposed by any possible science, including any sociological or historical claim about the nature of evidence. Furthermore, although science can be studied for its aesthetic, moral, and even literary qualities, it remains possible at every moment to ask of it another question: Is it knowledge? The argument here, then, is identical to the earlier one made against Dilthey.

It does seem necessary, before concluding, to say something of what might be distinctive about these late writings of Husserl and what would at least suggest a motivation for the above misreadings. Husserl strove in his career to defend the possibility of philosophical knowledge. He pictured this effort, almost always in his writings, as that of individual thinkers pursuing reflectively and rigorously, guided by methodological supports, the pure analysis of experience. He furthermore held that the proper understanding of transcendental subjectivity, the domain of this research, was that of a solitary, reflective inquiry. I believe that later in his life he chose to emphasize that philosophical clarification demanded and required a civilization or cultural tradition. In that way the weaknesses of each thinker as a "born dogmatist" would be checked again, and it would extend the methodological constraints already outlined.

Husserl had raised this concern, however, early in his career in bemoaning the absence in philosophy of "mutual study carried on with a consciousness of responsibility . . . to produce Objectively valid results." Conflicting philosophical voices produced, in his view, "pseudo-criticizing . . . a mere semblance of philosophizing seriously with and for one another" (CM 5). But this concern grew in his late writings, for reasons sketched above, and he there tries to explicate precisely how the project of philosophy could be understood as carried out by a culture, instead of individuals.

I suppose that those who misread Husserl's early work as consisting of some sort of subjectivism were thereby convinced that these later writings marked a decisive philosophical change. If they were wrong in the first place, as I hold they were, Husserl's shift of emphasis, though rightly a topic for specialists and commentators, is neither inconsistent with his earlier positions nor a repudiation of them.

Critical Friendship and Enmity

This section reviews those criticisms of Husserl's phenomenology that were historically significant for the development of continental philosophy.[29] Though the criticisms by Maurice Merleau-Ponty and Jean-Paul Sartre were more deeply influenced by Martin Heidegger, the subject of the next chapter, their assessments of Husserl's transcendental idealism will provide a picture of the early reception of Husserlian phenomenology even before we discuss the impact of Heidegger.

Husserl was well aware, toward the end of his life, that much of his original project was being abandoned and thus proclaimed, with that distinct gloom that pervades the *Crisis* volume: "Philosophy as science, as serious, rigorous, indeed apomictically rigorous, science—*the dream is over*. . . . A powerful and constantly growing current of philosophy which renounces scientific discipline, like the current of religious disbelief, is inundating European humanity" (Crisis 389–390). Here and elsewhere, Husserl expressed deep misgivings about the philosophical preoccupations of his contemporaries and followers; and he was largely correct about the fate of his ambitious agenda.

I begin with a characteristic criticism of Husserl's idealism. Marvin Farber, who studied with Husserl at Freiburg in the 1920s, argued, as many others have done since, that the phenomenological method was not neutral. As discussed above, Husserl denied at length that the phenomenological reduction assumed solipsistic idealism. But Farber's criticism takes a slightly different tack. The reduction excludes philosophical materialism, or what is today often called simply physicalism. If Farber were correct, that would amount to showing that the phenomenological method could neither adjudicate between philosophical disputes nor, according to Farber, defend the kind of realism Husserl began his career defending with the slogan "Back to the things themselves." Husserl's later transcendental idealism is then "methodogenic," in Farber's words, since it reflects the implicit bias of the phenomenological method.

> The promise of pure subjectivism, that a universal suspension of beliefs and a retirement to immanent experience would bring to light all influences and all conditions bearing on experience, is not fulfilled. For a larger realm is needed, in which the mind and all experiences are contained—the infinite realm of existence, antedating the relatively recent development of human beings and continuing after the possible disappearance of life as we know it from the cosmos. The transmogrification of real existence to accommodate the central position accorded to minds, selves, or egos, is a methodological achievement of philosophical subjectivism, which is at times concealed linguistically by describing its determinations as "objective."[30]

Farber goes on to hypothesize that Husserl's "subjectivism" should be explained sociologically by a combination of class interests, religious motives, and the ideological purpose of "an ingenious philosophy of renunciation which leaves the *status quo* unexamined and unchallenged." A very similar criticism of Husserl, with the same appeal to its underlying ideological motivation, was made by Theodor Adorno.

But, given my exposition of Husserl, this line of criticism (even leaving aside the claimed sociological explanation of Husserl's views) fails. Husserl's concept of the reduction does not deny the existence of a "wide realm," for instance, or specifically that the subject's mental life is materially, causally, or biologically dependent on the natural world. Nor could the reduction alone serve the ideological purpose of defending the status quo, since the method suspends claims about what is or is not the status quo of the social world, as well as how and even whether such a world could causally change (nor is it, as already stressed, an expression of skepticism concerning any such social realities).

Neither causal relations nor actual physical or social objects as such are within the noematic realm. Transcendental reflection converts claims about causal change, whether physical, psychological, or sociological, into a study of essential structures of meaning of these phenomena; this meaningful structure is accessible to reflection and concerns what is necessarily the case for any experience whatsoever. Even if Husserl were correct about his version of idealism, nothing would thereby follow from that analysis about the nature of social or physical causation itself; such features of the world are matters settled by whether there is empirical evidence and are not settled by philosophical idealism as Husserl understands it; phenomenology contests nothing of the scientific method. Thus his idealism could not provide an ideological defense of the status quo, since what constitutes the reality of the social world is a social-scientific rather than a philosophical problem.

Farber might, therefore, be better read as criticizing Husserl's basic distinction between philosophical and empirical inquiry, rather than the method itself. In other words, Farber's criticism is a defense of epistemological naturalism against Husserl's efforts to carve out a domain of philosophy apart from the sciences. But if the thrust of Farber's objection is to deny this basic distinction, Husserl still would not have committed the sins Farber condemns. Husserl's claims about the constitution of knowledge, if they turn out to be mistaken and if it turns out that epistemology is properly subsumed under naturalism, are still not ontological, causal, or empirical claims about the world. If it turns out that his theory of knowledge fails, Husserl still can be credited with having argued that naturalism is a philosophical, not a scientific, view; and he could still be defended for proposing a method that did not presuppose it.

Also, Farber's sociological explanations are premature, since the debate over this separation of philosophical from scientific inquiry continues to this day. Also, the challenges to even making such a distinction are again philosophical, not sociological, challenges. Farber may be justified in wanting to debate the distinction itself before embracing Husserl's method, but he is not justified in holding that the method, given that distinction, excludes physicalism or is, as he and Adorno claim, insidiously ideological.

French Phenomenology

I will now turn to a more immanent line of criticism of Husserl. Some of the detail and background of the views of both Merleau-Ponty and Sartre will not be fully clear until I discuss Heidegger in the next chapter, as I already state above. But even without those details, the following criticisms of Husserl's transcendental idealism and transcendental ego can give a clearer indication of how Husserl was understood by his near contemporaries.

The reader may have already been uneasy with some of these ideas in Husserl, an uneasiness I sidestepped in my exposition. Though I stressed Husserl's aim of defending empirical or perceptual realism and his claim that the reduction leaves the world as it is, both of these relatively accessible points rest on Husserl's more difficult and obscure notion of there being something he called "transcendental subjectivity." What does he intend by postulating a "transcendental ego"?

I begin with Merleau-Ponty's account of the relationship between philosophy and science since that relationship was central to Husserl's project. Merleau-Ponty challenges both the Husserlian account of philosophy's relationship to the sciences and specifically how this relationship between philosophy and science arises in criticizing psychological studies of perception. These challenges then sustain Merleau-Ponty's more general criticism of Husserl's transcendental idealism, a criticism somewhat similar to Farber's objection. Merleau-Ponty believed that Husserl changed his philosophical position in his late writings. Since I have already disagreed with that reading, I present Merleau-Ponty as a critic of the Husserl I focused upon, the "early Husserl," as Merleau-Ponty calls him, the Husserl he then dismisses as "logicistic."

Merleau-Ponty's philosophical work grew from detailed commentaries on scientific work in psychology, physiology and experimental work on the brain, cognition, and sensory systems. These reflections occupied him in his two central philosophical works, *The Structure of Behavior* and *Phenomenology of Perception*. He strove in these works, by immanent criticism, to demonstrate the inadequacy of scientific psychology and its failure to account for the phenomena of consciousness and human action.

He describes his project as descriptive in contrast to the causal explanations of scientific psychology. "It tries to give a direct description of our experience as it is, without taking into account its psychological origin, and the causal explanations which the scientists, the historian or the sociologist may be able to provide" (PP vii). Merleau-Ponty then connects this criticism to Husserl's view of science, but in a way that immediately gives rise to serious misunderstandings.

> It is a matter of describing, not of explaining or analyzing. Husserl's first directive to phenomenology, in its early stages, to be a "descriptive psychology" or to return to the "things themselves" is from the start a foreswearing of science. I am not the outcome or the meeting-point of numerous causal agencies which determine my bodily or psychological make-up. I cannot conceive myself as nothing but a bit of the world, a mere object of biological, psychological or sociological investigation. I cannot shut myself up within the realm of science. All my knowledge of the world, even my scientific knowledge, is gained from my own particular point of view, or from some experience of the world without which the symbols of science would be meaningless. (PP viii)

The problem with this passage, at least as an account of Husserl's views, lies in the second sentence. In asserting "I am not the outcome or the meeting-point of numerous causal agencies" *(Je ne suis pas le résultant ou l'entrecroisement des multiples causalités)* Merleau-Ponty has misstated, in an especially crucial way, the strategy of the phenomenological reduction, and thus he has misstated Husserl's conception of the relationship between science and philosophy. The bracketing of the phenomenological reduction does extend to causality, but that would include a claim that causality did *not* hold for the self, as would appear to be Merleau-Ponty's point. Merleau-Ponty confuses, characteristically, the procedure of the reduction to bracket causal or ontological claims with denying causal or ontological claims—a difference Husserl repeatedly pointed out and a misreading he continually warned against. In this manner Merleau-Ponty conceives of the reduction as a direct challenge to scientific research and as demanding a philosophical alternative to scientific psychology.

The third sentence, which uses the verb "cannot conceive," restores in a sense Husserl's strategy since only the meaning of any such claims would be in question. But the concluding sentence in which knowledge (if meaningful) is said to presuppose "my own particular point of view" distorts Husserl once again. The use of the word "particular" strongly suggests that the phrase "my own point of view" refers to an actual, "situated" observer's point of view, in the natural sense of having a factual location and identity. But even in his late writings (those writings Merleau-Ponty claims as his guide) Husserl says of the reduction: "This is not a 'view,' an 'interpretation' bestowed upon the world ... every opinion about 'the' world, has its ground in the pregiven world. It is from this very ground that I have freed myself through the epochē" (Crisis 152).

Merleau-Ponty's careless wording converts Husserl's position into a version of traditional phenomenalism or subjectivism, a common misreading. Husserl makes all too clear that whenever he uses the phrase "transcendental reflective ego," he is not speaking of any actual observer or any empirical matter of fact about an observer. Merleau-Ponty's wording, to be fair, may reflect deeper objections to Husserl's idealism, criticisms I will discuss in a moment. But I believe these misstatements were unintended since I am quoting from passages in which he claims he is merely summarizing Husserl's views. If that is the case, such missteps (including the unintended banality of the concluding sentence that states "All my knowledge of the world ... is gained from ... experience of the world"), by one of phenomenology's most famous proponents, go some way toward justifying Husserl's repeated warnings about how easy it was to misunderstand, trivialize, and carelessly misidentify his method with past philosophical views.

Merleau-Ponty's central theme in *Phenomenology of Perception* is that "empiricistic" psychology and "intellectualistic" psychology "are incapable of expressing the peculiar way in which perceptual consciousness can constitute its object. Both keep their distance in relation to perception, instead of sticking to it" (PP 26). Contrary to experimental psychology's assumption of scientific "objectivity," perception and consciousness are, as Merleau-Ponty often puts it, "embodied" as "forms of existence." Why does perception being embodied or existing as "being-in-the-world" constitute a criticism of or rejection of scientific causal analysis? (Merleau-Ponty's use of hyphens is a stylistic device adopted from Heidegger and this device will be discussed in Chapter 2.)

Merleau-Ponty accuses the sciences of "schematization." The schemata of the sciences are designed to abstract their topic, such as perception and its relationship to the human body, from what Merleau-Ponty calls its "fundamental ontology" and in that way make its object suitable for naturalized inquiry. It is this schematization that allows for causal studies of psychology and the brain. The understanding or comprehension of the body and perception in a way that does not schematize it as a physical object turns out to be difficult to formulate and rather obscure, as Merleau-Ponty willingly admits.

> How significance and intentionality could come to dwell in molecular edifices of masses of cells is a thing which can never be made comprehensible. . . . But there is, in any case, no question of any such absurd undertaking. It is simply a question of recognizing that the body, as a chemical structure or an agglomeration of tissues, is formed, by a process of impoverishment, from a primordial phenomenon of the body-for-us, the body of human experience or the perceived body, round which objective thought works, but without being called upon to postulate its completed analysis. As for consciousness, it has to be conceived, no longer as a constituting consciousness and, as it were, a pure being-for-itself, but a perceptual consciousness, as the subject of a pattern of behavior, as being-in-the-world or existence, for only thus can another appear at the top of his phenomenal body, and be endowed with a sort of "locality." (PP 350)

I emphasized in my account above that Husserl begins his inquiry from the stance of perceptual realism; the object of normal perception is the real object. Merleau-Ponty properly emphasizes that such perceptual realism, as in Husserl's slogan "Back to the things themselves," should not be understood as providing a causal account of realism. Merleau-Ponty agrees with Husserl's opposition to naturalizing epistemology.

> Science has not and never will have, by its nature, the same significance *qua* form of being as the world which we perceive, for the simple reason that it is a rationale or explanation of that world. I am, not a "living-creature" nor even a "man," nor again a "consciousness" endowed with the characteristics which zoology, social anatomy or inductive psychology recognize in these various products of the natural or historical process—I am the absolute source, my existence does not stem from antecedents, from my physical and social environment; instead it moves out toward them and sustains them, for I alone bring into being for myself (and therefore into being in the only sense that the word can have for me) the tradition which I elect to carry on, or the horizon whose distance from me would be abolished. . . . To return to things themselves is to return to that world which precedes knowledge, of which knowledge always speaks, and in relation to which every scientific schematization is an abstract and derivative sign-language. (PP viii–ix)

Accordingly, Merleau-Ponty's point concerning psychology is that no accumulation of evidence through such cognitive research could establish that an object, understood factually, is the cause of one's perception of it, if that claim is to have any epistemological significance. But that criticism, if for the moment it is accepted, would hold for any possible psychology, including the phenomenologically reformed psychology Merleau-Ponty appears to promote.

Merleau-Ponty offers in contrast to both naive realism and naturalism what he calls an "ontological" account of perception. Perception and consciousness ontologically precede and are more basic than the causal relations studied by the sciences. Perception, in his usage, is a form of existence or a kind of being, not a physiological mechanism or a cognitive system. Though this view may sound rather occult at first, I think the strangeness of Merleau-Ponty's point can be lessened somewhat.

Chapter 2 will discuss the origin of this approach in Heidegger's defense of the possibility of fundamental ontology, a defense Merleau-Ponty is largely assuming in these passages. But setting aside that question for the moment, Merleau-Ponty is making a defensible distinction between ontological and causal dependence. For example, physicalism, as a philosophical view, amounts to the claim that all states of the world are ultimately, in their kind of being, physical states; "physical" is then the way to characterize the being of the world. But in making that metaphysical claim about the nature of the world, and some may believe the sciences lend support to it, one is not stating what as a matter of fact causes what or in what manner such and such a state is a physical state. Rather, physicalism concerns only how the world must be for there to be any possible causes, regularities, and dependencies. Thus a philosophical position such as physicalism concerns ontological dependency, in Merleau-Ponty's language, not a specification of causal dependencies.

In a parallel way, though sensory activity is realized by complex psychophysiological processes and therefore involves causal dependencies, Merleau-Ponty shifts attention to perception as a way of being in the world. In that sense of what is perceptual, a conscious body is a way of being, among other ways of being in the world, and makes possible the schematic conception that physically realized sensation can make present to consciousness an object of knowledge. As I said in discussion of Farber's objection above, this position need not deny that human sensations are causally dependent on biological and physiological facts of the matter. Thus in discussing this ontological dependence Merleau-Ponty is doing philosophy, not psychology or physiology. Confusing the study of ontology with that of causal dependence is a symptom of naturalism, in his view.

But, in this way, Merleau-Ponty's stance as a critic of modern psychology, and as offering an alternative approach by way of phenomenology, is both confusing and somewhat misleading. Psychology as science ought not to have been in question. The study of psychology does not, any more than that of physics, resolve questions in the theory of knowledge; that was Husserl's central point. Thus, to adopt Merleau-Ponty's wording, fundamental ontological questions cannot be settled from within any of the sciences.

For example, Merleau-Ponty says that action is *ontologically dependent* on perception. In this way he defends his claim that the proper study of how action depends on perception is not any possible scientific study. "Perception is not a science of the world, it is not even an act . . . it is the background from which all acts stand out, and is presupposed by them" (PP x–xi). Husserl would have preferred to put this point by saying that what he was proposing was the study of the sense or meaning of action, but Merleau-Ponty's approach at least shares some of Husserl's intent.

Thus Merleau-Ponty's distinction between ontological and causal dependence echoes, in part, Husserl's distinction between factual contingency and meaningful necessity. But Merleau-Ponty's modification of Husserl's language of sense and meaning with the language of fundamental ontology does finally depart significantly from Husserl's project. Husserl explicitly treats ontological questions as problems relegated to the empirical sciences, not philosophy (except for formal aspects of ontology that arise in logic). Again quoting from the late Husserl, those writings Merleau-Ponty considers authoritative, the contrast is obvious:

> Thus we are not concerned with whether and what the things, the real entities of the world, actually are (their being actual, their actually being such and such, according to properties, relations, interconnections, etc.): we are also not concerned with what the world, taken as a totality, actually is, what in general belongs to it in the way of a priori structural lawfulness or factual "natural laws." We have nothing like this as our subject matter. (Crisis 156)

Merleau-Ponty, in contrast, holds that although the sciences determine whether or not some entity exists and what its properties are, these causal, physical analyses presuppose and depend upon a fundamental ontology whose defense falls to philosophy. Therefore, it is not the psychological and physiological realization of perception as matters of fact, but perception as "being-in-the-world," an ontology preceding such scientific account, that is the topic of philosophy. He then wants to show how this type of philosophical reflection reforms psychology.

How does Merleau-Ponty's account, therefore, amount to a criticism of Husserl's earlier position? The focus of Merleau-Ponty's criticism is on Husserl's idealism. Merleau-Ponty considers Husserl to have become fixated on a pseudoproblem: How can private experiences represent a public, external world? Husserl wrongly thought that this problem had either an idealist or realist solution. But the "hook" onto the external world that Husserl's transcendental idealism strives to establish is already provided by what Merleau-Ponty prefers to call the "lived" body. This phrase and many other ontological expressions characterizing the nature of perception show that distinctions between object and subject or mind and world, all those separations that bedeviled Husserl, are presuppositions of the sciences.

Thus the problem of how the world can be represented in thought, if that were Husserl's problem, is a pseudoproblem generated by the very naturalistic psychology he began criticizing. Husserl was finally naturalism's secret agent and his philosophical project an uncritical extension of the scientific worldview.

Perception, for Merleau-Ponty, is neither a physiological nor an epistemological issue (epistemology is no more than naturalism); it is an ontological issue. Perception must of necessity be embodied consciousness and such a consciousness must already be there in the world before the above questions can be posed. Merleau-Ponty's "deflationist" account of epistemological problems, as it might be called, bears some comparison with the efforts of such analytic philosophers as G. E. Moore and Gilbert Ryle. However, neither Moore nor Ryle sought an alternative philosophical project, such as the study of fundamental ontology, to replace these traditional, discredited themes. Whether Husserl's turn to idealism can be deflated in this way, and whether epistemology is in this fashion subsumed within the somewhat mysterious study of ontology outlined above, must await a fuller discussion of Heidegger's defense of fundamental ontology as the central philosophical task and Heidegger's similar criticisms of Husserl.

No Raison d'Être?

In an early essay, "The Transcendence of the Ego," Jean-Paul Sartre also criticizes Husserl's idealism by objecting to the notion of a "transcendental ego." This criticism of Husserl can be considered apart from the rest of Sartre's influential *Being and Nothingness,* which is the focus of the final section of Chapter 2.

After introducing the phenomenological method to his readers as a "descriptive science," Sartre turns to his criticism, which is that the transcendental ego is incompatible with what is valuable about the phenomenological reduction. "Like Husserl, we are persuaded that our psychic and psycho-physical *me* is a transcendent object which must fall before the εποχη. But we raise the following question: is not this psychic and psycho-physical *me* enough? Need one double it with a transcendental I, a structure of absolute consciousness?" (TE 36).[31]

Sartre accuses Husserl of postulating the existence of a transcendental ego due to his later turn to idealism; thus his specific arguments for this notion will prove weak. Sartre notes that Husserl defends his introduction of a transcendental ego because of the need to preserve the "unity of consciousness." The expression "unity of consciousness" has been already encountered in Brentano, who argued that mental experiences "belong to one unitary reality only if they are inwardly perceived as existing together." Thus the so-called problem of the "unity of consciousness" concerns determining what criteria guide one in assigning experiences to one's self and not to another. How is it possible for my consciousness, for instance, to belong to me?

Intentionality (Sartre uses the term interchangeably with "consciousness") is "directedness" toward an object, and Sartre asserts that the unity of consciousness is built into any intentional state whatsoever, though it occurs impersonally and anonymously. The point of this claim is to convince his readers that the unity of consciousness does not require postulating a self or the transcendental ego. Sartre treats Husserl as bothered by a traditional philosophical misconception that there must be some relationship of "ownership" of consciousness. "The ego is not the owner of consciousness, it is the object of consciousness" (TE 97).

Thus, the transcendental ego has no raison d'être with regard to phenomenology. The unity that Husserl is trying to account for with the transcendental ego is already present by way of the spontaneous (and yet anonymous) nature of mental activity: "The ego is the spontaneous, transcendent unification of our states and our actions. In this capacity, it is no hypothesis" (TE 76). Therefore, "consciousness is simply consciousness of its object—whatever that object is—consciousness is aware of itself *in so far as it is consciousness of a transcendent object*" (TE 40).

Sartre's central argument is that if the ego is simply another intentional object of consciousness, it is subject to the same bracketing as any intentional object and ought not to be postulated as a "thing-in-itself," as he claims it is by Husserl. But on this point Sartre is confused in both his understanding of the reduction and the transcendental ego. Sartre, like Merleau-Ponty, treats the phenomenological reduction as a form of skepticism about the existence of "transcendent objects." As I have argued already, the reduction is a methodical device, not a substantive position concerning ontology. Thus, even if Sartre were correct about his point concerning the self and the procedure of reduction, it would not allow him to conclude that the self does not exist.

Assuming for the moment Sartre's misunderstanding of the reduction, Sartre considers Husserl's transcendental ego in *Ideas* as an ontological claim against which there are two objections. First, it ought to be treated as all other ontological claims are, namely, suspended by the *epochē*. Second, Husserl has wrongly assumed that an ego or self, like consciousness, is a sort of state of the world, whereas in Sartre's view the ego or the self is a construction of consciousness.

First of all, these two criticisms are at odds with one another. The first point simply recommends that one suspend judgment about the reality of the natural ego (which is, after all, Husserl's procedure), whereas the second criticism concludes that the ego is "not real"; it is some sort of invented effect of consciousness. But Sartre is simply confusing here questions about the existence or nonexistence of entities (or what causes what) with the task of analyzing phenomena.

Sartre's entire account of this issue goes astray because Husserl's transcendental ego is not an ontological claim at all; it is not a claim about the natural world, nor does it postulate any mysterious entity. The transcendental domain is the domain of meanings, and none of its claims, including the necessity of the reflective or transcendental ego, are about the existence of entities or understood by Husserl as competitive with the ordinary, empirical world. Asking whether Husserl's transcendental ego really exists suggests a conceptual confusion on a par with asking, as Husserl used the example, whether numbers enter into causal relations with objects.

Sartre's criticism is guided by a central conviction, also found in Merleau-Ponty, that Husserl's realism and idealism are deeply irreconcilable; Husserl appears to both as a prisoner rather than a critic of obsolete, traditional metaphysics. Husserl's detailed project for philosophical reform, misunderstood and then dismissed as insufficiently radical, would as a result of these kinds of criticisms and pronouncements not survive in the form he had envisaged. As though cursed, however, what Husserl attacked as the "bewitching routine of resurrected metaphysics" would not only replace his dream of philosophy as a rigorous science, but do so under his name.

Notes

1. Franz Brentano, *The True and the Evident* (New York: Humanities Press, 1966), p. 10.

2. "In this unhappy present, is not our situation similar to the one encountered by Descartes in his youth? If so, then is not this a fitting time to renew his radicalness, the radicalness of the beginning philosopher: to subject to a Cartesian overthrow the immense philosophical literature with its medley of great traditions, of comparatively serious new beginnings, of stylish literary activity (which counts on 'making an effect,' but not on being studied), and to begin with a new *meditationes de prima philosophia*" (CM 5).

3. "It should be noted, however, that our aim here has not been to . . . project a new 'theory of knowledge' pertaining to the various spheres of reality; our aim has been instead only to bring about insight into certain general thoughts which can help one to acquire the idea of transcendentally pure consciousness" (Ideas 130).

4. Though I will avoid discussion of translation problems in my exposition, Husserl's term "intuition," the usual English translation for *Anschauung*, tends to mislead English readers due to some unintended associations. "Intuition" is a technical term in German philosophy after Kant and the expression "intuition of essence" *(Wesenschau)* has no irrational or mystical implications as used by Husserl.

5. The terms "internalism" and "externalism" are currently used to contrast two responses to skepticism (social externalism is also the topic of Chapter 3). Internalism refers to those philosophical positions in which justification of knowledge is due to some feature of a subject's inner mental states apart from whatever lies external to those mental states. Tyler Burge, writing in opposition to internal-

ism, calls it a type of "individualism": "According to individualism about the mind, the mental natures of all of a person's or animal's mental states (and events) are such that there is no necessary or deep individuative relation between the individual's being in states of those kinds and the nature of the individual's physical or social environments." "Individualism and Psychology," *Philosophical Review* 95 (1986), p. 4. Also see Burge, "Individualism and the Mental," in *Studies in Metaphysics,* ed. Peter A. French et al., *Midwest Studies in Philosophy* 4 (1979), pp. 73–121.

6. The most influential version of these attacks is to be found in W. V. O. Quine, *From a Logical Point of View* (Cambridge, Mass.: Harvard University Press, 1953). Quine directed his criticism to these distinctions within logical positivism, not within Husserl's writings. But Quine's objections, if sound, would bring down the project of phenomenology as well. Quine's critical strategy continues, however, to be a lively topic of debate in philosophy.

7. Husserl considers his project of providing philosophy secure foundations and a method as making possible a philosophical "science." *Wissenschaft* in German has a much broader use than "science" in English. Since the repeated use of "science" would only serve to obscure, for the English reader, Husserl's distinction between philosophy as a priori inquiry and the empirical inquiry of science (unless I repeat that science can also refer to systematic a priori inquiry), I will, whenever possible, avoid this phrasing.

8. Husserl warns, "I avoid as much as possible the expressions *'a priori'* and *'a posteriori'* because of the confusing obscurities and many significations clinging to them in general use, and also because of the notorious philosophical doctrines that, as an evil heritage from the past, are combined with them" (Ideas xxvii). Though Husserl's warning about this terminology and its "evil heritage" are worth bearing in mind, it is difficult to take seriously Husserl's pledge to avoid these terms or see how his usage finally diverges significantly from the philosophical tradition.

9. Hilary Putnam, "Why Reason Can't Be Naturalized," *Realism and Reason, Philosophical Papers,* vol. 3 (New York: Cambridge University Press, 1983), pp. 229–247.

10. In his review of various arguments against the project of a naturalized epistemology, W. V. O. Quine also cites circularity as a traditional objection. "Why not settle for psychology? Such a surrender of the epistemological burden to psychology is a move that was disallowed in earlier times as circular reasoning. If the epistemologist's goal is validation on the grounds of empirical science, he defeats his purpose by using psychology or other empirical science in the validation." *Ontological Relativity and Other Essays* (New York: Columbia University Press, 1969), pp. 75–76. Quine dismisses such concerns by dismissing the entire project of providing epistemological foundations.

11. "We protect ourselves methodically against these confusions so deeply rooted in us as born dogmatists; in no other way could we avoid them" (Ideas 141).

12. Kah Kyung Cho, "Phenomenology as Cooperative Task: Husserl-Farber Correspondence during 1936–37," *Philosophy and Phenomenological Research* 1, Supplement (Fall 1990). Emphasis added.

13. Franz Brentano, *Psychology from an Empirical Standpoint*, ed. Oskar Kraus (New York: Humanities Press, 1973), p. 88.

14. Brentano, *Psychology*, p. 164.

15. Brentano distinguishes "mental phenomena" from "physical phenomena." But this language is confusing since by "physical phenomena" he does not mean actual objects referred to in the world, but the qualitative experiences of color, sound, or odor. These internal phenomena, according to Brentano, lack intentionality and hence are not strictly "mental phenomena" after all; they are nonrepresentational, physical phenomena.

16. Gilbert Ryle's essays on Husserl stress the connection between his theory of meaning and a defense of the autonomy of philosophy. "Husserl at the turn of the century was under many of the same intellectual pressures as were Meinong, Frege, Bradley, Peirce, G. E. Moore, and Bertrand Russell. All alike were in revolt against the idea-psychology of Hume and Mill; all alike found in the notion of meaning their escape-route from subjectivist theories of thinking; nearly all of them championed a Platonic theory of meanings, i.e., of concepts and propositions; all alike demarcated philosophy from natural science by allocating factual enquiries to the natural sciences and conceptual enquiries to philosophy; nearly all of them talked as if these conceptual enquiries of philosophy terminated in some super-inspections of some super-objects, as if conceptual enquiries were, after all, super-observational enquiries." Ryle, *Collected Papers,* vol. 1 (London: Hutchinson, 1971), p. 180.

17. For a further discussion of Husserl's theory of meaning, see Chapter 5.

18. J. A. Fodor's "Methodological Solipsism Considered as a Research Strategy in Cognitive Psychology," *Behavioral and Brain Sciences* 3 (1980), pp. 63–72, defends constraining psychological explanations to what is "in the head" of the individual. Fodor borrows the phrase "methodological solipsism" from Rudolf Carnap, who in turn cited Husserl. "The autopsychological basis is also called *solipsistic.* We do not thereby subscribe to the solipsistic view that only one subject and its experiences are real. ... At the beginning of the system, the experiences must simply be taken as they occur. We shall not claim reality or nonreality in connection with these experiences, rather these claims will be 'bracketed' (i.e., we will exercise the phenomenological 'withholding of judgement,' *epochē*, in Husserl's sense." R. Carnap, *The Logical Structure of the World,* trans. Rolf A. George (Berkeley: University of California Press, 1969), p. 101.

19. In recent philosophy of mind it has become common to distinguish mental sensations from propositional attitudes. The distinctive ways such sensations look or feel, sensations such as hearing a sound or feeling nauseous, are called *qualia,* or "raw feels"(see Colin McGinn, *The Character of Mind* (Oxford: Oxford University Press, 1982). Some of Husserl's terminology fits this picture, but Husserl does not consider speculating about the nature of cognitive structure as a properly philosophical concern.

20. "Philosophy simply puts everything before us, and neither explains nor deduces anything—since everything lies open to view there is nothing to explain. For what is hidden, for example, is of no interest to us. One might also give the name 'philosophy' to what is possible *before* all new discoveries and inventions." Ludwig Wittgenstein, *Philosophical Investigations,* trans. G. E. M. Anscombe (New York: Macmillan, 1953), p. 50.

21. Husserl eventually has the intuition of essences displace argument. For example, in *Crisis* he speaks of studying the "a priori accomplishments" of "our intentional life" as "exhibited rather than argumentatively constructed or conceived through mythical thinking" (Crisis 181).

22. An often repeated criticism of Husserl is that the method of the reduction fails at preserving philosophical neutrality. I will discuss this line of criticism later in this chapter, in Chapter 2, and again in Chapter 5. For a lengthy defense of this objection see Herman Philipse, "Transcendental Idealism," in *The Cambridge Companion to Husserl*, ed. Barry Smith and David Woodruff Smith (New York: Cambridge University Press, 1995), pp. 239–322.

23. Husserl's characteristic shift in this passage between "our" and "my" transcendental ego demonstrates some carelessness about how to state his point. A footnote in this edition reports that in later editorial comments Husserl crossed out the word "my" in the second to the last sentence and wrote, "The dangerous first person singular! This should be expanded terminologically."

24. Husserl characterizes the reduction as "immanent," "within experience," interior, pure, or an "abstractive restriction to the pure contents of 'internal' or purely psychological self-experience . . . *purely internal experience*" (CM 25).

25. "By explaining Intentionality in terms of language I do not mean to imply that Intentionality is essentially and necessarily linguistic. . . . Language is derived from Intentionality and not conversely. The direction of pedagogy is to explain Intentionality in terms of language; the direction of logical analysis is to explain language in terms of Intentionality." John Searle, *Intentionality: An Essay in the Philosophy of Mind* (New York: Cambridge University Press, 1983), p. 5.

26. "Even an absolute God cannot create a 'feeling of evidence' that absolutely guarantees the being of Nature—or, in a better formulation, a self-contained process of external experience that, no matter how different it might conceivably be from 'our' sensuous experience, would give something—itself apodictically and adequately" (FTL 284).

27. Wilhelm Dilthey, *Selected Works*, vol. 1, *Introduction to the Human Sciences*, ed. Rudolf A. Makreel and Frithjof Rodi (Princeton: Princeton University Press, 1989).

28. Karl Schuhmann, "Koyré et les phénoménologues allemands," *History and Technology* 4 (1987), pp. 149–167.

29. "Everyone has the sense of philosophy's end . . . and, in the same way, obviously, he understands the others in whose company, in critical friendship and enmity, he philosophizes" (Crisis 394).

30. Marvin Farber, "The Philosophic Impact of the Facts Themselves," *Essays in Honor of Dorion Cairns*, ed. Richard Zaner and Fred Kersten (The Hague: Martinus Nijhoff, 1973), p. 36.

31. The phrase "must fall before the εποχη" echoes a formulation from Husserl. "But when I practice the reducing epochē on myself and my world-consciousness, the other human beings, like the world itself, fall before the epochē; that is, they are merely intentional phenomena for me" (Crisis 256). However, the phrase "intentional phenomena for me" does not mean for Husserl, as Sartre assumes, that the phenomena in question are thereby nonexistent.

Suggested Readings

The following collections of articles on Husserl are representative of central disputes concerning his work: Frederick A. Elliston and Peter McCormick, eds., *Husserl: Expositions and Appraisals* (Notre Dame, Ind.: University of Notre Dame Press, 1977); Hubert L. Dreyfus, ed., *Husserl, Intentionality and Cognitive Science* (Cambridge, Mass.: MIT Press, 1982); J. N. Mohanty and William R. McKenna, eds., *Husserl's Phenomenology: A Textbook* (Washington, D.C.: University Press of America, 1989); Barry Smith and David Woodruff Smith, eds., *The Cambridge Companion to Husserl* (Cambridge: Cambridge University Press, 1995).

Two informative book-length accounts focusing respectively on Husserl's philosophical background and his current philosophical significance are: Barry Smith, *Austrian Philosophy: The Legacy of Franz Brentano* (La Salle, Ind.: Open Court, 1994); and David Woodruff Smith and Ronald McIntyre, *Husserl and Intentionality: A Study of Mind, Meaning, and Language* (Boston: Reidel, 1982).

An influential and characteristic work within the continental tradition, though excruciatingly written, that criticizes Husserl's idealism by way of Marxist sociology is Theodor Adorno, *Against Epistemology, A Metacritique: Studies in Husserl and the Phenomenological Antinomies* (Oxford: Blackwell, 1982). This kind of approach receives more critical discussion in Chapters 3 and 5.

The work of Maurice Merleau-Ponty and what I called "French phenomenology" have occasioned a vast but wildly uneven secondary literature. A useful though not especially critical overview of Merleau-Ponty's major works can be found in James Schmidt, *Maurice Merleau-Ponty: Between Phenomenology and Structuralism* (New York: St. Martin's Press, 1985). J. N. Mohanty, *The Possibility of Transcendental Philosophy* (Boston: M. Nijhoff, 1985), compares and contrasts Husserl with, among others, his French interpreters.

Bibliography

CM: Husserl, E. *Cartesian Meditations: An Introduction to Phenomenology.* Translated by Dorion Cairns. Boston: Kluwer Academic Publishers, 1995.

Crisis: Husserl, E. *The Crisis of European Sciences and Transcendental Phenomenology.* Translated by David Carr. Evanston, Ill.: Northwestern University Press, 1970.

FTL: Husserl, E. *Formal and Transcendental Logic.* Translated by Dorion Cairns. The Hague: Martinus Nijhoff, 1969.

Ideas: Husserl, E. *Ideas Pertaining to a Pure Phenomenology and to a Phenomenological Philosophy.* First Book. Translated by Fred Kersten. Boston: Kluwer Academic Publishers, 1982.

PP: Merleau-Ponty, M. *Phenomenology of Perception.* Translated by Colin Smith. London: Routledge & Kegan Paul, 1962.

PRS: Husserl, E. "Philosophy as a Rigorous Science." In *Phenomenology and the Crisis of Philosophy.* Translated by Quentin Lauer. New York: Harper Torchbooks, 1965.

TE: Sartre, J-P. *Transcendence of the Ego: An Existential Theory of Consciousness.* Translated by Forrest Williams and Robert Kirkpatrick. New York: Hill and Wang, 1990.

2

ONTOLOGY

Martin Heidegger's studies of Husserl's *Logical Investigations* when he was a student led him from the study of theology to philosophy. At the University of Freiburg Heidegger had already attended lectures of the Neo-Kantian Heinrich Rickert, whose chair of philosophy, after 1911, Husserl occupied. In Husserl's seminars, which Heidegger eventually joined, participants were trained exclusively through phenomenological exercises. Aside from the obligatory ancient Greek terminology, Husserl kept his distance from the details or difficulties of understanding the history of philosophy and did not think such matters resolved deep philosophical debates. Husserl's technique of phenomenological description was introduced not only as the way to ultimately decide philosophical issues, but as a means of creating among his students a commitment to philosophy as a professional discipline requiring training and aiming at "scientifically" rigorous results.[1]

Though Heidegger wrote to Karl Jaspers as early as 1923 with a surprisingly harsh dismissal of Husserl's personal and professional significance, it is likely that this letter is less reliable than Heidegger's repeated public acknowledgments of Husserl's intellectual influence.[2] Specifically, the effect of Husserl's teachings on Heidegger's break with traditional philosophical approaches, eventually including Husserl's own transcendental idealism, cannot be underestimated.

Husserl also held Heidegger in very high regard, at least until shortly before his own death, and considered him his most significant student and follower.[3] The dramatic events behind the deterioration of their friendship are summarized below. However, even during that period after 1918 marking their closest personal and professional friendship, these two thinkers were already divided by temperament and a basic conception of the task of philosophy.

Husserl's philosophical interests had been stamped by his early work in mathematics, logic, and psychology, and his approach relegated as largely

irrelevant both interpretative textual debate about the history of philosophy and stylistic innovation. Heidegger, on the other hand, connected his
philosophical views intimately to historical, artistic, poetic, theological,
and even literary preoccupations, concerns that gradually came to dominate his later writings. Heidegger did identify with Husserl's efforts to dis-
lodge naturalism, and they agreed on the sterility of contemporary philosophical debate, including typical studies of the history of philosophy. But
Heidegger held, even when under Husserl's influence, that concentration
on theoretical, scientific, and mathematical issues deeply distorted genuine philosophical inquiry.

Heidegger embraced phenomenology as the method guiding his critical
reappropriation and revival of philosophy (and he agreed with the sense of
a crisis with regard to this task), eventually claiming leadership of this intellectual movement poised to realize Husserl's "dream." But, as I will argue
below, Heidegger's method proved not to be Husserl's phenomenology, and
that would have been clear to any attentive and careful reader at the time.
Being and Time, Heidegger's first major published work, even criticizes fundamental details of Husserl's views (though not by name). But Heidegger's
announced embrace of the phenomenological method was taken rather uncritically by most readers, perpetuating misunderstandings of both these
figures. As a result, Husserl's conception of philosophy and its proper
method gradually disappeared from continental philosophy, swept aside by
Heidegger's agenda, "flashier" style, and public claim that he was merely
following in his teacher's path.

Finally, these thinkers were divided in their sense of philosophy's cultural
role. Heidegger wrote for a wider audience than Husserl did, even as he
wrote difficult and intentionally obscure works. Though Husserl also appreciated philosophy's cultural relevance and specifically addressed what he
considered the crisis of relativism gripping European society, Husserl was
an insular, self-directed, and self-absorbed thinker. He wrote as if in a continual monologue. Heidegger, on the other hand, was from the very beginning of his career oracular, emotive, and grandiose. Apparently a skilled
lecturer, he mastered the literary and rhetorical techniques of philosophizing in the "grand style" while at the same time cultivating the dramatic
stance of a radical and an outsider.[4]

Unlike Husserl, Heidegger was keenly aware of and attentive to the social, cultural, and political issues that lurked beneath the surface of even
rarefied debates. In 1928, after Husserl retired from the University of
Freiburg, Heidegger (with Husserl's support) replaced Husserl as professor
of philosophy at Freiburg. In 1933 Heidegger was elected rector of the University of Freiburg and in that same year joined the National Socialist
Party. During November 1933, on the eve of the Reichstag elections, he
gave public speeches supporting Hitler and his policies. Though Heidegger

resigned from both the party and the rectorship in 1934, he defended and implemented during the period of his rectorship the *Gleichschaltung* legislation within universities barring Jews and others deemed "undesirable" from the civil service.

Heidegger remained silent for the rest of his career about this period except for an interview for *Der Spiegel* in 1966. Even in that interview, which appeared only after his death, he remained evasive and self-serving concerning the details of those past events. In recent years a number of works have appeared detailing Heidegger's involvement with German fascism and exhibiting a range of views about the nature of his complicity and what relationship, if any, exists between Heidegger's philosophical views and these political misadventures.[5]

Though the connection of these events to his philosophical views would take me beyond the limits of this work, these events raise serious questions, at the very least, about the many moral and political pronouncements Heidegger scatters throughout his writings. He could not claim to have been unaware, for instance, of Husserl's situation, and he even acted at the time of his rectorship in what seems both a petty and symbolic manner to deny Husserl library privileges. But Heidegger also exhibited during this period, and in his subsequent frustrating quiescence, a somewhat traditional view about the relationship between intellectual life and politics, one at odds with his supposed political and philosophical radicalism. Although adherence to such a tradition scarcely absolves him of responsibility, a recently translated 1941 lecture finds Heidegger crafting, in passing, a self-justification based on picturing political and historical events as so many transient realizations of deep metaphysical battles.

> It is something else when world dominions are knowingly planned to last millennia and the assurance of their existence is undertaken by that will whose essential goal is the greatest possible duration for the greatest possible order of the largest possible masses. This will has been the concealed metaphysical essence of modernity for at least the last three centuries. . . . However, where one interprets the execution of this metaphysical will as a "product" of selfishness and the caprice of "dictators" and "authoritarian states," there speak only political calculation and propaganda, or the metaphysical naivete of a thinking that ran aground centuries ago, or both. Political circumstances, economic situations, population growth, and the like, can be the proximate causes and horizons for carrying out this metaphysical will of modern world-history. But they are never the foundation of this history and therefore never its "end."[6]

Because of Heidegger's public actions during and after the war and his withdrawal from political life, there arose an image of him (often with his encouragement) as the stereotypically naive academic at the mercy of political forces and ends he barely comprehended. Though Heidegger's politics can likely be described as naive, using the term in its normal rather than Husserlian sense, this picture of him as detached from and oblivious to the events in which he participated simply finds no support in his own words or in the historical evidence. Yet, ironically enough, this image of academic detachment fits Husserl only too well. It was only shortly before Husserl's death that he finally grasped, with shocked indignation, that his intellectual reputation and lifelong patriotism counted for nothing against a Jewish heritage—even, as he then further understood, in the calculations of his most famous student.

In discussing the development of continental philosophy in the twentieth century, this chapter focuses on Heidegger's *Being and Time,* his most influential work. Although Heidegger's style may be largely an acquired taste, the terminology and organization of *Being and Time* have a certain rationale and sense once the strangeness of the initial encounter wears off. The obscurity arises at the level of grasping the overall problem being discussed and his reasons for pursuing the project as he does. The very few defenses he does offer of his approach are unfortunately always sketchy; often he appeals only to some repetitive syntactic devices (especially the passive-voice construction so common in German), an excessive use of hyphens by which phrases are converted into mysterious "substantives," and numerous neologisms. I will try to avoid, whenever possible, Heidegger's cumbersome hyphens and passive-voice syntax.[7]

Though I also use the recently published lectures he gave on the topic of phenomenology during the period in which he was composing *Being and Time,* I will ignore Heidegger's later publications. The distinction between ontic and ontological questions is the main theme, and after outlining his concepts of "Dasein" and temporality my exposition leads back to a line of criticism concerning this central distinction. At the end of *Being and Time,* Heidegger grants that there may be other ways to pose these questions he believes Western philosophy has forgotten. "We must look for a way to illuminate the fundamental ontological question and follow it. Whether that way is at all the *only* one or even the *right* one can be decided only after we have *followed* it" (BT 398, SZ 437). If the philosophical problem he attempted to make central again for philosophers were really only accessible by way of some of the idiosyncratic German he invents, then its importance would be extremely doubtful. Though I want to convey this effort, warts and all, my emphasis is on the philosophical position and not on contorted efforts at paraphrasing it.

Jean-Paul Sartre's *Being and Nothingness* receives a briefer discussion. Sartre's widely known philosophical work is deeply Heideggerian in theme and language, but fundamentally abandons, as Heidegger would claim in his "Letter on Humanism," the central question as Heidegger understood it.

Being, Not Beings

Chapter 1 ended with various critical assessments of Husserl focusing on the metaphysical commitments that some critics charged survived and compromised the claimed neutrality of the phenomenological reduction. Husserl never wavered from the view, however, that phenomenology was distinct from the adoption of a philosophical position, a point he stressed when he discussed ontology, perhaps even more strongly given his own idealism.

> The object of research, to make assertions about what belongs eidetically to these sort of physical—thing—intentions as such . . . is not to explore physical things, physical things as such. A 'physical thing' as correlate is not a physical thing; therefore the quotation marks. . . . For phenomenology it is not ontological Intuition, but rather, phenomenological Intuition that here has to make the final decision. Ontology itself, with all its ontic positings, is really something irrelevant for precisely such performances.[8]

The phenomenology of intentional objects is not the study of physical objects; philosophy is not strictly the study of objects at all. Husserl could be described as proposing an intellectual division of labor between philosophy and the sciences. The sciences determine what ontology (objects or states of affairs) is required for its theoretical accounts of the natural world. Philosophy reflects upon the essential meaning of objectivity, necessity, causality, or physical things, independently of those posited theoretical objects and accounts; philosophy's a priori inquiry in this way precedes and is independent of any specific scientific theories and ontologies.[9] Thus philosophers only need speak of "physical objects."

In contrast, Heidegger begins *Being and Time* announcing that he aims to reinvigorate the study of ontology and what he specifically calls the question of being. But, at the same time, he indicates that he is abandoning the metaphysical tradition. *Being and Time* starts, then, with Husserl's reform of philosophy in view, but a reform with regard to ontology as the central philosophical problem of the tradition.

Heidegger's defense of this topic presupposes a basic distinction, continually stressed and repeated in his work, between ontic and ontological questions. This distinction is meant to preserve the autonomy of philosophy with respect to the sciences by distinguishing two different tasks that the philosophical tradition has persistently confused. But it also undercuts Husserl's restriction on what is the proper topic of philosophy. Without this distinction, or lacking a clear grasp of it, Husserl failed, in Heidegger's view, to grasp the deep connection between phenomenology and ontology. "Ontology and phenomenology are not two different disciplines which among others belong to philosophy. Both terms characterize philosophy itself, its object and procedure. Philosophy is universal phenomenological ontology ... " (BT 34, SZ 38).

Heidegger uses the term "ontic" for what in his view has wrongly been considered ontology and is the traditional topic of metaphysics. Traditionally, philosophy has identified itself with practical and theoretical inquiry into what are the structures, properties, dispositions, or states of the various natural and social entities found in the world. These ontic questions range from practical tasks to theoretical explanations as found in the advanced sciences and are wrongly assumed to be the equivalent of philosophical ontology. In this sense, Heidegger continues Husserl's effort to sharply distinguish philosophical from scientific questions.

Ontological questions, in contrast, do not elicit inquiry into a catalog of entities or their properties; inquiry into the being of things is not inquiry into the properties of entities. Being is not an entity, nor is it a property of an entity. Also, the question of being can be investigated independently of the extent of technical or theoretical knowledge about the world. In other words, although the answers to ontic questions do depend on what is the state of technical and theoretical inquiry, ontological inquiry is possible pretheoretically and pretechnically. Even were entities and their properties, as a matter of contingent fact, other than they are in this world, or even were they, in some possible world, wholly inaccessible, the question of ontology would remain possible and would remain distinct. Being is what is common to entities whatever their nature and whether or not their nature is empirically accessible.

For example, in Heidegger's conception physicalism (as discussed in the previous chapter) would be an ontological, not an ontic claim about the world. Physicalism is thus a type of metaphysics and concerns, as Heidegger prefers to state it, "being-in-the-world," not a list of the actual beings in the world. In this way physicalism, properly understood, exhibits the conceptual priority of the question of being over the question of what beings there are. Also physicalism, in this sense, is presupposed by any scientific success, because it states some a priori conditions holding for all possible worlds, to use a more recent way of speaking, as being physical worlds. Though Heidegger thinks physicalism is deeply mistaken metaphysics, for reasons to be discussed, he would likely consider it a properly ontological position and thus an answer, however much a failure, to the question of being. In disputing physicalism, then, the issue concerns the question of the being of the world, not the beings in the world. The latter form of inquiry Heidegger gives over to the sciences.

Scientific inquiry has made enormous progress with regard to ontic questions and thus with regard to knowledge of the properties and causal powers of a vast range of entities. But that progress, if Heidegger is right, is not progress in the question of ontology; in fact ontological questions are not only independent of advances in technology and empirical research, but such success proves an obstacle to ontological inquiry. Heidegger argues that ontic inquiry blinds thought to the separate question of being. Yet ontic responses (such as scientific explanations) presuppose, both theoretically and practically, ontological clarification. "What is decisive about the mathematic project of nature is again not primarily the mathematical element as such, but the fact that this project *discloses a priori* ... that in it the thematic beings are discovered in *the* only way that beings can be discovered: in the prior project of their constitution of being" (BT 332, SZ 363).

But Heidegger's question about the meaning of being remains strikingly odd, and much of Heidegger's writing embraces how strange an inquiry it is. The question of being is unavoidable and yet demands a unique type of inquiry. The question of being is prone to misunderstanding and confusion precisely because it seems indistinguishable from explaining or controlling the beings (entities) in the world.

> The first philosophical step in understanding the problem of being consists in avoiding ... "telling a story," that is, not determining beings as beings by tracing them back in their origins to another being—as if being had the character of a possible being. As what is asked about, being thus requires its own kind of demonstration which is essentially different from the discovery of beings. Hence what is to be *ascertained,* the meaning of being, will require its own conceptualization, which again is essentially distinct from the concepts in which beings receive their determination of meaning. (BT 5, SZ 7)

A full account of the nature of entities may be the ideal task of science, but even the completion of such a task (even were a "final theory of everything," as physicists now call it, possible) would not constitute an answer to the question of being. In this way Heidegger's distinction produces a kind of Husserlian bracketing. If Heidegger is correct about this separate, independent inquiry into ontology, he can place all ontic results, no matter how secure, and disputes, no matter how pressing, within parentheses.

As evidence of this implicit Husserlian strategy, Heidegger uses the same language as Husserl, which is actually rare in *Being and Time,* when he characterizes both the distinction itself and what constitutes the subject matter of ontology. He describes the inquiry he hopes to defend as a priori inquiry, as inquiry into the *meaning* of being, as a *pure science* of ontology, and as an investigation into the precondition for or possibility of both mundane and scientific understanding.

The sciences, however, are treated by Heidegger as merely an extension of the kind of mundane involvement with the world characteristic of everyday life, and therein lies the first hint of a difference with Husserl. Encountering the world is, Heidegger emphasizes, primarily the use and manipulation of and involvement in the world as those occur in the most pedestrian of actions and encounters. The tendency to picture encountering the world only through theoretical inquiry, as in the sciences, is in Heidegger's view a deep error. In fact, it is primarily in the mundane involvement with the world (not the disinterested act of theoretical reflection) that the being of the world is "disclosed," rather than the properties of beings. Heidegger characterizes his project as a concern with "being as *it is initially and for the most part—in its average everydayness.* Not arbitrary and accidental structures but essential ones are to be demonstrated in this everydayness . . ." (BT 15, SZ 17). The being of entities makes possible encountering and thus using the world. That is why, as regards ontology, the ontic inquiry of the sciences neither takes priority over nor has greater significance than the tasks of everyday life.

> It is true that ontological inquiry is more original than the ontic inquiry of the positive sciences. But it remains naive and opaque if its investigations into the being of beings leave the meaning of being in general undiscussed. And precisely the ontological task of a genealogy of the different possible ways of being (a genealogy which is not to be construed deductively) requires a preliminary understanding of "what we really mean by this expression 'being.'"
>
> The question of being thus aims at an a priori condition of the possibility not only of the sciences that investigate beings of such and such a type—and are thereby already involved in an understanding of being—but it aims also at the condition of the possibility of the ontologies that precede the ontic sciences and found them. *All ontology, no matter how rich and tightly knit a system of categories it has at its disposal, remains fundamentally blind and perverts its innermost intent if it has not previously clarified the meaning of being sufficiently and grasped this clarification as its fundamental task.* (BT 9, SZ 11)

In bracketing the ontic response, however, Heidegger runs the risk of denying himself any access to his topic. If the nature of beings is properly the object of either the sciences or simple practical involvement and does not thereby belong to the task of *Being and Time,* what kind of inquiry concerning the being of entities remains possible? Even given the distinction between being and beings (entities), it remains obscure as to what would even constitute the answer to the question "What is the meaning of being?"

Before discussing Heidegger's strategy for ontological inquiry, I want to look more closely at his intent. (I will return to this basic distinction and its possible problems in the section criticizing Heidegger.) Given the above constraint, what genuine philosophical task survives? First, it does not involve, as would be expected, the traditional questions of whether certain problematic or controversial objects exist or not. For example, Heidegger does not classify as genuinely ontological questions such traditional philosophical topics as those concerning the nature or existence of the soul, numbers, relations, other minds, or substances. These traditional questions are irremediably ontic. *Being and Time* (and I will treat that discussion in detail later) does discuss the persistence of the self in time and traditional quandaries about personal and material identity. But even when Heidegger flirts with how his approach might contribute to the discussion of these traditional philosophical problems, he thinks his analysis reveals that the underlying presuppositions of traditional thought confuse the ontic with the ontological.

Thus, Heidegger's ontology makes no "radical" proposals. He does not make dramatic declarations about, for instance, the existence of minds, material objects, or artifacts. In fact, many of his ontic claims are conservative and rely mostly on common sense. He thinks, for example, that there are artifacts, persons, and causal relations, just to mention some examples of traditional controversies in which Heidegger comes out on the side of common sense. Heidegger treats such claims as questionable only to the extent that they presuppose, and yet fail to clarify, an understanding of what is meant by the concept of being and that such clarification must precede any decision about whether existence extends to "immaterial" objects or to such abstractions as minds and numbers.

Second, Heidegger does not argue, for instance, that the normal, ordinary, or, as he often prefers, "vulgar" account of objects and entities is entirely wrong or needs to be completely replaced. In spite of his extravagant vocabulary for ontological inquiry, he does not present common sense as deeply mistaken on its fundamental categories, for instance, the basic typology of artifact, material object, and experience. His extravagant vocabulary in fact seems parasitical on such ordinary claims, and in the end he seeks to salvage some of this common sense against what he calls our philosophical confusions.

"Idle talk," as Heidegger calls the verities of common life, is not treated by him as the philosophical equivalent of believing in the "humors" of ancient medicine or the "phlogiston" of pre-Lavoisian chemistry. But in spite of my comments about Heidegger's conservative attitude toward challenging basic ontological assumptions, he does challenge the vocabulary of mental states (including Husserl's concept of intentionality) for concealing an ontology. These suspicions do then play an important role in why he crafts the strange language of *Being and Time,* as explained below.

For the most part Heidegger simply does not enter into familiar philosophical disputes, dismisses most of them as merely ontic when he does mention them, and considers them apart from and secondary to the question of the meaning of being.

Always, We Ourselves

Let me return to questions raised above. Is such ontological inquiry, irreducible to ontic inquiry, possible? Where does inquiry into the being of the world begin, if it cannot begin with actual entities? How do we investigate the being of the world while suspending questions about either the existence or properties of whatever beings there are? How can inquiry into being not presuppose the sciences?

Heidegger defends the significance and possibility of this ontological inquiry in two ways, only the second of which I can discuss in this chapter. First, he proceeds on the basis of the argument in *Being and Time* to recount, in a series of later books and lectures, the history of philosophy as the history of "forgetting" this question about the being of beings. That is, he examines major philosophers (Kant, Leibniz, Hegel, Schelling, Parmenides, and Heraclitus, among others), uncovering within their work various strategies (both latent and manifest) to avoid, suppress, or misconceive the question of being. It is this long history of misunderstanding in philosophy that has made the question of being disappear and dissolve into ontic study of entities. "We understand this task as the destructuring of the traditional content of ancient ontology which is to be carried out along the *guidelines of the question of being*. This destructuring is based upon the original experiences in which the first and subsequently guiding determinations of being were gained" (BT 20, SZ 23).

Second, Heidegger answers the above question by a reflective strategy reminiscent of Husserl. Ontological inquiry could begin with an entity, if there were an entity such that asking about it was necessarily asking about the meaning of being. The problem raised above was that the study of ontology seemed impossible to carry out since it could not begin with any contingent entity within the world. The question of being is autonomous, after all, from the question of the nature of the beings that happen to exist in the world. But, fortunately enough, there is an exception. Something in the world encounters the world and thereby asks both ontic and ontological questions about it. Though the nature and properties of that questioner are likewise contingent, ontic features of it, asking about its ontic features is necessarily also asking about its kind of being. There is one entity for which the ontic and ontological questions coincide. "Thus to work out the question of being means to make a being—he who questions—transparent in its being" (BT 6, SZ 8). Ontology thus begins with "ourselves." "The being whose analysis our task is, is always we ourselves. The being of this being is always *mine*" (BT 39, SZ 42). The being that serves as the entity through which the question of ontology is asked is that being whose kind of being poses ontological questions by way of its involvement with the world. "We" ask such questions, thus "we" are where ontological inquiry begins.

The term "we," however, is only provisional and is potentially misleading as a beginning; it is after all only "our" *kind of being* that makes ontological inquiry possible, not "our" human nature. Heidegger thus introduces a neutral term, *Dasein*, for the kind of being "we ourselves are"; and it is now common in commentaries and discussions of this work to continue to use the German term, as I will do.[10] "We shall call the very being to which Da-sein can relate in one way or another, and somehow always does relate, existence *[Existenz]*. And because the essential definition of this being cannot be accomplished by ascribing to it a 'what' that specifies its material content, because its essence lies rather in the fact that it in each instance has to be its being as its own, the term Da-sein, as a pure expression of being, has been chosen to designate this being" (BT 10, SZ 12).

Dasein is the being for whom inquiry into its being is inquiry into the question of being. Being reveals itself to Dasein by way of Dasein's "encountering" the world. Other entities do not encounter the world, not in this ontological sense of the term, and thus inquiry into their nature as an entity does not concern being itself. Not all entities disclose the being of the world; only Dasein does. In encountering beings, including itself, Dasein "understands" being. "There exists no comportment to beings that would not understand being. No understanding of being is possible that would not root in a comportment toward beings. Understanding of being and comportment to beings do not come together only afterward and by chance" (BPP 327).

Heidegger's formulations are peculiar and curiously cautious. There is little time spent defending or explicating this beginning point or, as I already said, the ontic-ontological distinction at its base. In fact, the fortunate coincidence of the ontic and ontological in Dasein seems no more than begging the question of the possibility of ontological inquiry as separate and autonomous. Furthermore, Heidegger's caution with regard to not straightforwardly speaking of "humans" or "persons" who have experiences about the world, think about the world, and distinguish, for example, the world's objectivity from their subjectivity is not defended. The introduction of the neutral term "Dasein" thus is made somewhat surreptitiously and its full implications do not emerge until the entire argument of the book is grasped. I will try to explain this caution about terminology in a moment.

But Heidegger's idea for this project can be stated a bit less contentiously. Dasein, like all other beings, is both a kind of being and an entity. Its status as an entity is not the concern of ontology; thus Heidegger often repeats that he is not doing philosophical anthropology. What is distinct with regard to this entity, and finally why it alone receives this special name, is that it is an entity whose interactions with the world are unique. These interactions or encounterings—Heidegger prefers to use a verb that distinguishes Dasein's involvement with the world from that of other entities—make it possible for entities, including Dasein itself, to also appear as *kinds of being* and not just kinds of beings. Thus Dasein allows for being "to be dis-

closed," another new verb that Heidegger often substitutes for "to experience" or "to appear."

Heidegger does not deny that the world is also studied by making observations and that the properties of objects can thereby be known and used
through the fashioning of artifacts or the simple accumulation of empirical
evidence. But the properties of things and whether those properties are accessible to observers are contingent matters of fact. What is necessary and
what precedes such familiar acts of observation or measurement is that in
all such encounters a kind of being is disclosed to Dasein. The topic of ontology is the a priori necessity of such disclosure of being. Hence this inquiry can be undertaken apart from the state and extent of knowledge of
those ontic matters of fact.

Heidegger warns that common ways of speaking ("The table stands next
to the wall" and "The chair touches the wall") are misleading about this
point. "The presupposition for that would be that the wall could be *en-
counterable* 'by' the chair. A being can only touch an objectively present being within the world if it fundamentally has the kind of being of being-in—
only if with its Da-sein something like world is already discovered in terms
of which beings can reveal themselves through touch and thus become accessible in their objective presence" (BT 52, SZ 56).

Encountering the world, in the ontological use of the term, is only possible for Dasein, and encountering the world, in this sense, is not a disposition
or capacity of this entity. Having a sensory experience of the world, for example, is an ontic feature of many entities, a feature shared, for instance, by
many animals and perhaps, controversially, by such artifacts as future com-
puters. Of course, ontic features of Dasein could be the object of scientific
study. For example, the properties enabling an entity to represent the world
to itself might turn out to be biological structures. Likewise, there could be
studies of how such representations of the world causally malfunction, arise
from evolutionary adaptation, or are mechanically replicated.

But, for the purposes of Heidegger's project, debates about such matters
can be set aside. Specifically, as I shall discuss, the skeptical worry that the
world fails to resemble the way it is disclosed or appears by way of Dasein's
comportment is a symptom of past philosophical confusion. Global skepticism concerning whether access to the external world is even possible, let
alone reliable, is an ontic topic. Heidegger thinks any worries about these
physical processes leave the question of being unanswered, since that question neither depends upon nor presupposes reliable access. For instance, the
possibility that representations of the world might "misfire" due to deviant
causal processes is not an ontological problem, though it may be a significant ontic one. Even given such a massive misfire, Dasein encounters being.

In Heidegger's somewhat classic view on this point, then, fundamental
ontology is prior to epistemology. In fact, whether or not knowledge of the

world is possible, encountering the world is always encountering something such that the question of being becomes possible. That would remain the beginning point even were the properties of that something inaccessible. It would remain even if one were encountering only phenomena. Ontic limits do not limit ontology.

Also, it does not matter which actual beings (entities) are included under the term "Dasein." There has been a long and contentious philosophical debate about whether animals and robots are also persons or subjects as mentioned above. All that matters ontologically, however, is that Dasein is a kind of being that makes the question of being possible. Whether "personhood" is the reality of Dasein and in fact what entities are Dasein are secondary matters. Heidegger's project can thereby ignore biology, physiology, neurology, or even machine intelligence. Though "we ourselves" make the project of *Being and Time* possible, "we ourselves," for the purpose of this project, need not be specified in any way; for all we know, we may not be living, biological, mental, or even human beings. Nothing else about "us" needs to be fixed but that "we are Dasein."

Not only is specification of our ontic features not required for fundamental ontology, Heidegger claims repeatedly that such ontic concerns prove an obstacle. The question of being is not answered by causal analyses, such as those of biological evolution, or by any empirical study of cognitive and sensory systems. Heidegger's investigation of Dasein is a type of a priori inquiry, as Husserl claimed was the topic of phenomenology. Ontology is a study of the precondition for the naturalistic causal investigations listed above.

Not only does Heidegger avoid the language of "living entities" or "experience" when he characterizes Dasein as "we ourselves," he banishes mentalistic expressions as well. It is that abolition that partly accounts for the utter "strangeness" of the vocabulary he does introduce. Heidegger believes he must replace both familiar and traditional philosophical concepts that have to do with thought, reason, and emotion. For example, even Husserl's central concept of intentionality does not appear as a technical term in *Being and Time,* in spite of the claim that the book is predicated on the phenomenological method. But, likewise, the ordinary language of feeling pains, thinking thoughts, or having desires proves equally misleading.

Thus it is a mistake to read Heidegger as appropriating the "folkish" expressions of common sense because they escape philosophical contamination. It is, rather, the contrary. The deep philosophical positions he is attempting to uncover extend insidiously into the language of everyday life. Thus Heidegger's expressions, even when they are colloquial, are always used in an uncommon fashion. Heidegger's vocabulary in *Being and Time* is thereby simultaneously, at least for a German speaker, common and strange. For instance, the German word *Dasein* is not an uncommon one in either German philosophy or common speech for referring to objects or to something existing. But Heidegger's use of it adds a mysterious dimension. Dasein functions as a noun anonymously replacing a whole range of concepts: humankind, person, human being, subject, rational animal, soul, living being, thinker, consciousness, intentional agent.

Though it does not matter what entities are Dasein, Dasein lacks as yet ontological clarification. Our "whatness," as Heidegger calls concern with Dasein's ontic features, must be put into parentheses to make possible a phenomenology of being. Such a phenomenology is not a report on subjective or psychological states and experiences of the world; *Being and Time* is deeply opposed to both subjectivism and what Heidegger repeatedly dismisses as psychology or philosophical anthropology. Rather, it studies how the being of the world must appear to Dasein or, as he also puts it, how the world is *necessarily* disclosed whenever Dasein encounters the world. In his lectures Heidegger states, "The *method of ontology* is nothing but the sequence of the steps involved in the approach to being as such. . . . We call this method of ontology *phenomenology*" (BPP 328). In this way Heidegger connects the phenomenological method and his philosophical project and simply calls phenomenology "the name for the method of ontology, that is, of scientific philosophy" (BPP 17).

Heidegger took from Husserl's phenomenology, then, at least two points. First, he stresses that phenomenology reveals what is essential and a priori, and that dimension provides the link to the subject of ontology as distinct from ontic inquiry. The very central distinction between being and beings, as shown, emphasizes that the question of ontology is not a question of matters of fact. The inquiry that such a distinction makes possible, that of being disclosed phenomenally to Dasein, is then not an inquiry into the natural world or an inquiry into the things of that world, strictly understood.

Second, Heidegger emphasizes that phenomenology is neither a subjective nor a psychological method; that is why he, more than Husserl, cautiously avoids all those mentalistic expressions. To say that it is necessarily the case that Dasein encounters beings, and thus raises the question of being, makes neither a psychological nor a subjective claim about the world. Thus, the very idea of appearance does not have its traditional philosophical significance in Heidegger; it does not mean, for instance, the sensory appearance of things.

Heidegger excludes not only psychology but any biological facts of the matter that might suggest themselves as capturing Dasein's being in the world; hence the concepts of life, consciousness, or human nature are likewise strictly avoided (though less strictly by the many commentators on Heidegger who reach for such concepts as for so many floating clichés in evoking Heideggerian profundities). The question of being necessarily requires that something encounter the world; but naturalistic questions concerning how that might actually occur are for disciplines other than philosophy.

> Therefore, in distinction from the sciences of the things that are, of being, ontology, or philosophy in general, is the critical science, or the science of the inverted world. ... We are surmounting beings in order to reach being. Once having made the ascent we shall not again descend to a being, which, say, might lie like another world behind the familiar beings. The transcendental science of being has nothing to do with popular metaphysics, which deals with some being behind the known beings. (BPP 17)

Specifically, then, ontology must take no standpoint with regard to any fact of the matter; ontology abandons the guidance of all sciences, including psychology, and thereby abandons the security of ordinary ontic inquiry.

> In suggesting that anthropology, psychology, and biology all fail to give an unequivocal and ontologically adequate answer to the question about the *kind of being* of this being that we ourselves are, no judgement is being made about the positive work of these disciplines. But, on the other hand, we must continually be conscious of the fact that these ontological foundations can never be disclosed by subsequent hypotheses derived from empirical materials. Rather, they are always already "there" even when that empirical material is only *collected*. The fact that positivistic investigation does not see these foundations and considers them to be self-evident is no proof of the fact that they do not lie at the basis and are problematic in a more radical sense than any thesis of positivistic science can ever be. (BT 46–47, SZ 50)

Heidegger's term "Dasein" is also connected with his project of the "destruction of the history of ontology." The failure of ontology in the history of philosophy rests on the philosophical tradition beginning with things, entities, or objects, not with Dasein. In that way the tradition does reflect how Dasein comports itself in the world, since Dasein always comports itself toward other beings or things. But the tradition thereby confuses the study of the being of Dasein (ontology) with the study of these beings. Philosophy traditionally confused itself with the natural sciences, because philosophy misconceived the being of Dasein as that of an entity. "The distinction between the being of existing Da-sein and the being of beings unlike Da-sein (for example, reality) may seem illuminating, but it is only the *point of departure* for the ontological problematic; it is nothing with which philosophy can rest and be satisfied" (BT 397, SZ 437).

In his lectures, where Heidegger is somewhat freer with his terminology, he characterizes his study of ontology as "transcendental," using the term in partly its traditional philosophical sense. He chooses that word not only to link his approach to Husserl's, but to emphasize that ontology is the study of what makes it possible for there to be either the manipulation or understanding of entities encountered in the world. The same point is also made, more obscurely, in *Being and Time*.

> Fundamental concepts are determinations in which the area of knowledge underlying all the thematic objects of a science attain an understanding that precedes and guides all positive investigation. Accordingly these concepts first receive their genuine evidence and "grounding" only in a correspondingly preliminary research into the area of knowledge itself. But since each of these areas arises from the domain of beings themselves, this preliminary research that creates the fundamental concepts amounts to nothing else than interpreting these beings in terms of the basic constitution of their being. (BT 8–9, SZ 10)

Existential Analysis

Heidegger calls his analysis of Dasein's way of being "existential analysis." That phrase presupposes another basic distinction in the text between "categorical" and "existential" ontological inquiry. These inquiries are both a priori possibilities of being in the world; again the distinction is not ontic.

> Existentials and categories are the two fundamental possibilities of the characteristics of being. The being which corresponds to them requires different ways of primary interrogation. Beings are a *who* (existence) or else a *what* (objective presence in the broadest sense). It is only in terms of the clarified horizon of the question of being that we can treat the connection between the two modes of characteristics of being. (BT 42, SZ 35)[11]

Traditional metaphysics has been dominated, to its detriment, by the study of *essentia*, namely, the categorical study of being. My previous example of physicalism would be a case of such traditionalism in metaphysics, according to Heidegger, since it subordinates the question of being to physical things. But before there can be a debate about physicalism, Heidegger stresses, we must clarify what kind of a metaphysical claim is being made by the physicalist. At least initially, Heidegger declares himself neutral between these two projects of fundamental ontology; the categorical and the existential are both "equiprimordial."

The categorical, however, largely disappears from *Being and Time,* and Heidegger ends up defending, for purposes of this inquiry and the method he has adopted, the priority of existential analysis. He does not fully argue for this decision, and he seems to simply ignore his previous declaration that the two positions are "equiprimordial." In giving the priority to existential analysis, Heidegger repeats in effect that Dasein (whose kind of being is existence) *uniquely* makes the question of being possible and that Dasein is *uniquely* the kind of object from which ontology always begins.

In announcing that Dasein is the only entity that will allow ontology to begin, he asserts that Dasein has no other essence than existence, a claim that means that with regard to Dasein there could only be an existential ontology: "The whatness *(essentia)* of this being must be understood in terms of its being *(existentia)* insofar as one can speak of it at all" (BT 39, SZ 42). What kind of being consists of *existentia,* but not *essentia?* As already mentioned, "we" are such a being. But for purposes of existential analysis, what requires clarification, then, is what makes it possible for us to be.

Heidegger's terminology, however, has proved misleading to readers on this central point. The term "existential" sounds to some readers as though Heidegger is characterizing Dasein as a wholly contingent being, a mere matter of fact. But if that were what he meant in the above sentence, then "existential" analysis would not constitute a type of a priori analysis. To study what is contingent about Dasein would be, on the contrary, an ontic topic. Also, when Heidegger declares that Dasein does not have an "essence," it ought not be concluded that what Heidegger means is that Dasein is incomprehensible or impossible to discuss. Also, the term "existential" apparently acquired associations, subsequent to Heidegger's work, of irrationality and "absurdity" that seriously distort his present project.

Existential analysis does not mean analysis of what is contingent, accidental, or merely matter of fact about any entity, including Dasein; nor does it mean that the analysis undertaken is irrational or mystical. As Heidegger puts it in his lectures: "Anyone who gets his information about phenomenology from newspapers and weekly reviews must let himself be talked into the notion that phenomenology is something like a mysticism, something like the 'logic of the Indian contemplating his navel.' This is not just a matter to be laughed at; it is actually current among people who wish to be taken in scientific earnest" (BPP 114). In a later passage he speaks of philosophy as threatened by three intellectual movements: "the formation of world-views, magic, and the positive sciences that have forgotten their own limits" (BPP 328).

Existential analysis is a type of ontological analysis; it is a way of answering the question about the meaning of being. If one followed Heidegger's distinction between such inquiry and ontic questions, the misreadings discussed above could not arise. Though Dasein is also, like all kinds of being, an entity or a being, perhaps sharing some of its ontic features with other entities, what concerns existential analysis (as fundamental ontology) is its kind of being, not its properties. Heidegger's basic strategy, as stated, is that Dasein's encountering other beings of the world in terms of their being necessarily (essentially) raises the question of being; all factual contingencies about encountering are to be set aside.

Heidegger also warns the reader at length about how the philosophical tradition has misunderstood Dasein specifically by reducing its kind of being to that of other beings, for example, conceiving Dasein categorically as "soul," "subjectivity," "mind," or "reason." By maintaining inquiry into the being of Dasein, Heidegger hopes to guard against and avoid such pitfalls. "This insight will keep us from failing to see this structure or from previously cancelling it out, a procedure motivated not ontologically, but 'metaphysically' in the naive opinion that human being is initially a spiritual thing which is then subsequently placed 'in' a space" (BT 53, SZ 57).

The existential analysis of the being of Dasein begins with another of Heidegger's ubiquitous distinctions. He claims that there are two ways the world appears to Dasein. ("Appearance" and "disclosure," as used by Heidegger, are never to be understood as reporting psychological experiences.) Being is disclosed to Dasein as "what is at hand" and "what is objective presence," meaning, roughly, a distinction between how the being of the world can appear as equipment for our uses or as something simply present and apart.[12] Thus, there are three kinds of being in the world: objective presence, being at hand, and Dasein. Dasein does not reduce or collapse into either objective presence or what is at hand; rather, Dasein is the kind of being through which these kinds of being are disclosed phenomenally.

Heidegger's example of "being at hand" is an artifact, namely, a hammer. But the example should not become too central; otherwise one might conclude that this kind of being concerns only physically realized equipment or tools. Heidegger, on the contrary, considers linguistic signs, numbers, and representations in general as "equipment" even when they lack, in his language, objective presence. This difficult, new way of speaking is in part meant to demonstrate the inadequacy of the traditional philosophical vocabulary. Traditional concepts such as subject, object, mind, and matter will prove, in comparison, to blur the ontic and ontological distinction and presuppose, for instance, the kind of reductionist strategies rejected above. Also, Heidegger intends that his unfamiliar and cumbersome language will provide an obstacle to the many theoretical explanations of these questions. "As opposed to the theoretically concocted 'explanations' of the objective presence of others which easily urge themselves upon us, we must hold fast to the phenomenal fact which we have indicated of their being encountered in the *surrounding world*" (BT 112, SZ 119).[13]

Existential analysis begins with "what is at hand." Heidegger takes this beginning as a challenge to a core assumption of the philosophical tradition, which he holds, without examining this step, begins with the world as an object apart, that is, as objective presence. Heidegger considers his contrary stress on the priority of involvement or concern with the world as immediately vaulting over traditional philosophical confusions and pseudoproblems.

The philosophical tradition, when understood as a tradition of metaphysics, can then be said to have failed in three ways, to briefly summarize

Heidegger's later and intricate historical essays. First, in ancient philosophy objective presence was uncritically adopted as the meaning of being (thereby ignoring how being manifests itself as equipment and of course how the being of Dasein is neither equipment nor objective presence). Second, in the modern tradition, though the availability of being (its equipment-like nature) in the world was recognized as such (for instance, the knowledge of technique was not considered inferior), it detached itself from Dasein's concern with the being of the world and became uncritically identified with the being of nature itself (much as objective presence had been projected onto the natural world in ancient thought). Third, in both modern and ancient metaphysics Dasein was reduced to either what is at hand or objective presence. Heidegger sees his work as challenging all three of these deeply embedded interpretative tendencies and the associated failure to start with this pretheoretical involvement; hence the need for the "folkish" terminology.

> Phenomenologically pre-thematic beings, what is used and produced, becomes accessible when we put ourselves in the place of taking care of things in the world ... everyday Da-sein always already *is* in this way; for example, in opening the door, I use the door-knob. Gaining phenomenological access to the beings thus encountered consists rather in rejecting the interpretational tendencies crowding and accompanying us which cover over the phenomenon of 'taking care' of things in general, and thus even more so beings *as* they are encountered of their own accord *in* taking care. (BT 63, SZ 68)

When first characterizing Heidegger's project, it is irresistible to simply use natural objects, artifacts, and living beings as examples, but that approach soon proves both misleading and inadequate. The distinction between objective presence and being at hand is meant to replace, however clumsy it is to use this language, such examples. Also using such examples would only reinforce stubbornly persistent ontic tendencies and thus the appeal of reduction and theoretical explanation Heidegger opposes. The point is that in saying that something appears as objectively present or as being at hand, the topic no longer concerns the properties of whatever entity is in question. Because the topic ceases to concern the entity in question, the task ceases to be one that could appeal to theoretical science or even practical experience. What this new language forces us to keep considering is the being of many and various beings.

In the same fashion, the phenomenological analyses (by which Heidegger claims to be guided, but which he neither discusses nor carries out in his writings) that characterize existential ontology are not about what mental states occur when having an experience or thinking about the world. Psychological interpretations of the world are on par with the physical properties of the hammer; it would be deeply confused to take ontology as the equivalent of such reports.

Given all of the above, what, ontologically, is Dasein? Heidegger answers, enigmatically again, that Dasein is *Das Man,* using the German in-
definite article "the they."[14] Dasein is then not "myself" or "we," the provisional beginning claim, nor is it a substitute for some collective subjectivity
or mind. Heidegger claims enigmatically that by "the they" he also does
not intend to appeal to the sum total of selves. "The 'who' is the neuter, *the
they*" (BT 119, SZ 127). This strange usage seems part of a continuing effort to distance the reader from this project's language.

Heidegger is of course avoiding the available vocabulary of "subject,"
"person," "self," or "mind," concepts that are "ontically contaminated,"
to coin a phrase. He later uses "the they" in rather contorted punlike arguments to show that concepts such as person, ego, or subjectivity, all used
uncritically by Husserl in his view, are complicitous with failing to grasp
the question of being. The point, as far as I grasp it, is that in traditional
terminology what is lost is that the being of Dasein precedes its being a person or self. Thus Heidegger says in the following passage that Dasein
makes possible not only the appearance in the world of equipment and ob-
jectness, as kinds of being, but the existence of itself and others. "These beings are neither objectively present nor at hand, but they *are like* the very
Da-sein which frees them—*they are there, too, and there with it.* So, if one
wanted to identify the world in general with interworldly beings, one
would have to say the 'world' is also Da-sein" (BT 111, SZ 118).

Other Minds

The above quotation introduces one of the few passages in which Heidegger actually discusses a traditional and recognizable philosophical problem
at any length. After the above passage, Heidegger turns to "the problem of
other minds," as it is widely referred to in philosophy. Though, as I have already said, Heidegger provides little argumentative defense for the above
distinctions, except to treat them as phenomenologically given and thus
philosophically neutral, he does, in this context, give the reader some reasons for accepting his approach by claiming that it resolves or clarifies a famous philosophical issue. What Heidegger actually claims is that the problem of other minds dissolves as a serious debate once the misconceptions at
its root are revealed and thus abandoned.

The traditional issue of "other minds" concerns dissimilarities between
one's own mental experiences and one's experience of the behavior of others. These dissimilarities can be stated in two ways. First, it can be said that
one has "privileged access" to only one's own mental states and not the
mental states of others, which are, for oneself, merely analogous to one's
own. Second, whereas the fact of another person having a mind is a contingency about that entity being a person, it is necessarily the case for oneself

that one's mental experiences are real. It is this kind of necessity, as Descartes argued, that makes the claims about one's own experience indubitable. The problem is also sometimes stated epistemologically: Can one know with certainty that others also have minds?

Much analytic philosophy contemporary with Heidegger's early work was devoted to clarifying the language in which this problem is stated, a language that turns out to be surprisingly complicated. Heidegger's language can also be used to restate the issue if it is remembered, however, that Heidegger formulated a new vocabulary for philosophy precisely against the assumptions behind this classic problem. Are Dasein's encounters with entities in the world distinguishable from its encounters with other Dasein? The issue as so stated is not irrelevant to Heidegger's project. Heidegger, as discussed above, began his work with the idea that Dasein's encountering the world is unique and distinct; it is not, for example, like a chair touching a wall. But the problem of other minds doubts such a distinction by asking whether one could know that encountering other persons is distinct from encountering other objects or whether one could know that relations between persons are distinct from relations between objects. Why do I believe that others have an inner mental life like my own? How is it possible that I can thus speak of "we"?

Heidegger repeats that the traditional solution to this skeptical problem about what can be known about others, as I mentioned above, is an analogy between Dasein's being toward others, namely, other Dasein, and Dasein's reflective understanding of itself. Since Heidegger began the project with the reflective claim that ontology concerns "we ourselves," this traditional reflective response to the problem of other minds might seem the path he ought to defend. But Heidegger rejects this solution and intends to replace it with a deeper rejection of the entire problem of other minds.

Heidegger rejects the traditional reply, that we know ourselves and thus indirectly we know others in a way we do not know things within the natural world, for two reasons. First, Heidegger's concerns are ontological rather than epistemological, and many commentaries on Heidegger appear to fail to grasp this difference. What Heidegger wants to ask about is the being of Dasein, not whether there is access to those features of other entities, including properties of Dasein itself. Second, the reply claims to answer the quandary by proposing that Dasein already understands itself in such a way that it is able to distinguish itself from other beings like and unlike itself. But that answer presupposes, Heidegger claims, that Dasein does understand, even in this naive manner, its kind of being, a being it then determines is either shared or not shared with others. But such a response leaves presupposed and unanswered the very inquiry Heidegger has initiated: Can Dasein grasp the meaning of being?

Should the reader conclude, therefore, that there is a real skeptical doubt concerning the existence of other minds (other Dasein)? Heidegger answers no. By rejecting the above strategy of reasoning by analogy with one's own being, he has shown that the problem, as traditionally considered, is not properly formulated. (It is only properly formulated as an ontological problem; it is in fact the problem of the meaning of being, misstated as an epistemological quandary about whether there is access to the ontic features of various beings.) Ontological analysis, as Heidegger defends it, begins prior to the concepts of mind, self, and person. Thus whether ontically there are or are not any beings like Dasein, ontologically Dasein is already "being-with-others" and hence no serious *philosophical* problem about other minds arises (there could of course be psychological and sociological problems concerning other minds). In using one of his phrases turned into a substantive by hyphens ("being-with-others"), Heidegger claims to abolish or leap over a perennial philosophical worry. By beginning with Dasein already in the world, he sweeps away as a pseudoproblem the problem of other minds.

> The phenomenological statement that Da-sein is essentially being-with has an existential-ontological meaning. It does not intend to ascertain ontically that I am factically not objectively present alone, rather that others of my kind also are. If the statement that the being-in-the-world of Da-sein is essentially constituted by being-with meant something like this, being-with would not be an existential attribute that belongs to Da-sein of itself on the basis of its kind of being, but something which occurs at times on the basis of the existence of others. (BT 113, SZ 121)

Heidegger's reply sounds similar, in this way, to Husserl's account in *Cartesian Meditations*. Phenomenological reflection, it was argued there, necessarily requires that experiencing the world is an experience for others, not as a matter of fact, but as a matter of conceptual necessity with regard to evidential experience. Similarly, Heidegger holds that for purposes of ontology, the a priori study of being, skepticism about the reality of other Dasein can be set aside; on this issue Heidegger retains an Husserlian approach.

Understanding

Previously I presented Dasein as both comportment toward the world and understanding of the world. The notion of understanding the world involves understanding the question of being. Thus, to follow the pattern already repeated, the being of Dasein necessarily makes possible understanding the question of being. Specifically, the way Dasein exists in the world makes such inquiry possible.

Dasein has two modes of being in the world that make possible this kind of inquiry into the world: *Befindlichkeit* and *Verstehen*. *Verstehen* ("understanding") was at the time a familiar term in Neo-Kantian philosophy (and of course in Kant's philosophy) and specifically, during Heidegger's youth, was used to identify the mode of cognition appropriate to the social sciences. (The term was used and discussed extensively, for example, by Heinrich Rickert, whose lectures Heidegger attended at Freiburg.) Though Heidegger does not use understanding as a method for the social sciences, he does assume the reader's familiarity with understanding as a general concept of inquiry that carries certain epistemic baggage and specifically challenges the priority of the scientific method.

But *Befindlichkeit* is hardly a familiar philosophical concept at all; rather, it is formed from a colloquial greeting and altered by Heidegger for heavy and deeply obscure philosophical use. It is also particularly difficult to translate.[15] It identifies, ontologically, Dasein's comportment toward or involvement in the world when that comportment is viewed as a type of inquiry.

How did Heidegger arrive at this distinction between *Befindlichkeit* and *Verstehen?* This distinction is simply introduced, as though it were obvious or hardly deserving of any discussion or defense. It seems to be modeled, as I suggest above, on the traditional distinction between theory and practice, though that would be a misleading assumption. Heidegger does occasionally claim that these various distinctions are the result of unidentified phenomenological exercises, but such exercises are not even vaguely discussed. Whatever phenomenological exercises allowed for these results to be "seen," Heidegger must intend that by suspending efforts to conceptualize or explain the world (namely, efforts to take the study of beings for the question of being), the being of the world simply and necessarily discloses itself in these two distinct ways. I will return to problems about these distinctions in my criticisms of Heidegger.

The whole picture, then, looks as follows. Heidegger is engaged in what he calls existential analysis, which takes as its starting point nontheoretical, nonreflective involvement with the world by the kind of being, that is, Dasein, that necessarily questions the being of the world in its various involvements with the world. Furthermore, he is led to distinguish between those states in which Dasein is wholly involved with the world, as when engaged and preoccupied by things, and those states in which it is interpreting or understanding the world, as, for example, in seeking an explanation or theorizing. These distinctions, as I already said, are hardly that strange in traditional philosophy.

In his description of what he means by *Befindlichkeit*, Heidegger introduces yet another special term: Dasein has "moods." Heidegger stresses, though many readers ignore his comments, that the word "mood" is devoid of psychological or emotive meaning. A mood is the state of finding oneself fully engaged in some situation. Another way to put the point is that even a theoretical interpretation of the world, which is a type of understanding, is a mood. From Heidegger's vantage point in which the priority is always given to pretheoretical involvement with the world, theorizing is simply finding oneself engaged in a certain kind of activity and thus in a certain mood with regard to the world. Thus the way Heidegger uses the term "mood" tends to blur the distinction between understanding and involvement with the world. Heidegger's point is that the world discloses itself to Dasein by way of (or appears to Dasein by way of) these moods ("stances" or "attitudes" might be better so as to avoid the psychologistic associations of "mood"), whether Dasein's encounter with the world is considered an act of understanding or involvement.

Moods are such that the world is also concealed through such disclosure. Heidegger uses numerous paradoxical expressions to make this point, but it seems no more paradoxical than the prosaic insight that emphasis on one topic is only possible if one is distracted with regard to many other topics. Heidegger's concern, however, is ontology, not epistemology; thus he wants to drive home that this feature of moods to "conceal" while disclosing being ought not to be taken as a limitation on ontological inquiry.

Heidegger emphasizes this point about concealment, I believe, because he takes it as the ontological "explanation," though that is not the right word, for the "forgetting of being" characterizing both the philosophical tradition and modern culture. Ontic inquiry, in other words, necessarily ignores or actively suppresses ontological inquiry, because it is focused on precisely those aspects that conceal the being of objects; the more ontic access the less ontological access, as it might be put. Anyway, neither disclosure nor concealment plays a cognitive or empirical role in Heidegger.

> Phenomenally, *what* mood discloses and *how* it discloses would be completely misunderstood if what has been disclosed were conflated with that which attuned Da-sein "at the same time" is acquainted with, knows, and believes. Even when Da-sein is "sure" of its "whither" in faith or thinks it knows about its whence in rational enlightenment, all of this makes no difference in the face of the phenomenal fact that moods bring Da-sein before the that of its there, which stares at it with the inexorability of an enigma. (BT 128, SZ 136)

Authenticity and Inauthenticity

All of the above distinctions and terminology are somewhat stipulative. The reasons given for these distinctions are extremely elusive, except for a general defense of the entire approach, and thus the reader has no choice but to follow the path Heidegger sketches. As I suggested above, once the terminology has been deployed by Heidegger, the picture often is not as radically distinct from the tradition as Heidegger advertises it to be.

As an example of the weakness of this style, Heidegger connects mood, in his account of understanding, to the concepts of authenticity and inauthenticity and attempts to drive his discussion toward some claims about the nature of social life and politics. The concepts of authenticity and inauthenticity do considerable work in Heidegger's overall argument, and he attempts to use them to squeeze substantive conclusions from the text's baroque and somewhat arcane classifications.

Heidegger introduces the idea of authenticity by claiming that the being of Dasein has in addition to what was above called its "concealment-function," in the account of mood and the reduction of the question of being to the nature of beings, a second feature that Heidegger characterizes as the "levelling down" of being; it is this aspect that he also calls "inauthenticity." "The care of averageness reveals, in turn, an essential tendency of Da-sein, which we call the *levelling down* of all possibilities of being" (BT 119, SZ 127).

What, then, do "authentic" and "inauthentic" mean when used as ontological rather than moral concepts? Dasein projects itself on the being of those entities it encounters in the world. Heidegger describes this projection (which he also claims forms the key activity of understanding) as Dasein "losing" the question of being or "forgetting" the question of being. By mistaking the being of the world in this way, Dasein is inauthentic (does not ask the question of being). Hence, the state of authenticity might be said to one of hypervigilance concerning the question of being by maintaining the distinction between ontic and ontological questions, both theoretically and practically, for example, by resisting projection. Inauthenticity then constitutes, ontologically, the replacement of ontic concerns for the question of being by strategies such as reduction or appeals to common sense.

> First and mostly, we take ourselves much as daily life prompts; we do not dissect and rack our brains about some soul-life. We understand ourselves in an everyday way or, as we can formulate it terminologically, *not authentically* in the strict sense of the world, not with constancy from the most proper and most extreme possibilities of our own existence, but *inauthentically,* our self indeed but as we are *not our own,* as we have lost ourself in things and humans while we exist in the everyday. . . . Dasein's inauthentic understanding of itself via things is neither ungenuine nor illusory, as though what is understood by it is not the self but something else, and the self only allegedly. Inauthentic self-understanding experiences the authentic Dasein as such precisely in its peculiar "actuality," if we may say so, and in a genuine way. (BPP 160–161)

When Heidegger speaks of Dasein "choosing," he must have in mind a special sense of the verb "to choose." The acts of forgetting and inauthenticity are not choices in the normal or pedestrian sense. They are, therefore, not properly faults or failures of some effort, but simply more aspects of Dasein's being. What is inauthentic is not, for example, some unfortunate limitation of one person, and yet not of another. Inauthenticity is not dishonesty, nor is it a brand of self-deception. As he notes, though the word "inauthentic" carries certain moral implications, those implications are not in his special usage.

> Because selfhood belongs to existence, as in some manner "being-one's-own," the existent Dasein can *choose itself on purpose* and determine its existence primarily and chiefly starting from that choice; that is, it can exist authentically. . . . We have already said that inauthentic existence does not mean an apparent existence or an ungenuine existence. What is more, inauthenticity belongs to the essential nature of factical Dasein. Authenticity is only a modification but not a total obliteration of inauthenticity. (BPP 170–171)

The concept of authenticity has in addition played a large role for those followers and commentators who, ignoring Heidegger's explicit warnings, imbue the term with sociological, moral, and psychological significance. Though Heidegger takes quite seriously his ontological analysis of inauthenticity, his choice of language and subsequent comments do encourage the confusion he warns against. Heidegger appears concerned in the central passages of this section with what would appear to be ontic problems such as the threat of conformism to personal and cultural vitality, the various insidious effects of modern mass culture, and the moral concept of personhood.

But this political or cultural understanding of the idea of authenticity, as far as I can grasp it, would constitute a misconception of the project of fundamental ontology, as Heidegger has so far presented it. The ontological analysis of Dasein as being in the world concerns what Dasein is essentially, a priori; it constitutes answering the question of the meaning of being. In that sense, though the options or choices of a person living within some historical culture are made possible by this structure of being, in some special sense of "making possible" that would need to be clarified, such actions are distinct from the questions Heidegger hopes to tackle, in much the way that Dasein's biological features are contingent and thus independent, in his usage, from the being of Dasein. Therefore, when using terms such as "concealment," "levelling," or "inauthentic" as characterizing the being of Dasein, Heidegger could not be analyzing, at least if he were being consistent, a failing, weakness, limitation, or success of any particular plan of action, set of choices, or "way of life" an individual or culture might aspire to realize. These choices and their subsequent causal effects would be matters of fact appropriate to other disciplines, for instance, sociology, but not properly the concern of ontology. In fact, it is precisely such an error that Heidegger repeatedly cites as the bankruptcy of the philosophical tradition in facing this question of being. But I still cannot deny that Heidegger lapses into discussions that do, for all these warnings, amount to cultural and sociological criticism.

Back to the Things Themselves

The terms *Befindlichkeit* and *Verstehen* identify Dasein's two essential modes of being and these modes constitute together what Heidegger calls "care." Heidegger once again distinguishes the ontological and "vulgar" meanings of "care": "In contrast to these prescientific ontic meanings, the expression 'taking care' is used in this inquiry as an ontological term (an existential) to designate the being of a possible being-in-the-world. . . . The expression has nothing to do with 'distress,' 'melancholy,' or 'the cares of life' which can be found ontically in every Da-sein" (BT 53, SZ 57). The notion of care captures in ontology Dasein's encountering other beings, including other Dasein. Heidegger summarizes his account up to this point.

> In the foregoing interpretations, which finally led to exposing care as the being of Da-sein, the most important thing was to arrive at the appropriate ontological foundations of the being which we ourselves actually are and which we call "human being." For this purpose, it was necessary from the outset to change the direction of our analysis from the approach presented by the traditional definition of human being, which is an approach ontologically unclarified and fundamentally questionable. In comparison with this definition, the existential and ontological interpretation might seem strange, especially if "care" is understood ontically as "worry" and "troubles." (BT 183, SZ 197)

Heidegger is led by these comments to a second perennial philosophical problem; this second problem allows him to make more explicit his underlying criticisms of Husserl.[16] In Chapter 1 I recounted Husserl's concern with the "problem of reality," by which I meant such epistemological questions as: Is there a reality outside consciousness? Can skepticism concerning the reality of the external world be answered? Is knowledge of entities as they are in themselves possible? Heidegger's aim with regard to such traditional problems is similar to his approach to the problem of other minds; he claims that fundamental ontological analysis dissolves traditional philosophical problems. Thus, ontologically, questions about the possibility of knowledge are converted into questions about the being of that being that has access to entities in the world. "The question of whether there is a world at all and whether its being can be demonstrated, makes no sense at all if it is raised by Da-sein as being-in-the-world—and who else should ask it?" (BT 188, SZ 203).

The "scandal of philosophy" does not consist in the fact that this proof is still lacking up to now, but *in the fact that such proofs are expected and attempted again and again*. Such expectations, intentions, and demands grow out of an ontologically insufficient way of positing *what it is from which*, independently and "outside" of which, a "world" is to be proven to be objectively present. It is not that the proofs are insufficient, but that the kind of being of the being that does the proving and requests the proofs is *not definite enough*. For this reason the illusion can arise that with this demonstration of the necessary objective presence together of two objectively present things something is proved or even demonstrable about Da-sein as being-in-the-world. Correctly understood, Da-sein defies such proofs, because it always already *is* in its being what the later proofs first deem necessary to demonstrate for it. (BT 190, SZ 205)

In this way Heidegger claims to avoid the philosophical quandaries of realism and idealism, though he stresses some points of agreement with both positions. For example, existential analysis shares with realism the thesis that the world is objectively present; that is, the world is encountered as it is in itself. The difference is that realism takes this claim as involving an explanation of how the world can be "given" on the basis of such ontic features as causal connections between objects and the sensations. Ontological analysis is, however, strictly pretheoretical, precausal, and precedes the distinction between person and object.

Existential analysis, therefore, agrees with idealism that being cannot be explained by way of such natural relations as causality or by way of the various properties of entities. Heidegger makes a strong statement of his agreement with idealism. "If the term idealism amounts to an understanding of the fact that being is never explicable by beings, but is always already the 'transcendental' for every being, then the sole correct possibility of a philosophical problematic lies in idealism" (BT 193, SZ 208).

This passage evolves, for the careful reader, into a discussion of Husserl (though Husserl's name is not mentioned). The critical comments that immediately follow the above concession of the importance of idealism constitute Heidegger's indirect discussion and criticism of Husserl in *Being and Time*. Heidegger qualifies the above agreement with idealism by rejecting efforts to eliminate ontological questions from the topic of philosophy, a stance that I have argued represents Husserl's position. "If idealism means the reduction of all beings to a subject or a consciousness which are only distinguished by the fact that they remain *undetermined* in their being and are characterized at best negatively as 'unthinglike,' then this idealism is methodologically no less naïve than the grossest realism" (BT 193).

Heidegger takes it that phenomenology frees the notion of appearance from theoretical assumptions. Entities appear or disclose their being to Dasein by way of Dasein's concern for them as useful, accessible, and available to Dasein, but not by way of any conceptual elaboration of this concern.

Thus Heidegger puts emphasis not on thinking or theorizing about the world, but on this pretheoretical and precognitive "encountering" of the world. Dasein's comportment with, involvement in, and encounter with the world are stressed, while observing, reflecting upon, or examining the world are presented as secondary and thus presuppositional stances.

The shortcomings of Husserl's project and his very conception of phenomenology are foreshadowed by Heidegger's account. Since the concepts of subjects and objects are deeply presuppositional, Husserl has failed to be radical enough. His method ignores the fundamental questions of ontology by both taking over problematic concepts, such as those of intentionality and subjectivity, and by asking only epistemological questions about the topic, attempting unsuccessfully to bracket the problem of ontology. Without explicitly mentioning Husserl, Heidegger has two particularly vivid rejections of the very idea of transcendental subjectivity.

> Every idea of a "subject"—unless refined by a previous ontological determination of its basic character—still posits the *subjectum (hupokeimenon) ontologically* along with it, no matter how energetic one's ontic protestations against the "substantial soul" or the "reification of consciousness." Thingliness itself needs to be demonstrated in terms of its ontological source in order that we can ask what is now to be understood *positively* by the nonreified *being* of the subject, the soul, consciousness, the spirit, the person. All these terms name definite areas of phenomena which can be "developed." But they are never used without a remarkable failure to see the need for inquiring about the being of the beings so designated. Thus we are not being terminologically idiosyncratic when we avoid these terms as well as the expressions "life" and "human being" in designating the beings that we ourselves are. (BT 43, SZ 46)

> In directing itself toward . . . and in grasping something, Da-sein does not first go outside of the inner sphere in which it is initially encapsulated, but, rather, in its primary kind of being, it is always already "outside" together with some being encountered in the world already discovered. Nor is any inner sphere abandoned when Da-sein dwells together with a being to be known and determines its character. Rather, even in this "being outside" together with its object, Da-sein is "inside," correctly understood; that is, it itself exists as the being-in-the-world which knows. Again, the perception of what is known does not take place as a return with one's booty to the "cabinet" of consciousness after one has gone out and grasped it. Rather, in perceiving, preserving, and retaining, the Da-sein that knows *remains outside as Da-sein*. (BT 58, SZ 62)

These passages sweep aside Husserl's two central philosophical strategies: epistemological internalism and transcendental idealism. For Heidegger, these two commitments are linked by Husserl's generally uncritical appropriation of bits and pieces from the philosophical tradition, especially Kant. Once the priority is given to ontology and to Dasein, Husserl is found to have merely redressed pseudoproblems. Furthermore, the focus on Dasein replaces Husserl's study of how we might come to represent the world outside of us with a beginning in which already we are "everyday and average being-with-one-another" (BT 114, SZ 122).[17]

Nonnaturalistic Time

My outline now arrives at the end of the "analytic of Dasein." *Being and Time* began with a "provisional aim . . . the interpretation of time as the possible horizon for any understanding whatsoever of being" (BT xix, SZ 1). In Division Two of the book, Heidegger connects the previous ontological investigation of Dasein to temporality. He holds that temporality has already appeared, implicitly, in the categories of "care" and "everydayness" with regard to Dasein-analysis.

> We must go back and free the ontological structures of Da-sein already gained with regard to their temporal meaning. Everydayness reveals itself as a mode of temporality. But by thus repeating our preparatory fundamental analysis of Da-sein, the phenomenon of temporality itself will at the same time become more transparent. In terms of temporality, it becomes intelligible why Da-sein is and can be historical in the ground of its being and, being *historical,* it can develop historiography. (BT 216–217, SZ 235)

I can give only a brief account of Heidegger's attempt, in the second division of *Being and Time,* to connect his fundamental ontology to the concept of time. This final part of the book is even harder to follow than the earlier sections and seems a kind of patchwork of material that looks to have been designed for publication elsewhere and hints concerning the direction of future work. Heidegger would expand on this sketch in a later book on Kant and in his study of Husserl's analysis of temporality in consciousness. The question of how temporality fits into fundamental ontology, and specifically how temporality constitutes answering the question of being, remains the least accessible part of an already forbidding philosophical project. Specifically, the notion of temporality, which Heidegger again warns is distinct from the "vulgar" notion of time, is not clarified beyond repeated assertions that it is being used ontologically and the use of the particularly unhelpful syntactic device of the verb "to temporalize."

What I wish to provide is enough of his suggested analysis of time so as to complete, within the limits of my study, the outline of Heidegger's account of metaphysics as existential analysis. My exposition will then turn to a critical discussion of this attempt at fundamental ontology. Therefore, I will take the liberty of extrapolating much of the following from Heidegger's lectures on phenomenology. I prefer the discussion in those lectures to that in *Being and Time* on this topic, because Heidegger states the issue, in his lectures, in terms of how time figures in ontology by way of the concept of the a priori. This approach has two advantages. It relates the discussion of time directly to his central philosophical topic, namely, how the meaning of being is an a priori analysis. Second, it avoids the excessive and indulgent vocabulary that Heidegger deploys in *Being and Time*. Specifically, the later material on death, anxiety, fear, and historicity proliferate misreadings both because the analysis is compressed and because of the confusions generated by an increasingly idiosyncratic usage. Heidegger implicitly recognizes the inadequacy of this attempt and with it most of the current interpretation of his views in his 1947 "Letter on Humanism," a recognition that eventually led him away from philosophy entirely.

To begin, then, the concept of time as used in Heidegger's book is not that of "calendar" or strictly historical time; nor is it the concept of time found in either the natural or social sciences. Thus this ontological sense of time cannot be identified with cultural or intellectual history, which would be perhaps the natural interpretation, given Heidegger's admiring comments on Dilthey's historicism. Specifically, when Heidegger makes the statement that "Dasein is historical," he is making an ontological, not an ontic statement; he means that Dasein's kind of being makes historicity possible. It would be a misreading, therefore, to conclude that Heidegger's argument at the end of *Being and Time* amounts to the ultimately naturalistic and prosaic reminder that the study of Dasein is found in history or that philosophy ought to be studied as a cultural, historical discipline. Such bromides and clichés concerning the "history of ideas" are deeply contrary to Heidegger's intent.

What, then, does the notion of time mean? Temporality, Heidegger claims, constitutes Dasein's specific difference from all other entities. In a famous discussion of death in *Being and Time* Heidegger makes the following point, though I am now quoting from his lectures.[18] "A thing that is not temporal, whose being is not determined by means of temporality, but merely occurs within time, can never have-been, because it does not exist. Only what is intrinsically futural can have-been; things, at best, are over and done with" (BPP 290). In this quotation the word "temporal" is contrasted with "merely occurs in time." Naturalistically many entities "occur within time," but there is a being who is "determined by means of temporality." What does it mean to say that Dasein's being is determined by the means of temporality (and is in that sense historical)? The answer is found by turning to the associated notion of transcendence.

Heidegger uses "transcendence" to mean that which is independent of or outside of the worldly experience of beings. In this sense the term is used to indicate that something exists as a "thing-in-itself," using Kant's famous phrase, the being of that which humans encounter and understand. As already stressed, Heidegger opposes the Kantian view that such things-in-themselves are separate from phenomenal experience of the world, since existential analysis begins with Dasein involved with or encountering being by way of beings. Therefore, given Heidegger's conception of ontology, a Kantian skeptical worry that the thing-in-itself may differ fundamentally from the thing as phenomenally given marks another philosophical pseudoproblem.

Heidegger's concept of being is not then transcendent in this strict Kantian sense of the term, since Heidegger is not concluding that being is inaccessible to Dasein (human beings). But Heidegger does consider transcendence the key to understanding why being does not reduce to its ontic determinations within the world. Things in the world are not transcendent; they are always intraworldly, whereas being is transcendent.

Dasein encounters things, but it is the world itself, the "worldliness" of being, that is existentially Dasein's way of being. In other words, the world discloses its different ways of being by way of how Dasein encounters the world; what is disclosed thereby is the being of the world, not the beings in the world. Heidegger concludes then that the transcendent nature of being of the world, to which he has directed philosophy's attention, turns out to be Dasein itself. Dasein is in effect the "thing-in-itself," to speak somewhat improperly, and that accounts for Dasein's raising the question of being through its efforts at reflection.

> Only a being with the mode of being of the Dasein transcends, in such a way in fact that transcendence is precisely what essentially characterizes its being. . . . Because the Dasein is constituted by being-in-the-world, it is a being which in its being is out *beyond* itself. . . . Only a being to whose ontological constitution transcendence belongs has the possibility of being anything like a self. . . . The Dasein is the transcendent being. Objects and things are never transcendent. (BPP 299–300)

Heidegger's strategy is to somehow connect this account of being as transcendence to the notion of temporality. I confess that I do not fully understand the above account of transcendence or how he claims to work out the connection between the notions of temporality and transcendence. I suppose the best I can offer in summary is that Heidegger thinks "temporality," in this special sense, makes it possible for being to disclose itself to Dasein and for Dasein to thereby understand the question of being. Thus even those beings who "merely occur in time" are not "determined by temporality" and that is why the being of the world does not appear to those beings, but only to Dasein. I will discuss problems with Heidegger's appeal to appearance and disclosure in the following critical section.

> If, then, philosophical investigation from the beginning of antiquity . . . oriented itself toward reason, soul, mind, spirit, consciousness, self-consciousness, subjectivity, this is not an accident and has so little to do with world-view, that, instead, the admittedly still hidden basic content of the problems of ontology as such pressed and directed scientific inquiry. The trend toward the "subject"—

not always uniformly unequivocal and clear—is based on the fact that philosophical inquiry somehow understood that the basis for every substantial philosophical problem could and had to be procured from an adequate elucidation of the "subject." (BPP 312)

It might be thought at this point, wrongly it will turn out, that Heidegger is appropriating some kind of Hegelian metaphysics. Hegel thought that philosophical inquiry somehow required and was made possible by the actual course of events in history. Hegel argued, for instance, that such specific political and social events as the rise of the modern state and the occurrence of the French Revolution were part of and made possible a certain level of philosophical reflection and clarification. Thus, additionally, Hegel famously argued that his own objective idealism could only have been conceived in his own historical moment; and, thereby, Hegel reached the seemingly outrageous conclusion that history itself must come to an end with his own philosophy, since there could be no higher level of philosophical reflection than his own.

But identifying Heidegger with Hegelian historicism would be a mistake. The way in which Hegel's metaphysics converts the variety of ontic facts about human history and the natural world directly into ontological claims, thus ignoring the basic distinction between ontic and ontological inquiry, is wholly incompatible with Heidegger's approach. Collapsing ontic and ontological inquiry in such a way that actual, contingent historical events are necessary for raising the question of being is simply the other side of denying the possibility of ontological inquiry as such; Hegel's brand of historicism is a different version of forgetting ontology.

> As long as this original belonging together of comportment toward beings and understanding of being is not conceived by means of temporality, philosophical inquiry remains exposed to a double danger, to which it has succumbed over and over again in its history until now. Either everything ontic is dissolved into the ontological (Hegel), without insight into the ground of possibility of ontology itself; or else the ontological is denied altogether and explained away ontically, without an understanding of the ontological presuppositions which every ontical explanation already harbors as such within itself. (BPP 327)

Ontological analysis is prior to and independent of the historicity of events or cultures. "We have seen that all comportment toward beings already understands being, and not just incidentally: being must necessarily be understood precursorily (pre-cedently)" (BPP 325). Also Heidegger distrusts, as Husserl did, the idea of worldviews. "The conflict is carried on with what today more than ever before threatens philosophy from all the precincts of intellectual life; the formation of world views, magic, and the positive sciences that have forgotten their own limits" (BPP 328).

The only argument I can find for the above connection is that temporality and the a priori are etymologically linked; a priori means "earlier than," he claims. This attempted analysis is confusing at best, even if we grant Heidegger the etymological speculation. Heidegger's point must be that since the phrase "earlier than" contains a temporal reference, therefore he has shown that a priori is a temporal concept. But he has already said that "temporal" in its ontological sense is distinct from its everyday, "calendar" meaning. Thus this etymological point concerning "early," whether or not it is correct, is beside the point.

Also, Heidegger cites, as evidence for his connection between the a priori and temporality, a definition of a priori by Kant that states that "to cognize something a priori means to cognize it from its mere possibility" (BPP 324). Heidegger concludes that "mere possibility" as used by Kant is again a temporal concept. But, on the contrary, the passage Heidegger quotes from Kant concerns what is *conceptually possible,* not what is temporally prior. Since Heidegger has not clarified what the ontological sense of temporality means, even this criticism of his reading of Kant fails to shed any light on the issue; perhaps "conceptually possible" is "temporal" in Heidegger's very special sense of the term. At any rate, neither of these points is either convincing support for a connection between the a priori and the temporal, nor do they clarify Heidegger's aim.

> To be sure, as long as we orient ourselves toward the common concept of time we are at an impasse, and negatively it is no less than consistent to deny dogmatically that the a priori has anything to do with time. However, time in the sense commonly understood ... is indeed only one derivative, even if legitimate, of the original time, on which the Dasein's ontological constitution is based. *It is only by means of the Temporality of the understanding of being that it can be explained why the ontological determinations of being have the character of apriority.* (BPP 325)

A Criticism

In contrast with the critical discussion of Husserl, the reaction to Heidegger has tended, historically, to split into two equally unhelpful extremes. Either his work has met with the kind of uncharitable hostility and dismissal exemplified by Carnap's essay, cited earlier, or it is reverentially summarized in ever uglier pastiches (if such can be imagined) as the work of genius. Thus I cannot begin by surveying critical objections. Instead, I will sketch a criticism that tries to attack the very core of the project of a fundamental ontology, as Heidegger proposed it, a criticism that I also believe provides some understanding of Heidegger's abrupt abandonment of philosophy.

My criticism of the distinction between the ontic and ontological involves showing that Heidegger's appeal to being as appearing or disclosing itself to Dasein in the form of presence or what is at hand cannot be made distinct from the appearance of beings or entities. By saying "it cannot be made distinct," then, I mean that is not a failing of any particular philosophical tradition or set of assumptions. Thus this criticism also gives reasons for doubting Heidegger's perplexing confidence that the question of the meaning of being does not depend upon or presuppose the question of whether access to the nature of beings is reliable or not.

I begin with some positive comments. The distinction does introduce a way to consider ontic commitments critically. In other words, it draws our attention to the difference between a debate about the existence of some entity, neutrinos for example, versus a debate about physicalism, the ontological position underlying much of modern physics. Thus a defense of physicalism, to return to my usual example of an ontology, could be undertaken even by those who might consider any current scientific theory and its various theoretical entities as fallible or in need of revision, or even by those wholly ignorant of contemporary physics. Heidegger's distinction allows one to defend physicalism as a philosophical matter, for instance, without defending the specific results of any current sciences. It is the distinction between determining the nature of things, the task of science and practical inquiry, and determining the kinds of things there are, the task of philosophy. That effort is certainly debatable, though the weight of opinion these days is against it (hence Heidegger's strenuous opposition to the existing philosophical traditions). Nevertheless, the way the distinction is presented and used by Heidegger is fraught with difficulties.

My argument against Heidegger's distinction is that he cannot both maintain the distinction and the phenomenological method. The reason that he cannot maintain both of these commitments is that the phenomenological method involves examining the meaning of how the world appears, not psychologically, but as a study of the conceptual necessities for any possible experience. However, the meaning of the world of things and objects, though autonomous from matters of fact, is always the meaning of something, of some referent, of some object or state of affairs.

The distinction between being and beings, or things and kind of things, could only be introduced into phenomenology by distinguishing between the meaning involved in speaking of neutrinos versus speaking of the physical world as a whole. Thus phenomenally Husserl could discuss the meaning-correlates of the distinction in question by discussing global ontological claims versus specific ontological commitments. But of course the phenomenological method requires that the meanings are examined first in terms of pure conceptual relations before one lifts the veil of ignorance and asks whether there is evidence for the validity of either the ontic or ontological commitments.

It is possible that when Heidegger speaks of the "meaning of being," he is not using "meaning" in Husserl's fashion at all then, that he does not consider meaning as the sense or way in which the world is presented to thought. Perhaps he merely wants to say by that phrase that the question of being is not "meaningless." But, if the question of being, as he defends it, is a properly philosophical question, a question independent of what beings there are and their properties, Heidegger must provide some reason to accept his view that these questions are dramatically distinct phenomenally, if that is the way in which he recommends we study philosophical questions. But not only does he not defend this fundamental claim, it seems clearly not to follow from Husserl's method.

Heidegger, I suspect, is aware of this problem. "Can ontology be grounded *ontologically* or does it also need for this an *ontic* foundation, and *which* being must take over the function of this foundation?" (BT 397, SZ 437). Heidegger's answer to this question must be that Dasein provides the proper kind of foundation, namely, one that is both ontic and ontological, as I noted in the beginning of this chapter. But that implicit response, which his entire book indirectly defends, demonstrates that this distinction precedes the apparent adoption of the phenomenological method. Thus the method, and Heidegger's appropriation of it, is not neutral between philosophical positions, as Husserl intended, but has built into it a way to exclude certain possible philosophical positions, namely, those positions in which ontological disputes reduce to or are only resolved by further ontic inquiry.

Husserl's intent was not to refute naturalism by way of some sort of sleight of hand. Husserl sought to treat naturalism as a competing philosophical position assessed in terms of its account of the necessary aspects of how the world appears in experience. Though Husserl thought it would ultimately prove a failure when tested against phenomenological analyses, the *lingua franca* for all philosophical debate, the only form of naturalism that needed to be excluded before the debate was the one in which philosophical questions were dismissed as misunderstood scientific questions concerning matters of fact. Since this position presupposed the truth of naturalism, it would prevent even the exercise of the phenomenological reduction.

Heidegger is introducing, in contrast, simply another version of presuppositional philosophical debate. Phenomenological analyses are thus irrelevant to such a strategy, and hence they do disappear from Heidegger's work. The fundamental distinctions at issue are established independently of or are prior to any such phenomenological reflection or any appeal to pure intuitions. Hence, how things are given as existing is phenomenally identical to how kinds of things are given as existing; bracketing would suspend either claim. Of course, Heidegger may have other reasons for defending the distinction between ontic and ontological questions, reasons he conceals in *Being and Time*. But since no defense of it is provided, this central distinction of Heidegger's project acts as an unquestioned and unexamined assumption of the entire project. In this way it challenges the book's claimed radicalism and refusal to countenance buried assumptions.

Popular Existentialism

Jean-Paul Sartre's *Being and Nothingness* is arguably one of the most famous and widely known philosophical works of the twentieth century. It was largely responsible for introducing the term "existentialism" into both academic and popular culture. Yet the apparent fascination with this work and its notoriety is rather curious when one considers its inhospitable nature. Perhaps Sartre's literary career or status as a public intellectual in Cold War Europe explains the success of what is in fact a largely unedited, rambling book whose philosophical content often lies buried beneath an impenetrable tangle of old and new terminology, discussions that read as though they are being worked out on the page as written, critical comments that are difficult to follow and do not clarify Sartre's views, numerous political and literary digressions, authoritative pronouncements of all sorts, and a great deal of repetition.

Sartre begins *in media res* with the problem of ontology, which he specifies as the tension between Husserl's realism, captured in the slogan "Back to the things themselves," and Husserl's transcendental idealism, which Sartre had already rejected in an early essay on Husserl's concept of the transcendental ego discussed in the previous chapter. *Being and Nothingness* opens with the claim that Husserl began a new direction in the study of philosophy, but left it unresolved; Sartre calls the problem "the pursuit of being."

Since Sartre defines an idealist as one who holds that "'to appear' supposes in essence somebody to whom to appear" (BN 4), Sartre calls idealism the "relativistic" aspect of phenomenology and contrasts it with phenomenology's "absoluteness" or realism. "The phenomenon can be studied and described as such, for it is *absolutely indicative of itself*" (BN 4). Though in this fashion Sartre's whole reading of Husserl, as can be gleaned from these definitions, is deeply wrong (as discussed in the previous chapter), Sartre thinks he has arrived at a central ontological question: What is "the being of this appearing"? Sartre's reliance on Heideggerian language is immediately apparent, since Sartre then speaks of how this question allows being to "disclose itself."

Sartre's terminology, wildly uneven in the book, often shifts from Husserl's usage to Sartre's own use of "phenomenon" as that which concerns an entity's properties or nature. Sartre's special usage consists of what Husserl dismissed as traditional phenomenalism and repeatedly and carefully contrasted with his use of the term. Sartre, however, remains oblivious to these differences. "The existent is a phenomenon; this means that it designates itself as an organized totality of qualities. It designates itself and not its being. Being is simply the condition of all revelation" (BN 8).

Sartre declares Husserl's project of philosophical reform a failure because it presupposes a fundamental ontology. Sartre thus follows Heidegger's criticisms of Husserl by focusing on the transcendental subject as symptomatic of this presupposed ontology and Husserl's failure to grasp the connection between phenomenology and ontology. However, even to a greater extent than Heidegger, Sartre abandons even making a gesture toward the phenomenological method or reduction (though, like Heidegger, he occasionally calls some psychologically descriptive passages "phenomenological" analyses). In addition, he declares that the problem of ontology is "transphenomenal" without being clear about which sense of "phenomenal" he has in mind.

> What is implied by the preceding considerations is that the being of the phenomenon, although coextensive with the phenomenon, cannot be subject to the phenomenal conditions—which is to exist only in so far as it reveals itself—and that consequently it surpasses the knowledge which we have of it and provides the basis for such knowledge. (BN 9)

Sartre intends to criticize the philosophical form of idealism in which the existence of entities depends on epistemic access (this form of idealism does not, of course, properly capture Husserl's view). For Sartre, then, the question concerning the being of appearance challenges phenomenalism. He also states that, in asking about the being of appearance, one is asking about the being of consciousness. To ask what kind of being phenomena have is to ask what makes it possible for being to appear; that question is identical in Sartre to asking what consciousness is. Though Sartre is not following Heidegger in the latter's wariness concerning either ontic or psychologistic expressions (for instance, Sartre freely uses the terms "consciousness," "human," and "mind" as though interchangeable and, more seriously, as though philosophically innocuous), he pursues something equivalent to Heidegger's Dasein-analysis. But Sartre immediately qualifies his agreement with Heidegger.

> Certainly we could apply to consciousness the definition which Heidegger reserves for *Dasein* and say that it is a being such that in its being, its being is in question. But it would be necessary to complete the definition and formulate it more like this: *consciousness is a being such that in its being, its being is in question in so far as this being implies a being other than itself.* (BN 24)

The last clause holds that the being of consciousness "implies a being other than itself," and Sartre sounds as though he intends this additional comment as a clarification. But Sartre's formulation immediately introduces some confusion. Heidegger did analyze Dasein as "being-with" in his discussion of the problem of other minds. But Heidegger does not argue that Dasein "implies" the existence of others. There is no analogical, logical, or causal implication in "being-with"; Heidegger's usage is specifically designed to avoid such formulations.

But more significantly, Sartre is not clear whether he intends to follow Heidegger in making a strict distinction between ontic and ontological questions. Whether "a being" (i.e., an entity) exists or not, in Heidegger's conception at least, is a separate matter from the subject of ontology. Ontology is a priori inquiry into being regardless of the beings (entities) that happen, as a contingent matter of fact, to exist. Sartre's reformulation, if the final clause is stressed, thus reverts to a confusion of traditional metaphysics from Heidegger's viewpoint. Also, as I already noted above concerning the term "existential," Sartre was among those who read the term, as is implicit in the above passage, as referring to the contingency or arbitrariness of a being, as appears in the phrase "without a foundation."

Sartre's ontology is built from a distinction between the being of phenomenon, which throughout the book he calls the "in-itself," and the being of consciousness, which he calls the "for-itself." The in-itself, by which Sartre replaces Heidegger's distinction between objective presence and being at hand, is simply what is. The for-itself is whatever is as it is in relation to consciousness. Being in-itself is then independent of whatever appears to consciousness as being for-itself.[19] This entire presentation presupposes Sartre's Heideggerian reading of Husserl in which the task of phenomenology is fundamental ontology.

> The phenomenon of being is not being. . . . But it indicates being. . . . The phenomenon of being, like every primary phenomenon, is immediately disclosed to consciousness. We have at each instant what Heidegger calls a pre-ontological comprehension of it; that is, one which is not accompanied by a fixing in concepts and elucidation. For us at present, then, there is no question of considering this phenomenon for the sake of trying to fix the meaning of being. . . . In particular the preceding reflections have permitted us to distinguish two absolutely separated regions of being: the being of the *pre-reflective cogito* and the being of the phenomenon. But although the concept of being has this peculiarity of being divided into two regions without communication, we must nevertheless explain how these two regions can be placed under the same heading. That will necessitate the investigation of these two types of being, and it is evident that we cannot truly grasp the meaning of either one until we can establish their true connection with the notion of being in general and the relations which unite them. (BN 25–26)

Sartre's position that being for-itself and being in-itself constitute an "unbridgeable gulf" becomes the guiding theme and guiding problem for the rest of the book. Sartre thus embraces, at least early in the text, a kind of dualism (a kind of "property dualism," to use a perhaps misleading phrase, since the in-itself and for-itself are both kinds of being). He claims that "the being of phenomenon can on no account act upon consciousness" (BN 26) and he rules out what he calls any "realistic" account of their relation. Though the language of causality does creep back into later passages of the book and even, inconsistently, eventually comes to characterize the sought after "connection" between these two regions, Sartre initially labels causal interactionism as a "realistic" solution that collapses the two distinct "regions of being" and is illicit. Sartre's occasional comments about the sciences reinforce that reading, since he claims the sciences are constitutionally unable to bridge the gulf between the for-itself and the in-itself.[20]

Sartre's ontology abandons Heidegger's problem of the meaning of being. Sartre's question is: How is consciousness "connected to" (understanding "connected to" in some nonnaturalistic fashion) the world outside of it? In Sartre's language, how does the in-itself (or what he often calls "transcendent being") manifest itself to the for-itself? Since Sartre rejects scientific answers to this question about the relationship between consciousness and the world, he says he is seeking an ontological or simply metaphysical account.

Sartre's problem concerning a "connection" between these regions of being requires quotation marks around the term. It is not a question psychologists or neurologists would ask, for example. But on this central point Sartre is deeply confusing. Since he allows himself the use of the language of causality and naturalism in later sections of the text, it becomes increasingly difficult to understand how Sartre's question about the "connection" between consciousness and the external world is, in the final analysis, different from the same question asked by the sciences. I think this confusion is the central obscurity of the book, reinforcing, but in some ways underlying, the other obscurities of Sartre's style.

The central problem of the book thus proves either unsolvable or trivial. If "regions of being" are not connected by any naturalistic relation, because being precedes and makes possible causal relations, and if idealism is ruled out because, in Sartre's account, it denies the autonomy and independence of the in-itself from the for-itself, then the problem (if it is a problem at all) is simply unsolvable. Consciousness cannot "act upon," modify, transform, or even aim at "transcendent being," as Sartre often repeats. Thus, ontological analysis of this "connection" becomes a wholly mysterious and apparently pointless task.

But if all Sartre is saying is that both the in-itself and for-itself are kinds of being, the sought after connection is trivial. As different kinds of being, they are connected because that is how Sartre has stipulated it. In either case, Sartre seems alternately confused or quiescent about the obvious clash between the way he has stated this philosophical dualism animating his work and the commonsense realism, to which he also often appeals, wherein causal connections between consciousness and the world are simply obvious and denied only at the peril of a puerile skepticism.

Sartre echoes passages from Heidegger by beginning his analysis of this "immediate relationship" between consciousness and transcendent being as a relation of "questioning." Consciousness questions the being of the world, he states. The notion of questioning leads Sartre to an infamous account of how the "nothingness" of the being (the for-itself, or simply consciousness) is "the worm in the heart of being."

The manner in which Sartre uses the term "nothingness" and the florid, metaphorical language that proliferates in much of this part of the book strongly suggest that Sartre enjoyed making himself obscure. But we need not throw up our hands just yet. At least two points will help recover some kind of central theme from the mass of Sartre's paradoxical formulations. First, Sartre's topic is that of fundamental ontology and, and if we set aside disputes about the viability of such a topic, the focus is thereby not on the nature of beings as such. Therefore, the concept of "nothingness" is not functioning as it would normally or practically in everyday life. Second, "nothingness," as an ontological concept, unifies a diverse range of activities by saying that these activities share this kind of being, that which Sartre also calls the "for-itself." "Nothingness" is not a thing, an entity, or something that occurs during those actions. It could not somehow be found among those activities or located anywhere in the world; nor is it "nihilating," a causal action like that of "mashing" or "crushing." Nothingness is not then the opposite of being; it is properly an ontological category. In view of these two points, I can try to restate Sartre's approach without the contentious phrases.

Sartre is concerned with a group of phenomena he identifies as "nihilating activities." These include such "activities," metaphorically understood, as absence, possibility, differentiation, distinction, negation, denial, doubt, and deception. Sartre also refers to such activities, understood ontologically, as "negativities": "a swarm of ultra-mundane beings which possess as much reality and efficacy as other beings, but which enclose within themselves non-being" (BN 56).

One ought not to think naturalistically about that sentence, though the words "as much reality and efficacy" do make it difficult to resist collapsing again the ontic and ontological points. Sartre claims he is providing an ontological explication of how being can appear to consciousness by showing how it is possible for consciousness to question being. Such questioning occurs by way of stressing that being for-itself is, for instance, a set of possibilities. Questioning then presupposes, in Sartre's conception, the ontological concept of nothingness. These "negativities," such as denying or criticizing what is, are possible, understanding the word "possible" in a philosophical manner, because nothingness is an existential feature of being for-itself; that is, it is an a priori possibility of being for-itself and not some fact about the world or property of being in-itself. This whole account is not so much an analysis as an interlocking set of metaphors.

> The relations of man in the world, which the *négatités* indicate, have nothing in common with the relations *a posteriori* which are brought out by empirical activity. We are no longer dealing with those relations of *instrumentality* by which, according to Heidegger, objects in the world disclose themselves to "human reality." Every *négatité* appears rather as one of the essential conditions of this relation of instrumentality. In order for the totality of being to order itself around us as instruments, in order for it to parcel itself into differentiated complexes which refer to one another and which can *be used*, it is necessary that negation rise up not as a thing among other things but as the rubric of a category which presides over the arrangement and the redistribution of great masses of being in things. Thus the rise of man in the midst of the being which "invests" him causes a world to be discovered. But the essential and primordial moment of this rise is the negation. Thus we have reached the first goal of this study. Man is the being through whom nothingness comes to the world. (BN 59)

Despite my comments above, I do not think Sartre's views can be fruitfully discussed by following him in his use of the term "nothingness." The central problem is how many distinct topics he strives to cover using the term and how he then ceases to defend his conclusions once he puts this vocabulary in place. For instance, the statement that "consciousness is nothingness" could be understood as suggesting some argument against reductive accounts of consciousness in the physical or biological sciences (and Sartre does explicitly take it this way). It could also be said to capture the point of Sartre's argument against the reality of the ego, already discussed in Chapter 1. Yet these positions are distinct, since agreeing with Sartre on the failures of scientific reduction does not entail accepting his view about the nonexistence of the ego. Furthermore Sartre's opposition to the reduction of consciousness by the sciences confuses ontic and ontological questions (which is one reason why Heidegger avoided the term "consciousness") as well as simply assuming that the kind of physicalism presupposed in the sciences is necessarily reductionist. Sartre's cryptic, metaphorical pronouncements, especially characteristic of this book, leave even the most tenacious reader quite confused, less because of the doctrine's subtleties than Sartre's unforgiving style. Rather than remain on a windy and rather barren ontological plane, I would prefer to explicate Sartre's view by way of two examples in which the ontology outlined above is pressed into service answering two traditional philosophical problems. These two examples also conveniently involve the most often quoted passages of *Being and Nothingness*.

First, Sartre claims to solve the traditional metaphysical quandary concerning freedom and determinism. Second, Sartre analyzes and claims to solve the problem of other minds. I have already followed the thread of the second problem through Husserl and Heidegger, and this example will usefully include Sartre's criticisms of Husserl and Heidegger. Sartre extends his comments on the problem of other minds into a larger account of human action, for which his work is very well known, involving, as it does, the concepts of "bad faith" and "the look."

The metaphysical problem of free will and determinism can be stated as a dilemma. Either the natural world is deterministic or indeterministic with regard to whatever are its basic processes and interactions. This "either-or" is a priori since there is no other way for the world to be. The dilemma then arises because freedom appears incompatible with either determinism or indeterminism. This clash between our understanding of the world and our intuition about the nature of our own actions is thus apparently both immune to any further empirical evidence and yet the kind of dilemma that demands a solution.

To deny human freedom, as some philosophers have found themselves forced to do, leaves a philosophical account of human behavior deeply inconsistent with entrenched and perhaps "ineliminable" concepts of action and personhood. Though this would hardly be the only issue on which philosophy finds itself at odds with common sense, there appear here no attractive ways to fully abandon common sense and the concept of freedom. The tension between philosophy and common sense on the issue of freedom has thus traditionally seemed more troubling and fundamental than the tensions between philosophy and common sense over issues in epistemology or ethics.

Philosophers have held three positions concerning this metaphysical quandary. First, determinism (or indeterminism) is affirmed and freedom of the will is simply denied, as noted above. Second, free will is defended by some notion of primary "uncaused" actions that escape any and all dependence on the natural world. Third, both free will and determinism are affirmed together in a position often called "compatibilism." The compatibilist position seems an attractive option and has been supported by a very wide range of past philosophers; for example, such otherwise remarkably diverse thinkers as Hobbes, Mill, and Hegel were compatibilists. But it remains a controversial and, to some, suspicious type of compromise; Kant, for instance, labeled it a "wretched subterfuge." Sartre also rejects it. Thus the quandary is all the more pressing since the remaining two options are then equally unattractive; one violates our deepest intuition and the other any possible understanding of the natural world.

Given this very brief account, Sartre holds that his ontology can contribute to clarifying and resolving this famous problem in a manner more satisfying than traditional answers. Before attempting to explicate Sartre's position, I should note that Sartre presents the debate between determinists and proponents of free will in a peculiar fashion by making certain restrictive assumptions about determinism. For example, he assumes that a determinist must exclude the reality or efficacy of mental states, namely, whatever people believe or intend concerning some state of affairs. When Sartre argues against determinism, then, he claims that a situation becomes wholly "indeterminate" once the beliefs of the participants are included. Sartre even asserts that no given state of affairs, even one including those relevant psychological state of affairs, is "capable by itself of motivating any act whatsoever" (BN 562).

Since it is hard to see how Sartre could hold both of these points or what else motivation could amount to in such a context, Sartre must mean in the second quotation that even a complete account of the relevant facts of the matter leaves it impossible to *predict* what any agent will do. But if that is what he means, then Sartre is confusing determinism, as a metaphysical claim about the world, with the separate, epistemic question about whether human actions can be predicted, even given complete information. Obviously one could be a determinist in one's metaphysics and yet agree that such prediction is impossible. Due to his restrictive assumptions and his shift to the problem of prediction, Sartre does not raise clear objections in these passages to a properly formulated determinism. Setting aside that confusion, here is Sartre's account of the debate:

> The latter [proponents of free will] are concerned to find cases of decision for which there exists no prior cause, or deliberations concerning two opposed acts which are equally possible and possess causes (and motives) of exactly the same weight. To which the determinist may easily reply that there is no action without a cause. . . . To speak of an act without a cause is to speak of an act which would lack the intentional structure of every act. (BN 563–564)

Sartre presents us with a stark choice. If any human action is possible, it apparently must be part of the causal, world order. If an action is part of the causal order, whether the world is deterministic or indeterministic, that action cannot be free. Yet if our actions are not free, then they are not in effect actions at all. In the passages that follow the above statement, Sartre argues that his ontology involves an analysis of motivation (motivation turns out to be a species of negativity in Sartre's language) that resolves this stark dilemma.

The naturalistic concept of cause, Sartre argues, concerns only the in-itself, but motivation includes the for-itself, and thus another structure of negativity. Motivation "nihilates," metaphorically, the in-itself; hence free action is "made possible" by the being of consciousness. But Sartre's effort to distinguish motivation from cause simply restates rather than resolves the question. It asserts that motivation escapes the causal world order, whereas both the determinist (indeterminist) and compatibilist would deny such a distinction and thus such a possibility.

Sartre's point is to understand determinism as an ontological position and claim that, since it requires reducing being for-itself to being in-itself, it is somehow ontologically suspect; determinism then excludes the category of being for-itself. Thus Sartre's argument against determinism, even given his restrictive understanding of it, consists of his reminding the reader that if being for-itself were so reduced or eliminated, "genuine human action" would not be possible. Sartre returns then to characterizing determinism as a position that must deny the efficacy or reality of intentional actions and, thereby, the reality of consciousness (consciousness is likewise reduced to the in-itself, to a thing).

Does Sartre's reiteration of his ontological separation between these two "regions of being" contribute to resolving the debate concerning the possibility of freedom? I do not see how this discussion moves the debate much further. Sartre warns that his account of the debate will not be easy to follow and that freedom as understood philosophically is different from freedom in its practical or vulgar use. But, in the final analysis, Sartre's position amounts to a bald assertion that there are free, uncaused actions or an assertion of his initial distinction between being in-itself and for-itself. His defense of either assertion amounts to no more than repeating his definitions; but his definitions do not move the debate beyond its traditional stalemate.

> We stated that this permanent possibility of nihilating what I am in the form of "having-been" implies for man a particular type of existence. We were able then to determine by means of analyses like that of bad faith that human reality is its own nothingness. For the for-itself, to be is to nihilate the in-itself which it is. Under these conditions freedom can be nothing other than this nihilation. (BN 567)

Sartre's claims about human beings are not supposed to be competitive with those of psychologists, neurologists, anthropologists, or biologists concerning human beings (though Sartre is not as consistent as Husserl and Heidegger in keeping these issues separate). His claim that there is no human nature must therefore be understood as ontological, not ontic. To claim, as he does, that human beings are endless concatenations of actions is to make an ontological statement, not a claim about any fact of biology, physiology, or psychology.

But such an ontological analysis does not constitute a defense of freedom against determinism. The determinist could agree with Sartre about this "plasticity" of human beings, as behaviorists actually did (assuming such theorists would accept talk distinguishing ontological and ontic inquiry), and yet continue to insist that all actions are determined (or statistically indeterminate), setting aside the limits of human access to such knowledge.

Sartre approaches the debate as though the ontological category of the for-itself, which he claims he gained by phenomenological analysis, establishes that determinism is somehow *phenomenally* incoherent. Yet, the proponents of determinism and compatibilism, as even Sartre grants in describing the debate, could reformulate their positions in such a way as to be compatible with Sartre's ontological language. In this fashion the debate for him is the following kind of squabble: There are free actions because there is being for-itself.

To be fair to Sartre, there are points he makes in the course of his account of the metaphysical debate concerning freedom and determinism that are worthwhile making and insightful, though they are barely developed. He notes that the concept of action has many subordinate concepts that need to be carefully analyzed before trying to settle the question. He correctly notes that his brand of ontological dualism necessarily excludes compatibilism.

> Thus any synthesis of two types of existents [free will and determined passion] is impossible, they are not homogeneous; they will remain each one in its incommunicable solitude. . . . This discussion shows that two solutions and only two are possible: either man is wholly determined . . . or else man is wholly free. (BN 570–571)

In addition, the concept of "free will" is misleading. "Willing" is just another mental event, and what must constitute a defense of freedom is not the special or unique mental event of "willing," but any human intentional action at all. Sartre also wisely and usefully distinguishes between determinism and fatalism and thus notes that in seeking a "reason" for an action, and as long as those "reasons" can include intentional action, determinism is compatible with his own account of human action (BN 583). Finally, Sartre properly focuses the debate on the claim that: "A choice is said to be free if it is such that it could have been other than what it [was]" (BN 584). Sartre's analysis of this claim leads him to conclude that there are truly free acts. Certain actions that he calls "radical conversions" alter not simply the choices possible, given the facts of the matter (that would be an alteration in outcome compatible with determinism), but change the very meaning and purpose of the entire situation. Such acts are "gratuitous," as Sartre says; they are primary, uncaused, free acts.

Sartre's position is thus a rejection of both determinism and indeterminism. Normally or ordinarily, he could agree, the account of human action is determinist. Such determinism could include mental deliberation, for instance, as part of the reasons for an action. But there are radical conversions, rooted in the ontological split between in-itself and for-itself, where actions escape both determinism and the indeterminism of probability. Hence Sartre is not an "indeterminist," as some may mistakenly describe his view, but a defender of a possible uncaused action.

I now turn to the second philosophical problem leading to Sartre's theory of action. As mentioned already, Sartre introduces the notion of "negativity" to encompass, among other phenomena, such actions as doubting, differentiating, and denying. Sartre, in the section I will now discuss, extends this point to a larger account of human actions.

He calls the central feature of his account "bad faith," which I will explain shortly, and includes within it those cases in which "consciousness instead of directing its negation outward turns it toward itself" (BN 87). Sartre distinguishes "bad faith" from "ordinary lying." Both are negativities of course, but bad faith has an ontological significance quite distinct from the practical or everyday act of lying.

> We shall willingly grant that bad faith is a lie to oneself, on condition that we distinguish the lie to oneself from lying in general. Lying is a negative attitude, we will agree to that. But this negation does not bear on consciousness itself; it aims only at the transcendent. . . . The ideal description of the liar would be cynical consciousness . . . all the negations which constitute it bear on objects which by this fact are removed from consciousness. The lie then does not require special ontological foundation, and the explanations which the existence of negation in general requires are valid without change in the case of deceit. (BN 87–88)

What is bad faith if not simply lying? Sartre focuses on examples of human behavior that Aristotle described with the term *akrasia,* or "weakness of the will." The problem of *akrasia* has led some theorists to postulate a divided mind in the hopes of providing, as Aristotle also hoped to provide, a naturalistic or even purely psychological account of such behaviors.[21] Sartre's answer, as will be shown below, has some similarities with these accounts, though he claims that bad faith is ontologically important independent of the need for psychological or physiological explanations. Bad faith is a case in which one deceives oneself while simultaneously being in a state of self-awareness. It is in effect having the "plan" to systematically self-deceive.

> That which affects itself with bad faith must be conscious (of) its bad faith since the being of consciousness is consciousness of being. . . . We must agree in fact that if I deliberately and cynically attempt to lie to myself, I fail completely in this undertaking; . . . it is ruined from behind by the very consciousness of lying to myself which pitilessly constitutes itself well within my project as its very condition. (BN 89)

Though Sartre describes this condition as "evanescent," he also describes it as autonomous, durable, and frequent. What makes a case of bad faith possible? Suppose someone knows that smoking cigarettes is bad for health, has formed the intention not to smoke, and does value his or her long-term good health over the momentary pleasure of smoking, but smokes anyway. Sartre stresses that his analysis of such actions concerns not just the fact that the person fails to do what he or she has intended to do, but that the failure is brought about in an effort to "fool" or "trick" oneself about the nature of the action. Thus bad faith is "weakness of the will" manifesting itself in "sneaking" smokes, treating each failure to quit as an accident, interpreting each relapse as "being overpowered," or simply denying to oneself that one has smoked. Naturalistically our impulse is to approach the problem from the perspective that cigarettes are addictive substances. But let us assume, even if it attributes a rigor to Sartre's discussion that it lacks, we were bracketing such physiological explanations in discussing the meaning of such behavior.

Sartre pictures this behavior as one in which the mind becomes divorced or divided against itself, and in which the subject is aware of itself both as a bodily system of desires and as a mental system of plans, projects, or judgments. As Sartre states the essential feature of such situations: "The basic concept which is thus engendered utilizes the double property of the human being, who is at once a *facticity* and a *transcendence*" (BN 98). Sartre presents bad faith, therefore, as exemplifying the ontological dualism with which the book itself began. It is a special form of duplicity involving looking at one's own behavior as for-itself and then looking at oneself as in-itself, as though at another person.

> We can equally well use another kind of duplicity derived from human reality which we will express roughly by saying that its being-for-itself implies complementarily a being-for-others. Upon any one of my conducts it is always possible to converge two looks, mine and that of the Other. The conduct will not present exactly the same structure in each case. (BN 100)

Bad faith arises, then, because of the following two ontological features of consciousness. First, consciousness is transparent to itself and has "privileged access" to its own contents. Sartre argues against the psychoanalytic theory of the unconscious based on this first feature of consciousness, though he does agree that persons can *act* as though (or pretend in the manner of being in bad faith) their own intentions or desires are not apparent to themselves. Second, consciousness is unlike any being in-itself that it encounters in the world. It is not a thing or property of the world, but, as Sartre likes to state it, a "structure of negativities." Thus no human action can be said to be determined by even the totality of factual matters, since actions are simply not features of the world as being in-itself.

Bad faith is then inevitable and that gives human action its distinctive and unique profile in the world. The normal explanations of bad faith, naturalistic or causal claims about human psychology or addictive personalities, are ontologically misleading. Such explanations either violate the transparency of consciousness with regard to its own content (which is what Sartre accuses psychoanalysis of doing) or deny the ontological for-itself of actions as fundamentally free and uncaused.

Human beings are the sum total of their actions; there are neither inherent guides nor natural limits for actions (though there are such limits for the factual aspects of human behaviors). Human actions continually fail to both fully explicate themselves to the subject while simultaneously remaining self-aware. Paradoxically, then, freedom is something the subject seeks to escape from and such total honesty is, at least in Sartre's conception, a sign of some kind of disturbed and curiously dissociated self.

Sartre's account of human behavior became widely discussed because of what Sartre encouraged many to consider as its political and social implications. These political implications appear in the following famous passage and were then echoed in one of Sartre's most widely read essays on the problem of prejudice and tolerance:[22]

> A homosexual frequently has an intolerable feeling of guilt, and his whole existence is determined in relation to this feeling. . . . Here is assuredly a man in bad faith who borders on the comic since, acknowledging all the facts which are imputed to him, he refuses to draw from the conclusion which they impose. His friend, who is his most severe critic, becomes irritated with this duplicity. The critic asks only one thing . . . that the guilty recognize himself as guilty. . . . Who is in bad faith? The homosexual or the champion of sincerity?
>
> The homosexual recognizes his faults, but he struggles with all his strength against the crushing view that his mistakes constitute for him a *destiny*. He does not wish to let himself be considered as a thing. He has an obscure but strong feeling that a homosexual is not a homosexual as this table is a table or as this red-haired man is red-haired. (BN 107)

Times have changed and much of the above, not only the reference to "faults," but also Sartre's final implicit claim that being homosexual is *not* like being "red-haired," would ironically be considered factually if not politically incorrect, at least by some. Though Sartre, as a result of such an account, condemned the treatment of homosexuality as an illness or disability (which partly explains his moral language in the above quotation), his conclusion seems dependent on a rather direct factual question, whether homosexuality is a physiological condition on a par with having red hair. But if the issue rests on empirical evidence, it resists an a priori ontological analysis anyway.

The reason for the confusion is that Sartre fails to either discuss or clarify how he distinguishes actions (which have at least the possibility of being free and uncaused in the fashion he wants) from other behaviors or functions that are not actions. It is obvious from the quotation that Sartre thinks inheriting red hair is not an action, whereas drinking coffee in a cafe, for instance, constitutes his archetype of an action. However, these obvious cases leave others indeterminate and specifically leave something as complex as homosexuality as a blur of actions and physiological conditions.

Equally problematic are behaviors that have historically shifted from one category to the other, normally as a result of the empirical information that has been learned about the natural world. Puberty, for example, may have appeared to a previous age as a series of actions, but it now is securely understood as a physiological change. Therefore, puberty is no more an action than the proper function of one's liver.

The same story is now being told about being homosexual. The cultural and political changes that have occurred since Sartre wrote the above sentences raise the uncomfortable point that factual issues do have a significant impact on philosophical debate. However, debates concerning the political and cultural analyses based on the concept of bad faith lie outside the scope of this book.[23]

Toward the end of *Being and Nothingness,* Sartre extends the above account of human action to the philosophical problem of other minds. "Therefore, if realism bases its certitude upon the presence 'in person' of the spatio-temporal thing in my consciousness, it cannot lay claim to the same evidence for the reality of the Other's soul since by this very admission, the Other's soul does not give itself 'in person' to mine" (BN 304). Furthermore, causality could not provide that link and thus solve the problem of other minds. "Causality could in fact link only phenomena to each other . . . in this sense I am not prevented from considering the redness of Paul's face as the effect of his anger. . . . But, on the other hand, causality has meaning only if it links phenomena of one and the same experience and contributes to constituting that experience. Can it serve as a bridge between two experiences which are radically separated?" (BN 307–308).[24] At best, Sartre thinks, there are common sense and "deep-rooted tendencies" to oppose skepticism about the existence of other minds.

Having revived the philosophical problem of solipsism, Sartre uses it to critically assess Heidegger and Husserl. Though Sartre grants that Husserl's account in *Cartesian Meditations* is an advance over the tradition and says that he agrees with Husserl's rejection of any solution based on reasoning by analogy with knowledge of one's own mind, he concludes that Husserl's account is faulty. Husserl's transcendental ego, Sartre argues, only deepens the problem of skepticism. "The true problem is that of the connection of transcendental subjects who are beyond experience" (BN 317). Sartre holds that Husserl's recourse to the transcendental ego exacerbates the problem.

> Consequently the only way to escape solipsism would be . . . to prove that my
> transcendental consciousness is, in its very being, affected by the extra-

mundane existence of other consciousnesses of the same type. Because Husserl
has reduced being to a series of meanings, the only connection which he has
been able to establish between my being and that of the Other is a connection
of *knowledge*. (BN 318)

As I discussed in Chapter 1, Sartre collapses the neutrality of the phenomenological reduction with regard to solipsism with the separate question, which Husserl does not consider in *Cartesian Meditations,* whether
philosophical solipsism is correct. But Sartre is simply mistaken. Husserl
does not attempt to answer the problem of other minds by providing some
"connection" between oneself and others; this misreading vitiates much of
Sartre's criticism of Husserl on this point and I refer the reader to my account of Sartre's criticism at the end of the previous chapter.

Sartre characterizes Heidegger's approach as exemplifying Heidegger's
"barbaric fashion of cutting Gordian knots rather than trying to untie
them." Sartre claims that Heidegger's dismissal of solipsism rests on two aspects of his ontology: "(1) the relations between human-realities must be a
relation of being; (2) this relation must cause 'human-realities' to depend
on one another in their essential being" (BN 330). Putting aside for the moment the apparently careless use of "cause" in the second phrase, Sartre
agrees that Heidegger dismisses the problem of other minds as a "false
problem." But Sartre's reasons for why it is a false problem hardly resemble
Heidegger's reasons. Sartre claims that it is a false problem because the
other self is no longer a particular existence encountered in the world, apart
from my existence, but "contributes to the constitution of my being." I discussed Heidegger's analysis at greater length above and Sartre's summary
hardly does it justice.

Sartre rejects Heidegger's conclusion because it amounts to no more than
defining Dasein as "being-with"; such a solution, Sartre responds, lacks a
foundation. Though Sartre appreciates Heidegger's wish to sidestep traditional philosophical issues by beginning his analysis prior to the distinctions that generate those problems, he thinks that in this case Heidegger has
cheated by simply introducing the solution in the definition of Dasein.

But Sartre's objection begs clarification of what Sartre means here by a
"foundation." For example, Sartre repeatedly describes the "for-itself" as
"without foundation" and uses the same strategy as Heidegger in the debate
on freedom and determinism when he simply defines the "for-itself" as the
possibility of free, uncaused actions. Sartre's proposed account of the problem of other minds, then, abandons Heidegger's fundamental ontology.

To say that human reality . . . "is-with" by means of an ontological structure
is to say that it is-with by nature—that is, in an essential and universal capacity. Even if this affirmation were proved, it would not enable us to explain any
concrete being-with. In other words, the ontological co-existence which ap-

pears as the structure of "being-in-the-world" can in no way serve as a foundation to an ontic being-with, such, for example, the co-existence which appears in my friendship with Pierre. . . . But this is impossible from the point of view which Heidegger has adopted. (BN 334)

Sartre thinks the problem of other minds fails to admit of Heidegger's ontological analysis because the problem only concerns a "particular ontic relation between me and Pierre." However, this account of the debate is wrong both in its reading of Heidegger and as an account of the philosophical problem itself. The philosophical problem is distinct from practical, sociological, psychological, or historical questions about relationships between persons. The philosophical problem concerns the criteria for the identity of the self. Neither psychological nor sociological information as such would contribute to providing those criteria (unless the entire philosophical problem is rejected as misconceived and thereby without a solution).

Second, Heidegger is not proposing a solution to the problem of other minds at all. He is, as Sartre previously agreed, dismissing the problem as confused, based on misunderstandings, and a symptom of traditional confusions over fundamental ontology. The problem of other minds is the price paid for a naive metaphysics, a naïveté Heidegger hopes to uncover and by that effort dismiss. Thus criticizing Heidegger for not solving the problem is tantamount to misunderstanding Heidegger.

Sartre's answer, then, is both confused and inadequate.

> It is here that we can derive a new and valid insight as the result of our critical examination of Heidegger's teaching: Human-reality remains alone because the Other's existence has the nature of a contingent and irreducible fact. We *encounter* the Other; we do not constitute him. And if this fact still appears to us in the form of a necessity, yet it does not belong with those "conditions of the possibility of our experience" or—if you prefer—with ontological necessity. If the Other's existence is a necessity, it is a "contingent necessity": that is, it is of the same type as the factual necessity which is imposed on the *cogito*. If the Other is to be capable of being given to us, it is by means of a direct apprehension which leaves to the encounter its character of facticity, just as the *cogito* itself leaves all its facticity to my own thought, a facticity which nevertheless shares in the apodicticity of the *cogito* itself—*i.e.*, in its indubitability. (BN 336–337)

Sartre has shifted the dispute to "ontic questions" and thus "contingent" or factual necessity. That could mean that the problem of other minds is, as a philosophical problem, a pseudoproblem and simply resolves into further psychological or sociological issues. This point is not properly an objection to Heidegger's analysis, but there is even a deeper confusion.

Sartre does have an answer to the problem he states in the second part of the above passage. The other is "directly apprehended" as the other. But that formulation restates rather than resolves the problem. The philosophical problem arises precisely because the other cannot be "directly apprehended," given the assumption that consciousness has "privileged access" to only its own mental states. Sartre has challenged neither privileged access nor its being ego-specific. In fact, he continually affirms both views. His needlessly confusing digression concerning Descartes's *cogito* highlights Sartre's commitment to "privileged access." What makes the knowledge claim of Descartes's *cogito* "indubitable" is that it is wholly internal to the thinking subject and thus immune to any doubts concerning external reality.

Thus the appeal to direct apprehension alone, if it is understood in the way Sartre states it (the way he thinks Descartes and Husserl understand it), could not amount to an answer to the problem of other minds. The problem can either be dismissed, as Husserl and Heidegger hoped to do, or solved by abandoning some or all of the assumptions about mental experience that characterize a kind of "Cartesian internalism." Sartre does not provide, however, a third way between these two options in which he embraces such internalism and yet does not have to accept any limits concerning knowledge of the external world and specifically knowledge of other minds. Finally, his solution amounts to the argument from analogy in which knowledge of other minds is based on knowledge of one's own mind, an answer Sartre earlier dismisses.

The Last Word

Sartre's famous book is so wholly at odds with Heidegger's defense of the possibility of a fundamental ontology that it is difficult to appreciate today that Sartre's contemporaries and his many readers failed to see any of these glaring differences. It was deeply frustrating to Heidegger who, like his own teacher, began to realize that he could not control the way his words were appropriated (even though he had anticipated and predicted some of this misuse while still enthusiastically composing his work and planting inside it those various "pitfalls" for the unwary).

The philosophical revolution he had launched was slowly but surely regressing to traditional themes and positions, much as he had warned it would. In 1947, responding to a student's request, Heidegger expressed his views about what was then popularly called existentialism, but which Heidegger dubbed "humanism." The focus of his reply was primarily to Sartre, but Heidegger intended the argument to apply more widely to what he considered the new resistance to thinking ontologically.

Sartre had just published a widely discussed article called "Existentialism Is a Humanism"[25] and that gave Heidegger an opportunity to link the uncritical way in which Sartre used such concepts as "man" and "consciousness" with the belated revival of traditional philosophy that Heidegger found in Sartre's cultural and political views, specifically Sartre's Kantian ethics.

Heidegger's essay begins, in an apparent debate with Sartre's account of human action, by contrasting work and thinking. Efficacy is a matter of cause and effects, whereas thinking is concerned with truth. Work is directed toward beings, thinking toward being. Heidegger describes the effort to treat thinking as theoretical research as an inadequate effort to rescue thinking and preserve its autonomy from both technology and work. These often repeated themes of his philosophy are summarized usefully as follows:

> Since then "philosophy" has been in the constant predicament of having to justify its existence before the "sciences." It believes it can do that most effectively by elevating itself to the rank of a science. But such an effort is the abandonment of the essence of thinking. . . . Being, as the element of thinking, is abandoned by the technical interpretation of thinking. (LH 195)

Predictably, Heidegger treats talk of "humanism" as "idle talk," a public discourse that "under the dictatorship of the public realm . . . decides in advance what is intelligible and what must be rejected as unintelligible" (LH 197). But Heidegger accepts that humanism raises a legitimate question, albeit in a confused manner, concerning the "essence of man." He then reviews different answers to this question contrasting Marxism, which appeals to society, with Christian theology, for which "man is not of this world." Heidegger's aim here is not to choose between these conceptions, but to show that they share an unexamined metaphysics; they are different but equally naive ontology.

> But if one understands humanism in general as a concern that man become free for his humanity and find his worth in it, then humanism differs according to one's conception of the "freedom" and "nature" of man. So too are there various paths toward the realization of such conceptions. The humanism of Marx does not need to return to antiquity any more than the humanism which Sartre conceives existentialism to be. In this broad sense Christianity too *is* a humanism, in that according to its teaching everything depends on man's salvation *(salus aeterna)*; the history of man appears in the context of the history of redemption. However different these forms of humanism may be in purpose and in principle, in the mode and means of their respective realizations, and in the form of their teaching, they nonetheless all agree in this, that the *humanitas* of *homo humanus* is determined with regard to an already established interpretation of nature, history, world, and the ground of the world, that is, of beings as a whole. (LH 201–202)

Heidegger proceeds to characterize this entire approach as metaphysics, using the term in the pejorative sense as imprisoned within the philosophical tradition. Specifically, it fails to grasp the distinction between ontic and ontological, it takes essences as perceived in experience, and it makes assumptions about nature and physical things that Heidegger believes *Being and Time* had already shown to be problematic. Humanism is not a serious questioning of ontology, it is mere projection.

> Nor is the error of biologism overcome by adjoining a soul to the human body, a mind to the soul, and the existentiell to the mind, and then louder than before singing the praises of the mind—only to let everything relapse into "life-experience," with a warning that thinking by its inflexible concepts disrupts the flow of life and that of Being distorts existence. The fact that physiology and physiological chemistry can scientifically investigate man as an organism is no proof that in this "organic" thing, that is, in the body scientifically explained, the essence of man consists. That has as little validity as the notion that the essence of nature has been discovered in atomic energy. It could even be that nature, in the face she turns toward man's technical mastery, is simply concealing her essence. (LH 204–205)

Heidegger repeats that existence, as part of ontology, does not refer to any matter of contingent fact about a being. Existence is the proper ontological response to the poorly stated question of the essence of man. Heidegger also stresses, again, his rejection of subjectivism.

> By way of contrast, Sartre expresses the basic tenet of existentialism in this way: Existence precedes essence. In this statement he is taking *existentia* and *essentia* according to their metaphysical meaning, which from Plato's time on has said that *essentia precedes existentia*. Sartre reverses this statement. But the reversal of a metaphysical statement remains a metaphysical statement. . . . Concealed in its essential provenance, the differentiation of *essentia* (essentiality) and *existentia* (actuality) completely dominates the destiny of Western history and of all history determined by Europe. (LH 208)

The possibility of ontology, he repeats, involves abandoning sociological, anthropological, or moral-evaluative concepts. He concludes that his way of thinking about being is not humanism, which is simply traditional metaphysics; nor is it existentialism, which deeply misunderstands *Being and Time*. In view of the degeneration of philosophy in Europe, where idle talk and technical success prevail, Heidegger offers only what he considers the superior access of poetry to the question of being; philosophy is now apparently a lost cause.

Existentialism, which Heidegger so roundly disparaged, disappeared almost as quickly as it appeared, at least among philosophers. Merleau-Ponty and Sartre went on to embrace different types of historicism, largely leaving phenomenology and existentialism behind, in their mutual exploration of how a theory of knowledge becomes part of a broader sociological theory, a position I discuss in Chapter 3. Ironically, Heidegger had predicted this nascent direction when he pointed out that "the Marxist view of history is superior to that of other historical accounts. But since neither Husserl nor—so far as I have seen till now—Sartre recognizes the essential importance of the historical in Being, neither phenomenology nor existentialism enters that dimension within which a productive dialogue with Marxism first becomes possible" (LH 219–220).

Heidegger was also to abandon the philosophical project of *Being and Time*. As Heidegger's work had ended Husserl's dream, Heidegger turned his thoughts to what would prove ever more obscure poetic and mystical gestures. As the catastrophe of World War II receded and European intellectual life began to renew itself, philosophy's "inextinguishable task," that demand for rational criticism Husserl had begun the century defending and whose misunderstanding he prophetically warned would be practically and theoretically disastrous, was abandoned once and for all by friend and foe alike.

Notes

1. "[Husserl] regarded himself as a master and teacher of patient, descriptive, detailed work, and all rash combinations and clever constructions were an abomination to him. In his teaching, whenever he encountered the grand assertions and arguments that are typical of beginning philosophers, he used to say, 'Not always big bills, gentlemen; small change, small change!' This kind of work produced a peculiar fascination. It had the effect of a purgation, a return to honesty, a liberation from the opaqueness of the opinions, slogans, and battle cries that circulated." H-G. Gadamer, "The Phenomenological Movement," in *Philosophical Hermeneutics*, trans. David E. Linge (Berkeley and Los Angeles: University of California Press, 1977), p. 133.

2. Hugo Ott, *Martin Heidegger: A Political Life*, trans. Allan Blunden (New York: Basic Books, 1993), p. 182.

3. "Spiegelberg recounts that at the beginning of the 1920s Husserl used to say, 'Phenomenology: that is I and Heidegger, and no one else.' As illusory as this assertion was, inasmuch as Husserl misjudged the original intentions of his follower of that time, nevertheless such an assertion was not as completely fantastic as it might seem. Rather, it indicates the fact that the majority of phenomenologists had reservations regarding Husserl's development of transcendental phenomenology. . . . To many, this development seemed to be nothing more than an inexplicable relapse into Neo-Kantian idealism." Gadamer, "Phenomenological Movement," p. 143.

4. Hannah Arendt links the impact of Heidegger's *Being and Time* to the notoriety Heidegger had already gained from his lectures. She compares his reputation to the "rumour of the hidden king." "Heidegger's fame predates by about eight years the publication of *Sein und Zeit* in 1927; indeed it is open to question whether the unusual success of the book—not just the immediate impact it had inside and outside the academic world, but also its extraordinarily lasting influence, with which few of the century's publications can compare—would have been possible if it had not been preceded by the teacher's reputation among the students, in whose opin-

ion, at any rate, the book's success merely confirmed what they had known for many years." Gadamer also emphasizes the impact of Heidegger as a lecturer, noting that with him "lecturing as such became something altogether new. . . . It was the full concentration of all the powers—powers of genius—in a revolutionary thinker who actually seemed himself to be startled by the intensity of the questions growing more and more radical in himself." These reminiscences are quoted in *Martin Heidegger: Basic Writings,* ed. David Farrell Krell (New York: Harper & Row, 1977), pp. 15–16.

5. The contrast between the following two studies is worth noting. Richard Wolin's *The Politics of Being* (New York: Columbia University Press, 1990) argues that the concepts of *Being and Time* are saturated with the political theory of "decisionism," an interpretation put forward by Jürgen Habermas in the 1950s. Wolin fleshes out the details by emphasizing the emotive and evaluative meanings associated with Heidegger's ontological terminology. In contrast, Hans Sluga's *Heidegger's Crisis: Philosophy and Politics in Nazi Germany* (Cambridge, Mass.: Harvard University Press, 1993) disagrees with this general approach but nevertheless agrees that there are some connections between Heidegger's politics and philosophy. "He understood that philosophical knowledge consisted in questioning, not having ready-made answers. He distrusted the formulas of objective values and organic totalities, of heroic realism and populist holism, of the unity of philosophy and politics in the idea of the Reich. He rightly distrusted all these inventions and yet, because he wanted his thinking to have some effect in the political and philosophical struggle for power, he fell into the trap of inventing an original order on which one could ground and justify a political system. There was, he said, only questioning, but there was also a primordial questioning, a language in which such a questioning could be asked, and a people who could ask it because they spoke a primordial language. On this principle of an origin, . . . Heidegger hoped to ground the political order that was emerging in Germany in 1933" (*Heidegger's Crisis,* p. 231). A clear and detailed history of these events can be found in Ott, *Heidegger: A Political Life.* The various documents concerning Heidegger's speeches and their critical evaluation can be found in *The Heidegger Controversy: A Critical Reader,* ed. Richard Wolin (Cambridge, Mass.: MIT Press, 1993). The work that began this recent reexamination is Victor Farias, *Heidegger and Nazism,* ed. Joseph Margolis and Tom Rockmore, trans. Paul Burrell and Gabriel Ricci (Philadelphia: Temple University Press, 1989). Also, Berel Lang, *Heidegger's Silence* (Ithaca: Cornell University Press, 1996).

6. Martin Heidegger, *Basic Concepts,* trans. Gary E. Aylesworth (Bloomington: Indiana University Press, 1993), pp. 14–15.

7. Heidegger often warns the reader about his language and his special usages. For example, in introducing the odd term *Verfallen* (translated as "falling prey to") as an essential structure of Dasein, Heidegger quickly warns the reader that he is not making a "negative value judgement" (BT 164, SZ 176). Other examples include: "The expression 'idle talk' is not to be used here in a disparaging sense" (BT 157, SZ 168); "With regard to these, the remark may not be superfluous that our interpretation has a purely ontological intention and is far removed from any moralizing critique of everyday Da-sein and from the aspirations of a 'philosophy of culture'"(BT 156, SZ 167); "In contrast to these prescientific ontic meanings, the

expression 'taking care' is used in this inquiry as an ontological term (an existential) to designate the being of a possible being-in-the-world. We do not choose this term because Da-sein is initially economical and 'practical' to a large extent, but because the being of Da-sein itself is to be made visible as *care*. Again, this expression is to be understood as an ontological structure concept. . . . The expression has nothing to do with 'distress,' 'melancholy,' or 'the cares of life' which can be found ontically in every Da-sein. These—like their opposites, 'carefreeness' and 'gaiety'—are ontically possible only because Da-sein, *ontologically* understood, is care" (BT 53, SZ 57). These warnings about colloquial usage, and the examples could be multiplied, suggest that in this sense the English reader, for example, may be in a better position than the average German reader in appreciating Heidegger's text (not being distracted, in other words, by those associations Heidegger wishes to ignore). It is, however, rather perverse to choose words for technical purposes that carry heavy evaluative or interpretative baggage whose effects must then be countered by these cautions. I suspect that this strategy may be explained in part by the various "pitfalls" Heidegger intentionally plants for the careless or unwary reader.

8. Edmund Husserl, *Ideas: Book III, Phenomenology and the Foundation of the Sciences*, trans. E. Klein and William F. Pohl (The Hague: Martinus Nijhoff, 1980), pp. 72, 79.

9. Husserl's strategy of salvaging philosophy by abandoning its traditional competition with the sciences paralleled a dominant approach in twentieth-century philosophy in which metaphysical claims were, on the whole, treated as illicit. For example, the movement of logical positivism classified the claims of metaphysicians as "meaningless" statements. Such quibbles might turn out to be empirically meaningful, but that would entail bequeathing them to further scientific research rather than further philosophical debate. Rudolf Carnap, a leading proponent of positivism, wrote a critical examination of Heidegger's 1929 lecture "What Is Metaphysics?" in which Carnap applied his own technique of "radically eliminating" metaphysical claims. In rejecting what he considered Heidegger's effort to revive metaphysics, Carnap emphasized that the "metaphysician himself states that his questions and answers are irreconcilable with logic and the scientific way of thinking." Carnap, "The Elimination of Metaphysics Through Logical Analysis of Language," in *Logical Positivism*, ed. A. J. Ayer (New York: Free Press, 1959), pp. 60–81.

10. Joan Stambaugh follows a recommendation by Heidegger to always add a hyphen to the term, Da-sein. Albert Hofstadter, on the other hand, translates it as "the Dasein." I will not, however, follow either of these devices, which are intended to distance the reader from how the German expression normally functions; English readers are already sufficiently distanced. What this term allows Heidegger to do is rid philosophical discussion of the concepts of "self," "person," "ego," or "human," all of which he considers irremediably ontic and misleading.

11. This passage suggests either sloppiness with regard to terminology on Heidegger's part or an unintentionally revealing misstep. The distinction between "categorical" and "existential" is a distinction within the subject of ontology. Each aspect would apparently have an "analytic," as Heidegger calls it. He thus characterizes the distinction by identifying the "who" as an aspect of "existence" and the "what" as a feature of categorical objects in general. But "objective presence" is a concept within the existential analytic, since it is how being appears to

Dasein. Thus, it ought not consistently to also characterize the categorical ontology, unless the categorical account does reduce, against Heidegger's insistence that it does not, to the existential. But this slip may be revealing since it shows that Heidegger is not being purely descriptive in these passages, but presupposes, without argument, that the question of being can only be answered by existential, not categorical, analysis. Heidegger treats the categorical approach to being, which reaches its zenith in the sciences, as a deep obstacle and a "forgetting," the neologism he prefers, of the questions of fundamental ontology.

12. These English phrases translate *Zuhandenheit* and *Vorhandheit* (or *Zuhandensein* and *Vorhandensein*). The above English expressions of Stambaugh replace the clumsy but still widely used "ready-to-hand" and "present-at-hand" from the original Macquarrie and Robinson translation. Neither effort, however, can convey the familiarity and naturalness of Heidegger's original terms. Hubert Dreyfus has recommended "availableness" and "occurrentness." Though still stiff, Dreyfus's version allows for some preferable formulations in saying, for example, that entities other than Dasein have a way of being in which they are "available" to Dasein and a way of being in which they are "occurrent" to Dasein.

13. "And we may not advance any kind of theory. There must not be anything hypothetical in our considerations. We must do away with all *explanation*, and description alone must take its place. And this description gets its light, that is to say its purpose, from the philosophical problems. These are, of course, not empirical problems; they are solved, rather, by looking into the workings of our language, and that in such a way as to make us recognize those working: *in despite of* an urge to misunderstand them. The problems are solved, not by giving new information, but by arranging what we have always known. Philosophy is a battle against the bewitchment of our intelligence by means of language." Ludwig Wittgenstein, *Philosophical Investigations*, trans. G. E. M. Anscombe (New York: Macmillan, 1953), p. 47.

14. *Das Man* provides another translation problem, and Hubert Dreyfus suggests, I think helpfully, that "the one" is a preferable way to convey the point in English and allows clearer translations of other terminology based on Heidegger's use of *Das Man*.

15. *Befindlichkeit* is translated as "attunement" in the English version I am using, but I choose to avoid that translation. Hubert Dreyfus suggests "affectedness" and I think the term "disposition" might suit some passages.

16. When Heidegger identifies the phenomenological method with the "science of being," in defense he offers an etymological discussion of the Greek *logos* and *phenomena*. This invented etymological digression allows Heidegger to set aside discussing Husserl's method and the device of bracketing. A story about the linguistic origin of the word "phenomenology" could hardly settle what appears to be a deep philosophical dispute between Husserl and Heidegger, and therefore the story seems a mere evasion or perhaps a kind of joke.

17. "What divided the [Heideggerian and Husserlian] schools was the question: is the true transcendental a universal pure subjectivity understood as consciousness, or an entity with a mode of being other than the mode of being of all that is a positive matter of fact (thing or tool)? In a letter to Husserl, dated October 22, 1927, Heidegger expresses his agreement with Husserl that the transcendental constitution of the world, as understood by Husserl, cannot be clarified by taking recourse

to a being of exactly the same mode of being as that of entities belonging to the world. However, he adds, that does not imply that the locus of the transcendental is not a being at all." J. N. Mohanty, *The Possibility of Transcendental Philosophy* (Boston: Dordrecht, 1985), p.155.

18. Though their intents are not the same, a passing comment in Wittgenstein on death is not unlike Heidegger's ontological one. "Death is not an event in life. It is not a fact of the world." Ludwig Wittgenstein, *Notebooks 1914–1916*, ed. G. H. von Wright, trans. G. E. M. Anscombe (Chicago: University of Chicago Press, 1979), p. 75.

19. Sartre's language is an amalgam of Heidegger, Hegel, and Husserl. The following passage from Husserl's *Cartesian Meditations* does suggest the approach Sartre is adopting: "Everything that exists is 'in-itself', in a maximally broad sense, and stands in contrast to the accidental being 'for me' of the particular acts; likewise every truth is, in this broadest sense, a 'truth in itself'" (CM 61).

20. For example, in a later passage Sartre asserts: "Necessity concerns the connection between ideal propositions but not that of existents. An existing phenomenon can never be derived from another existent *qua* existent. This is what we shall call the *contingency* of being-in-itself. But neither can being-in-itself be derived from a *possibility*. The possible is a structure of the *for-itself*; that is, it belongs to the other region of being. Being-in-itself is never either possible or impossible. It *is*" (BN 29).

21. Al Mele, *Irrationality: An Essay on Akrasia, Self-deception, and Self-control* (New York: Oxford University Press, 1987).

22. Jean-Paul Sartre, *Anti-Semite and Jew,* trans. George J. Becker (New York: Grove, 1962).

23. Simone de Beauvoir, *The Second Sex,* trans. H. M. Parshely (New York: Knopf, 1953).

24. This passage again shows how Sartre, either through carelessness or confusion, uses causality to characterize the answer to his question about what connects consciousness and the world at the same time that he proceeds, at other points in the text, as though causal relations and the work of the sciences are suspended when the topic is fundamental ontology.

25. Jean-Paul Sartre, *Existentialism*, trans. Bernard Frechtman (New York: Philosophical Library, 1947).

Suggested Readings

Some comments on Heidegger's writing style are in order here. Perhaps more than his precise philosophical aims, Heidegger bequeathed, for better or worse, a distinct style of writing to the continental tradition, the results of which already appear in the previous chapter's discussion of Merleau-Ponty. He crafted this style for the difficulties of his theme and against what he considered a persistent indifference and resistance to ontology. Though notoriously obscure, unlike Husserl's clumsy academic prose, Heidegger's work has a distinctive "voice" that some find irresistible, mysteriously convincing, and unfortunately easy to imitate, though whatever elegance it has mostly evaporates in English.

Heidegger's collected works began to appear in 1975 and the lectures he presented at both Marburg and Freiburg have now appeared in English translation. These lectures, under the titles *The Basic Problems of Phenomenology*, trans. Albert Hofstadter (Bloomington: Indiana University Press, 1988), and *History of the Concept of Time: Prolegomena*, trans. Theodore Kisiel (Bloomington: Indiana University Press, 1992), are useful since they were delivered during the preparation of *Being and Time* and contain supplementary arguments, analyses of classic philosophers such as Kant, Aristotle, and Husserl, and discussions of specific philosophical concepts such as the transcendental, a priori, and intentionality. Also the lectures do not exhibit the degree of stylistic innovation found in *Being and Time*. I think they are central to any future philosophical assessment of Heidegger.

I benefited in preparing this chapter from a new translation of *Being and Time* by Joan Stambaugh (Albany: State University of New York Press, 1996). The older version translated by John Macquarrie and Edward Robinson (New York: Harper & Row, 1962), though still used, is often very misleading and unreliable; however, I do provide the page numbers to *Sein und Zeit* (as SZ after BT) so that quotations can then be located in either translation.

Hubert Dreyfus's discussion of translation and interpretation problems concerning Heidegger in *Being-in-the-World: A Commentary on Heidegger's Being and Time, Division I* (Cambridge, Mass.: MIT Press, 1995) is recommended. Three collections of essays on Heidegger's philosophical works are: *Heidegger and Modern Philosophy*, ed. Michael Murray (New Haven: Yale University Press, 1978); *Heidegger: A Critical Reader*, ed. H. Dreyfus and H. Hall (Oxford: Blackwell, 1992); and *The Cambridge Companion to Heidegger*, ed. Charles B. Guignon (Cambridge: Cambridge University Press, 1993). Also recommended for a certain clarity and critical engagement are Frederick Olafson's *Heidegger and the Philosophy of Mind* (New Haven: Yale University Press, 1987) and *What Is a Human Being? A Heideggerian View* (New York: Cambridge University Press, 1995).

Since I have presented Sartre as a variant of Heidegger, I will not even comment on the vast secondary literature he has occasioned. But a survey of Sartre's central philosophical ideas clearly traced throughout his writings can be found in Peter Caws, *Sartre* (London: Routledge & Kegan Paul, 1979).

Bibliography

BPP: Heidegger, M. *The Basic Problems of Phenomenology*. Translated by Albert Hofstadter. Bloomington: Indiana University Press, 1988.

BN: Sartre, J-P. *Being and Nothingness: An Essay on Phenomenological Ontology*. Translated by Hazel E. Barnes. New York: Washington Square Press, 1971.

BT: Heidegger, M. *Being and Time*. Translated by Joan Stambaugh. Albany: State University of New York Press, 1996. (SZ: Heidegger, M. *Sein und Zeit*. Tübingen: Max Niemeyer, 1953.)

LH: Heidegger, M. "Letter on Humanism," in *Martin Heidegger: Basic Writings*. Edited and translated by David Farrell Krell. New York: Harper & Row, 1977.

3

SOCIAL EPISTEMOLOGY

Whatever their other differences, Husserl and Heidegger (at least prior to Heidegger's turn away from philosophy) defended the autonomy of philosophy with respect to the social or natural sciences. Such a defense of philosophy, however, has been a minority viewpoint throughout most of the twentieth century when compared to epistemological naturalism. With few exceptions (the ordinary language movement within analytic philosophy also criticized philosophers' exclusive emphasis on science in the theory of knowledge), the reigning assumption has been that such disciplines as cognitive psychology or evolutionary biology will eventually supplant traditional epistemology. If Husserl's resistance to such proposals can be called internalist, then the twentieth century has been predominantly externalist.[1]

Internalism, as I am using the term, consists of approaching epistemological questions from at least two assumptions. First, the content of thought or consciousness can be examined independently of any claims about the external world. Second, the content of one's thoughts, to which one has direct access, constitutes the domain for the analysis of knowledge. A characteristic attack on these assumptions, useful for purposes of this chapter, can be found in the work of Hilary Putnam.[2] Putnam imagines two worlds in which observers are physiologically and psychologically identical, but where some physical feature differs between the two worlds. In his often cited example, there is imagined a twin earth of people identical, molecule for molecule, with those on earth (earth people and their twin-earth doubles have, therefore, internally identical mental states). Water on the twin earth, however, turns out to have a different microstructure; it is not H_2O, but XYZ. Putnam defends the following conclusions concerning this thought experiment.

The underlying physical structure fixes the extension of natural kinds such as water (there is a longer discussion of the concept of natural kinds in

Chapter 5). Therefore, if water on earth and "water" on the twin earth do not share the same underlying physical structure, that fact is independent of whether or not the internal thought contents about them are the same. (It is a feature of the thought experiment that the experience of water on the two earths is phenomenally identical.) The discovery, then, that twin earth's "water" is not the same as earth water is not a discovery within thought. For Putnam the meaning of a term such as "water" is not determined, then, by examining intentional mental states about it, but rather by what causes the thought and thereby fixes the meaning of the term. Whether phenomenally or as representations, thoughts about these kinds as similar is trumped in this way by an external worldly difference. As he puts it, "Meanings ain't just in the head." Donald Davidson expands on this argumentative strategy by stressing how meaning and content rest upon "linguistic practices" that are likewise not "internal to the individual" and about which the individual has no privileged access. Thus what he calls the "causal history of the individual," in its broadest terms, will eventually replace traditional philosophical inquiry.

In the continental tradition, Karl Mannheim's philosophical writings represent an early version of this same strategy and will be the focus of this chapter. I have been struck in my readings in the continental tradition how often these kinds of arguments and conclusions are repeated, though rarely acknowledging a debt to Mannheim. Also, as will be noted at the end of this chapter, similar claims are now associated, curiously enough, with those calling themselves postmodernists and poststructuralists (terms never likely to become any clearer), for whom philosophical inquiry is treated as wholly ideological and political. Therefore after sketching Mannheim's position and its weaknesses, I turn to Georg Lukacs's equally influential Marxist version of how social practices might be said to shape knowledge. Though Lukacs's conception of philosophy as a social ideology properly belongs within political philosophy, my concern is limited to his claims about epistemology, the philosophy of science, and metaphysics. The chapter concludes with a discussion of structuralism, another intellectual movement influential in continental philosophy after World War II, which challenged both social epistemology (the viewpoint called historicism at that time) and phenomenology.

Epistemology as Sociology

The essential thrust of Karl Mannheim's conception of the obsolescence of epistemology anticipates Putnam, as suggested, because Mannheim claims that social conditions external to the subject (and external to the subject's awareness) determine "assertions." Mannheim champions sociology, not psychology or the physical sciences, for the study of the causal determinations on knowledge and as a replacement for theory of knowledge: "Theoretical and intellectual currents of our time seem to point toward a temporary fading out of epistemological problems, and toward the emergence of the sociology of knowledge as the focal discipline."[3]

Mannheim adopts the term "psychologism" to refer to the thought of those who wish to restrict their study of cognition to either psychological or neurophysiological topics. Though Mannheim claims Husserl's support on this point, he is actually in disagreement with Husserl. For Husserl, psychologism exemplified only a specific case of the general strategy of naturalism.[4] In contrast, Mannheim considers psychologism the wrong kind of causal account; it restricts itself to causes "internal" to the thinker. Mannheim's defense of broad sociological, causal explanations of knowledge fails to grasp that Husserl would have opposed them as well.

> The two methods of studying cultural phenomena dealt with above, the epistemological and the psychological, had in common an attempt to explain meaning from its genesis in the subject. ... Thereby they unwittingly brought false assumptions into the fundamental problems of epistemology and psychology which the sociological approach has had to correct. What is most important about the latter is that it puts an end to the fiction of the detachment of the individual from the group, within the matrix of which the individual thinks and experiences. (IU 28)

Mannheim conceives of sociological analysis as supplanting epistemology in two ways. First, sociological studies collect empirical evidence concerning a person's interests, biases, evaluations, unconscious dispositions, and so forth, which are generated and shaped by external social structures and then influence or determine thinking. Mannheim's causal language is somewhat vague here, but he often stresses that these causal determinations normally escape a person's awareness. These causal features are not psychological facts about the individual; they are sociological facts. Mannheim denies that this argument involves hypothesizing supra-individual structures such as a "collective mind" or "world spirit." His point is that an individual's capacities for experience and reasoning are not entirely internal capacities of a psychological or physiological sort, though such internal structures are necessary conditions for acquiring knowledge. The broader sociological factors and causes then enter into a complete explanation of how knowledge is acquired.

Second, sociological explanations introduce wider theoretical frameworks for understanding cognition. Mannheim singles out two sociological theories, which he calls genetic and functionalist theories, that have special relevance for the study of cognition. Genetic theories (Mannheim alternatively calls them "psychogenetic" theories) casually trace the assertions of social agents back to the "social determinations" that "brought about" or "produced" those assertions. Mannheim groups under the rubric of genetic studies those concerning the formation of a personality or learning. The central point is that individual desires, beliefs, or choices are formed, constrained, and made possible by the social environment.

Following Max Weber, Mannheim treats reasons as the causes of behavior.[5]

> In this approach, by use of the technique of understanding, the reciprocal functional interpenetration of psychic experiences and social situations becomes immediately intelligible. We are confronted here with a realm of existence in which the emergence of psychic reactions from within becomes evident of necessity and is not comprehensible merely as is an external causality, according to the degree of probability of its frequency. (IU 45)

Since the contents of beliefs and desires are socially determined rather than being a matter of psychological states, Mannheim is led to criticize genetic theories for their individualistic biases.

> The most essential limitation of the psychogenetic approach is the important observation that every meaning is to be understood in the light of its genesis. ... But this observation contains within it the injurious constriction that this approach will be found only in an individualistic application. In most cases the genesis of a meaning has been sought in the individual context of experience rather than in its collective context. (IU 26–27)

The second approach Mannheim considers, as suggested in the above comment about a "collective context," is sociological functionalism. In this approach the assertions of social subjects (the sociological data) are examined in terms of their "expressive function," by which they generate social stability. Such an expressive function can be studied apart from the question of the assertion's validity. "It [sociology of knowledge] points rather to a research interest which leads to the raising of the question when and where social structures come to express themselves in the structure of assertions, and in what sense the former concretely determine the latter" (IU 266).

Functionalist explanations, which are ubiquitous in the social sciences, analyze social phenomena in terms of their disposition to produce beneficial effects for the social system. This causal disposition then enters into an explanation of the existence or persistence of the social practice, institution, or system of beliefs.

For example, religious belief could be studied sociologically not in terms of whether the religious beliefs were true, but in terms of how their expression causes those asserting such beliefs to act in ways that reinforce social stability and order. If such social stability were in fact a beneficial consequence, then it would explain the presence of religious beliefs in society by virtue of a causal disposition.

Even if all the meaning conveyed by the magical-religious view of the world had been "false," it still served—when viewed from a purely functional stand-point—to make coherent the fragments of the reality of inner psychic as well as objective external experience, and to place them with reference to a certain complex of conduct. We see ever more clearly that from whatever source we get our meanings, whether they be true or false, they have a certain psychological-sociological function, namely to fix the attention of those men who wish to do something in common upon a certain "definition of the situation." (IU 21)

Though Mannheim's analyses often utilize the notion of how beliefs may benefit some social stratum, he also expresses reservations concerning functionalism. He criticizes such theories for idealizing social conditions and for introducing an assumption concerning the objectivity of certain ends or goals in society. "If to-day one inquires concerning the ends served by analysis, the question is not to be answered with reference to either nature or the soul or society, or else we formally posit a purely technical, psychical, or social optimum condition, as, for example, the most 'frictionless functioning'" (IU 19–20).

These criticisms, though quite sketchy, arise in part because Mannheim properly distinguishes (unfortunately not consistently) between sociology's contribution to the empirical study of knowledge and its contribution to strictly epistemological questions concerning truth and objectivity. He grants, then, that one might accept sociology's contribution to the former, but not to the latter.

The sociology of knowledge is on the one hand a theory, and on the other hand an historical-sociological method of research. As theory it may take two forms. In the first place it is a purely empirical investigation through description and structural analysis of the ways in which social relationships, in fact, influence thought. This may pass, in the second place, into an epistemological inquiry concerned with the bearing of this interrelationship upon the problem of validity. It is important to notice that these two types of inquiry are not necessarily connected and one can accept the empirical results without drawing the epistemological conclusions. (IU 266–267)

How might sociology contribute to the epistemological conclusions? Before discussing Mannheim's position, I want to distinguish a modest from an ambitious thesis concerning sociology and epistemology. The modest thesis would hold that there are some cases in which causal, sociological explanations may resolve traditional epistemological issues. The ambitious thesis holds that *only* sociological explanations of the formation of thought content constitute what should be salvaged of traditional epistemology; philosophy disappears into sociology. Though Mannheim occasionally wavers, he generally defends the modest thesis, whereas Georg Lukacs, as will be seen, defends the ambitious thesis. But even the modest thesis leads

Mannheim to oppose the concept of the a priori and the contempt, as he sees it, for what is "merely fact-minded" in philosophy, thereby using Husserl's own words.

> Our point is not, therefore, that the sociology of knowledge will, by its very nature, supplant epistemology . . . , but rather that it has made certain discoveries which have more than a mere factual relevance, and which cannot be adequately dealt with until some of the conceptions and prejudices of contemporary epistemology have been revised. . . . Under the dominant presuppositions of present-day philosophy it will be impossible to utilize this new insight for epistemology, because modern theory of knowledge is based on the supposition that bare fact-finding has no relevance to validity. . . . Once it is decided and elevated into the realm of the *a priori* that nothing can come out of the world of empirical facts which has relevance for the validity of assertions, we become blind to the observation that this *a priori* itself originally was a premature hypostatization of a factual interrelationship which was derived from a particular type of assertion and was formulated over-hastily into an epistemological axiom. (IU 287)

Mannheim's account of how sociology contributes to epistemology is "relationalism," a view not to be confused, he insists, with relativism.

> A modern theory of knowledge which takes account of the relational as distinct from the merely relative character of all historical knowledge must start with the assumption that there are spheres of thought in which it is impossible to conceive of absolute truth existing independently of the values and position of the subject and unrelated to the social context. Even a god could not formulate a proposition on historical subjects like 2 x 2 = 4, for what is intelligible in history can be reformulated only with reference to problems and conceptual constructions which themselves arise in the flux of historical experience.
>
> Once we recognize that all historical knowledge is relational knowledge, and can only be formulated with reference to the position of the observer, we are faced, once more, with the task of discriminating between what is true and what is false in such knowledge. The question then arises: which standpoint *vis-à-vis* of history offers the best chance for reaching an optimum of truth? (IU 79–80)

The claim that "all historical knowledge is relational knowledge" is stronger than the claim that "there are spheres of thought in which it is impossible to conceive of absolute truth." The latter is hardly controversial. Even well-supported scientific theories, for instance, are treated as fallible, since the search for confirmatory evidence never ends. But being a fallibilist and thus doubting "absolute truth" is compatible with also rejecting Mannheim's statement that "all knowledge is relational."

I think Mannheim must have meant the phrase with the following emphasis: "all *historical* knowledge is relational knowledge." Only claims involving a necessary reference to historical conditions are subject to his relational analysis. Historical knowledge concerns context-sensitive assertions. For example, a historian reconstructing the beliefs of an eighteenth-century physician concerning the human body must carefully attribute only those beliefs historical evidence suggests were possible. But with regard to the nonhistorical study of any knowledge, not just mathematical or logical truths, such a constraint can be ignored. This contrast is often stressed by Mannheim in what he calls the "structural-relativity" of assertions. "Whereas the assertion (to cite the simplest case) that twice two equal four gives no clue as to when, where, and by whom it was formulated, it is always possible in the case of a work in the social sciences to say whether it was inspired by the 'historical school,' or 'positivism,' or 'Marxism,' and from what stage in the development of each of these it dates" (IU 272).

In contemporary philosophy, context-sensitive assertions are called "referentially opaque" in contrast with those that are "referentially transparent." In referentially transparent contexts, such as those of mathematics, the truth of a claim is not altered by substituting within it equivalent expressions: thus, if $2 \times 2 = 4$ and $2 + 2 = 4$, then $2 \times 2 = 2 + 2$. Similarly, if "Socrates was sentenced to death" is true and it is also a fact that Socrates was married to Xanthippe, then substituting "Socrates" for "the husband of Xanthippe" would not alter any truths about Socrates. But that substitution only holds if the context if referentially transparent. In a referentially opaque context, such as a claim concerning what someone historically believed about Socrates, the same substitution may fail to preserve truth. For example, if the original sentence were "Descartes believed that Socrates was sentenced to death," the equivalent substitution may fail due to the historical, relational fact (if it is a fact) that Descartes did not know Socrates was the husband of Xanthippe.

If that is the issue, Mannheim must distinguish between "historical" and "nonhistorical" knowledge rather than merely cite examples. The problem is how far relational sociology extends, and he has not made that clear, nor what is guiding him in these distinctions. He does, however, make clear that sociological analysis aims at more than documenting how a claim originated and that the basic questions within traditional epistemology must be taken seriously; specifically Mannheim sees his analysis as showing whether knowledge is justified, or "valid" as he prefers to state it. Though Mannheim concedes that sociology alone cannot answer all these questions, it provides a method of critical assessment.

> By particularizing, the sociology of knowledge goes a step farther than the original determinations of the facts to which mere relationalism limits itself. Every analytical step undertaken in the spirit of the sociology of knowledge arrives at a point where the sociology of knowledge becomes more than a sociological description of the facts which tell us how certain views have been derived from a certain *milieu*. Rather it reaches a point where it also becomes a critique by redefining the scope and the limits of the perspective implicit in

given assertions. The analyses characteristic of the sociology of knowledge are, in this sense, by no means irrelevant for the determination of the truth of a statement; but these analyses, on the other hand, do not by themselves fully reveal the truth because the mere delimitation of the perspectives is by no means a substitute for the immediate and direct discussion between the divergent points of view or for the direct examination of the facts. (IU 285)

The closest Mannheim comes to grappling with the central problem raised by this quotation is when he asks: "What can it [sociology of knowledge] tell us about the validity of an assertion that we would not know if we had not been able to relate it to the standpoint of the assertor?" (IU 283). Mannheim considers three possible answers. First, the validity of any assertion might be found to be illusory or self-deceptive. This answer characterizes theories of ideology such as Marxism. Second, sociological analysis might make no contribution to determining the validity of a statement, "since the manner in which a statement originates does not affect its validity." Finally, Mannheim identifies his position.

> There is a third possible way of judging the value of the assertions that the sociologist of knowledge makes, which represents our own point of view. It differs from the first view in that it shows that the mere factual demonstration and identification of the social position of the assertor as yet tells us nothing about the truth-value of his assertion. It implies only the suspicion that this assertion might represent merely a partial view. As over against the second alternative, it maintains that it would be incorrect to regard the sociology of knowledge as giving no more than a description of the actual conditions under which an assertion arises (factual-genesis). Every complete and thorough sociological analysis of knowledge delimits, in content as well as structure, the view to be analyzed. In other words, it attempts not merely to establish the existence of the relationship, but at the same time to particularize its scope and the extent of its validity. (IU 283–284)

Assuming that "relationalism does not signify that there are no criteria of rightness and wrongness," Mannheim's term "particularize" is critical and means that the target assertion is reformulated in such a way that it is identified as the expression of some social group's beliefs. Before criticizing Mannheim's attempted solution, I think an example would be helpful.

Suppose I were attempting to give a Mannheim-inspired, relational, sociological account of the specific assertion in Machiavelli's *The Prince* that immoral rulers are more politically successful than moral ones. I would "particularize" that claim, in a sufficiently complex and detailed manner, by studying how it arose, biographically and historically, within Renaissance Florence. After such an analysis, the claim is both reformulated and restricted. It is not the validity of Machiavelli's original assertion that is now in question, but the validity of the properly "relativized assertion," which asks whether a specific type of person (and member of some specified social group), given certain experiences, interests, upbringing, education, and so forth, would be caused by those social circumstances to have the belief that a moral ruler was at a disadvantage when compared with an immoral ruler. In some such fashion relationalism answers critical questions concerning the assertion's justification, scope, and validity.

But Mannheim's analysis has unwittingly changed the content of the assertion in question, and thus the sociological explanation he proposes, even were it more than a mere description, misses the target assertion. The validity of the so-called particularized claim leaves the validity of Machiavelli's original claim undetermined, since the content of these two claims is different. Machiavelli's original claim was about the advantages of immoral conduct. The scope of the particularized sociological claim concerns not the truth or falsity of the disadvantages of moral conduct, but the truth or falsity of whether some specified social conditions causally produced a state of belief in a Florentine of a certain background; the content of the state of belief (the belief about the disadvantages of moral conduct with regard to political power) has been in effect put into parentheses. In determining as a sociologist the causes or functions of beliefs, Mannheim is not, as he admits elsewhere, judging them as knowledge claims.

I now turn to Mannheim's confusing efforts to distinguish relationalism and relativism. Husserl's favorite objection to sociological and historical accounts of cognition, as noted in the discussion of Dilthey in Chapter 1, was that they are self-defeating. The sociologist of knowledge is deprived of the "right," Husserl argues, to sociological knowledge; the "deflation" of knowledge to the status of a social expression necessarily extends to the claims of sociology itself. But Husserl's argument only applies to the ambitious thesis, not the modest thesis, wherein only selected assertions admit of sociological analysis; the weaker thesis need not entail self-defeating confusions.

Mannheim, however, struggles with the threat of relativism precisely because he occasionally shifts between the modest and ambitious theses concerning a sociological analysis of knowledge. Though he asserts that relativism is not implied by relationalism, he countenances accepting that objective knowledge is not possible. He reaches this conclusion because of his holism concerning belief. Sociological analyses concern belief systems, not individual beliefs. Mannheim often warns against assuming, for example, that the occurrence of the same word guarantees the occurrence of the same belief.

But Mannheim's point concerning belief or meaning does not affect the validity or objectivity of the claims at issue. Even if one must proceed holistically in determining what the concept of virtue means for Machiavelli, it remains a separate question whether whatever Machiavelli believed about virtue is true. Similarly, even if Mannheim worries that it may be impossible in some cases to settle what a concept means or what a thinker believes, it does not follow that the truth or falsity of these assertions (even were their meaning indeterminate) is likewise indeterminate. Since Mannheim thought otherwise, he came to doubt his confident distinction between relationalism and relativism.

These worries about relativism led him to propose a weak and inconsistent sociological solution for which his work was widely criticized. Since he had concluded that "points of view" are caused socially (and represent the interests of that community whose dispositions generate beliefs of those sorts), the possibility of objective claims about the world depends on there being a community of inquirers socially conditioned or caused to seek the truth, a group he called "socially unattached intellectuals."

The weaknesses of this attempted solution are so legion that the strategy smacks of some desperation on Mannheim's part. First, it salvages objectivity at the cost of denying the core idea of his sociological program. Even given the modest sociological thesis, sociological analyses of knowledge would be wholly idle with respect to epistemology if one were to take seriously Mannheim's hypothesis. Second, the objectivity or truth of a point of view concerns its content and not *who* asserts the claim, let alone to which social group they belong. Mannheim has been led to confuse what he insisted initially on keeping separate—the empirical and epistemological aspects of his sociology.

Mannheim often speaks metaphorically of "partial aspects" within different "styles of thought" or "points of view." But if sociologists were able to determine which views were "partial" and thereby contrast them with the "whole view," then points of view would not be incomparable or holistically indeterminate; holism and relationalism would again be idle with regard to the study of knowledge. If, on the other hand, points of view are indeed incomparable and internally valid, then no amount of sociology could detect partiality within or between points of view. His position, then, would amount to the relativism he resists, at least in his theory of knowledge. Even assuming relativism were his position concerning the validity or truth of beliefs, then whether or not a class of "socially unattached intellectuals" exists could have no bearing on this epistemological limit. The depth of Mannheim's confusion is brought out by realizing that the existence of this unattached group of intellectuals, whatever he precisely means by that, appears equally irrelevant if relativism were, as he originally thought, false. In that case, knowledge claims would be true or objective independent of whether claims originated within that group.

Mannheim's position simply fails to cohere, and that makes it difficult to understand the extent of his influence or why these ideas have remained so central to the continental tradition (and are so often repeated). I think there may be two reasons. First, as occurs in the next two sections, there is the appeal to "fancier" accounts (structuralist, semiological, dialectical) that claim to salvage Mannheim's core insight while avoiding relativism and the hypothesis concerning intellectuals. Second, the collapse of projects for a purely philosophical theory of knowledge (specifically Husserl's project) made it seem all the more plausible that scientific disciplines such as sociology were the alternative. If the details remained fuzzy, the consensus was that this was the right kind of solution.

Social Ontology

Georg Lukacs's philosophical defense of Marxism exercised an especially powerful, if somewhat underground, influence on a whole generation of philosophers in the continental tradition, coinciding, it would seem, with the quick rise and fall of existentialism and phenomenology. An appreciation of this influence requires a brief sketch of the unique intellectual influence of Marxism in European philosophy.

Merleau-Ponty coined the term "Western Marxism" to capture the way in which Marx influenced European intellectual life after World War II but contrast it with the kind of Marxism-Leninism officially canonized as the state ideology of the Soviet Union.[6] Merleau-Ponty introduced Marx's work as concerning philosophical debates about historical explanation, the possibility of social-scientific laws, and the relationship between theoretical and practical inquiry.

The complete edition of Marx's writings began to appear only after World War II and its first volumes contained Marx's early writings, specifically unpublished notes and manuscripts he composed in Paris during 1848. These writings had a dramatic impact on philosophers in those days. Marx's later political philosophy, on the evidence of these manuscripts, evolved more from studies of Hegel and Kant than from economics, an intellectual background not at all obvious in Marx's published writings. These youthful writings brought to Marx a certain respectability and theoretical relevance. Even Heidegger, as quoted at the end of Chapter 2, treated Marx as a sophisticated philosophical materialist and protophenomenologist. A revival of interest in Hegel in France (due in part to lectures by Alexander Kojeve before the war) also contributed to this particular kind of philosophical interest in Marx. With an explosion of Hegelian studies, interest shifted to how Hegelianism shaped the antiphilosophical diatribes of Nietzsche, Feuerbach, and Kierkegaard. Within such a story of late-nineteenth-century philosophy, Marx suddenly appeared center stage.[7]

More central to my topic, Marx had influenced Max Weber's sociology and philosophy of social science. Intellectuals such as Mannheim and Lukacs, both of whom matured intellectually as Weberians, took this influence for granted. Though Mannheim was to remain a faithful partisan of

Weberian sociology, Lukacs abandoned it for ideological reasons.[8] *History and Class Consciousness*, Lukacs's defense of Marxism on philosophical grounds, is to a large extent a debate with Mannheim. Lukacs attacks both Mannheim's theoretical account of sociology and his defense of the objectivity of "socially unattached intellectuals." Lukacs's motivation for his ambitious but rigidly doctrinaire version is partly a concern with the problem of causality in social theories of knowledge.

Mannheim raised cautions against misunderstanding the causal language pervading his essays (terms such as "produce," "reflect," "generate," "condition," "determine," "influence"): "Here we do not mean by 'determination' a mechanical cause-effect sequence: we leave the meaning of 'determination' open, and only empirical investigation will show us how strict is the correlation between life-situations and thought-process, or what scope exists for variations in the correlation" (IU 267, n. 1). Mannheim's comment appears attached to the phrase "existential determinations of knowledge" and he clearly signals the need for a new conception of causality distinct from those he calls "mechanical."

Lukacs introduces a cumbersome and complicated terminology extracted from Hegel for this very purpose. The concept of dialectic (and the associated terms "mediation" and "immediacy") serve to relate thought to social conditions in the proper interactive fashion. This embrace of Hegel may seem odd for a Marxist, but Lukacs thought it orthodox and justified. Marxism, he reasoned, was canonized officially by Lenin after the Russian Revolution as "dialectical materialism," and Lenin had even written that Hegel's *Logic* was as significant for studying and understanding dialectical materialism as was Marx's *Capital*. Lukacs, emphasizing how Marx cut his philosophical teeth on Hegel and Hegelianism, interprets Marxism as an effort to translate traditional philosophical questions into political philosophy. Lukacs often speaks of how philosophical "antinomies" (he uses Kant's name for those interminable disputes of traditional philosophy) are expressions of social conflicts and contradictions.

Lukacs restricts orthodoxy in Marxism to its method, not to any specific claims. Thus he considers the central issues of Marxism not to be its economic analyses, such as the falling rate of profit, but epistemology and ontology (namely, defending materialism and epistemological realism). Lukacs states this methodological doctrine quite strongly when he asserts that all Marx's empirical claims might prove false, and yet the method remain scientific. Though it exhibits an admirable amount of fallibilism about Marx's economic views, Lukacs's shift to purely philosophical topics becomes rigidly doctrinaire and dogmatic. Since it is dialectic that constitutes this irrefutable philosophical method, not a narrower scientific method, Lukacs understands Marx as primarily a philosopher.

Engels . . . contrasts the ways in which concepts are formed in dialectics as opposed to "metaphysics"; he stresses the fact that in dialectics the definite contours of concepts (and the objects they represent) are dissolved. Dialectics, he argues, is a continuous process of transition from one definition into the other. In consequence a one-sided and rigid causality must be replaced by interaction. But he does not even mention that the most vital interaction, namely the dialectical relation between subject and object in the historical process, let alone give it the prominence it deserves. Yet without this factor dialectics ceases to be revolutionary, despite attempts . . . to retain "fluid" concepts. For it implies a failure to recognize that in all metaphysics the object remains untouched and unaltered so that thought remains contemplative and fails to become practical; while for the dialectical method the central problem is *to change reality.*" (HCC 3)

This contrast leads Lukacs to an expanded account of causal interaction.

But even the category of interaction requires inspection. If by interaction we mean just the reciprocal causal impact of two otherwise unchangeable objects on each other, we shall not have come an inch nearer to an understanding of society. . . . The interaction we have in mind must be more than the interaction of *otherwise unchanging objects.* It must go further in its relation to the whole: for this relation determines the objective form of every object of cognition. Every substantial change that is of concern to knowledge manifests itself as a change in relation to the whole and through this as a change in the form of objectivity itself. . . . Thus the objective forms of all social phenomena change constantly in the course of their ceaseless dialectical interactions with each other. The intelligibility of objects develops in proportion as we grasp their function in the totality to which they belong. This is why only the dialectical conception of totality can enable us to understand *reality as a social process.* (HCC 13)

Lukacs's distinction between the dialectical method and the traditional scientific method involves criticizing traditional theories of scientific knowledge, specifically empiricism.

It thus appears extraordinarily "scientific" to think out the tendencies implicit in the facts themselves and to promote this activity to the status of science. . . . The unscientific nature of this seemingly so scientific method consists, then, in its failure to see and take account of the *historical character* of the facts on which it is based. . . . As the products of historical evolution they [the "facts"] are also precisely in their objective structure the products of a definite historical epoch, namely capitalism. Thus when "science" maintains that the manner in which data immediately present themselves is an adequate foundation of scientific conceptualisation and that the actual form of these data is the appropriate starting point for the formation of scientific concepts, it thereby takes its stand simply and dogmatically on the basis of capitalist society. It uncritically accepts the nature of the object as it is given and the laws of that society as the unalterable foundation of "science." In order to progress from these "facts" to

the facts in the true meaning of the word it is necessary to perceive their historical conditioning as such and to abandon the point of view that would see
them as immediately given: they must themselves be subjected to a historical
and dialectical examination. (HCC 6–7)

The central criticism is that the sciences assume reality is "immediately
given" in perception, and such a naive version of empiricism is attacked as
both ideological as well as unscientific. But all traditional accounts of science and the scientific method were not empiricist. In fact, Lukacs appears
in the above to treat empiricism and "representational realism" (normally
seen as opposed views) as the same view. He is also unclear as to what assumption he is criticizing in what he calls the "immediacy of perception."
For instance, Lukacs argues elsewhere that Marx's theory of society has extensive evidential support. Therefore, the central weakness of empiricism
must lie in claiming that such evidence is purely perceptual or that empirical evidence *alone* determines whether a theory is correct. But what in addition to empirical evidence is required for deciding a theory is correct remains vague, though Lukacs often offers the term "dialectical" as the
answer. He argues, for instance:

> The blinkered empiricist will of course deny that facts can only become
> facts within the framework of a system—which will vary with the knowl-
> edge described. He believes that every piece of data from economic life,
> every statistic, every raw event already constitutes an important fact. In so
> doing he forgets that however simple an enumeration of "facts" may be,
> however lacking in commentary, it already implies an "interpretation." Al-
> ready at this stage the facts have been comprehended by a theory, a method;
> they have been wrenched from their living context and fitted into a theory.
> (HCC 5)

This kind of argument, which also appears within the analytic tradition,
states that evidence or factual data is itself theoretically contaminated and
thus cannot directly confirm or disconfirm theories.[9] The problem with
Lukacs's statement of it above is that he simply assumes that the "theory-
laden nature of facts," setting aside the need for some defense of this thesis,
is inconsistent with empiricism. But that assumption is unwarranted. First,
empiricism, broadly understood, need not claim that observations or perceptions are uncontaminated by any theoretical hypotheses, though historically empiricists such as Francis Bacon made that assumption. Second, this
argument that facts are theory-laden would apply to any theory of scientific
knowledge, even anti-empiricist ones. The argument establishes a limit with
regard to evidence for a sufficiently complicated theory that does not depend on what the nature of evidence is stipulated to be (whether purely perceptual or "mediated," as Lukacs claims). Thus the limit holds for Lukacs's
dialectical conception.

Furthermore, if evidence were theory-laden in the manner Lukacs suggests, it would leave the question open as to why one theory is preferable to another. Since the question would remain open, nothing prevents the empiricist from providing a more complicated account, an account as complex as dialectics claims to be. Thus, Lukacs's argument does not settle the question of choosing between the traditional and dialectical methods of science. In fact, the point could be put more strongly. Excluding idealism, to which Lukacs claims to be opposed, there seems no clear alternative to empirical evidence in choosing between competitive theories.

But Lukacs has a second defense of the superiority of dialectics, and that defense involves reintroducing the concept of ideology. Mannheim had dismissed sociological studies of knowledge that relied on the concept of ideology. As a theoretical term, the concept of ideology is due to Marx, who reasoned, plausibly enough, that societies develop complex systems of thought whose function it is to perpetuate and maintain the social structure. These systems of thought were of central significance, in Marx's view, when considering societies characterized by deep internal inequalities and yet structured in such a way as not to resort to coercion, at least not directly. Marx considered the role of ideologies a measure of how advanced a society was and that they constituted the core of what he called the society's "superstructure." He included in the superstructure, among other examples, law, literature, art, and philosophy. Thus the function of these systems was not their stated intent, but their effect of rationalizing and thereby making acceptable features of society that otherwise would be questioned or actually changed. In this manner ideological analysis and functional analysis were intertwined in Marxist sociology.

Lukacs's demonstration that the "myth of immediacy," as he calls the faulty assumption of empiricism discussed above, is bad epistemology while being good social ideology is an example of this kind of ideological analysis. The assumption of the direct perception of facts, he argues, arises because of how social phenomena ought to appear to members of that society if the social relations that make up that society are to be taken as natural, permanent, and universal. This complex functional role of philosophy is of course not at the level of awareness. Hence I include Lukacs as a social externalist.

Lukacs's attempt to demonstrate this complex functional role for philosophy has two parts. He argues against empiricism by claiming to demonstrate, by broadly metaphorical arguments, that empiricism rationalizes the interests of the ruling class in modern society. Second, Lukacs argues that even highly reflective and critical philosophers (Kant is his prime example) do not escape this ideological function. He thinks this proves that the ideological function of philosophy is a matter of the social structure, not the individual philosopher's lack of rigor or honesty.

This function is called "false consciousness," and Lukacs speaks of it as producing "ghostly objectivity." In an extended treatment Lukacs claims that the exchange of commodities in capitalist economies generates the appearance of lawlike regularities in social life, the reduction of social relations to relations between individuals, and the separation of mental and physical states as captured in the traditional mind-body problem.

> The movement of commodities on the market, the birth of their value, in a word, the real framework of every rational calculation is not merely subject to strict laws but also presupposes the strict ordering of all that happens. The atomisation of the individual is, then, only the reflex in consciousness of the fact that the natural laws of capitalist production have been extended to cover every manifestation of life in society; that—for the first time in history—the whole of society is subjected, or tends to be subjected, to a unified economic process, and that the fate of every member of society is determined by unified laws. (HCC 91–92)

The social phenomenon of "reification," which "sinks more deeply, more fatefully, and more definitively into the consciousness of man" (HCC 93), is the central theme by which Lukacs links philosophical views and ideological effects.[10] These ideas, especially reification and alienation, became popular in the same period as existentialism. For my purpose, however, since I am ignoring political philosophy and ethics, the point is to show that traditional epistemology must be eliminated in the name of a science of society.

> For we are not concerned to present a history of modern philosophy, not even in a crude outline. We wish only to sketch the *connection* between the fundamental problems of this philosophy and the *basis in existence* from which these problems spring and to which they strive to return by the road of understanding. However, the character of this existence is revealed at least as clearly by what philosophy does *not* find problematic as by what it does. At any rate it is advisable to consider the interaction between these two aspects. And if we do put the question in this way we then perceive that the salient characteristic of the whole epoch is the equation which appears naïve and dogmatic even in the most "critical" philosophers, of formal, mathematical, rational knowledge both with knowledge in general and also with "our" knowledge. . . . It can similarly be taken as read that the whole evolution of philosophy went hand in hand with the development of the exact sciences. These in turn interacted fruitfully with a technology that was becoming increasingly more rationalised, and with developments in production. (HCC 112–113)

But Lukacs does not view himself as entirely dismissing philosophy. He thinks his work is partly a defense of the contribution of philosophy to the emergence of Marx's thought. The positive aspect of philosophy (and thus what distinguishes philosophy from most other ideologies) is its reflective and critical stance, but not as those ideas are traditionally understood. For instance, Kantianism is thought to be an investigation of the a priori conditions of any possible knowledge. Rather, for Lukacs, the critical function of philosophy is the incipient social criticism that is found metaphorically in philosophical reflection and that a politically attuned interpreter can extract from its otherwise obscure metaphysics.

> Nevertheless classical philosophy is able to think the deepest and most fundamental problems of the development of bourgeois society through to the very end—on the plane of philosophy. It is able—in thought—to complete the evolution of class. And—in thought—it is able to take all the paradoxes of its position to the point where the necessity of going beyond this historical stage in mankind's development can at least be seen as a problem. . . . That is to say, classical philosophy mercilessly tore to shreds all the metaphysical illusions of the preceding era, but was forced to be as uncritical and dogmatically metaphysical with regard to some of its own premises as its predecessors had been toward theirs. (HCC 121)

Even setting aside debates concerning the status of Marx's work and its philosophical importance, there are serious problems with Lukacs's position. For my purposes two problems are central. First, the distinctions between scientific, philosophical, and ideological systems of thought are entirely undefended. Second, Lukacs mounts a deeply confused defense of nonindividualized conscious states.

Lukacs contrasts standpoints or points of view of social classes as objective, scientific, or ideological. He identifies this difference with the conceptual schemes used by these social groups in understanding the world and the way in which the world, as a matter of social conditioning, is caused to appear. Conceptual elaboration has then in some cases this ideological function, and all conceptual elaboration represents the interest of some social class. Thus, in Lukacs's account, whether claims are ideological or scientific rests upon the interests of the class those claims represent.

But this claim clearly states that the external facts about social classes determine, in some sufficiently complex fashion, the difference between objective and ideological mediations (understanding "mediation" as another term for "conceptual elaboration"). Since social causality brings about all mediation, given Lukacs's position, it is also determining which concepts or beliefs are objective and which are not. Husserl's objection was simply that to reach such a conclusion demands more than a story about causation. It requires some criteria (and also a defense of those criteria) for distinguishing between these causally produced mediations or concepts. Lukacs simply asserts that some beliefs are caused to reflect and others are caused to distort the external social structure. For this claim to amount to more than a mere assertion, and to be even minimally convincing, it requires a distinction between "mirroring" and "distorting" arrived at independently of the causal account. If that difference is also accounted for by referring to what caused the beliefs in the first place, then Lukacs's argument chases its tail. To claim that certain views are objective or scientific is to claim that, whatever caused them, those views are true, accurate, objective, or evidentially justified; Lukacs wishes to make that claim and yet also wishes to dismiss any philosophical discussions of it.

Lukacs distinguishes class consciousness, a category that bridges sociological and philosophical functions of thought, from psychological states. He speaks therefore of an "imputed consciousness." "This consciousness is, therefore, neither the sum nor the average of what is thought or felt by the single individuals who make up the class. And yet the historically significant actions of the class as a whole are determined in the last resort by this consciousness and not by the thought of the individual—and these actions can be understood only by reference to this consciousness" (HCC 51).

The plausibility of this claim cuts to the heart of Lukacs's audacious and reductionist account of philosophy. First, what is meant by "imputed"? When a historian speculates about what someone did or did not believe or when anyone empathizes with others, the procedure could be called "imputing" thoughts to others. However, that usage does not entail the conclusion that "actions of the class as a whole are determined in the last resort by this consciousness and not by the thought of the individual." In this first sense "imputed" merely means guessing about what the thoughts of someone else actually are. In the second sense, which Lukacs seems to have in mind, "imputed" involves identifying some collective belief apart from and apparently independent of what individuals think. Apparently, then, actions and behavior can be determined by a system of thought that neither the agent is aware of as such nor consists of the agent's reasons. This second sense would allow the above conclusion concerning what determines action "in the last resort" and constitutes an example, at least for Lukacs, of how a metaphysical problem (namely, the mystery of causal interaction between mind and body) gives way to a sociological solution.

But this second sense of an imputed consciousness is deeply unclear and irrelevant to the mind-body problem. Though it is plausible that social practices play a role in how knowledge is acquired even if thinkers are not aware of these practices, Lukacs's "imputed consciousness" is put forward as an account of social actions. The original question was to explain how social externalism could fit the interaction between mind and the world. Part of the interaction between mind and the world is, importantly for Lukacs, the critical or reflective stance that allows for questioning concepts and even recommending their replacement. Thus Lukacs leaves mysterious both his own critical discussions as well as the social externalism he claims to defend.

Furthermore, the argument that the content of a person's beliefs is socially determined is not relevant to the classical mind-body problem. This philosophical problem concerns the criteria for identifying one's self as opposed to one's body and whether causal interaction between these distinct mental and physical states is possible. Although I agree that the problem is suspicious, the introduction of social determinations on thought makes no difference to such a dissolution of the problem, since what precisely causes the content of thought, assuming reduction is not an option, and whether those causes are inside or outside the mind do not resolve the traditional mind-body problem.

It has been a dogma of the continental tradition since the postwar period that one's philosophical and political position in some fashion coincide. Thus it is often repeated among its thinkers that empiricism and political conservatism are internally linked. If we set aside criticisms of such views, such a project of social criticism has little or nothing to do with the phenomenological reform of philosophy. It is thus an utter mystery, at least to me, why the above kinds of arguments, with additionally precious little critical reflection upon them, were widely proclaimed during this period in various efforts to amalgamate phenomenology and sociology or phenomenology and Marxism.[11] What remains at issue is that the efforts of Mannheim and Lukacs to subsume philosophy within some conception of social science fail to confront the sustained questions Husserl had begun to pose concerning any possible theory of knowledge and philosophy of science. Within the continental tradition, however, the most influential response to the above brand of social externalism requires discussing, unfortunately, another "ism."

"Against the Observer, the Native"

Easily the most influential opposition to both Mannheim and Lukacs was ironically another naturalistic project. During the 1960s and 1970s, the intellectual movement called structuralism, like existentialism before it, gained as much popular cultural notoriety as it did theoretical and philosophical influence. Also, like existentialism, it was embedded in French intellectual and cultural life.

After 1950, Claude Lévi-Strauss defended the status of the social sciences in terms of a broad position he called "structuralism," which in turn asserted the hegemony of the sciences over philosophy. Unlike Mannheim, however, Lévi-Strauss opposed a distinction between the natural and social sciences and opposed both historicism and relativism.[12]

Lévi-Strauss abandoned philosophy, even though he was preparing for an advanced degree, to enthusiastically embark on anthropological research in 1934. As strikingly stated in his 1960 Collège de France inaugural lecture: "Against the theoretician, the observer should always have the last word, and against the observer, the native" (SA2 7). Nevertheless, he retained an interest in the theory of knowledge and the philosophy of science.

Lévi-Strauss always begins, as is typical in this tradition, attacking empiricism, even though that might seem contrary to the above quotation. Lévi-Strauss thinks empirical inquiry is decisive, and that philosophers, not scientists, introduce confusions concerning it. Specifically, the social sciences have been confronted with a "false dichotomy" in the claim that they differ from the natural sciences.

> In thus completing what Durkheim envisioned, Mauss freed anthropology from the false dichotomy, introduced by thinkers such as Dilthey and Spengler between explanation in the physical sciences and explanation in the human sciences. The search for causes ends with the assimilation of an experience, but an experience at once external and internal. . . . We can already discern the originality of social anthropology. Instead of opposing causal explanation and understanding, it brings to light an object which may be at the same time objectively very remote and subjectively very concrete, and whose causal explanation could rest upon that understanding which is, for us, but an additional form of proof. (SA2 9)

Though the above quotation makes clear that understanding and explanation ought not to be opposed as methodological tasks, Lévi-Strauss does not embrace a traditional view of the social sciences. He thinks that the history of science reveals both "reductionist" and "structuralist" programs. A science pursues a "structuralist" approach when there are "phenomena too complex to be reduced" and when the aim is "understanding what kind of original system they [phenomena] make up" (MM 10). "Several among us hold more modest views on the future of social anthropology. . . . They do not picture social anthropology modelled after the inductive sciences . . . rather see it as a taxonomy whose purpose is to identify and to classify types, to analyze their constituent parts, and to establish correlations between them" (SA2 12).

Initially, at least, structuralism has a rather straightforward meaning in Lévi-Strauss. Concern with structure is a stage in science in which the focus is upon taxonomy and classification and both theory construction and empirical confirmation operate. But this structural stage is temporary. Anthropology, for instance, awaits the day when the strategy of reduction will make it a mature science.[13] "But if it [anthropology] is resigned to being in a purgatory next to the social sciences, it is because it has not yet lost hope of awakening in the hour of the last judgement, among the natural sciences" (SA2 18–19).

In striving for correlations between constituent units of classification, anthropology follows advances in linguistics. The contribution of linguistics is not merely substantive; it is a success story in formal modeling, in keeping syntactic regularities distinct from psychological generalizations, and in marrying formal analyses with empirical research.

To speak of rules and to speak of meaning is to speak of the same thing; and if we look at all the intellectual undertakings of mankind, as far as they have been recorded all over the world, the common denominator is always to introduce some kind of order. If this represents a basic need for order in the human mind and since, after all, the human mind is only part of the universe, the need probably exists because there is some order in the universe and the universe is not a chaos. (MM 12–13)

He calls anthropology a "semiological science" because its phenomena (social practices and rules) exhibit meaning, syntactic structure, and systematic connections.

This convergence of scientific perspectives is very reassuring for the semiological sciences, in which social anthropology is included, since signs and symbols can only play their part insofar as they belong to systems regulated by internal laws of implication and exclusion; and since the property of a system of signs is to be transformable, in other words *translatable*, into the language of another system with the help of substitutions. (SA2 18–19)

An example of this approach may allow for a more forceful critical assessment of Lévi-Strauss's philosophical views. His essay "The Effectiveness of Symbols" (SA1 186–205) is supposed to exemplify both the empirical and formal techniques of social anthropology. His topic is South American tribes in which songs play a magical-religious role in difficult childbirth. Lévi-Strauss reviews interpretations of these songs, including one in which supernatural forces are referred to as "represent[ing], literally, the vagina and uterus of the pregnant woman," thereby allowing the shaman to battle "malevolent spirits" preventing the woman from giving birth. Lévi-Strauss's hypothesis is that this literal interpretation can be confirmed by a structural study of the song's terminology. He thinks that even though the "song constitutes a purely psychological treatment . . . nevertheless it involves, directly and explicitly, the pathological condition and its locus" (SA1 191).

The social practice of shamanism is described by him as "effective," therefore, in representing the pregnancy to the woman herself in mythological terms. This representation indirectly produces the hoped for physiological responses. The reason for its "effectiveness," Lévi-Strauss hypothesizes, is that the pregnant woman believes in the mythological beings referred to in the song though "she does not accept . . . the incoherent and arbitrary pains which are an alien element in her system but which the shaman, calling upon myth, will reintegrate within a whole where everything is meaningful" (SA1 197).

Lévi-Strauss proceeds to consider an objection to his hypothesis. In modern society, representing the illness to the patient in the concepts or theories of medicine is irrelevant to whether the patient's physiology changes. How can this kind of change be the explanation for the shamanistic practice?

We shall perhaps be accused of paradox if we answer that the reason lies in the fact that microbes exist and monsters do not. And yet, the relationship between germ and disease is external to the mind of the patient, for it is a cause-and-effect relationship; whereas the relationship between monster and disease is internal to his mind, whether conscious or unconscious: it is a relationship between symbol and thing symbolized, or, to use the terminology of linguists, between sign and meaning. The shaman provides the sick woman with a language, by means of which unexpressed, and otherwise inexpressible, psychic states can be immediately expressed. And it is the transition to this verbal expression—at the same time making it possible to undergo in an ordered and intelligible form a real experience that would otherwise be chaotic and inexpressible—which induces the release of the physiological process, that is, the reorganization, in a favorable direction, of the process to which the sick woman is subjected. (SA1 197–198)[14]

The above account awaits a longer analysis and discussion than I can provide here. Lévi-Strauss begins with a traditional distinction between external causal connections and internal conceptual connections. His point must be, however, that there is some interaction between the two kinds of connections and, furthermore, that it would be premature for anthropology to assume that because the "relationship between symbol and thing symbolized" is "internal to the mind," it is causally epiphenomenal or relegate it to a social ideology. Thus Lévi-Strauss's hypothesis could be understood as holding that if there is some causal interaction between these internal and external events, then it is possible that physical or physiological changes could occur indirectly by way of a purely symbolic relation (and he thinks that is what happens in psychoanalytic cures, for instance).

The way in which Lévi-Strauss states this position is fraught with some deep philosophical confusions. First, he often characterizes his view as one in which subjective experiences, mental states, and human subjectivity are dismissed from the domain of social science (as behaviorism also argued). If structuralism holds that mental states are not real, it is difficult to see why he would assume both their reality and effectiveness in this example. Second, assuming such states are real and part of the phenomena of social science, his account collapses two distinct issues. First, there is the point that the terminology of internal mental life may diverge from the terminology of external events. Second, there is the problem that the relationship between signs and their meanings is not a causal relationship, and yet meanings play some kind of causal role in social events and actions. Lévi-Strauss collapses these topics in part because he appears to assume, at least in this article, that the meaning of a sign is a type of connection found only inside of mental states, that meaning is a subjective, psychological phenomenon. It would have been preferable, given his aim in this article and his overall views, to begin by distinguishing between intentional and nonintentional types of causation and emphasize that meaning is a matter of a social practice, at least for his brand of structuralism. This distinction would then avoid the very mysterious appeal to some sort of interaction between conceptual and physical connections. But his failure to make these distinctions properly suggests greater underlying confusions about the central concepts of causality and structure.

Finally, this article highlights his problematic and contentious view of the scientific status of anthropology. Lévi-Strauss thought his discipline was, at the end of the day, a natural science, but he wanted to resist reductionist theories of meaning; specifically he gives this as a reason to oppose behaviorism. In distinguishing external and internal phenomena in the manner in which he does above, Lévi-Strauss classifies meaning as a "rational phenomenon."

He says of anthropology, "The question we asked ourselves was that of the *meaning* of the incest prohibition . . . and not that of its *results*, real or imaginary" (SA2 19). From this statement he concludes, "Between the solution of the riddle and incest, a relation exists, not external and of fact, but internal and of reason; and this is indeed why civilizations as different as those of classical antiquity and indigenous America can associate them independently" (SA2 23). Although he agrees that the social sciences have their own "laboratory," he seems to be making the highly debatable claim that anthropology can arrive at purely conceptual truths. "In the absence of an inaccessible factual truth, we would have arrived at a truth of reason" (SA2 20–21). It is difficult to grasp how "truths of reason," other than those formal necessities common to any and all scientific hypotheses, could arise where "factual truth" is "inaccessible" or how "truths of reason" explain social phenomena such as kinship systems.

From Mannheim to Lévi-Strauss, therefore, problems in the philosophy of science are curiously suppressed. Both treat the scientific status of their chosen field as either obvious or unproblematic (in much the same manner Lukacs does not argue for the scientific status of Marxism). This same confidence extends to the structuralists, who appeal either simply to the collection of evidence and hypothesis testing or mysteriously to "rationality" and "truth." But given their protonaturalism, especially the distrust of traditional epistemology found in all of these thinkers even when they otherwise disagree, these appeals are neither convincing nor as uncontroversial as they claim. I will examine, at the end of this chapter, the only structuralist who tries to answer, unsuccessfully I believe, such questions.

But to provide a broader picture of the appeal and enthusiasm for the structuralist approach, as well as anticipate themes covered in Chapter 5 under the rubric "poststructuralism," I will consider, albeit very briefly, the philosophy of language (broadly characterized) of Julia Kristeva. The philosophy of language has been the central topic of much of twentieth-century philosophy and attempts to outline a theory of meaning have occasioned its richest developments within the last four decades. Kristeva shares the view that the philosophy of language is central, but she does not think it can directly settle broader philosophical issues. She distrusts such a view because she distrusts Husserl's efforts, among others, to suspend metaphysical assumptions. Thus in Kristeva's account, the philosophy of language does not have the adjudicating role it had for Husserl. Rather, it is part of a larger semiology, a new science subsuming eventually both traditional philosophy and sociology.

Kristeva's central influence is Lévi-Strauss's structural anthropology. "One can say consequently that, without presenting itself explicitly as a semiotics and without giving itself up to thinking and exploration about the nature of the sign, structural anthropology *is* a semiotics, to the extent that it considers various anthropological phenomena as languages and applies to them the descriptive procedure specific to linguistics" (LU 300). She thinks of a language as any system of signs (gestures, foods, clothing, photographs, and paintings can all be studied as languages) functioning as a social practice. Although Kristeva credits Lévi-Strauss with reforming the social sciences on this basis, she has two disagreements with his brand of structuralism. First, she stresses that the central feature of these systems of signs or linguistic practices is communication.

> All language that is produced is produced to be communicated in social exchange. The classic question "What is the primary function of language: to *produce* a thought or to *communicate* it?" has no objective foundation. Language is all that at once, and cannot have one of these functions without the other. All the evidence that archaeology offers us of language practices is found in social systems, and consequently is of a communicative nature. (LU 7)

Second, she argues against what she identifies as a structuralist dogma that there are really no human subjects who use and think with these signs. She holds, therefore, that these general inquiries into semiotic systems raise rather than settle central philosophical questions about the nature of thought, representation, reality, and the self. Though I think these are the right challenges to make against structuralism as a movement, Kristeva's answers unfortunately involve too little clarification of the issues or her appeal to Marxist sociology and Freudian psychoanalysis as sciences of social practices and the causal relationship between language and thought.

Before discussing these objections, however, Kristeva's terminology requires some explanation. As many French theoreticians and philosophers did during the 1960s and 1970s, Kristeva borrows her terminology from Ferdinand de Saussure's *Course in General Linguistics*. Specifically, she distinguishes between the "signifier," or sign vehicle (word or sound), and the "signified" concept the word or sound stands for. The real or actual object also designated by a sign is in turn distinguished from the signified conceptual content and called the "referent."

Saussure held that the systematic study of signs concerns only the relationship between the signifier and the signified, not the relationship of the sign to the referent. I think Saussure's terminology is quite confusing on this and many other points, and I will have occasion to return to that criticism of Saussure in Chapter 5 when discussing Jacques Derrida's attempt to employ this same vocabulary in discussing Husserl. But I want to set aside that issue for now.

Given this terminology, Kristeva raises what she considers the central question: What kind of a relation holds between the signifier and the signified?

> One of the founding postulates of linguistics is that the sign is arbitrary. That is to say, there is no necessary relation between the signifier and the signified: . . . This does not mean that the signifiers are chosen arbitrarily by a single voluntary act, and that consequently they can be changed just as arbitrarily . . . the word "arbitrary" signifies more exactly *unmotivated*, that is to say, there is no natural or real necessity linking the signifier and signified. (LU 14)

This passage is frustratingly unclear. The term "arbitrary," which is called a "founding postulate," is qualified as "unmotivated," which in turn is explicated as denying "natural or real necessity." But unmotivated and arbitrary are not the same concepts at all, and since there are different forms of necessity, it is not clear how "real" serves to qualify necessity in the above quote.

Kristeva agrees, however, that these issues are confusing and she even grants that the central notion of arbitrariness is unclear. Therefore she suggests the following modification:

> Basically . . . it is not the relationship between the signifier . . . and the signified . . . that is arbitrary. The link . . . is necessary: the concept and the sound-image are inseparable and are in an "established symmetry." What is arbitrary is the relation between the sign (signifier/signified . . .) and the reality it names, in other words, the relation between the language symbol in its totality and the real outside it that it symbolizes. It seems that we have here a contingency for which no philosophical or theoretical explanation can be found in the current state of linguistic science. (LU 16)

Though I sympathize with Kristeva's struggles over Saussure's terminology, her suggested modification is not plausible. The relationship between signs and whatever reality they stand for could not be arbitrary in the way that she has defined that concept at the cost of making rudimentary practices of communication, the phenomena she wishes to study, impossible. Since the relationship between a sign and its referent is a causal one for her, and she properly calls it "contingent" in the same passage, she would be further committed to holding that such causal relations are arbitrary, non-explanatory, and nonlawlike.

But it is difficult to understand why she would embrace such a conclusion. Both Marxism and Freudianism consider the causal, contingent relations in their respective domains as lawlike (assuming these disciplines are sciences, a controversy I am setting aside for the moment). Also Kristeva appeals to the putative psychological and sociological laws of Marx and Freud in her own studies of "signifying practices" and the relations between thought and language. But such analyses and laws would not be possible, if I am understanding her properly, were the relations in question arbitrary. Simply put, if her statement that there is no "theoretical explanation" of the relationship between symbols and the external realities they represent is taken seriously, then Marxism, psychoanalysis, and her own criticisms of structuralism are decisively weakened.

The problem is exacerbated since the term "arbitrary" also covers other aspects of her account. First, she adopts the view that meaning resides not at the level of words, but at the level of sentences. Kristeva understands that position to entail that with regard to the systematic nature of language words are arbitrary as referring expressions. She also thinks this arbitrariness of words supports her strict distinction between meaning and reference. Kristeva's version thereby assumes that whereas the syntax of language is systematic and formally necessary, its semantics (which includes reference) is arbitrary. It is this assumption that makes communication and the simple phenomena of meaningful words utterly mysterious and need not follow from a proper understanding of the distinction between meaning and reference.

The second use of "arbitrary" is for the distinction between formal and physically contingent necessities (or between a priori and a posteriori necessities). Since I assume that causal necessities are a posteriori for Kristeva, the term "arbitrary" thereby expands to all physically contingent relations (only the syntax of language as formally necessary escapes this expanded sense of arbitrariness). Kristeva would thereby not be setting a limit for linguistics or semiotics, but raising a skeptical challenge concerning causality and lawlikeness in general.

Kristeva defines the science of language as disinterested in reference. "Linguistics is not concerned with the referent; it is interested only in the signifier, the signified, and their relation" (LU 14). Yet, simultaneously, she insists that the study of language must include communication, the relationships between human subjects and sign systems, and the social realities causally producing such communication systems. "For one cannot assign a place to linguistics, much less make a science of signification, without a theory of social history as the interactions of various signifying practices" (LU 328). Kristeva's efforts to reconcile these seemingly opposed themes makes her, in my view, characteristic of those philosophers in the continental tradition for whom structuralism, even if they criticized it, signified that philosophical problems from now on were the province of the social sciences (for example, Mannheim's position with which this chapter began).

This combination of the philosophy of language and political philosophy would also become, partly through Kristeva's work, characteristic of a distinctly European brand of feminism involving debates far outside the limits of this study and specifically emphasizing criticisms of philosophy through notions of ideology and gender. Kristeva's literary and cultural criticism therefore has been, at least in the context of the United States, the port of entry for continental philosophy to a larger academic audience. I briefly mentioned this fact in my Introduction when noting the largely literary interpretations that currently appear of many thinkers discussed in this work. Also Kristeva's work is often considered representative of a style of philosophical criticism identified now with Jacques Derrida, whom I discuss at greater length in Chapter 5.

What is significant about Kristeva's efforts for the main theme of this chapter is that her dependence on the social sciences, specifically Marxism and psychoanalysis, is both ambiguous and dogmatic. As noted above, Kristeva pictures Marxism and psychoanalysis joining with linguistics into a new semiotic science. But she neither asks about nor clarifies the concept of science at issue or the kind of explanations expected by such a new discipline, assuming, as she does, that they are not causal or lawlike explanations. More problematically, Kristeva's analyses often contrast the "science" of Marx, Freud, or Saussure with the "ideology" of others. The question such a strategy raises, and a question implicit through the development of structuralism, is how this contrast between science and ideology is drawn and defended nondogmatically while sidestepping the philosophical challenges to such naturalistic strategies already posed by Husserl.

Scientific Holism

Louis Althusser's *Reading Capital* enlists Lévi-Strauss's approach in the debate concerning Marxism and philosophy begun by Mannheim and Lukacs. Althusser defends two epistemological positions he considers implicit in Marx.[15] First, Marx defends an anti-empiricist philosophy of science. Althusser uses the term "empiricism" to refer to any position in which theories are confirmed (or refuted) by empirical data. Although I think it highly implausible that Marx's defense of the importance of theoretical economics implied that his own theory was not to be judged in terms of evidence for or against it, I am ignoring questions about the interpretation of Marx. Second, Althusser argues that Marx's science of history is a matter not of scientific method, but the discovery of the correct conceptual scheme making possible this new science.[16]

Althusser's ideas about the history and philosophy of science are borrowed from Gaston Bachelard's *La Formation de l'Esprit Scientifique.* Bachelard's work was lionized by structuralists. (I will consider these ideas further in the discussion of Michel Foucault in Chapter 5.) However, as will become apparent, Bachelard's ideas were not entirely in harmony with the main theme of structuralism, as far as that is characterized by Lévi-Strauss's views.

Bachelard coined the terms "epistemological break" and "epistemological obstacle" in his case studies in the history of science. Bachelard pictures scientific progress in acquiring knowledge as occurring against a background of "obstacles" or "problem situations" *(la problématique).* Though Bachelard was a realist with regard to the physical sciences, his realism involved distinguishing between the real objects (conceptual or abstract objects) discovered by the sciences and the world of objects manifested in everyday experience. The object of science is not the object of experience. It is, however, like the object of experience, always conceptually elaborated.

Scientific thinking arises against ingrained and embedded "belief systems" that constitute a complex of interests, images, prejudices, and "folkish" theories. It is against this complex of beliefs that science shapes itself by in large part a conceptual effort of clarification. Bachelard's case studies are often warnings about how the way in which the objects of experience manifest themselves in thought brings about occasional regressions in the sciences to prescientific conceptions.

For example, some of his studies focus on the role of common sense as an epistemological obstacle to scientific reasoning. Bachelard claims that the "utility" of material objects produces misleading "mental blocks" concerning the object's underlying structure. Scientific inquiry is, in contrast with "folkish" theories and popular conceptions, explicitly and consciously constructive with regard to data.

> Above all knowledge necessitates posing problems. And, whatever one may say, in science problems do not pose themselves. It is precisely this sense of problems that is the true mark of the scientific mind. For science, all knowledge is a response to a question. If there are no questions, there can be no scientific knowledge. Nothing proceeds from itself. Nothing is given, all is constructed.[17]

Epistemological obstacles are not, however, restricted to common sense. Even mature scientific theories continue to rely on images, assumptions, and metaphors that occasionally block needed theoretical innovation. The relevance of Bachelard to Althusser is that Bachelard sees no methodological device for preserving or picking out scientific innovation and thereby distinguishing the scientific from the prescientific and the pseudoscientific.[18]

Althusser adopts Bachelard's emphasis on realist epistemology and his opposition to methodology in the philosophy of science. First, Althusser holds that there is no special philosophical knowledge separate from the sciences. Thus, epistemology involves no more than the philosophy of science. Second, sciences also always contain, albeit implicitly, philosophical conceptions that need to be criticized, especially at the birth of a science. The implicit philosophical views, also, always lag behind the science itself; even in a developed science philosophy can halt theoretical advances.

From this perspective Althusser considers efforts to revive the concept of dialectic as precisely a hidden philosophical imagery interfering with the advance of a new science, in this case the science of history. Althusser claims, in reply, that the concept of structure, and more precisely "structural causality," provides the proper response to the problems discussed above.

Whatever else structure means, Althusser takes it as a reason to reject the individual as the unit of analysis for epistemology. Althusser refers to history as a "process without a subject" and claims that both with regard to the nature of society and the nature of knowledge (science), the tendency to focus upon the individual subject is a philosophical assumption (or an ideological conception). For example, Althusser often makes this kind of argument against empiricism in the theory of knowledge. Knowledge is a social practice, or "mode of production" of conceptual objects. The spontaneous philosophical position for understanding this practice is empiricism, and Althusser hopes to defeat it.

> When Marx tells us that the production process of knowledge, and hence that of its object, as distinct from the real object which it is its precise aim to appropriate in the "mode" of knowledge takes place entirely in knowledge, in the "head" or in thought, he is not for one second falling into an idealism of consciousness, mind or thought, for the *"thought"* we are discussing here is not a faculty of a transcendental subject or absolute consciousness confronted by the real world as *matter;* nor is this thought a faculty of a psychological subject, although human individuals are its agents. This thought is the historically constituted system of an *apparatus of thought,* founded on and articulated to natural and social reality. It is defined by the system of real conditions which make it, if I dare use the phrase, a determinate *mode of production* of knowledge. (RC 41)

Althusser connects this passage with a more general statement concerning his reasons for rejecting individualism.

> The structure of the relations of production determines the *places* and *functions* occupied and adopted by the agents of production, who are never anything more than the occupants of these places, insofar as they are the "supports" *(Träger)* of these functions. The true "subjects" (in the sense of constitutive subjects of the process) are therefore not these occupants or functionaries, are not, despite all appearances, the "obviousness" of the "given" of

naive anthropology, "concrete individuals," "real men"—but *the definition and distribution of these places and functions. The true "subjects" are these definers and distributors: the relations of production* (and political and ideological social relations). But since these are "relations," they cannot be thought within the category *subject*. And if by chance anyone proposes to reduce these relations of production to relations between men, i.e., "human relations," he is violating Marx's thought, for so long as we apply a truly critical reading to some of his rare ambiguous formulations, Marx shows in the greatest depth that the *relations* of production . . . are irreducible to any anthropological inter-subjectivity—since they only combine agents and objects in a specific structure of the distribution of relations, places and functions, occupied and "supported" by objects and agents of production. (RC 180)

This passage is not as persuasive as it needs to be. Althusser seems to defend a socially external account of knowledge. But such an effort, as already noted, requires a distinction between knowledge and ideology, assuming it is not to reduce to relativism. Althusser is justified in warning that the crude philosophical conceptions of ideas "inside the head" mirroring or representing states of affairs outside in the world are inadequate, misleading, and conceptually confused. But having said that, Althusser presents a conception of knowledge that is barely preferable. To say, as he does, that knowledge is a practice or a mode of production is a metaphor and, as such, harmless. However, such a metaphor is being overworked if it is supposed to lead automatically to the conclusion that knowers are mere "occupants" or "functionaries" of an anonymous, somewhat mysterious "historically constituted system of an apparatus of thought founded on and articulated to natural and social reality." The truth of this view does not follow from the inadequacies of empiricism or representational realism.

Even if one were to agree with Althusser's embrace of such an ambitious holistic conception of knowledge, the hypothetical apparatus does not provide the required distinction between ideology and knowledge. In his other writings Althusser argues, for instance, that the concept of subjectivity, including the very idea of there being a subject of knowledge claims, is ideological. But this is an assertion, not an argument. It simply repeats that the conception of a subject representing states of affairs in the world is a misleading or faulty philosophical conception of knowledge. But it is attacked by another philosophical conception, as outlined briefly above. What ought to have been added is some reason to accept the one philosophical account as superior to the other. Either Althusser would need to provide some account of what it is to be scientific or of how social realities determine the so-called thought apparatus.

The concept of ideologies concerns those ideas that play a justificatory role with regard to the existing social structure. Althusser's central example of an ideology is a religion, and he glosses religions as belief systems metaphorically addressing themselves to the individual. Althusser must think, therefore, that epistemology is an ideology in a similar way, as when empiricism convinces those studying the world that the way the world appears coincides with social relations as they really are. But that kind of argument repeats the concern raised above. Althusser can assert that traditional epistemologies serve to justify the existing theory of property or legal system and claim thereby that certain philosophical categories are contaminated. But how has he determined that they are so contaminated? The picture is that an autonomous and anonymous structure produces knowledge and social relations simultaneously determining, in that way, that an individual is a "bearer" of these functions. In turn, certain ideas are then generated to justify this entire structure and its modes of production. This kind of argument is a bad armchair imitation of the job of the social sciences. The issue remains: Why is Kant's theory of a transcendental subjectivity ideological and Althusser's appeal to an "apparatus of thought" not?

With the notion of "structural causality" Althusser introduces the machinery of a somewhat traditional externalist epistemology. But there are two problems. First, there remains the traditional objection that causal analysis is irrelevant, since epistemology concerns the justification of knowledge and causality concerns the facts, whether sensory, mental or social, of its actual occurrence. Though Althusser considers such Husserlian objections wrongheaded, he does not say why, aside from a circular accusation that they are also ideological. Second, assuming that Husserl's objection to the relevance of any causal analysis for epistemology could be answered, the causality Althusser introduces is very perplexing. The burden falls to Althusser to explicate how causality can be said to operate at the level of abstract structures and practices, given that these structures are not physical features and are not reducible to the beliefs or mental states of individuals. Lévi-Strauss, as discussed, identified structure with ways of classifying and organizing phenomena. He further hypothesized that classification systems such as kinship were structures the society's members were not conscious of (such abstract structures did not constitute part of their explicit concepts or beliefs), yet determined their behaviors and perhaps related beliefs. But this hypothesis, whatever its other weaknesses, involved no mysterious form of causality. Nor does it, as Husserl charged his own opponents long before this movement, commit the fallacy of attributing causal powers to abstract objects such as numbers. The reason it is not mysterious is that Lévi-Strauss assumes there must be wholly material features of the world, for instance, the biophysiological features of the brain, that someday will provide the "reductionist" phase replacing structuralism in social science.

In contrast, Althusser allows himself the very confusing philosophical strategy of treating real causal relations in the world, which are independent of how the world is described or conceptualized, as identical to theoretical devices. Theoretical devices are what epistemological debates are supposed to assess; their job is to understand and explain the world. The theoretical device of structural causality both accounts for the scientific character of some claims about the world and yet serves also to show that the study of knowledge claims, apart from the sciences, is ideological.

How to Read

Though I think these continental versions of social externalism in epistemology are deeply flawed, I am even less enthusiastic about Althusser's particular structuralist variant. Lévi-Strauss raised proper concerns about the contemporary understanding of the social sciences, and only time will tell whether he was correct about the future of the social sciences. But I can think of no philosophical way to predict the development of the social sciences or distinguish scientific from nonscientific theories (aside from very general and unhelpful comments about how evidence might confirm or refute certain theoretical choices). For all the effort to be hardheaded and rigorous (and that was probably the best contribution the movement of structuralism made to these intellectual debates), the work of Althusser, and many others, falls far short of the level of philosophical innovation and engagement that at least held out some promise in the phenomenological movement. Although not everyone finds the study of philosophy worth pursuing or even important, such an attitude is normally not a good reason to actually study and write about it. As I will discuss again in Chapter 5, antiphilosophical arguments, at least when put forward with such dogmatic enthusiasm, are nevertheless philosophical arguments.

I have left aside, in the above, another way in which Althusser claims to defend the scientific status of Marxism. This second defense points to a quite different conception of philosophical debate. Althusser outlines a "theory of reading." He simply means by "reading" the interpretation of passages, and he attempts to make a complex case for being allowed to treat Marx's own statements about philosophy and economic theory selectively. Althusser thereby introduces by way of this controversial defense the broader question of a theory of interpretation, which will be the focus of Chapter 4.

Althusser rejects what he calls "innocent" or "theological" readings. His main characterization of either of these categories of interpretation is that they equate "reading" with "seeing." The error Althusser has in mind is thus somewhat reminiscent of what Husserl called "objectivism." Althusser raises a complex objection. These innocent readings are dogmatic since they claim to be correct because the truth manifests itself without the intermediary of criticism. Once again empiricism will turn out to be an example of a "theological" approach to the world, since it assumes a direct, unquestionable contact with reality by whatever is given to the senses. Despite his deep distrust of the continental tradition and the concept of ideology, Karl Popper adopts an oddly similar criticism of traditional empiricism and is even led to use the term "religious" in making his point.

> We can see more clearly how, in this optimistic epistemology, the state of knowledge is the natural or pure state of man, the state of the innocent eye which can see the truth, while the state of ignorance has its source in the inquiry suffered by the innocent eye in man's fall from grace; an inquiry which can be partially healed by a course of purification. And we can see more clearly why this epistemology, not only in Descartes' but also in Bacon's form, remains essentially a religious doctrine in which the source of all knowledge is divine authority.[19]

Althusser then contrasts the innocent reading with two more properly interpretative strategies. In the first, the interpreter's current standpoint is taken as the standpoint from which to judge others. The present conception acts as a "grid," as he prefers to call it, indicating where competitive or proceeding theories accord and where they conflict. This reading is called "retrospective," and Althusser claims it always seeks continuity in the history of thought.

Althusser finds examples of this retrospective reading in his discussion of how Marx has been variously understood to fit within the history of political economy. Althusser suggests that these retrospective accounts find that: "What Smith did not see, through a weakness of vision, Marx sees . . . this reduces Marx to Smith minus the myopia" (RC 18–19). Though Althusser ultimately rejects the retrospective reading, for reasons to be discussed, he claims it is superior to an innocent reading because it is explicitly critical.

The retrospective reading, however, betrays its own dogmatism. Every searchlight casts shadows, and every perspective is selective. By taking the present as its unquestioned reference point, the retrospective reading fails to become fully self-critical. It reduces then, he argues, to another version of the manifest account of truth lying behind the innocent or theological reading. It takes it for granted, in other words, that the "grid" that is derived from the assumptions of the present is authoritative for deciding these questions.

Althusser's final model is a "symptomatic reading." In a symptomatic reading, all theories, including the theories we take as correct in the present, are merely conceptual schemes constituting their own theoretical objects and problematics, not "some pre-existing object which it could have seen but did not." The symptomatic reading must then reconstruct each theory's problematic without assuming that the truth manifests itself to us in the present. This account would appear to be a highly fallibilistic attitude toward the history of thought and our own present theories, but it becomes in Althusser's hands a weapon of dogmatism.

Since the symptomatic reading does not assume there is a common object, missed in the past, it does not assume that intellectual history follows a smooth path from past confusion to present clarity. These "lapses" in continuity are not, however, matters of psychological failings or simple oversights. The idea is, naturally enough, that Althusser's own study of Marx exemplifies a symptomatic reading and thus should be taken as superior to others. Marx's thought emerged from a set of anomalies or problems in theoretical economics. The reader of Marx must exercise the same attention to inconsistencies and misunderstandings of the sort Marx detected in the work of economists in Marx's own writings.

> In the papers you are about to read . . . we simply have tried to apply to Marx's reading the "symptomatic" reading with which Marx managed to read the illegible in Smith, by measuring the problematic initially visible in his writings against the invisible problematic contained in the paradox of *an answer which does not correspond to any question posed.* (RC 28)

Althusser was forced to develop these metaphors of reading in defense of his conclusions concerning the scientific status of Marxism and his orthodoxy, because he is explicitly anti-experimental in his account of what constitutes a scientific theory; in fact he sets a rigid distinction between the theoretical and experimental sciences. A science is described by him as a "theoretical practice" for the production of a "theoretical object" and as such is to be considered apart from whatever results emerge from experimental practices.

> We must completely reorganize the idea we have of knowledge, we must abandon the mirror myths of immediate vision and reading, and conceive knowledge as production. . . . This introduces us to a fact peculiar to the very existence of science; it can only pose problems on the terrain and within the horizon of a definite theoretical structure, its problematic, which constitutes . . . *the form in which all problems must be posed,* at any given moment in science. (RC 24)

Having disallowed appeal to prediction, confirmation, refutation, or evidence, Althusser defends the scientific status of Marxism by specifying that its "conceptual object" is scientific and branding as "unorthodox" any alternative account. But neither concepts nor readings are inherently scientific (or ideological). Althusser's claim that by his interpretation of Marx he secures the theory's scientific status is either relativism or a mere confession of faith in Marxism's status as a science. But an expression of faith is no longer a matter of philosophical debate. Although Althusser's efforts to defend the scientific reform of philosophy fail, he does raise in this way the issue of whether disagreement about philosophical issues admits of some further interpretative clarification.

Notes

1. Donald Davidson identifies two forms of externalism in recent epistemology. First, "the idea that the meanings of a person's words, and the contents of that person's thoughts, depend in part on the linguistic practices of the person's community, even in cases where the individual is mistaken about the relevant practices." Second, "the contents of utterances and thoughts depend on the causal history of the individual, particularly in connection with perception." Davidson characterizes the part of this position with which he agrees: "The contents of our . . . basic sentences . . . must be determined by what it is in the world that causes us to hold them true." "Epistemology Externalized," *Dialectica* 45, no. 2–3 (1991), pp. 197–198. The following further definition by Davidson is particularly helpful with regard to my presentation: "Externalism makes clear how one person can come to know what someone else thinks, at least at the ground level, for by discovering what normally causes someone else's beliefs, an interpreter has made an essential step toward determining the content of those beliefs. . . . Reflecting on how externalism operates in interpretation, we can partly explain the asymmetry between first person and third person knowledge of thoughts. For where the interpreter must know, or correctly surmise, the events and situations that cause a verbal or other reaction in another person in order to fathom her thoughts, no such nomic knowledge is needed for the thinker to decide what she thinks. Causal history partly determines what she is thinking, but this determination is independent of any knowledge of the causal history she may have." "The Conditions of Thought," in *The Mind of Donald Davidson,* ed. Johannes Brandl and Wolfgang L. Gombocz (Amsterdam: Rodopi, 1989), pp. 195–196.

2. Hilary Putnam, "The Meaning of 'Meaning'," in *Mind, Language and Reality, Philosophical Papers,* vol. 2 (Cambridge: Cambridge University Press, 1975), pp. 215–271. See the anthology *The Twin Earth Chronicles,* ed. Andrew Pessin and Sanford Goldberg (Armonk, NY: M. E. Sharpe, 1996).

3. Karl Mannheim, *From Karl Mannheim,* ed. Kurt Wolff (New York: Oxford University Press, 1971), p. 61.

4. Mannheim understands Husserl's attack on psychologism as tantamount to defending a sociological conception of cognitive inquiry, because he thinks that the difference between the natural and phenomenological attitudes is comparable to different "points of view" on the same topic, and because he treats the phenomenological method as a scientific method. Karl Mannheim, *Structures of Thinking,* ed. David Kettler, Volker Meja, and Nico Stehr (London: Routledge & Kegan Paul, 1982), p. 132, n. 11. Though these misunderstandings are not particular to Mannheim, as already discussed, the popularity of his work had the effect of reinforcing them.

5. *Max Weber on the Methodology of the Social Sciences,* trans. Edward Shils. (Glencoe, Ill.: Free Press, 1949).

6. Maurice Merleau-Ponty, *Adventures of the Dialectic,* trans. Joseph Bien (Evanston, Ill.: Northwestern University Press, 1973), pp. 30–58. Merleau-Ponty uses Lukacs's early writings as his example of Marxism as "an integral philosophy without dogma." Though Merleau-Ponty cautiously suggests, without clarification, that "there was something justified in the opposition it encountered" (p. 57), he

clearly sides in the essay with Lukacs's brand of philosophically engaged Marxism against Communist Party orthodoxy. This essay spurred a revival of interest in Lukacs's writings of the 1920s, which spread in France through a pirated translation. Lukacs, who had become more orthodox over time, suppressed at that time republication or translation of the original German edition of *History and Class Consciousness.*

7. Karl Löwith, *From Hegel to Nietzsche: The Revolution in Nineteenth-Century Thought* (New York: Holt, Reinhart & Winston, 1964). Marx and Hegel play central roles in Löwith's account, written under Heidegger's influence, of nineteenth-century philosophy, which is seen as preoccupied with the problems of ontology in the clash between materialism and idealism as well as science and philosophy.

8. Georg Lukacs, a Hungarian intellectual who precociously advanced in the circle of students and colleagues around Max Weber, wrote a successful first book, *The Theory of the Novel,* which was widely reviewed as an example of Weberian sociology of literature. Mannheim, Lukacs's younger fellow countryman, reviewed *The Theory of the Novel,* calling it a major "aesthetic interpretation" of the philosophy of history through Weber's theory of ideal types. But Mannheim criticized Lukacs for ignoring "sociological conditions" in his study of literature and for emphasizing "the spirit that we can describe only metaphysically." *From Karl Mannheim,* p. 6.

9. For this debate, see *Can Theories Be Refuted?: Essays on the Duhem-Quine Thesis,* ed. Sandra Harding (Boston: Reidel, 1976).

10. Either the notion was in the air at the time or Heidegger had read Lukacs's writings, because in *Being and Time* the phrase "reification of consciousness" appears with roughly Lukacs's intent (BT 43, 385, 397). For a discussion of connections between these thinkers, see Lucien Goldmann, *Lukacs and Heidegger,* trans. William Q. Boelhower (London: Routledge & Kegan Paul, 1977).

11. An example of this confused and confusing subgenre in philosophy during this time that attempts to link all the names in continental philosophy with Marxist sociology is Enzo Paci, *The Function of the Sciences and the Meaning of Man,* trans. Paul Piccone and James E. Hansen (Evanston, Ill.: Northwestern University Press, 1972).

12. "In Sartre's terminology, I am therefore to be defined as a transcendental materialist. . . . I am a transcendental materialist because I do not regard dialectical reason as *something other than* analytic reason, upon which the absolute originality of a human order would be based, but as *something additional in* analytic reason: the necessary condition for it to venture to undertake the resolution of the human into the non-human. . . . I believe the ultimate goal of the human sciences to be not to constitute, but to dissolve man. The pre-eminent value of anthropology is that it represents the first step in a procedure which involves others." This statement is part of a sustained attack on Jean-Paul Sartre as a representative of historicism. The quotation is from the final chapter, "History and Dialectic," of Claude Lévi-Strauss, *The Savage Mind,* trans. George Weindenfield (Chicago: University of Chicago Press, 1968), pp. 246–247.

13. "The reductions I am envisaging are thus legitimate, or indeed possible, only if two conditions are satisfied. First, the phenomena subjected to reduction must not be impoverished; one must be certain that everything contributing to their distinc-

tive richness and originality has been collected around them. . . . Secondly, one must be ready to accept, as a consequence of each reduction, the total overturning of any preconceived idea concerning the level, whichever it may be, one is striving to attain. The idea of some general humanity to which ethnographic reduction leads will bear no relation to any one may have formed in advance. And when we do finally succeed in understanding life as a function of inert matter, it will be to discover that the latter has properties very different from those previously attributed to it. Levels of reduction cannot therefore be classed as superior and inferior, for the level taken as superior must, through the reduction, be expected to communicate retroactively some of its richness to the inferior level to which it will have been assimilated. Scientific explanation consists not in moving from the complex to the simple but in the replacement of a less intelligible complexity by one which is more so." *Savage Mind,* pp. 247–248.

14. Lévi-Strauss goes on in the article to draw the comparison between these conclusions about the practice of shamanism and psychoanalysis by claiming that, in a similar fashion, psychoanalysis achieves "cures" by manipulation of the patient's symbolic system and thereby is also a case of "symbolic effectiveness." I am ignoring the analogy both because it is contentious, assuming as it does that there are psychoanalytic "cures," and because I have excluded from my topic the rather heated debates about the status of psychoanalysis that occupied some of the philosophers discussed in this and Chapter 5.

15. Hilary Putnam cites Althusser as a critic of empiricism, because Althusser holds that theories are overthrown by other theories rather than recalcitrant evidence, in Putnam's "The 'Corroboration' of Theories," in *Mathematics, Matter and Method, Philosophical Papers,* vol. 1 (New York: Cambridge University Press, 1975).

16. Althusser calls those who oppose this second epistemological thesis the "historicists." The term "historicism" has had a long and confusing career in twentieth-century philosophy. It has been used to identify those for whom there are historical laws (a position with which Althusser appears to agree) as well as those who believe that history involves the meaning of events demanding the method of understanding rather than that of scientific explanation (a position with which he clearly disagrees). See Robert D'Amico, *Historicism and Knowledge* (New York: Routledge, 1988).

17. Gaston Bachelard, *La Formation de l'Esprit Scientifique* (Paris: Librarie Philosophique J. Vrin, 1980), p. 14.

18. There is a strong Baconian flavor to Bachelard's work in his continual warnings against the seductive appeal of these various "idols of the mind," the somewhat moralizing recommendation for vigilance against the "cult" of the natural and the obvious, and his effort to recount narratives about the history of science as a therapy against what he takes as prescientific fetishism. For example, in *The Psychoanalysis of Fire,* trans. Alan C. M. Ross (London: Routledge & Kegan Paul, 1964), Bachelard treats the persistence of prescientific conceptions of the "elements" as requiring complex psychological explanations.

19. Karl Popper, *Conjectures and Refutations* (New York: Harper & Row, 1968), p. 15. "In Bacon . . . Nature is an open book. He who reads it with a pure mind cannot misread it. Only if his mind is poisoned by prejudice . . ." (p. 7). "The

traditional system of epistemology may be read to result from yes-answers or no-answers to questions about the source of our knowledge. They never challenge these questions, or dispute their legitimacy; the questions are taken as perfectly natural" (p. 25).

Suggested Readings

Though Lukacs and Mannheim are my main examples, Sartre and Merleau-Ponty also embraced variations of the arguments discussed in this chapter: Jean-Paul Sartre, *Critique of Dialectical Reason,* ed. Jonathan Ree, trans. Alan Sheridan-Smith (London: New Left Books, 1976); Maurice Merleau-Ponty, *Adventures of the Dialectic,* trans. Joseph Bien (Evanston, Ill.: Northwestern University Press, 1973).

A useful account of their work and influence can be found in Mark Poster, *Existential Marxism in Post-War France: From Sartre to Althusser* (Princeton: Princeton University Press, 1975).

For the two figures I discussed, more information can be found in: H. E. S. Woldring, *Karl Mannheim: The Development of His Thought* (New York: St. Martin's Press, 1987) and *Georg Lukacs: The Man, His Work, and His Ideas,* ed. G. A. R. Parkinson (New York: Random House, 1970). For two defenses of social externalism explicitly using Mannheim, there is David Bloor, *Wittgenstein: A Social Theory of Knowledge* (New York: Columbia University Press, 1983), and Peter Berger and Thomas Luckmann, *The Social Construction of Reality: A Treatise on the Sociology of Knowledge* (Garden City, N.Y.: Doubleday, 1966).

For a critical reply to such antirealist epistemologies, see John Searle, *The Construction of Social Reality* (New York: Free Press, 1995). A useful collection debating social externalism can be found in *Socializing Epistemology: The Social Dimensions of Knowledge,* ed. Frederick F. Schmitt (New York: Rowan & Littlefield, 1994).

With regard to the final topics of the chapter, François Dosse's *History of Structuralism,* trans. Deborah Glassmann (Minneapolis: University of Minnesota Press, 1997), provides a useful if somewhat journalistic and thus uncritical narrative of the main figures and events, including political squabbles, of this intellectual movement in France. Dosse's account confirms that structuralism was understood by participants in vastly different ways, functioned more as a label than a basic agreement, and betrayed its promise of interdisciplinary research through an almost perverse inability among those involved in the many debates and excited pronouncements to be even minimally clear about what structuralism meant.

A different perspective on this whole period can be found in Louis Althusser's *The Future Lasts Forever,* ed. Olivier Corpet and Yann Moulier Boutang, trans. Richard Veasey (New York: New Press, 1993). It is a fascinating, if rather disturbing, confessional autobiography (Althusser murdered his wife and was held in a prison for the criminally insane toward the end of his life) narrating the intellectual and political context of philosophical study in France since the 1940s.

Finally, representative examples of the specifically European feminist movement in philosophy, mentioned briefly above in the discussion of Kristeva, are in *New French Feminism,* ed. Elaine Marks and Isabelle de Courtivron (Amherst: University of Massachusetts Press, 1980).

Bibliography

HCC: Lukacs, G. *History and Class Consciousness: Studies in Marxist Dialectics.* Translated by Rodney Livingstone. Cambridge, Mass.: MIT Press, 1971.

IU: Mannheim, K. *Ideology and Utopia: An Introduction to the Sociology of Knowledge.* Translated by Louis Wirth and Edward Shils. New York: Harcourt, Brace & World, 1966.

LU: Kristeva, J. *Language the Unknown: An Initiation into Linguistics.* Translated by Anne M. Menke. New York: Columbia University Press, 1989.

MM: Lévi-Strauss, C. *Myth and Meaning: The 1977 Massey Lectures.* New York: Schocken Books, 1979.

RC: Althusser, L., and E. Balibar. *Reading Capital.* Translated by Ben Brewster. New York: Pantheon Books, 1970.

SA1: Lévi-Strauss, C. *Structural Anthropology,* vol. 1. Translated by Claire Jacobson. New York: Basic Books, 1963.

SA2: Lévi-Strauss, C. *Structural Anthropology,* vol. 2. Translated by Monique Layton. New York: Basic Books, 1976.

4

INTERPRETATION

Consider the mundane hammer. Heidegger uses it as his example of how being appears in the world. Setting aside his contentious vocabulary, we can view hammers as artifacts.[1] Artifacts consist of stuff arranged for a function or purpose. An artifact's user or designer assigns or imposes such a function on whatever are the thing's physical features. Thus grasping that something is an artifact requires, in part, grasping that its identity is not merely its "objective presence," to use Heidegger's language once again, but this imposed function or purpose. In other words, what it means to identify something as an artifact is to understand a background of human ends and purposes expressed in and by this thing. Thus a world without humans is a world without artifacts.

Interpretation, the topic of this chapter, concerns features of the world that call for the above kind of understanding. It calls for a study of what something means, signifies, or represents, not what explains the properties it has. A theory of interpretation would therefore be proper to not only the study of artifacts, but to determining others' thoughts or making sense of their actions. Finally, philosophy and interpretation appear, to some at least, as one and the same inquiry; philosophy seeks intelligibility, not the explanatory scope characteristic of the sciences.

Suppose an archaeologist were to claim that some discovered artifact were a hammer. The archaeologist would not be making a claim about the object under the description "physical object," a task belonging to chemists, geologists, or physicists. Rather, the archaeologist would be making a discovery about the object under the description "having a function or purpose." The kind of evidence that guides the archaeologist in this discovery is, then, quite unlike the evidence that guides the chemist. Objects have these purposes and functions not simply in virtue of whatever are their fixed physical properties. Therefore, even if all the physical, chemical, and geological facts about such an object were known, there would still remain a separate question of determining whether the object were an artifact and, if so, what its purpose was or what meaning it had for those who made it.

In the following discussion, a theory of interpretation will bear some relation to a theory of meaning. For example, as already noted in Chapter 1, Husserl held that the study of meaning is not entirely a topic of the sciences and thus, in parallel with the above, is not strictly a matter for explanation. Also a theory of meaning might in turn serve to show why the study of certain features of the world, namely, artifacts, beliefs, sign systems, and intentionality, raise similar problems and make similar nonexplanatory demands. Wherever there are problems of meaning, there are problems of interpretation and understanding.

The claim that phenomena such as artifacts, actions, and sign systems are studied in a manner separate from physical phenomena recalls Husserl's assertion that meaning, like epistemology, cannot be naturalized. Husserl made that claim in defending the study of meaning as a predominately philosophical topic, one not belonging simply to psychology or linguistics. Thus, as suggested above, there seems to be a link appearing between the task of interpretation and the task of philosophy itself. But a question remains: If knowing all of an object's physical properties is not sufficient for determining its meaning, how is its meaning determined?

One way to approach such a question would be to concentrate first on linguistic phenomena and treat artifacts and actions as in some fashion extensions of the determination of meaning there. If it were clear how to determine the meaning of words, for instance, these other topics might fall into place. In the twentieth century, philosophers have generally adopted this strategy. In fact, there could be said to be a surprising consensus, across otherwise deep divisions, that progress in solving a whole range of traditional philosophical problems depends on progress on a theory of meaning. Since philosophy is about the nature of thought, the argument goes, it involves questions of understanding and intelligibility that, in turn, lead inquiry inevitably back to the concept of meaning.

In this chapter the defenses of interpretative inquiry that I will discuss follow this general approach. They focus on the kind of inquiries wherein humans exercise a skill at determining the meaning of linguistic signs. On the basis of this skill, interpretation extrapolates to wider practices. Within the analytic tradition, this practical skill is often called "folk psychology" or simply "commonsense psychology."[2] Though this phrase is not found in continental philosophy, and unfortunately identifies the skill as belonging to some sort of psychology, it nevertheless draws attention to what kind of skill theories of interpretation hope to capture.

The folk psychological skill at making the world intelligible presupposes the concept of intentionality, already discussed in Chapter 1. The ability to grasp or determine the meaning of something depends upon the intentionality of mental states. Intentionality also separates off understanding from explanation. For example, the fact that the liver secretes bile or that iron rusts is a matter of how the world is whether humans conceive it or represent it as such. But grasping that an act of infidelity arouses anger or that the circulation of counterfeit currency drives out real currency in a market is inseparable from how these aspects of the world are conceptualized, described, and represented. A world without intentional beings is necessarily a world without infidelity, anger, or currency, but it may very well contain rust and bile.

The way to see this fundamental asymmetry between, for instance, understanding an act of infidelity versus explaining the phenomenon of oxidation is to realize that the concept of anger or resentment cannot be eliminated from the concept of infidelity as long as the focus remains on determining what it means, that is, on understanding it or making it intelligible to oneself. The reason for that constraint is that an action such as "being unfaithful" is an action only if described or represented in the right way. But, in contrast, oxidation is whatever it is, has whatever fixed features it has, no matter how one might choose to describe or picture the phenomenon in question.

Another way to put the same point is that there are always other movements, behaviors, or responses occurring simultaneously with an action that do not admit of what I am calling this "folkish" understanding. If currency as the medium in which debts are paid also causes flu viruses to be transmitted in a given population, then the skill at making the function of money intelligible only holds for money under the description "paying debts," not under the description "vector for viral infection."

The mental attitudes, such as believing, fearing, hoping, or wanting, that make possible meaningfulness have, as already discussed, intentionality or "essential directedness," as Husserl also called it. Though this technical language is not at all familiar in everyday life, the skill it is supposed to capture and clarify is so pedestrian and ubiquitous for humans that only in very special circumstances (where an action, object, or sign is especially mysterious or strange) is the practice explicitly examined or even noticed as such.

An example of pedestrian success is the case of the archaeologist who discovers that some artifact was in fact an ancient hammer. She is likely guided in her inquiry by the following kind of generalization about artifacts and mentality. If people want to accomplish such and such a task and believe that such and such a tool will serve in doing that task, then they will make and use such and such a tool. How does intelligibility emerge from such banality? The key is apparently the logical or rational connection between the intentional content (those phrases referring to the content of beliefs and wants) and the subsequent action or artifact in question. The intentional states can be said to "rationalize" actions, artifacts, and signs as well. In this context, "to rationalize" does not mean "to excuse." Rather, it refers to the kind of relation between the contents in the mind, what the agent understands or conceives as the action, artifact, and sign, and the subsequent actions, artifacts, or sign systems in the world. What the agent believes and what the agent wants must cohere in this fashion with what the agent then actually says and does. Intentionality allows for meaning to extend into the world in this fashion; the Janus-faced intentional contents look within toward the agent's mind and without toward the world. In the absence of such coherence, the only response is a shrug: "I don't understand."

The same exercise extends to imputing the mental states of others by means of extrapolating the content of their intentional states from hearing their sentences and seeing their actions. The possibility of this kind of empathy, however, rests in turn upon the content of one's own mental state. In this same way, artifacts and signs are intelligible and meaningful for agents by a complex and indirect reconstruction of what others had in mind.

The effort to describe this exercise or practice of interpretation in more detail, however, quickly reaches some difficult theoretical questions. It may be that this skill at grasping meaning or understanding these actions and artifacts is something that humans are guided by through a procedure or method. Therefore, such questions as what the nature of this skill is, what it presupposes, how intentionality underlies meaning, and what distinguishes understanding from explanation strike some as archetypal philosophical ones.

Three aspects of this "folkish" skill can be isolated apart from the debate about whether this skill is based on some method or is a kind of natural ability. First, the practice of making actions, objects, or symbols intelligible proceeds by advancing tentative guesses concerning the meaning of objects, actions, or sign systems. These provisional interpretations are then revised and altered as they are used to allow more and more of the situation to become intelligible. I will discuss the implied circularity of this aspect below.

Second, understanding, as already noted, is the effort of determining ultimately what someone else had "in mind," or even what was in one's own mind in certain special circumstances, when making, using, saying, or doing such and such; to determine what something means and to determine what someone thinks about are related problems. Finally, determining the function or purpose of an object or action depends on determining a network of concepts, often called a conceptual scheme.

For example, if an archaeologist decides that something is a hammer, she also necessarily distinguishes functional from natural features of a thing and, in doing so, deploys a network of concepts concerning purpose, design, intent, and so on. Thus, the archaeologist's discovery of signs of "chipping" and not just erosion, for instance, necessarily entails that the peoples in question conceptually distinguished "chipping" from the natural features of the object, assuming the object is an artifact. As I said above, the evidence guiding the archaeologist in such a complex reconstruction will be distinct from the kind of evidence guiding chemists or geologists.

These points together, however, may raise a certain worry, specifically when it is realized that the necessary conceptual background, shared, for instance, by the ancient peoples and the archaeologist, is itself an object of interpretation. The worry is that the entire procedure seems hollow and circular. The evidence supporting the claim about intelligibility, for instance, is itself being made intelligible by the very guesswork the evidence is then invoked to support.

One way to see, rather quickly, how the worry arises is to imagine that the archaeologist, confronted by what she thinks is a hammer, were simply able to ask her ancient informants about it: "Did you design this object in this way and, if you did, what purpose did you have in mind when you made it?" But even were that contact possible, the archaeologist would have to interpret her informants' words correctly. If, on the other hand, she merely were able to observe what these ancient peoples did with the object, so as to avoid having to interpret their linguistic responses, she would still have to interpret their actions correctly. The problem is therefore the same: Is she any more confident that they are now engaged in chipping than she was that what they mean by hammer is what she means by hammer?

These embedded interpretations, the interpretation of utterances or actions as evidence for interpreting the content of mental states and thereby determining the meaning of an object as an artifact, presuppose the initial question "How is meaning determined?" If interpreting things involves appealing to features extrinsic to the thing's physical properties, then what does serve to fix assignments of meaning to the world?

The "hermeneutic circle," as this quandary about the determinateness of interpretation is often called, seems at first glance a kind of skepticism. Such skepticism is not due, however, to a scarcity of evidence. It is not, for instance, based on the archaeologist's inability to actually ask informants the above questions (or observe their actions) when studying ancient or prehistoric societies. The skeptical aspect of the claim is that, given all the information one could hope for, the determination of whether something is an artifact and what it means for those who made it cannot finally be settled. There would be, then, a principled limit to understanding the world. Responding to or clarifying this skepticism is another philosophical topic for the theory of interpretation.

Against Method

Hans-Georg Gadamer's *Truth and Method,* which appeared relatively late in his career, was inspired by the thought of Husserl and Heidegger during the 1920s and 1930s, when phenomenology emerged and changed philosophy in Europe. But Gadamer's work also maintains a certain critical distance from those early works. Though he explicitly adopts Heidegger's ontological project, Gadamer's approach is more conservative and integrative toward the philosophical tradition, and the tone of philosophical radicalism is considerably muted. Though Gadamer also identifies himself with the phenomenological method, he abandons much of Husserl's phenomenology and shows surprisingly little interest in the problems in the philosophy of mathematics, logic, and language that shaped Husserl's early thought.

Gadamer's way of discussing his own views does create some difficulties in assessing them. Specifically, Gadamer often makes it difficult to determine where his exposition of other thinkers ends and his own position begins. In *Truth and Method,* for instance, lengthy expositions of Schleiermacher, Dilthey, and Heidegger shade with far too little argumentative development into conclusions that either Gadamer later takes for granted as his own or leaves in question. Furthermore, Gadamer makes vague and shifting appeals to "the problem" or "the central question." Which of several central problems is being discussed at any given time in the book is, however, often unclear. In an effort to carve out of this lengthy and digressive work a manageable set of themes, I will divide my discussion between Gadamer's epistemological and ontological conceptions of philosophy as a type, perhaps the central type, of interpretative inquiry. This division will also allow me to discuss his relationship to both Husserl and Heidegger.

Truth and Method discusses interpretation in two contexts. First Gadamer focuses on aesthetics, which I will largely ignore, and second on the problem of "historical objectivity." With regard to the study of history, Gadamer combines, in a somewhat confusing fashion, both epistemological and ontological arguments. At certain points in the book the emphasis is on the problem of the objectivity of knowledge of history and at others points the issue is whether historicity is the being of human beings.

Gadamer uses the term *Geisteswissenschaften,* often translated as "human or cultural sciences," for the question of what subject matter is encompassed by "historical objectivity." With this term he emphasizes the broad range of topics he has in mind and connects his theme with what was a central preoccupation of late-nineteenth-century German philosophy.

John Stuart Mill's 1843 *A Method of Logic* appeared in a widely read German translation in the 1860s. Mill's position was that the "moral sciences" (Mill's phrase "moral sciences" was translated as *Geisteswissenschaften*), encompassing the fields of economics, history, sociology, and politics, were methodologically indistinguishable from physics, astronomy, and chemistry. Neo-Kantians and Neo-Hegelians were inspired by the book's argument to offer a variety of reasons for rejecting Mill's claim of methodological identity between the natural and social sciences. These critics asserted that the social sciences required a different method from the natural sciences, or, more radically, they claimed that the scientific study of history and society was impossible. These sciences were impossible, it was argued by some, because value judgments entered the study of society and not the study of nature, because human freedom was incompatible with scientific determinism, or because the study of mind was not reducible to the study of matter.[3]

Gadamer considers these late-nineteenth-century debates about the possibility of a science of history as precursors and historically preliminary exercises in the philosophical topic of "hermeneutics," a term he then uses synonymously with "the universal scope of interpretation." He treats hermeneutics, for instance, as clarifying, with regard to that debate, the preconditions for objectivity in inquiry whether or not such inquiries are classified as sciences. Though he dismisses the narrow concern in traditional philosophy with scientific methodology, he agrees that the human sciences are not sciences. He argues for this conclusion by repeating an often made Neo-Kantian distinction between studying particular, unique objects and seeking lawlike generalizations.

> But the specific problem that the human sciences present to thought is that one has not properly grasped their nature if one measures them by the yardstick of progressive knowledge of regularity. The experience of the sociohistorical world cannot be raised to a science by the inductive procedure of the natural sciences. Whatever "science" may mean here, and even if all historical knowledge includes the application of experiential universals to the particular object of investigation, historical research does not endeavor to grasp the concrete phenomenon as an instance of a universal rule. The individual case does not serve only to confirm a law from which practical predictions can be made. Its ideal is, rather, to understand the phenomenon itself in its unique and historical concreteness. However much experiential universals are involved, the aim is not to confirm and expand these universalized experiences in order to attain knowledge of a law—e.g., how men, peoples and states evolve—but to understand how this man, this people or this state is what it has become or, more generally, how it happened that it is so. (TM 4–5)

Gadamer is hardly clear in the above as to why the study of individual cases necessarily excludes the study of regularities or why such studies can admit of only understanding and not explanation. Also, his statement that "The individual case does not serve only to confirm a law from which practical predictions can be made" suggests that such confirmation does occur as long as practical predictions are ignored. His position would be stronger if he were consistently agnostic with regard to any possible social-scientific laws or explanations. He could then argue that, even were there social-scientific laws and explanations, there would remain the separate question of how the intentional characterization of actions and objects (the feature of their intelligibility) is determined. Understanding must then be presupposed, he could argue, whether or not there are any possible social-scientific regularities. It is this intentionality of historical or social phenomena that requires, in his view, a theory of interpretation.

One persisting difficulty in discussing Gadamer's defense of the theory of interpretation is that, although the book is organized against a "methodical approach" to truth and inquiry, he does not discuss what he means by the term "methodology." Ignoring the vast literature on this topic, especially during the years he prepared *Truth and Method,* Gadamer cites only a brief, occasional essay by the physicist Hermann von Helmholtz, and not a particularly clear essay at that, in which methodology is roughly pictured as the kind of hypothetical-deductive reasoning Mill championed. Gadamer cites the essay in support of the claim that "what is called 'method' in modern science remains the same everywhere and is only displayed in an especially exemplary form in the natural sciences" (TM 7).[4]

Without characterizing the position he opposes any further than the above, Gadamer's argumentative intent is often obscure.

> My revival of the expression *hermeneutics,* with its long tradition, has apparently led to some misunderstandings. I did not intend to produce an art or technique of understanding, in the manner of the earlier hermeneutics. I do not wish to elaborate a system of rules to describe, let alone direct, the methodological procedure of the human sciences. . . . My real concern was and is philosophic: not what we do or what we ought to do, but what happens to us over and above our wanting and doing. . . . The difference that confronts us is not in the method but in the objectives of knowledge. The question I have asked seeks to discover and bring into consciousness something which that methodological dispute serves only to conceal and neglect, something that does not so much confine or limit modern science as precede it and make it possible. (TM xxviii-xxix)

Methodological disputes "conceal and neglect" what makes science and knowledge in general possible. This concealed aspect emerges in the book's later sections as truth itself. Both aesthetics and what Gadamer calls the "effectiveness" of history are experiences in which "the being of that which is to be understood" is disclosed and thereby constitute what he calls "objectives of knowledge." The disclosure of being by understanding is treated as synonymous with truth, then, by Gadamer. Such Heideggerian phraseology, neither clarified nor critically examined, permeates Gadamer's entire defense of the philosophical significance of his study of interpretation and specifically motivates a central theme of opposing both subjectivism and scientism.

> In understanding tradition not only are texts understood, but insights are acquired and truths known. But what kind of knowledge and what kind of truths?
>
> Given the dominance of modern science in the philosophical elucidation and justification of the concept of knowledge and the concept of truth, this question does not appear legitimate. Yet it is unavoidable, even within the sciences. The phenomenon of understanding not only pervades all human relations to the world. It also has an independent validity within science and it resists any attempt to reinterpret it in terms of scientific method. The following investigations start with the resistance in modern science itself to the universal claim of scientific method. They are concerned to seek the experience of truth that transcends the domain of scientific method wherever that experience is to be found, and to inquire into its legitimacy. Hence the human sciences are connected to modes of experience that lie outside science: with the experiences of philosophy, of art, and of history itself. These are all modes of experience in which a truth is communicated that cannot be verified by the methodological means proper to science. (TM xxi-xxii)

Gadamer expands upon this philosophical focus later in the same introduction.

> At any rate, the purpose of my investigation is not to offer a general theory of interpretation and a differential account of its methods ... but to discover what is common to all modes of understanding and to show that understanding is never a subjective relation to a given "object," but to the history of its effects [*zur Wirkungsgeschichte*]; in other words, understanding belongs to the being of that which is understood. (TM xxxi)

This effort to distinguish a theory of interpretation from any methodological conception and his defense of truth in interpretation lead Gadamer to defend a version of epistemological realism, as revealed in the last sentence of the above quote. Interpretation is not inventing an account of things, rather, it is a way to disclose whatever is the world's being. Understanding the "meaning of being," disclosed in these special aesthetic or historical encounters with the world, is a matter of truth, not a matter of opinion, projection, or convenience. The being of the world is not just an account of the world as it is given, even in those accounts provided by the sciences.

Gadamer's philosophical realism is, however, not identified as such in the book. His comments occasionally blur matters since his defense of why the world is only intelligible given interpretation (the epistemological emphasis) sometimes slides into formulations to the effect that the world's being is made possible by interpretation (the ontological emphasis). But I take his repeated attacks on subjectivism as a reason for ignoring that slide for the moment; I will return to this blurring of the issue, however, in my criticisms of Gadamer.

This instinctive defense of realism leads him to raise, in the same introduction, the potential threat of relativism and skepticism.

> This raises a question about the extent to which the hermeneutic viewpoint itself enjoys historical or dogmatic validity. If the principle of effective history is made into a universal element in the structure of understanding, then this thesis undoubtedly implies no historical relativity, but seeks absolute validity—and yet a hermeneutical consciousness exists only under specific historical conditions. (TM xxxiii)

This passage, in a very muddy fashion, poses the book's central theme. Can realism, Gadamer's basic criticism of relativism and subjectivism, escape dogmatism? Can the claim of "absolute validity" in interpretation be reconciled with the claim that interpretations always presuppose "historical fore-understandings and prejudices"?

> Hence there is a certain legitimate ambiguity in the concept of historically effected consciousness *(wirkungsgeschichtliches Bewußtsein),* as I have employed it. This ambiguity is that it is used to mean at once the consciousness effected in the course of history and determined by history, and the very consciousness of being thus effected and determined. Obviously the burden of my argument is that effective history still determines modern historical and scientific consciousness; and it does so beyond any possible knowledge of this domination. Historically effected consciousness is so radically finite that our whole being, effected in the totality of our destiny, inevitably transcends its knowledge of itself. But that is a fundamental insight which is not to be limited to any specific historical situation; an insight which, however, in the face of modern historical research and of science's methodological ideal of objectivity, meets with particular resistance in the self-understanding of science. (TM xxxiv)

Gadamer's point, as far as it can be reconstructed here, is that history determines the possibility of knowledge in that all knowledge presupposes these cultural "fore-structures" of interpretation. This aspect of history is not itself knowable, however; "it does so beyond any possible knowledge of this domination." I take it that this separation of the being of the historical world from epistemological access to that world is symptomatic of what I am calling Gadamer's realism. Thus Gadamer's disinterest in traditional philosophical positions, such as the version of empiricism that logical positivism promoted in the years prior to the appearance of *Truth and Method,* is due to his suspicion that such accounts of the theory of knowledge are deeply relativistic. They reduce, in his view, the truth of the being of the world, and thus the understanding of the being of the world, to how the world appears to us.

Though one can sympathize with criticizing relativism and defending realism, and though Gadamer is correct to stress that empiricism is an archetype of epistemological antirealism, he is frustratingly evasive on precisely how a theory of interpretation provides an alternative account of knowledge, distinct from both the philosophical tradition and the claims of the sciences, that at the same time does not degenerate into dogmatism. If I understand Gadamer's reasons for rejecting empiricism, then his continuing to speak of the being of the world as disclosed in experience must somehow capture a sense of experience distinct from that of perceiving the world, as the term is normally used in philosophy. Though it is possible to appeal to "insights" transcending the sensory limitations of human knowledge, Gadamer's own position also excludes such appeals. "But in truth there is nothing that is simply 'there.' Everything that is said and is there in the text stands under anticipations" (PH 121).

Gadamer's central philosophical concern, however, turns out not to be skepticism or even relativism about knowledge. Rather, he seems at the same time to aim at the more modest project of arguing that interpretation theory is the proper prolegomena for any future philosophical study of knowledge and being. In this fashion, Gadamer adapts an aspect of Husserl's enterprise, though, as will be seen, leaving the bulk of the phenomenological apparatus behind. Similarly, though he wants to defend Heidegger's efforts to revive ontology, he does so in such a way as to show how the disclosure of being is, in effect, a prephilosophical interpretative result that makes philosophical debates, such as those between realists and empiricists, possible. Only on the basis of our already understanding the world in the way Gadamer hopes to capture can philosophical problems arise with regard to the justification of knowledge and its objectivity.

My intent is to outline Gadamer's views on these matters in three stages. I begin with his relation to Husserl and the problem of epistemological realism. I then turn to Gadamer's efforts to subordinate the theory of interpretation to a theory of truth. Finally, I discuss his specific dependence on Heidegger's conception of ontology and the problem of circularity and prejudgment in interpretation. It will emerge that Gadamer returns to the same response in these three different contexts, namely, to a particular kind of defense of tradition and prejudice that I have been calling externalist.

Bridge to Realities

Though Gadamer retains the term "phenomenology" and even refers to "phenomenological research" and "phenomenological exercises" within his work, Husserl's method is not quite the same as the theory of interpretation.[5]

> The idea of "phenomenology"—i.e., bracketing all positing of being and investigating the subjective modes of givenness ... was to make intelligible all objectivity, all being-sense. But human subjectivity also possesses being-value. Thus it too can be regarded as a "phenomenon" and can be explored in the various modes of givenness. This exploration of the "I" as phenomenon is not the "inner perception" of a real "I," nor is it the mere reconstruction of "consciousness"—i.e., the relation of the contents of consciousness to a transcendental "I" pole (Natorp), but it is a highly differentiated theme of transcendental reflection. In contrast to the mere givenness of the phenomena of objective consciousness, a givenness in intentional experiences, this reflection constitutes a new dimension of research. For there is such a thing as givenness that is not itself the object of intentional acts. Every experience has implicit horizons of before and after, and finally fuses with the continuum of the experiences present in the before and after to form a unified flow of experience. (TM 244–245)

This passage exemplifies the stylistic ambiguity I mentioned earlier. The third sentence, "But human subjectivity also possesses being-value," shifts from what appears to be an exposition of phenomenology to an implicit criticism of Husserl, because it raises the challenge, discussed at length in Chapters 1 and 2, as to whether transcendental subjectivity escapes bracketing. Yet Gadamer then freely characterizes Husserl's aim as to "grasp the mode of being" by way of the "flow of experience" and to "draw subjectivity into the intentional investigation of correlation." These passages, saturated with an ontological reading of Husserl's program, which I criticized in Chapter 1, lead to a claim that Husserl focuses on the concept of life. "'Life' is not just the unreflective living characteristics of the natural attitude. 'Life' is also, and no less, the transcendentally reduced subjectivity that is the source of all objectifications" (TM 248).

In the essay "The Phenomenological Movement," in which Gadamer sets out to dispassionately settle accounts with Husserl and Heidegger, he gives a slightly different version of the significance of Husserl's method.

> [Phenomenology] wanted to bring the phenomena to expression, that is, it sought to avoid every unwarranted construction and to subject the unquestioned domination of philosophical theories to critical examination. ... But above all, it aimed its attacks at the construction that dominated epistemology. ... When epistemological inquiry sought to answer the question of how the subject, filled with his own representations, knows the external world and can be certain of its reality, the phenomenological critique showed how pointless such a question is. It saw that consciousness is by no means a self-enclosed sphere with its representations locked up in their own inner world. On the contrary, consciousness is, according to its own essential structure, already

with objects. Epistemology asserts a false priority of self-consciousness. There are no representative images of objects in consciousness, whose correspondence to things themselves it is the real problem of epistemology to guarantee. The image we have of things is rather in general the mode in which we are conscious of things themselves. (PH 131)

First, this passage's way of characterizing Husserl's criticisms of traditional philosophy and science contrasts with Husserl's own statement in *Ideas:*

> It is not now a matter of excluding all prejudices that cloud the pure objectivity of research, not a matter of constituting a science "free of theories," "free of metaphysics," by grounding all of which go back to the immediate findings, nor a matter of means for attaining such ends, about the value of which there is indeed, no question. What *we* demand lies in another direction. (Ideas 62)

Husserl did not criticize scientific theories for "simplifying" reality, as Gadamer puts it. I believe there is a confusion in the above account between Husserl's warning against the role of presuppositions in the exercise of phenomenological descriptions, which precede serious philosophical and scientific debate, and the possibility of a phenomenological reconstruction of abstractions in both geometry and the physical sciences. These possible reconstructions, however, are not pursued by Husserl for the purpose of condemning geometry, or any theory for that matter; the problem of "unwarranted constructions" is only an issue for the philosophy of mathematics or science.

The central point of this discussion of Husserl, however, is epistemological realism. Husserl's realism, Gadamer claims, is in a response to the futility of traditional epistemology. "When epistemological inquiry sought to answer the question of how the subject, filled with his own representations, knows the external world and can be certain of its reality, the phenomenological critique showed how pointless such a question is" (PH 131). Though Husserl did hope to show the inadequacy of much traditional epistemology, it is too strong to present Husserl's realism as dismissing epistemology, even in its traditional form. Naive realism, as exemplified, for instance, in naturalism, is as anathema to Husserl as is most traditional philosophy.

What Husserl embraces from the tradition, as I presented him, is internalism with regard to epistemology and yet also realism ("the question of how the subject, filled with his own representations, knows the external world and can be certain of its reality"). But, in this way, Husserl's project can be described as continuous with the philosophical tradition; and I believe Husserl understood it in precisely that fashion, as I quoted him on the continuing significance of Descartes, Locke, Leibniz, Hume, and Kant. Gadamer's analysis of Husserl is, on the other hand, saturated with Heidegger's reconception of both philosophy and phenomenology and thus, implicitly, a deeper rejection of the philosophical tradition and its emphasis on epistemology (at the cost of ontology) as moribund and myopic.

Gadamer's answer to Husserl's internalism is to stress, against Husserl, the constitution of one's internal representations by external historical traditions. Gadamer's defense of justification is, then, externalist, to repeat the terminology introduced in Chapters 1 and 3. For this reason, Gadamer's thought abandons the very core of phenomenology. Rather than finding some feature of the internal mental states of the reflective subject, it is the authority of tradition (or the authority of "our prejudices," as Gadamer likes to counterintuitively make his point) that alone justifies knowledge claims and makes possible a representation of the world. Thus, the authority of cultural traditions is not merely a prejudice, as that term is normally used in its negative sense, but, as Hilary Putnam put it, the realization that meaning "ain't merely in one's head"; it is tradition and its social practices that bridge the mind and the world.

> The epistemological question must be asked here in a fundamentally different way. We have shown above that Dilthey saw this, but was not able to escape his entanglement in traditional epistemology. Since he started from the awareness of "experiences" *(Erlebnisse)*, he was unable to build a bridge to the historical realities, because the great historical realities of society and state always have a predeterminate influence on any "experience." Self-reflection and autobiography—Dilthey's starting points—are not primary and are therefore not an adequate basis for the hermeneutical problem, because through them history is made private once more. In fact history does not belong to us; we belong to it. Long before we understand ourselves through the process of self-examination, we understand ourselves in a self-evident way in the family, society, and state in which we live. The focus of subjectivity is a distorting mirror. The self-awareness of the individual is only a flickering in the closed circuits of historical life. *That is why the prejudices of the individual, far more than his judgements, constitute the historical reality of his being.* (TM 276–277)

Gadamer's defense of traditionalism as external justification of knowledge, though an interesting line of criticism against Husserl (downplayed in the above quote by directing his point against Dilthey), is not developed into a full response to the problem of realism as Gadamer poses it and as he claims it arises within Husserl's phenomenology. First, Gadamer does not consider how accepting the authority of prejudgment can be made distinct from, for example, the subjectivism he rejects. It falls to Gadamer to show that cases of acquiescing to external authority are distinguishable from those in which biases are imposed and thereby the being of the world "distorted" by prejudice in its negative sense.

Externalism, as that view has gained adherents within the naturalistic approach in the analytic tradition, answers this demand by allowing the sciences to determine external epistemic authority. For instance, a complex causal theory of perception or cognition supplies the proper response to any further demand for epistemological support and allows for a distinction between representations that distort and representations that "disclose." But such a solution is unavailable to Gadamer, who rejects epistemological naturalism and embraces the effort to purge bias through an entirely interpretative exercise.

The issue is that Husserl needs a defense of realism in the fully relational sense, not just the adverbial sense. By that I mean, he needs to defend not simply that there is always an object internal to our experience of the world, what he called an intentional object, but an object existing independently of that internal object of thought that is somehow disclosed through or captured by our representations of it.

There are usually thought to be two ways to respond to such a question. Either one produces some account of reference in both its adverbial and fully relational forms, and I believe Husserl attempted such a response. Or one rejects the question as pointless and thereby abandons the philosophical project of providing foundations for knowledge claims, as it appears to me was Heidegger's or Quine's strategy. But if the question about realism is pointless, as Gadamer claims in the above quote on Husserl when he says "the phenomenological critique showed how pointless such a question is," then the authority of tradition could not provide a justification for metaphysical realism or a defense of the possibility of fundamental ontology. In other words, there could be neither the separate task of justification nor the purely philosophical inquiry announced in Heidegger's early writings.

If the question is not pointless for Gadamer, then, as I argued above, somehow the authority of tradition has to be shown to provide the proper justification. But Gadamer does not provide that defense and, especially toward the end of the book, seems to arrive comfortably at some sort of historicism. But if he is a historicist, then the project of *Truth and Method* is deeply inconsistent; and if he is not, the project remains crucially incomplete.

What, then, makes Gadamer's response obscure is that he fails to explain how cultural traditions, as external to the subject, provide any kind of epistemic authority and specifically how they provide that foundation without adopting the assumptions of epistemological naturalism. The interpretative exercise is presented by Gadamer as similar to Husserl's effort at systematic reflection on meaning given the suspension of all prejudgment. But, at the same time, interpretation is presented as a criticism of that effort and a defense of the priority, even absolute priority, of certain prejudgment; nothing is "there" without anticipations, Gadamer warns, and thereby the very effort of any purely internal epistemological justification is belittled.

But can Gadamer have it both ways? Gadamer cannot make this case by simply appealing to the words "authority" and "prejudice," since they are ambiguous (as he admits) between their illicit and legitimate functions; for example, the distortion of the world by rampant subjectivity is as much a prejudice as is the proper prejudgment already there in a cultural tradition. Although it is of etymological interest that "prejudice" means both "bias" and "proper prejudgment," what is at issue and what is thus left mysterious is how to distinguish them on other than naturalistic, pragmatic, or subjective grounds.

Second, and perhaps more telling, Gadamer nowhere in his lengthy writings on these issues makes clear what he means by the key word "tradition." Gadamer mentions, as in the above quote, the "historical realities" of state, family, and society. But in other passages "tradition" stands for any kind of prejudgment, fore-meaning, or "fore-structure," including intellectual conceptions in philosophy, art, and science. These passing comments are hardly helpful, since they do not identify what specific aspect of any of these usages is claimed to be authoritative for purposes of justifying interpretations, let alone bridging internal representations and the world.

Gadamer has certain intuitions concerning proper and improper appeals to tradition and prejudice in the complex process of defending and explicating interpretative meaning. But his own intuitions provide as arbitrary an answer to the question of validity in interpretation as the subjectivism they are meant to replace. If tradition and prejudice simply stand for the "historical conditions," as the above quote concludes, then it is difficult to see how they also provide an epistemological justification at all, assuming Gadamer is not simply an epistemological naturalist in spite of himself. The external, causal process by which knowledge is in fact acquired is one way in which traditions function in the production of knowledge. But Gadamer appeals to tradition in the context of justifying the objectivity of knowledge, and he claims to have bracketed any claims made about how the world causally works.

Gadamer is correct to seek a defense against subjectivism and skepticism. The above line of response to the problem of realism, however, is simply not philosophically adequate to this defense. Gadamer, in effect, condemns naturalism while offering a quasi-naturalistic response to relativism and subjectivism. He escapes philosophical disputes, much as the naturalist does, by appealing to some fact about the external world; the difference is that Gadamer's facts about the world are not within the purview of science, but within his as yet undefended conception of history. Gadamer's position could be made more coherent if he were completely abandoning Husserl's attack on naturalized epistemology, but, as it stands, it's neither fish nor fowl.

Holding True

One of Gadamer's stronger arguments in the book is the case he makes for the dependence of interpretation on truth, rather than on method, a dependence, he argues, that properly checks both arbitrariness and dogmatism in interpretation.

> The hermeneutical task becomes of itself a questioning of things and is always in part so defined. This places hermeneutical work on a firm basis. A person trying to understand something will not resign himself from the start to relying on his own accidental fore-meanings, ignoring as consistently and stubbornly as possible the actual meaning of the text until the latter becomes so persistently audible that it breaks through what the interpreter imagines it to be. Rather, a person trying to understand a text is prepared for it to tell him something. That is why a hermeneutically trained consciousness must be, from the start, sensitive to the text's alterity. But this kind of sensitivity involves neither "neutrality" with respect to content nor the extinction of one's self, but the foregrounding and appropriation of one's own fore-meanings and prejudices. The important thing is to be aware of one's own bias, so that the text can present itself in all its otherness and thus assert its own truth against one's own fore-meaning. (TM 269)

There is much of Husserl in this passage: the search for secure foundations, the warning against naïveté, the strategy of excluding whatever is accidental or contingent, the notion of objective meaning, and the effort to systematically exclude presuppositions. The weakness in the passage is the striking absence of an explicit theory of meaning that his theory of interpretation presupposes.

For my purposes I simply take it as given that Gadamer's rejection of method is a rejection of the views, for instance, of the logical positivists (Weinsheimer repeatedly makes this claim in his account of *Truth and Method*). But a theory of meaning precedes a theory of method, even for the logical positivists. For instance, in logical positivism the theory of meaning consists of the manner in which a statement is verified, and it is explicitly presupposed within the positivist account of the scientific method. It was this explicitly presupposed theory of meaning that became the focus of a subsequent generation of philosophical dispute. One serious weakness of logical positivism, therefore, was its misplaced confidence that its theory of meaning would prove uncontroversial and that it carried no philosophical special pleading. Standing against methodology, if Gadamer is read as rejecting logical positivism, does not at all allow him to also likewise presuppose a theory of meaning sustaining the possibility of interpretation.

Second, the failure to discuss a theory of meaning raises the specter of the kind of naïveté Gadamer warned against in the above quotation. The criticism of the conception of meaning in logical positivism showed, as Husserl had been among the first to stress, how important such unquestioned presuppositions may be within philosophical debates and how they contribute to making such debates unresolvable. Gadamer's silence on this issue has a similar effect, as I will try to show.

I want to suggest two possible accounts of meaning that I believe could be taken to operate implicitly and unnoticed in much of Gadamer's characterization of interpretative understanding. Following a phrase suggested by Michael Dummett, I call the first model "the code theory of meaning," a conception that Dummett suggests pervades both philosophical and commonsense accounts of meaning. The second model is very briefly adapted from Donald Davidson's account of how a theory of truth can, by way of what is called the "principle of charity" (explained further below), fix interpretations of the actions or languages of others.[6] In particular, I think that Davidson's model, though not entirely harmonious with Gadamer's intent, suggests a plausible way in which truth, meaning, and interpretation might fit together supporting at least some of Gadamer's aims.

Before discussing the two models, I begin with a passage exemplifying the account of interpretation at issue. Though Gadamer is discussing Schleiermacher in the following passage, his other writings suggest (and most commentators agree) that this passage can be taken as also representing Gadamer's view. The central question I will raise about the passage is how precisely truth constrains such understanding of others.

> We begin with this proposition: "to understand means to come to an understanding with each other" *(sich miteinander verstehen)*. Understanding is, primarily, agreement *(Verständnis ist zunächst Einverständnis)*. Thus people usually understand *(verstehen)* each other immediately, or they make themselves understood *(verständigen sich)* with a view toward reaching agreement *(Einverständnis)*. Coming to an understanding *(Verständigung)*, then, is always coming to an understanding about something. Understanding each other *(Sichverstehen)* is always understanding each other with respect to something. From language we learn that the subject matter *(Sache)* is not merely an arbitrary object of discussion, independent of the process of mutual understanding *(Sichverstehen)*, but rather in the path and goal of mutual understanding itself. And if two people understand each other independently of any topic, then this means that they understand each other not only in this or that respect, but in all the essential things that unite human beings. Understanding becomes a special task only when natural life, this joint meaning of the meant where both intend a common *subject matter*, is disturbed. ... The real problem of understanding obviously arises when, in the endeavor to understand the context of what is said, the reflective question arises: how did he come to such an opinion? For this kind of question reveals an alienness that is clearly of a quite different kind and ultimately signifies a renunciation of shared meaning. (TM 180–181)

The above passage envisages what philosophers now call a situation of radical translation. Many contemporary philosophers with otherwise diverse aims appear to agree that thought experiments concerning reaching agreement or communicating under conditions of possible conceptual disagreement have great philosophical importance. They have the supposed advantage of posing recalcitrant questions concerning a theory of meaning in the form of more amenable questions concerning how to translate the expressions of others. We are thereby presented with thought experiments concerning Eden-like encounters with and observations of others whom we hope to understand, even though with whom we lack the background assumptions and agreements common to everyday life in societies much like our own.

The code model of language is one suggested answer to this question. How might language assist us in reaching agreements or understanding one another, as pictured above? Perhaps language is a substitute for telepathy, as Dummett boldly puts it. We seek understanding about some matter of fact by seeking to convey a preliminary understanding of our own thoughts to others. Thus, in communicating with others to reach agreement, it is first a matter of somehow externalizing one's thoughts, transmitting them, and determining whether these others can decipher the transmission. Given externalization, not only is agreement with others possible but, to speak a little nonsense, agreement with oneself is possible. One's own thoughts become subject to the same refinement and self-correction by externalization that is possible with regard to the thought of others; one's mind and thus the minds of others become in this way open to scrutiny.

The model suggests, then, that concepts, as the units of thought, are encoded into words and sentences, mirroring in some complex way the thoughts that are transmitted to and decoded by others. A passage in which Gadamer discusses how writing fixes thought content evokes precisely this model.

> Nothing is so purely the trace of the mind as writing, but nothing is so dependent on the understanding mind either. In deciphering and interpreting it, a miracle takes place: the transformation of something alien and dead into total contemporaneity and familiarity. This is like nothing else that comes down to us from the past. The remnants of past life—what is left of buildings, tools, the contents of graves—are weather-beaten by the storms of time that have swept over them, whereas a written tradition, once deciphered and read, is to such an extent pure mind that it speaks to us as if in the present. (TM 163)

There may be many weaknesses in this account of meaning, but I restrict myself to how the coding picture clashes with other desiderata of Gadamer's view, specifically with regard to interpretation and the aim of understanding.

The first objection to the code model of meaning is that it violates Gadamer's claim of the universal scope of interpretation. In other words, the model conceives of communication as translating another language on the basis of one's own language. But it leaves implicit the view that one's understanding of the meaning of one's own thought or language is direct and noninterpretative. Since understanding others is based on self-understanding in the code model, not only would the universal scope of interpretation contract, but also its philosophical significance would erode. The direct access to one's own thought would thus be the primary basis of knowledge and interpretative tasks a poor second cousin.

There are two kinds of response to this point. First, it could simply be held that Gadamer's theory must embrace this primitive level of understanding as the basis for any further interpretative understanding. But Gadamer does explicitly argue against such an idea when he ridicules positing any direct access to meaning, even internal to the subject, as discussed in the previous section on Husserl. The second response to the above objection might be to treat the understanding of one's own thought, as I did in my account above, as itself a provisional hypothesis open to the same interpretative pattern of understanding; one could be said to interpret oneself and one's own meanings as one interprets others. This second response seems more in harmony with Gadamer's overall account and is suggested by the quotation above.

But a second criticism of the code model shows the inadequacy of even this response. As I quoted above, Gadamer makes agreement involve not mere agreement about a given topic, but agreement on related matters and background assumptions: "Two people understand each other not only in this or that respect, but in all the essential things that unite human beings."

Broad agreement is required due to what he considers the holistic features of meaning, already discussed. Thoughts, even in the coding model, could not be grasped atomistically, one at a time, but only as systematically interrelated. To understand what another believes about a hammer involves understanding and reaching agreement about a vast web of related concepts concerning tools, purposes, human actions, design, nature, and even time. Furthermore, the meaning of our thoughts is for Gadamer, as it was for Husserl, an objective aspect of the world, not a private psychological datum.

But when holism is combined with a view of meaning as an objective, nonnatural feature of the world, it becomes difficult to see how a coding and decoding model of meaning accounts for understanding. The holism of meaning makes the picture of coding and decoding redundant. For the decodings to be successful, they would have to maintain or reproduce the holistic feature of the speaker's meaning (the thoughts of the one being decoded). The only way to impose that constraint would be to already grasp meaning independent of this coding and decoding of one's words and sentences. The code theory of meaning thus presupposes the understanding it is supposed to explicate. This type of circularity would, however, be vicious; and Gadamer agrees, as will be discussed in the next section, that interpretation is not viciously circular.

There is, however, another way to conceive the connection between interpretation and truth in which interpretation is constrained by a maxim to preserve and maximize truths with regard to the world between those with whom we reach an agreement or mutual understanding. This second model subordinates interpretation to truth, in a way developed below, allowing for the possibility of learning from others, as Gadamer puts it. Thus such an account, if it could be formulated, would allow for what Gadamer labels the "absolute validity" of interpretation, without it simply reducing to a matter of dogmatism.

The anthropological fantasy of translating native languages is meant to drive home a hermeneutic lesson. We can fail to understand aliens in two contrastive ways: by trying to become one with them, "going native" as it's called, or by maintaining an imperial distance above them. In either case, the hermeneutic goal of insight along with agreement is lost.

Thus, for Gadamer, the mere act of producing a translation is not what is philosophically important about the story. There may be many ways to translate what aliens say or do, and perhaps there is no way to determine which of these possible translations is the right one. But the deeper issue, presupposed in any translation, is understanding others. We must ask: How do we come to understand them, even if there are various ways to translate them?

Intelligibility, meaning, understanding, and translation are, then, a tight family of notions due, in part, to the holistic and circular features outlined in the introduction. This second model of meaning is supposed to provide some insight into what controls or constrains this tight circle of guesswork and therefore the projection and correction of provisional judgments concerning what these peoples are doing and saying. It is such provisional guesswork, recall, that is supposed to be refined into agreement and understanding.

The principle of charity is offered, then, as just the right sort of guide. Given the anthropologist's radical situation with regard to the natives, where does she begin? She begins by assuming that the natives share with her "all the essential things that unite human beings." Thus in asking how they came to their opinions, she is asking how she came to her opinions. What the principle then demands is that she understand them in such a way that what they believe about the world is largely true, just as what she believes about the world is largely true. That is a kind of respect for them.

Why, then, is the principle of charity not satisfied by "going native"? Because the aim is agreement, understanding, and insight. If the anthropologist simply abandons whatever she thinks about the world, then she is neither understanding the natives nor is she capable of learning from them; "going native" is imitation, not insight.

Truth enters this story in a special way. Truth usually has at least three distinct contexts in which it arises. First, some philosophers have been interested in describing how truth is customarily used or in answering more technical questions about how truth functions for formal languages. Second, and more ambitiously, there are traditional metaphysical problems concerning what makes truth possible. This more obscure project has often involved consideration of whether correspondence or coherence is the proper type of relationship for truth; it also includes disputes about what stands in the corresponding or cohering relation in the case of truth. Third, philosophers of science have been interested in the more practical or methodical question of how to determine the truth-value of empirical claims. This third project concerning evidence and justification is often dismissed by Gadamer as deeply mistaken. But these different questions can easily bleed into one another and it seems possible that philosophers could give different answers to such questions.

Gadamer introduces the concept of truth, I am cautiously suggesting, as the proper constraint on provisional guesswork in determining meaning for the purpose of understanding others. In saying that we understand others as truth-seekers, just like ourselves, a subjective or purely practical aim of interpretation is blocked. As Davidson puts it:

> This process of devising a theory of truth for an unknown native tongue . . . is intended to solve the problem of the interdependence of belief and meaning by holding belief constant as far as possible while solving for meaning. This is accomplished by assigning truth conditions to alien sentences that make native speakers right when plausibly possible, according, of course, to our own view of what is right. What justifies the procedure is the fact that disagreement and agreement alike are intelligible only against a background of massive agreement. Applied to language, this principle reads: the more sentences we conspire to accept or reject . . . the better we understand the rest, whether or not we agree with them.[7]

Therefore, this picture achieves two of Gadamer's goals. We dismiss a priori the possibility of massive error and massive disagreement with others. Interpretative understanding excludes, from the start, that those we understand have a great many false beliefs about the world or are utterly confused about the world. Fearing the possibility of such a discrepancy between minds and their common world is then merely a philosophical pseudoproblem. It marks a failure in understanding, not a new threat of skepticism.

Second, the traditional methodological approach to knowledge has the problem backward. It is not that there is a technique by which truths about the world are determined. Rather, it is truth or "the disclosure of the being of the world in our encountering the world," as Gadamer prefers to state it, that makes possible knowledge, thus making possible procedures for arriving at knowledge. It is truth that imposes upon the exercise of interpretation a deep and necessarily reflective constraint, not a method that could guarantee truth as its automatic result.

Though I think the above picture may plausibly fit some central passages in *Truth and Method,* the principle of charity is finally not strong enough, given all Gadamer's aims. In the charitable conception, the beliefs of others are preserved as *largely* true; thus there is a certain flexibility with regard to understanding others. What consists in the others' beliefs being largely true is in the end up to us. In other words, even if we are prepared to learn from others and change our beliefs as a result of such an encounter, it is only on the basis of their beliefs coming out largely true in agreement with us.

The ability to understand others, therefore, does not produce, all by itself, the kind of realism Gadamer entertains, but only the weaker claim that the belief systems we can understand are the belief systems largely like our own. This presupposition says nothing about the being of the world, at least not as such. Thus these epistemological reflections lead back to the problem posed in the introduction as to whether interpretative conclusions are deeply indeterminate. Even the constraint of truth, apparently, cannot establish "absolute validity" in interpretation.

Vicious and Virtuous Circles

Up to this point I have proceeded in a somewhat misleading fashion. I have presented Gadamer's thought as focused solely on epistemological questions. Specifically I have explicated his views in terms of the defense of realism and the validity of interpretation as making possible knowledge. But Gadamer speaks of his project as an ontological one. He speaks of prejudices not as judgments about the world, but as "our being." Furthermore, he thinks a philosophical preoccupation with epistemological issues is a symptom of "forgetting the question of being," to use the Heideggerian charge of philosophical myopia. I therefore turn to interpretation as the study of being.

Gadamer's vocabulary and central themes are taken wholesale from Heidegger's characterization of the "analytic of existence" as a "hermeneutic of Dasein." I did not explicitly cover this material in Chapter 2 and therefore will briefly discuss that aspect of Heidegger here. In the beginning of *Being and Time,* after reviewing various "crises in foundation" occurring in mathematics, physics, biology, and theology, Heidegger describes such crises as turning points at which mature disciplines question their fundamental concepts. These fundamental concepts require the pretheoretical activity of interpretation. "This preliminary research that creates the fundamental concepts amounts to nothing else than interpreting these beings in terms of the basic constitution of their being" (BT 8–9, SZ 10).

Heidegger considers an objection, in this context, to the way he is proceeding. "Asking this question, as a mode of being of a being, is itself essentially determined by what is asked about in it—being" (BT 6, SZ 7). Heidegger calls this objection an accusation that his effort is viciously circular. Though Heidegger's discussion of this objection and his subsequent reply to it are very sketchy, as usual, the idea behind the objection is worth attempting to expand a bit. The charge of vicious circularity is the claim that an inquiry is illicit because its conclusion has been assumed; it is often stated as a charge of "begging the question." What is illicit about it is that the argument establishes its conclusion by appealing, in an underhanded way, to assuming the truth of the conclusion. As can be seen, even stating the objection is difficult, since some properly structured and valid argument patterns can also be said to assume the truth of their conclusion.

In the case of Heidegger's discussion I would imagine the objection he is considering is that the conclusion of the existential analytic, which is the demonstration that the being of Dasein is to understand the meaning of being (its being is to ask the question of the meaning of being), is already found at the start of the book when Heidegger simply defines Dasein as "asking the question of the meaning of being." Since that definition leads to the existential analytic of Dasein, the procedure is circular.

Heidegger's reply to this objection is also traditional. He contrasts "vicious" with "virtuous" circularity. In benign, or virtuous, circularity, the tentative grasp or "preliminary look" concerning where the inquiry is headed, and even what makes such inquiry possible, is not explicitly presupposed but reflected upon within that inquiry; it is not smuggled in like contraband. "Beings can be determined in their being without the explicit concept of the meaning of being having to be already available" (BT 6, SZ 8). Furthermore, Heidegger notes that this virtuous circular pattern of understanding is common in everyday life. "This guiding look at being grows out of the average understanding of being in which we are always already involved *and which ultimately belongs to the essential constitution of Dasein itself*" (BT 6, SZ 8).

Heidegger repeats this distinction when he discusses the role of a "forestructure" in understanding or interpretation. Interpretation or understanding are what Heidegger calls the "fundamental mode of the being of Dasein." Understanding is thus an existential structure. Heidegger also discusses the category of "discourse," a third existential structure, which "articulates intelligibility." He calls the articulation of intelligibility "the study of meaning." This house of cards around the notion of meaning is supposed to fix Heidegger's central notion of disclosure or "disclosedness," the appearance of beings as the meaning of being. Hence, interpretation is, as Gadamer often repeats, nothing more than fundamental ontology.

Discourse articulates whatever is intelligible about the world through communication, which, as an ontological concept, is more than the transmission of information. Communication is Dasein's being in the world—so goes the Heideggerian mantra. Likewise, discourse is not simply a matter of expressing the content of one's mind to others, it is "being outside." "The communication of the existential possibilities of attunement, that is, the disclosing of existence, can become the true aim of 'poetic' speech" (BT 152, SZ 163).

To summarize, Heidegger says that the being of Dasein is disclosed by the structure of interpretation. But since interpretation has what Heidegger calls a "fore-structure," he must defend the virtuous circularity involved in the "preliminary look" ("fore-sight"). Therefore, the strategy is that discourse, understood ontologically, makes the fore-structure explicit and thereby makes explicit the question of being. Though the whole effort is reflective and circular, it is not vicious or illicit. The project makes explicit, by this reflective effort, the structure of "making intelligible." Though admittedly the project is not possible without some preliminary projection, this pattern of reflective circularity still serves to enrich inquiry.

Heidegger also warns against a negative feature of this circular structure that he calls "idle talk." In this way the "obviousness" of these assumptions leads away from self-reflection and clarification. "This closing off is aggravated anew by the fact that idle talk, in which an understanding of what is being talked about is supposedly reached, holds any new questioning and discussion at a distance because it presumes it has understood and in a peculiar way it suppresses them and holds them back" (BT 158, SZ 169).

Even the simplest, empirical statements about the world have this complex fore-structure and thus contain the possibility of both fundamental ontology (the interpretation of being that begins with the prosaic examples of hammers and everyday encounters) and the threat of "closing off" inquiry by "idle talk" as the mere presumption of understanding.

> The statement's pointing out is accomplished on the basis of what is already disclosed in understanding or what is circumspectly discovered. The statement is not an unattached kind of behavior which could of itself primarily disclose beings in general, but always already maintains itself on the basis of being-in-the world. . . . The fore-conception always also contained in the statement remains mostly inconspicuous because language always already contains a developed set of concepts. Like interpretation in general, the statement necessarily has its existential foundations in fore-having, fore-sight, and fore-conception (BT 146–147, SZ 157).

These are the basic ideas Gadamer weaves throughout his own work and with which he sustains his conclusion that "understanding is Dasein's mode of being" (TM 259).

> Heidegger's hermeneutical phenomenology and his analysis of Dasein's historicity had as their aim renewing the question of being in general and not pro-

ducing a theory of the human sciences as overcoming the aporias of historicism. These were merely particular contemporary problems in which he was
able to demonstrate the consequences of his radical renewal of the question of
being. But precisely because of the radicalness of his approach he was able to
move beyond the complication on which Dilthey's and Husserl's investigations
into the fundamental concepts of the human sciences had foundered. . . . Heidegger, however, was able to make a completely fresh beginning because, as we
have seen, Husserl had made it an absolutely universal working method to go
back to life and hence had abandoned for good the narrow approach of simply
inquiring into the methods of the human sciences. His analysis of the life-
world . . . gave the question of objectivity in the human sciences a completely
new background of making science's concept of objectivity appear to be a special case. Science is anything but a fact from which to start. Rather, the constitution of the scientific world presents a special task, namely of clarifying the
idealization that is endemic to science. But this is not the most fundamental
task. When we go back to "productive life," the antithesis between nature and
spirit does not prove to be of ultimate validity. Both the human and the natural
sciences are to be understood as achievements of the intentionality of universal
life—i.e., of absolute historicity. Only this kind of understanding satisfies the
self-reflection of philosophy. (TM 258–259)

Gadamer's contribution to this topic involves explicating interpretation as
the middle course between traditional metaphysical speculation and scientific naturalism. The validity of interpretation opens up the possibility of
doing fundamental ontology in way lost since the rise of scientism and the
"forgetting of being" that distorts the philosophical tradition. I already
made the point that Heidegger's defense of the possibility of ontology is un-
satisfying, since it leaves the crucial notion of how the being of the world is
disclosed to Dasein, rather than merely the properties of beings of the
world, mysterious and intuitive. Hence Heidegger's own lapse into mysticism is hardly surprising, at least from my criticism of him.

Gadamer does attempt to provide a nonintuitive alternative to either mysticism or scientism by outlining how the exercise of interpretation would be
the appropriate mode of disclosure of the world's being, a mode presupposed by science, intuition, or philosophy. It depends on there being historical traditions, which escape the narrow concerns of the sciences, and it aims
at an understanding that does not reduce to private or subjective ends and
interests; it is the understanding of all who share our essential nature.

The way Gadamer goes about this defense of ontology is to expand the
category of Dasein. He takes Heidegger's analysis of Dasein as demonstrating
that the being of Dasein is also the being of history. Thus, in a kind of
Hegelian fashion, Gadamer wants to bring us to the realization that these traditions, prejudices, cultural externalities, works of art, historical actions, and
so on that he has invoked as the necessary anticipations or fore-meanings of
any possible inquiry are none other than ourselves; they are Dasein itself. In

studying the world, we are studying our own being, the being of that being whose being it is to ask the question of the meaning of being.

I do not think, in the end, Gadamer leads philosophy to a deep or enduring insight concerning the problem of ontology. My objection is not with the above style, though it is often not a little pompous. The problem is the disjunction between interpretation as outlined in his work and the question Gadamer believes Heidegger has raised. I agree that defending fundamental ontology, as far as I understand it, would likely involve defending some version of realism (the way things are independent of our claims about the way things are), the way the world is "over and above our wantings and doings," as Gadamer puts it. Furthermore, there may well be a defense of the distinction between ontology, the being of the world, and ontics, the beings in the world, even though I objected to that distinction in Chapter 2.

The question of ontology as Heidegger posed it, however, forces an additional question: Is there a discursive access to that way in which the world is, not just the way things in the world appear to us to be? It is possible to answer no and thereby turn away from philosophical ontology toward either the sciences (which tell us how things are in the world) or to some nondiscursive answer to the question of being, as Heidegger did later in his life. If, on the other hand, the answer is yes, as I think it is for Gadamer, then I cannot see how any theory of interpretation could account for that access to the being of the world; nor do I see how it serves to clarify Heidegger's use of the term "disclosure." Interpretation concerns the meaning or intelligibility of things, how the world is represented to us and others. How can the study of these diverse modes of presentation of the world tell us about the world "over and above our wantings and doings"? Such a constraint would demand that we represent the world "over and above" any possible representation of it for ourselves.

I agree with Gadamer that the aims of predicting or controlling phenomena are not necessarily a guide to the being of the natural world; nor is it likely that whatever is independent of "our doings and wantings" is also accessible to our senses (a point about which much contemporary philosophy of science now agrees). But if we exclude whatever science can tell us about the entities in the world and we restrict ourselves to meaning, as Husserl directed, the object of study seems to be the world as intentional object or meaning-correlate of thought. But, for anyone who takes Husserl seriously, the veil of looking inward blocks any ontological conclusion about these intentional objects, other than purely formal constraints, which are not Gadamer's concern. Therefore, the study of the being of the world in its fully relational sense is not amenable to interpretative inquiry; interpretation is precisely a study of the world in relation to whatever are "our wantings and doings."

What is missing in Gadamer is any persuasive argument against this separation I am forcing between matters of meaning and matters of being. The problem is that the way in which Gadamer understands the tightly knit circle of concepts of understanding, meaning, and representation leaves no point at which to locate the ontological significance of interpretation he wishes to preserve. Gadamer asserts that our representations of the world have broad, external content, since they are made possible by the cultures and traditions that precede and shape internal mental content. But Husserl did not doubt that our mental content was causally shaped by whatever was external to the mind, including our culture. Nor did Husserl argue that a complete account of meaning was possible within the artificial limits of bracketing required by the reduction. But Husserl did conclude that a philosophical account of meaning required systematically suspending inquiry into those external conditions of thought.

Thus none of the points Gadamer stresses in defense of the ontological significance of interpretation are persuasive, given the philosophical project he claims as his own. He could have explicitly embraced externalism or naturalism and agreed with others concerning the obsolescence of philosophy, but he did not. How a purely philosophical study of meaning becomes a study of the being of the world (the topic Husserl left to the sciences and Heidegger, eventually, to poetry) is a critical gap Gadamer neither closes nor seems to fully appreciate.

Nothing If Not Critical

Jürgen Habermas has produced in the course of the last four decades an extraordinary body of work stretching from sociological research to philosophy. He has written on epistemology, the philosophy of language, political philosophy, the philosophy of science, and ethics. Adhering to the limits of this book, I will ignore much of this work, specifically ethics and political philosophy, though he holds the view that his epistemology and ethics (or political theory) are internally linked and ought to be studied together.

Habermas explicitly identifies himself as a follower of the Frankfurt School or, more familiarly, the critical theory of society. Habermas has, with respect to this movement, taken on the task of providing what he considers proper philosophical foundations for its political and theoretical aims, specifically defending its basic distinctions between critical and traditional theory, science and ideology, and emancipatory and authoritarian social structures. My focus will be exclusively on Habermas's epistemological writings and within those writings specifically his criticisms of Gadamer, Husserl, and Heidegger.

Before I turn to Habermas's thought it is necessary to say a few more words about the movement of logical positivism. Habermas, like many philosophers in the continental tradition, presents significant parts of his epistemological and philosophical writings as a response to or criticism of logical positivism, easily one of the most influential movements in philosophy before and after World War II.

Though positivism exercised its greatest influence in the postwar period, it was born contemporaneously with Husserl. It defended the priority of science over philosophy and the tools of logical analysis over stylistic devices. Its main proponents and defenders emigrated to the United States and England during the war, and thus positivism gained a significant theoretical following among philosophers and scientists in England and the United States. Positivism's spirited defenses of scientific naturalism and attacks on philosophical obscurantism gained a certain moral force for it due in part to its founders' opposition to German fascism. The criticism many subsequently made, echoed eventually by nonpositivist intellectuals, was that the behavior of German intellectuals during the rise of German fascism and the failure of the German educational apparatus in view of its wartime military and civilian behavior were in part explained by attacks on science, reason, and liberalism in German intellectual culture prior to the rise of fascism.

It is difficult to give a summary of positivism in its twentieth-century version, since it embraces a diverse range of positions and complicated internal debates. Also Habermas, like many other continental philosophers, often uses the term less as the identification of a particular position within philosophy than as a general condemnation for those philosophers he disagrees with or dislikes. Even a critic of positivism, namely, Karl Popper, is lumped under the rubric of "positivist" because Popper defends the hypothetical-deductive method for the social and natural sciences (or simply because he defends some form of naturalized epistemology). But such an approach is deeply misleading since it would make the term "positivism," which ought to refer to a very specific view about the nature of science and philosophy, synonymous with epistemological naturalism as a whole. It is once again to Husserl's credit that he avoided such an approach and always stressed the distinction between positivism, which he characterized as a position about the evidential nature of sensation, and the general position of naturalism, under which he could include those opposed to both positivism and empiricism.

In fact, positivism may be unique in having generated internally its most trenchant critics.[8] Also thinkers such as Habermas, and many who follow him in his comments, exaggerate the degree of homogeneity within those they group as positivists. They also assume, unfortunately, that analytic philosophy, which is an equally diverse intellectual movement, can be treated as smoothly continuous with the legacy of positivism. These assumptions lead to the idea that there is an automatic connection between positivism as a theory of science and "scientism," a prejudice Habermas also labels "objectivism." But exhibiting the bias of "scientism," which I understand as the uncritical and unjustified acceptance of scientific claims and promotion of the scientific method beyond its appropriate sphere, does not automatically follow from positivism; nor does being a positivist entail being scientistic.

There are, however, two features of positivism that are worth stressing, even in the absence of a full-scale exposition of it. First, positivism embraced epistemological empiricism and thus adopted an antirealist account of scientific knowledge. For example, positivists have traditionally argued that the theoretical entities postulated by scientific theories are not actual entities in the world, but devices or "constructions," the currently fashionable word, whose purpose is to produce theoretical explanations of phenomena rather than speculate about ontology. Also, in the spirit of its antirealism, positivism sought to dismiss traditional philosophical problems, specifically with regard to the topics of metaphysics and ontology. It rejected as equally metaphysical and therefore equally empty both naturalism (physicalism) and idealism. Hence Husserl's careful distinction between positivism and naturalism was in part based on the fact that positivism claimed also to criticize scientific naturalism, though a very different type of criticism from Husserl's.

Second, positivists attempted to account for the concept of meaning by explicating it in terms of what they considered the clearer, operational notion of verification. It was an audacious and ambitious program, as mentioned above, aiming at the solution of a vast array of recalcitrant, yet central, philosophical problems. But it is an effort that has been largely abandoned by contemporary philosophy of language. The failures and inadequacies of the verificationist theory of meaning, which was the positivist's central tool, have been repeatedly pointed out by critics (for example, both the later Wittgenstein and the early Popper made precisely these kinds of objections). However, philosophers generally do not consider the effort to carry out such an ambitious program a worthless exercise. The sustained work it required raised and helped clarify important problems in the philosophy of logic and language, and thus the program contributed to the shape of contemporary philosophy, even if it must be judged to have oversimplified the essential task.

Habermas seeks an epistemological response to both of these assumptions. He wants to demonstrate the errors of empiricism at both the level of a theory of knowledge and at the level of its political implications; empiricism, he claims, leads to a political acceptance of the status quo. I doubt that such a criticism of empiricism amounts to more than a rhetorical argument, since I can see no way in which empiricists would be constrained to adopt the same political or moral views because of their epistemology. But I am only concerned with his epistemological argument against empiricism and his defense of a "transcendental epistemology."

On the question of the theory of meaning, Habermas adopts the justified criticism that the positivist theory of meaning was too narrow and inapplicable to normal, everyday functions. He connects that criticism with his defense of the cognitive significance of interpretative inquiry and the importance of ordinary language in guiding philosophy in its task of justifying and providing a foundation for knowledge claims. With regard to my criticism of Gadamer in the previous section, Habermas has in his most recent work begun to explicitly discuss issues with respect to a theory of meaning.[9]

Habermas's epistemological criticisms and clarifications are carried out in a way that can prove forbidding. His approach, equal parts impressive and irritating, is to digest great masses of theoretical work in both sociology and philosophy that he then places within classificatory schemes of his own design. Driven, apparently, by the need to catalog and organize the myriad debates in contemporary philosophy, he summaries and criticizes these viewpoints in a characteristic style of staccato bursts of adjective-laden nouns. His subsequent criticisms, when unpacked, often amount to pointing out that a given view fails to realize its place within the classificatory scheme Habermas has invented for it, or that it fails to answer certain questions that such a classificatory scheme would stress.

Habermas intersperses his discussions with brief expositions of a diverse range of contemporary and historical philosophers. Like Gadamer, Habermas's own philosophical argument is frequently welded together with expositions of past and present thinkers. These expositions, though often insightful, are frequently contentious and sketchy. A commentator is then faced with not only assessing Habermas's position, but the accuracy of his account of another's position; and often, as with Gadamer, the line between these two tasks blurs.[10]

In Defense of a Method

With regard to Habermas's critical response to Gadamer, I begin with their points of agreement. Habermas agrees with Gadamer that the exercise of interpretation is a mundane, common, ordinary feature of language that cannot be captured by methodical rules or strictures. "Hermeneutics mistrusts any mediatizing of ordinary languages and refuses to step out of their dimension; instead it makes use of the tendency to self-transcendence embedded in linguistic practice" (RGTM 244). Second, hermeneutics makes explicit and self-conscious the features of interpretative understanding that are normally presupposed and implicit on the basis of studying those cases in which there is resistance to understanding or in which there is some "distance" between the interpreter and that which is to be understood. "Linguistic understanding *(Sprachverstehen)* is based not only upon a primary mutual understanding *(Verständigtsein)* but also upon a hermeneutic understanding *(Verstehen)* that is articulated only when there are disturbances in communication" (RGTM 248). Third, Habermas agrees that interpretation, or hermeneutics, exhibits the "virtuous" kind of circularity discussed above: "We can decipher the parts of the text only if we anticipate an understanding—however diffuse—of the whole; and conversely, we can correct this anticipation *(Vorgriff)* only to the extent to which we explicate individual parts" (RGTM 252).

These points of agreement extend to Habermas's enlisting Gadamer in his general criticism of the evils of scientism and objectivism with regard to the social sciences in particular and modern culture in general. Hermeneutics contributes to the assault against scientism by showing that the study of society and history cannot be modeled upon the study of the natural world. Thus, for example, historical research, according to Habermas, could not consist of descriptions representing what happened in the past, that is, the past as it really was. History consists, in contrast, in rendering those past events intelligible to us in the present. He also agrees with Gadamer that intelligibility is neither merely giving one's subjective opinion nor recording one's psychological responses; interpretation demands philosophical clarification.

> The historian does not observe from the perspective of the actor but describes events and actions out of the experiential horizon of a history that goes beyond the actor's horizon of expectations. . . . Thus the language in which the historian presents events does not primarily express observations but the interrelations of a series of interpretations. The interpretation of contemporary observers is the last rung on a ladder of interpretations. Its first rung is the reference system of the historian, which, insofar as he is himself an acting subject, cannot be independent of his horizon of expectations. The ladder itself is the relationship of tradition that connects the historian with his object. It is constructed from the retrojections of those coming later who, knowing better, have reconstructed what happened in the schema of possible action. The historian is no chronicler restricted to observation; he is engaged in communicative experiences. Instead of the uninvolved recording of events, we have the task of hermeneutic understanding. At the level of historical presentation it proves to be meaningless to want to separate something like a pure description of the chronicler from interpretation. (RGTM 258)

This passage is an example of one in which it is difficult to decide, even in context, whether Habermas is speaking of his own view or summarizing Gadamer's views. The point of disagreement between them, at any rate, seems to reside primarily in how to properly respond to the worry that interpretation does not admit of "correctness." Habermas does think that the validity of interpretation can be defended, though, like Gadamer, he is not clear what concept of meaning is presupposed by this task.

But Habermas is clear that defending the validity of interpretation cannot depend on naturalism; that is, it ought not to involve appealing to additional matters of fact concerning biological instincts, perceptual psychology, or the nature of the physical world as pictured in the sciences.[11] Rather, Habermas agrees that there can be, on the contrary, a separate and independent epistemological defense. Interpretations have meanings (whether involving actions, symbols, or texts) as their objects of study and about which they make knowledge claims. Habermas considers the necessity involved here as demanding a transcendental epistemology. "I find Gadamer's real achievement in the demonstration that hermeneutic understanding is linked with transcendental necessity to the articulation of an action orienting self-understanding" (RGTM 260).

The term "transcendental" has already been encountered in Husserl, where it is used to identify the dimension of philosophical inquiry concerning not the nature of objects and their causal relations, but the possibility of such matters of fact having the meaning they do as objects of knowledge. I will return below to a longer discussion of Habermas's use of this term and his epistemology. For the moment all I want to emphasize is that Habermas considers interpretations knowledge claims, admitting of truth and falsity, and bearing a necessary, a priori relation, not just a factual, causal relation, to their object.

I summarized and criticized Gadamer's answer to this epistemological question in terms of how the notion of tradition could provide the proper justification. My criticism of this strategy was that it amounted, albeit unintentionally, to a disguised naturalistic defense of interpretation. Gadamer's effort to enlist a tradition whose content amounts to some contingent facts about the world in the service of epistemological justification rests upon ambiguities about his use of the terms "authoritative" and "tradition."

Habermas's criticisms of Gadamer turn out to be just the opposite; Gadamer's account of tradition is not sufficiently empirical or sociological in Habermas's view. Gadamer fails to draw a distinction between the role of hermeneutics in everyday communication and the more rigorous, self-reflective, and methodical role it plays in social science. This criticism would appear to echo Habermas's continuing discontent with Gadamer's ban on methodology. "And even if it were feasible to remove the humanities entirely from the sphere of science, the sciences of action could not avoid linking empirical-analytic with hermeneutic procedures" (RGTM 267).

Though Habermas offers little in this context as an argument in defense of an interpretative methodology, he suggests that Gadamer's ban on the "business of methodology" is due to the latter's latent Heideggerianism. "The ontological—in Heidegger's sense—self-understanding of hermeneu-

tics that Gadamer expresses . . . does not, it seems to me, suit his intentions" (RGTM 267). Habermas's point is to contrast the approach to tradition in which critical reflection and "methodical distancing" predominate,
the approach he favors, and the approach of Gadamer, in which, Habermas
charges, tradition appears as a "naturelike substance."

> Even in traditions whose efficacy is unbroken, what is at work is not simply
> an authority detached from insight and blindly asserting itself. Every tradi-
> tion must be woven with a sufficiently wide mesh to allow for application,
> that is, for prudent transposition with regard to changed situations. But the
> methodic cultivation of prudence in the hermeneutic sciences shifts the bal-
> ance between authority and reason. Gadamer fails to appreciate the power of
> reflection that is developed in understanding. This type of reflection is no
> longer blinded by the illusion of an absolute, self-grounded autonomy and
> does not detach itself from the soil of contingency on which it finds itself.
> But in grasping the genesis of the tradition from which it proceeds and on
> which it turns back, reflection shakes the dogmatism of life-practices.
> (RGTM 268)

Habermas raises two objections to Gadamer's defense. First, he stresses
that there is a difference between the authority of knowledge and the authority of a tradition. This point is certainly pertinent and highlights ambiguities in the way in which Gadamer uses such terms as "authoritative,"
"tradition," and "validity," as I pointed out above. Second, though criticism and reflection on tradition can weaken traditional authority, as
Gadamer often warns, there is a manner in which criticism weakens traditional authority that is epistemologically proper.

There are, therefore, two ways to weaken tradition. First, tradition can
be simply rejected as biased. Gadamer often pictures both modernism and
subjectivism as adopting this negative view of tradition. The second way to
weaken tradition is to subject the standards offered by it to critical examination and judge them, as all standards are judged, by whether they preserve truth and objectivity. This second, proper criticism rests upon the
point that no matter of fact, whether of the past or present, constrains the
exercise of reason and critical evaluation. No matter of fact can simultaneously be a matter of principle. Hence Habermas's criticism of Gadamer is
that he fails to distinguish in his defense of the authority of tradition between matters of fact and matters of principle. As Husserl prophetically
warned, such confusion breeds relativism.

Habermas's diagnosis of why these basic points escape Gadamer's notice
is that Gadamer mistakenly characterizes tradition as consisting entirely of
linguistic phenomena. I already made the criticism that Gadamer does not
clearly characterize how he uses the term "tradition." Habermas, on the
contrary, takes it that Gadamer's usage is clear, but mistaken.

Habermas replies that a tradition includes nonlinguistic aspects. These nonlinguistic features appear to be certain causal features, but Habermas is neither clear nor explicit on that point. The two nonlinguistic features of tradition Habermas identifies in his argument against Gadamer are "labor" and "political domination." I take it that his argument must be that these features of tradition, for instance, are not properly linguistic phenomena and thus they do not function as support for the validity of tradition or as the "fore-structure" for any possible interpretation. Labor and political domination would seem to fit as part of a culture's ideology, an issue somewhat outside the topic of this book.

Though the argument is barely fleshed out, the idea appears to be that phenomena of labor and political domination, which do as a matter of fact sustain traditions in Habermas's opinion, are wholly inadequate obviously as guides to the "correctness" of the interpretations. By virtue of their functioning in this way, these nonlinguistic features of the tradition not only fail as standards for truth and objectivity, but they may surreptitiously support norms or principles that ought to be criticized.

Let me return for a moment to my example of the hammer. Suppose the archaeologist were to discover that the meaning of this artifact included, for the people of that ancient culture, a sexual division of labor with regard to its use. In this way, both the function of labor and a certain political form of control would in effect have become part of the meaning of that artifact for those people. In this fashion an ideology can be said to be internalized within the practices and interpretative features of the tradition.

> Sociology cannot, therefore, be reduced to interpretive sociology. It requires a reference system that, on the one hand, does not suppress the symbolic mediation of social action in favor of a naturalistic view of behavior that is merely controlled by signals and excited by stimuli but that, on the other hand, also does not succumb to an idealism of linguistically *(Sprachlichkeit)* and sublimate social processes entirely to cultural tradition. Such a reference system can no longer leave tradition as such and in its relation to other aspects of the complex of social life, thereby enabling us to designate the conditions outside of tradition under which transcendental rules of world comprehension and of action empirically change. (RGTM 273)

The above passage presents, in Habermas's usual compressed and jargonistic manner, a complex criticism appealing to the epistemological concept of "transcendental rules," for instance, which I will explicate later. But even before examining those ideas, Habermas's appeal to that which lies "outside" of the linguistic aspects of tradition and his subsequent contrast between linguistic and nonlinguistic features of tradition is, in the end, a very weak criticism of Gadamer. (Though I agree that Gadamer's position ought to be criticized, my objection is to the way in which Habermas proceeds.)

First, Habermas appears to be simply rejecting the "universal scope" of hermeneutics, though he embraces it in other passages. If he were correct, then aspects of the study of culture and society would escape interpretative understanding. But since he himself is not consistent on this point, it hardly constitutes a serious criticism of Gadamer. Second, by appealing to the phenomena of labor and political domination as exceptions to Gadamer's hermeneutic approach, Habermas must hold that labor and political domination are not properly human actions. The reason for that implication is that if they fall within the scope of human actions, then they are meaningful. It is the meaning of actions that allows them to be contrasted with the "naturalistic view of behavior that is merely controlled by signals and excited by stimuli."

But labor and political domination are archetypal cases of action, and Habermas provides no argument to the contrary. Since such actions are essentially constituted by intentional states, Gadamer's claim that all cultural phenomena are phenomena of meaning is very plausible. The assumptions that lead Gadamer to this conclusion about cultural phenomena are in fact assumptions that Habermas shares with him.

Perhaps, then, Habermas means that labor and political domination have specific causal effects that the other cultural phenomena, which are also meaningful, do not have. But that point is also not an effective criticism of Gadamer, since questions of causal interaction, though important to a naturalistic epistemology or sociology, are not relevant to the nonnaturalistic epistemology Habermas and Gadamer claim to embrace. Hence differences in the causal effects of these phenomena could not show that these cultural phenomena are not meaningful and in that sense nonlinguistic phenomena.

Transcendental Arguments

Though Habermas's specific criticisms of Gadamer do not appear to be very clear or persuasive, he offers an epistemological defense of interpretation quite distinct from what we have seen in Gadamer. The term "transcendental epistemology" characterized Husserl's philosophical idealism, but to properly discuss Habermas's use of this term I will need to add some details I avoided in Chapter 1. The idea of a transcendental strategy in response to skepticism and as a way to justify knowledge claims was a feature of Kant's philosophy and has been an object of controversy and discussion in both the continental and analytic traditions.[12] My summary of this strategy will of necessity be sketchy and steer around the complexities of Kant's work.

First, "transcendental" and "transcendent" should not be confused. A transcendental inquiry does not concern any separate, supernatural realm; it does not propose another world apart from or hidden behind the empirical world. What "transcendental" does involve is the study of those aspects of the object of knowledge independent of it as a sensory experience.

In other words, transcendental inquiry claims that there is a necessity to the way in which an experience is given and that necessity is, of course, not itself a contingent fact of any experience. This necessity is what Kant and subsequent philosophers have called the a priori. It identifies the pure structure of an experience or, as Kant puts it, what reason produces "after a plan of its own."[13]

But this way of stating such a study of knowledge raises another possible confusion. The transcendental account of knowledge is not an account of how, psychologically or physiologically, human experience is organized; it is not a speculation concerning the nature of cognitive structure or the neural network of the brain. The question is a matter of legitimacy or justification, not physiology or cognitive psychology. Hence claims about a priori features of knowledge are not matters of possible research, but matters of conceptual investigations seeking clarifications that support the possibility of sense experience being objective or true.

Habermas's first presentation of his philosophical and epistemological views, the basic structure of which has guided him ever since, is found in *Knowledge and Human Interests*. Though the work is constructed around expositions of Hegel, Marx, Kant, Comte, Peirce, Dilthey, Freud, and Fichte (to list only those to whom he devotes separate chapters), it also contains some unadorned statements of his own view, which, when combined with passages in other related publications, give a general picture of the transcendental epistemology Habermas has championed within continental philosophy and that he continues to defend, albeit in a revised fashion.

A proper place to begin is with Habermas's assessment of Husserl. Habermas agrees with Husserl's aim of criticizing epistemological naturalism. From the perspective of naturalism, objective knowledge consists of recording by sensation of the various matters of fact constituting the world. As against it, Habermas agrees with Husserl that "the possible objects of scientific analysis are constituted a priori in the self-evidence of our primary life-world" (KHI 304).

Husserl's phenomenological description is accused of being embedded within a traditional conception of theory, according to Habermas. The neutral attitude toward claims about the world and Husserl's efforts to free philosophy from biases fails; hence Habermas repeats criticism of Husserl discussed in Chapter 1. But Habermas's criticism is not that the reduction fails by letting in certain assumptions; rather, Husserl ignores how the very project of bracketing builds in a crucial ontological assumption.

Husserl rightly criticizes the objectivist illusion that deludes the sciences with the image of a reality-in-itself consisting of facts structured in a lawlike manner; it conceals the constitution of these facts, and thereby prevents consciousness of the interlocking of knowledge with interests from the life-world. Because phenomenology brings this to consciousness, it is itself, in Husserl's view, free of such interests. It thus earns the title of pure theory unjustly claimed by the sciences. . . . Husserl cannot expect self-formative processes to originate in a phenomenology that, as transcendental philosophy, purifies the classical theory of its cosmological contents, conserving something like the theoretical attitude only in an abstract manner. Theory had educational and cultural implications not because it had freed knowledge from interest. To the contrary, it did so because it derived *pseudonormative power* from the *concealment of its actual interest*. While criticizing the objectivist self-understanding of the sciences, Husserl succumbs to another objectivism, which was always attached to the traditional concepts of theory. (KHI 306)

This criticism, a heady mixture of Heidegger and Lukacs, is that the above ontological commitment not only is required for the reduction, but plays a certain ideological role in philosophy. Habermas calls "traditional theory" the view that a theory, sufficiently purified of bias and prejudice, accurately represents the external world. Truth about the world becomes manifest to an eye once that eye is purified of various "idols." But this defense of objectivity, for Habermas, is a mere rationalization of a particular social conception of knowledge.

The position Habermas identifies as ideological has hardly wholly escaped criticism by even those who support the objectivity of the sciences; nor can such a view be attributed to Husserl, even by the tortuous logic of this passage. But ignoring whether Habermas is correct in considering this form of empiricism as an unchallenged and ideologically powerful orthodoxy, the central question is, however, whether this unquestioned orthodoxy also amounts to evidence of an ontological assumption.

The commitment arises due to the kind of object bracketed. The world is assumed, ontologically, to be a world of object-states, as investigated by the sciences. Thus the latent ontological assumption Habermas locates is physicalism. It then is treated by him as encouraging "scientism" and in a complex sociological account strategies for manipulation and social control.

This argument against Husserl is peculiar for two reasons. First, Husserl identifies among the ontological assumptions bracketed those physicalistic assumptions of the natural sciences (Husserl called them naturalistic assumptions). But Husserl does not decide whether, once the limits of the reduction are lifted, physicalism remains an illicit view. One might assume that he does, given Husserl's commitment to idealism, but I have argued that Husserl's idealism is not competitive with the assumption about the nature of objects Habermas isolates. Second, Habermas dismisses ontological concerns anyway. When he restates his criticism, it becomes clear that his objection to Husserl is in fact an epistemological one. In the appendix to *Knowledge and Human Interests* Habermas asserts that philosophy can be preserved "only on the ruins of ontology." Thus what is at issue between Husserl and Habermas is not a hidden ontological commitment, but whether a transcendental, nonidealist epistemology could be outlined that dispenses with both Husserl's method of reduction and his form of idealism.

When Habermas first states this position in *Knowledge and Human Interests,* he uses the term "constitutive" rather than "transcendental" to characterize the epistemological role he envisages for these human interests. It is clear, even in this formulation, that the term "interests" is not to be taken naturalistically. They are part of the task of epistemological justification, hence constitutive of the possibility of objectivity and truth, not part of the psychological or biological study of humans. A summary by Habermas of this account in his later collection *Theory and Practice* makes this connection between constitutive and transcendental explicit.

> I have carried my historical investigations and exploratory considerations sufficiently far, that the program for a theory of science becomes clearly discernible, a theory which is intended to be capable of grasping systematically the constitutive conditions of science and those of its application. I have let myself be guided by the problem posed by the system of primitive terms (or the "transcendental framework") within which we organize our experience *a priori* and prior to all science, and do so in such a manner that, of course, the formation of the scientific object domains is also prejudiced by this. In the functional sphere of instrumental action we encounter objects of the type of moving bodies; here we experience things, events, and conditions which are, in principle, capable of being manipulated. In the interactions (or at the level of possible intersubjective communication) we encounter objects of the type of speaking and acting subjects; here we experience person, utterances, and conditions which in principle are structured and to be understood symbolically. The object domains of the empirical-analytic and of the hermeneutic sciences are based on these objectifications of reality, which we undertake daily always from the viewpoint either of technical control or intersubjective communication. . . . Empirical analytic knowledge can assume the form of causal explanations or conditional predictions, which also refer to the observed phenomena; hermeneutic knowledge as a rule has the form of interpretations of traditional complexes of meaning. There is a systematic relationship between the logical structure of a science and the pragmatic structure of the possible applications of the information generated within its framework. (TP 8)

I have already noted the broad discussion of and dependence upon transcendental arguments in this tradition, though their critical assessment has not been pursued as zealously. As discussed in Chapter 1, Husserl called his own position "transcendental," though again giving the term his own special meaning. His main idea was that the concepts of subjectivity and objectivity account for human experience as a priori conditions, not as matters of fact of possible experience, as naturalism wrongly assumes. Given any experience, a transcendental argument claims to show what must conceptually or necessarily be the case for that experience to have been possible. I provided the example of reasoning that for a world of objects to be given in experience there necessarily is a distinction between subjective recognition and the object as recognized; it is necessarily the case that the experienced object and the act of experiencing it are distinguished.

Or, to use another example, Husserl claimed that conceptually, not just factually, intentionality (directedness toward objects) is a precondition for the possibility of experience. Another way to put the conclusion of the argument is that such a precondition makes experience intelligible. Heidegger adopted the same strategy, as discussed, but characterized the precondition as concerning the meaning of being: "Transcendental knowledge relates not to objects, not to beings, but to the concepts that determine the being of beings. . . . Transcendental philosophy denotes nothing but ontology" (BPP 128).

Clarifying Habermas's appropriation of this strategy confronts two difficulties. First, Habermas admits his versions of the argument are bare sketches and promissory notes that have proved more difficult to pay off than he originally assumed. "The formula 'quasi-transcendental' is a product of an embarrassment which points to more problems than it solves" (TP 14). Second, Habermas inherits from the continental tradition a frustrating ambiguity about the target of these arguments. Kant intended the transcendental argument to be a reply to epistemological skepticism. But both Husserl and Heidegger abandoned debates over skepticism and focused on the conceptual preconditions shared by science and common sense. This ambiguity is critical, however, since the target of the transcendental argument has implications for its structure and thus its defense.

Habermas speaks of the transcendental as a "viewpoint" or "framework" that "discloses reality" and establishes the possibility for objective knowledge.

> Empirical analysis discloses reality from the viewpoint of possible technical control over objectified processes of nature, while hermeneutics maintains the intersubjectivity of possible action-orienting mutual understanding. . . . The rigorously empirical sciences are subject to the transcendental conditions of instrumental action, while the hermeneutic sciences proceed on the level of communicative action. (KHI 191)

Habermas connects the notion of a conceptual framework with his distinction between that which is transcendental and that which is empirical. The idea of a framework can be approached by recalling Heidegger's notion of ontology. Questions may arise as to existence, for instance, "Are there unicorns?" But there could also be a question concerning whether the world is a world of physical bodies independently of what particular entities exist in it. In this way two different questions are posed. One question is whether, given the framework of physical bodies, there are, among those bodies, ones having the features of unicorns. The second question is whether the framework of physical bodies is the correct framework, whether the world is, as a whole, a world of physical bodies at all (not just whether among those bodies there are unicorns). These questions are not only different, but philosophical debates are normally associated only with the second. One could even argue that the second question makes possible the first; thus frameworks are in that sense transcendental. Without some framework or coherent set of ontological commitments, the specific empirical questions that normally are posed about our world would not be intelligible.

Given this picture of how the notion of the framework and the transcendental fit together, the philosophical or epistemological questions concern the defense of or investigation of the transcendental framework that would make empirical inquiry into the world possible. Such an investigation or defense is a conceptual one, carried on a priori, and aiming at the intelligibility, comprehensibility, or meaning of experience.

Epistemological naturalism, which Habermas opposes, rejects both the distinction between transcendental and empirical inquiry as well as the possibility of the "external questions" as defined above. For naturalism, external questions are mere metaphysics; all answerable questions are empirical. Habermas's defense of transcendental epistemology involves, then, explicating the way in which it accounts for how we apprehend reality and objectivity.

The conditions of the objectivity of possible experience established by the transcendental framework of processes of inquiry, whether in the natural or cultural sciences, no longer explicate only the transcendental meaning of general finite knowledge restricted to phenomena. Instead, in accordance with the objective structure of human life that gives rise to the two orientations of inquiry they preform the specific meaning of the methodical cognitive modes themselves. Empirical-analytic sciences disclose reality insofar as it appears within the behavioral system of instrumental action. In accordance with their immanent meaning, nomological statements about this object domain are thus designed for a specific context in which they can be applied—that is, *they grasp reality with regard to technical control that, under specified conditions, is possible everywhere and at all times.* The hermeneutic sciences do not disclose reality under a different transcendental framework. Rather, they are directed toward the transcendental structure of various actual forms of life, within each of which reality is interpreted according to a specific grammar of world-apprehension and of action. Thus, in accordance with their immanent meaning, hermeneutic statements about structures of this sort are designed for a corresponding context in which they can be applied—*they grasp interpretations of reality with regard to possible intersubjectivity of action-orienting, mutual understanding specific to a given hermeneutic starting point.* Thus we speak of a technical or practical knowledge-constitutive interest insofar as the life structures of instrumental action and symbolic interaction preform the meaning of the validity of possible statements via the logic of inquiry in such a manner that, to the extent that these statements are cognitions, they have a function only in these life structures: that is to the extent that they are technically exploited or practically efficacious. (KHI 195–196)

Habermas's target is an account of the objectivity of the sciences, very broadly understood, as evidentially justified knowledge. The constraints on his account are, first, that scientific theories, broadly understood, are always open to revision. (Habermas considers modern science fallible.) The second constraint is that Habermas treats scientific results as operationally defined. By operationally defined, Habermas means that scientific theories are formulated in such a way that their explanations connect to experiments, possible control over phenomena, or predictions. Thus scientific knowledge concerns not the way things are ultimately or absolutely, but the best explanation for how the world works, given the data available to humans and given our interests in and possible manipulations of the world.

Perhaps both these points suggest why Habermas is usually suspicious of ontological inquiry. Scientific theories are models of how the world works as adjudicated by the court of human experience, and Habermas's instincts about science are resolutely antirealist; he does not take the entities postulated by scientific theories as real entities. He considers them posits that prove themselves as explanatory devices only; they prove themselves operationally then, not realistically. In this aspect, he is, ironically enough, at one with the positivists. The sciences are not concerned with reality as such, but with phenomenology, the world not as it is, but as it is humanly experienced.

Given these limits, Habermas hopes to show the inadequacy of two approaches. First, he opposes, as Husserl did, naturalistic epistemology. "The concept of 'interest' is not meant to imply a naturalistic reduction of transcendental-logical properties to empirical ones. Indeed, it is meant to prevent just such a reduction" (KHI 196). Second, and connected to the first point, Habermas attacks the Millian conception of a single method for the sciences, both natural and social. These two points are connected by Habermas in the following characteristic passage:

The reduction of theory of knowledge to philosophy of science first effected by early positivism was interrupted by a counter-tendency exemplified by Peirce and Dilthey. But the self-reflection of the natural and cultural sciences only interrupted the victorious march of positivism and did not stop it. Thus the knowledge-constitutive interests that had been discovered could be immediately misunderstood in a psychologizing manner and succumb to the critique of psychologism on whose basis modern positivism has been established in the form of logical empiricism and which has determined the scientistic self-understanding of the sciences up to the present.

The connection of knowledge and interest that we have discovered methodologically can be explained and preserved against misinterpretation through recourse to the concept of an interest of reason, developed by Kant and especially by Fichte. (KHI 189)

The discovery announced in this passage, and attributed to Kant and Fichte, is that a transcendental argument can establish that there are non-natural constitutive interests providing a conceptual foundation for objectivity in the sciences and supporting the distinction between methods in the natural and cultural sciences. How would such a argument work?

It begins by assuming the fact of there being objective knowledge about the external world. It then argues that such knowledge could only be possible if such and such concepts were necessarily involved in the production of that knowledge. Given the fact of the knowledge, the argument concludes that such and such concepts must necessarily be involved in the production of knowledge.[14]

Habermas's aim is to show that the natural sciences presuppose, in this transcendental-conceptual sense, that the object of scientific investigation is an instrumental, operationally defined object. The social sciences presuppose that the object of investigation is an action constituted by meaning and admitting of intelligibility. Thus his argument is able to produce additionally the distinction between the natural and social sciences, which he defends, and yet preserve philosophical inquiry from reduction to the sciences.

But there are some serious shortcomings with respect to Habermas's strategy. First, he does not demonstrate how he determines that these transcendental rules are the sole preconditions for existing sciences. This point raises two further problems with Habermas's approach. Since he does not explain how he arrives at this conclusion from the fact of the existing sciences, he does not show that these are the only conceptual preconditions making scientific knowledge possible. Lacking such a demonstration makes the claim, as he admits, "quasi-transcendental." But a quasi-transcendental defense of science fails in its epistemological task. It cannot claim, then, to be an effective alternative to naturalism. On the contrary, Habermas's demonstration of transcendental rules appears to be setting limits for the development of the sciences that may well prove unreasonable, as he does with regard to defending an instrumentalist interpretation of modern physics. But such disputes are thankfully beside the point for me. The problem is that Habermas's epistemology improperly excludes even the possibility of debating such an interpretation in the physical sciences.

Second, Habermas outlines different transcendental conditions for the natural and social sciences, as well as a third condition for what he calls emancipatory critique. But this approach requires an additional step that Habermas does not even attempt. To demonstrate the superiority of his transcendental argument over naturalism, he must block relativism. It must be the case that the transcendental claims concerning what makes knowledge possible are part of one and only one conceptual scheme; a plurality of conceptual schemes must not be possible.

The need for such an argument against relativism parallels the first weakness. Lacking such an argument leaves Habermas's strategy as quasi-transcendental and thus neither an adequate epistemological foundation nor an alternative to epistemological naturalism, even given its inadequacies. In fact, Habermas's undischarged defense of his nonnaturalistic epistemology lends plausibility to epistemological naturalism.

This chapter marks a loss of direction and focus within the continental philosophical tradition leading to fruitless efforts at redefining phenomenology and philosophical debate as a whole. Both Habermas and Gadamer, in their own fashion, are thinkers attracted to a promise of some special philosophical emancipation. Their efforts to harness the philosophical tradition in the name of an as yet unarticulated philosophical revolution, either by way of tradition or some brand of Kantian socialism, are largely unsuccessful. But perhaps worse than not succeeding in defending a compromise between the preservation and destruction of the philosophical tradition (either in the name of Heidegger or Marx), their efforts would dissipate the defense of philosophy's autonomy with which the entire continental tradition began. These interpretative conceptions of philosophy set the stage within the European context for a more audacious challenge of the very idea of philosophy. Philosophy awaits not a reformer, but a team of assassins.

Notes

1. Peter van Inwagen's *Material Beings* (Ithaca: Cornell University Press, 1990) defends denying existence to artifacts: "There are, therefore, no tables and chairs, and there are no other artifacts . . . the labors of Michelangelo and the most skilled watchmaker are . . . devoid of true metaphysical issue. . . . All these people are simply shoving the stuff of the world about" (p. 127). In a similar spirit, John Searle's *The Construction of Social Reality* (New York: Free Press, 1995) treats the functions of objects as always "observer relative" and "imposed upon" or "assigned to" things. "As far as our normal experiences of the inanimate parts of the world are

concerned, we do not experience things as material objects, much less as collections of molecules. Rather, we experience a world of chairs and tables, houses and cars. . . . All the terms I have just used involve criteria of assessment that are internal to the phenomena in question under these descriptions, but not internal to the entities under the description 'material object'" (p. 14). Gadamer's efforts, discussed in this chapter, to marry interpretative inquiry with Heidegger's study of fundamental ontology do not critically reflect on the ontological status of those objects (signs or actions) that admit of interpretation.

2. The notion of folk psychological understanding and the picture of the mind connected to it have been criticized in recent naturalistic philosophy of mind. See, for example, Paul Churchland, *Scientific Realism and the Plasticity of Mind* (Cambridge: Cambridge University Press, 1971) and Stephen Stich, *From Folk Psychology to Cognitive Science* (Cambridge, Mass.: MIT Press, 1983). A defense of intentional psychology can be found in Lynne Rudder Baker, *Saving Belief* (Princeton: Princeton University Press, 1987). Also see the following collections: *Folk Psychology and Philosophy of Mind,* ed. Scott M. Christensen and Dale R. Turner (Hillsdale, N.J.: Erlbaum, 1993); *The Future of Folk Psychology,* ed. John D. Greenwood (New York: Cambridge University Press, 1991); and *Mind and Common Sense,* ed. Radu J. Bogdan (New York: Cambridge University Press, 1991).

3. Heinrich Rickert, who influenced both Heidegger and Dilthey, argued for a variety of these objections in *The Limits of Concept Formation in Natural Science,* ed. and trans. Guy Oakes (New York: Cambridge University Press, 1986) and *Science and History: A Critique of Positivist Epistemology,* trans. George Reisman (New York: Van Nostrand, 1962). A discussion of the influence of these ideas on German sociology and philosophy can be found in Guy Oakes, *Weber and Rickert: Concept Formation in the Cultural Sciences* (Cambridge, Mass.: MIT Press, 1988).

4. Hermann von Helmholtz, "The Relation of the Natural Sciences to Science in General" (1862), in *Selected Writings of Hermann von Helmholtz,* ed. Russell Kahl (Middletown, Conn.: Wesleyan University Press, 1971), pp. 122–143. Helmholtz gives an essentially Millian account of his topic. "The moral sciences clearly have the loftier and more difficult task. They cannot afford, however, to lose sight of the example set by those branches of science which, because they deal with more manageable materials, have—at least in form—made greater progress. Not only have they something to learn from them concerning methods, but they may also draw encouragement from the richness of the results" (p. 137).

5. Husserl did not hold that interpretation was on a methodical par with phenomenology, nor did he think that the study of intentionality was circular even in the "virtuous" way Gadamer assumes it is. In the following quote Husserl treats the contrast between "empathy" and experimental accounts of psychology as misleading and offers a trenchant criticism of such ideas. "The experimentalists are not a little proud of the fact that they, as critics par excellence of introspection and of—as they call it— armchair psychology based exclusively on introspection, have so developed the experimental method that it uses direct experience only in the form of 'chance, unexpected, not intentionally introduced experience,' and that it has completely eliminated the ill-reputed introspection. Though in direction, despite strong exaggeration, there is in this something unquestionably good, still, on the other hand, there is a fundamental

error of this psychology that should be brought out. It places analysis realized in empathetic understanding of others' experience and, likewise, analysis on the basis of one's own mental processes that were unobserved at the time, on the same level with analysis of experience . . . proper to physical science, believing that in this way it is an experimental science. . . . Psychologists think that they owe all their psychological knowledge to experience, thus to those naive recollections or to empathetic penetration into recollections, which by virtue of the methodical art of the experiment are to become foundations for empirical conclusions. Nevertheless the description of the naive empirical data, along with the immanent analysis and conceptual gaps that go hand in hand with this description, is affected by virtue of a fund of concepts whose scientific value is decisive for all further methodical steps. These remain—as evidenced by a bit of reflection—by the very nature of experimental questioning and method, constantly untouched in the further procedure and they enter into the final result, which means into the empirical judgements, with its claim to be scientific. On the other hand, their scientific value . . . can in fact be obtained logically from no empirical determinations whatever" (PRS 97–98).

6. Michael Dummett, *The Seas of Language* (Oxford: Clarendon, 1993). Donald Davidson, *Inquiries into Truth and Interpretation* (Oxford: Clarendon, 1985).

7. Davidson, *Inquiries into Truth and Interpretation*, p. 137.

8. The *locus classicus* of these attacks is found in W. V. O. Quine, *From a Logical Point of View* (Cambridge, Mass.: Harvard University Press, 1953), and Thomas Kuhn, *The Structure of Scientific Revolutions* (Chicago: University of Chicago Press, 1962).

9. Jürgen Habermas, *The Theory of Communicative Action*, trans. Thomas McCarthy (Boston: Beacon, 1984).

10. Though these views may change in some details, I believe Habermas's core position and thus my criticisms of it are not altered by his ongoing work: "My research program has remained the same since the 1970s." Habermas, *Justification and Application: Remarks on Discourse Ethics*, trans. Careen Cronin (Cambridge, Mass.: MIT Press, 1993), p. 149.

11. There are naturalistic accounts of interpretation. For example, Daniel Dennett argues: "There are two paths to intentionality. The Darwinian path is diachronic, or historical, and concerns the gradual accretion, over billions of years, of the sorts of Design—of functionality and purposiveness—that can support an intentional interpretation of the activities of organisms (the 'doings' of 'agents'). Before intentionality can be fully *fledged*, it must go through its awkward, ugly period of featherless pseudo-intentionality. The synchronic path is the path of Artificial Intelligence: in an organism with genuine intentionality—such as yourself—there are, right now, many parts, and some of these parts exhibit a sort of semi-intentionality, or a mere *as if* intentionality, or pseudo-intentionality—call it what you like—and your own genuine, fully fledged intentionality is in fact the produce (with no further miracle ingredients) of the activities of all the semi-minded and mindless bits that make you up. . . . This is what a mind *is*—not a miracle-machine, but a huge semi-designed, self-redesigning amalgam of smaller machines, each with its own design history, each playing its own role in the 'economy of the soul.'" Dennett refers to this general strategy elsewhere as that of "interpreting organisms as if they were ar-

tifacts." *Darwin's Dangerous Idea: Evolution and the Meanings of Life* (New York: Touchstone Books, 1995), pp. 205–206.

12. Transcendental arguments are examined in the following works: Barry Stroud, *The Significance of Philosophical Skepticism* (Oxford: Clarendon, 1984); A. C. Grayling, *The Refutation of Skepticism* (La Salle, Ind.: Open Court, 1985); P. F. Strawson, *The Bounds of Sense* (London: Methuen, 1966).

13. Immanuel Kant, *Critique of Pure Reason,* trans. Norman Kemp Smith (New York: St. Martin's Press, 1965), p. 20 (B xiii). Kant defines the type of inquiry in question as: "I entitle *transcendental* all knowledge which is occupied not so much with objects as with our knowledge of objects in so far as this knowledge is to be possible *a priori*" (p. 59 [A 11–12, B 25]). He notes in another context that mere experience can indicate "that a thing is so and so, but not that it cannot be otherwise" (p. 43 [B 3]).

14. To repeat an earlier example, perceptual knowledge of the external world can be taken as given by "all those except confused philosophers," as Husserl put it. For there to be perceptual knowledge of the external world, it is conceptually necessary that there is a distinction between the object known and the subjective experience. Given that there is such knowledge, the distinction between the object of thought and subjective experience is an a priori condition for the possibility of perceptual knowledge; it is in that sense a transcendental rule, to use Habermas's phrase.

Suggested Readings

The following two book-length accounts of Gadamer provide different, but effective, overviews. The first approaches Gadamer largely from the concerns of literary criticism and consists of a step-by-step commentary on *Truth and Method:* Joel Weinsheimer, *Gadamer's Hermeneutics: A Reading of Truth and Method* (New Haven: Yale University Press, 1985). The second is a philosophical treatment of Gadamer that, though supportive on the whole, engages in some critical analysis and argument concerning his views: Georgia Warnke, *Gadamer: Hermeneutics, Tradition and Reason* (Stanford: Stanford University Press, 1987).

Jürgen Habermas's work is normally discussed as representative of the Frankfurt School, or what is also called the critical theory of society. This intellectual group or movement was briefly mentioned in Chapters 1 and 3, and the best survey of its influence and main ideas is found in Martin Jay, *The Dialectical Imagination: A History of the Frankfurt School and the Institute for Social Research, 1923–1950* (Boston: Little, Brown, 1973). The following two collections of essays on Habermas are recommended: *The Cambridge Companion to Habermas*, ed. Stephen K. White (New York: Cambridge University Press, 1995); and *Habermas and Modernity*, ed. Richard J. Bernstein (Cambridge, Mass.: MIT Press, 1985).

A collection of articles concerning the main topics of this chapter and focusing on the work of Habermas and Gadamer can be found in *Understanding and Social Inquiry,* ed. Fred R. Dallmayr and Thomas A. McCarthy (Notre Dame, Ind.: Notre Dame University Press, 1977).

Bibliography

BT: Heidegger, M. *Being and Time*. Translated by Joan Stambaugh. Albany: State University of New York Press, 1996. (SZ: Heidegger, M. *Sein und Zeit*. Tübingen: Max Niemeyer, 1953.)

KHI: Habermas, J. *Knowledge and Human Interests*. Translated by Jeremy J. Shapiro. Boston: Beacon, 1971.

PH: Gadamer, H-G. *Philosophical Hermeneutics*. Translated and edited by David E. Linge. Berkeley and Los Angeles: University of California Press, 1977.

PRS: Husserl, E. "Philosophy as a Rigorous Science." In *Phenomenology and the Crisis of Philosophy*. Translated by Quentin Lauer. New York: Harper Torchbooks, 1965.

RGTM: Habermas, J. "A Review of Gadamer's *Truth and Method*." In *Hermeneutics and Modern Philosophy*. Edited by Bruce R. Wachterhauser. Albany: State University of New York Press, 1986.

TP: Habermas, J. *Theory and Practice*. Translated by John Viertel. Boston: Beacon, 1973.

TM: Gadamer, H-G. *Truth and Method*. Second edition, revised. Translated and edited by Joel Weinsheimer and Donald G. Marshall. New York: Crossroad, 1989.

5

THE NEW SOPHISTS

The previous chapters discussed those efforts in the continental tradition to defend the autonomy of philosophy against reduction to scientific explanation while also criticizing traditional philosophical approaches to ontological and epistemological problems. The continental tradition had not sought to eliminate the discipline of philosophy, in other words, though it criticized the current state of philosophy.

In contrast, both the analytic and positivist traditions during these same decades had begun to consider arguments rooted in the philosophy of language, seeking, as Ludwig Wittgenstein put it, to "break the spell of philosophical bewitchment." A version of this attempt to step beyond or outside of philosophy, rather than literally solve philosophical problems, found its most penetrating and influential form in Wittgenstein's later writings, in which he proposed to dismantle the very idea of the theory of knowledge and such central philosophical concepts as analyticity and the a priori.

While holding, as Gadamer does, that philosophy amounts to a kind of clarification rather than explanation, Wittgenstein sought to abandon the notion of there being distinct philosophical topics or themes. Philosophy, he concluded, has no specific task, produces no system of thought; thus criticism of it cannot proceed in the normal manner of disciplines in which one aims to correct errors or make new discoveries. Philosophy discovers nothing concerning the world; nor does it secure principles, essences, or truths about the topics of ontology or the theory of knowledge; nor, therefore, does it somehow fail in these tasks. It is not a superior or inferior form of common sense or science. Thus Wittgenstein was led to conclude that even the effort to criticize metaphysics, as practiced by positivism or pragmatism, proceeds within and thereby perpetuates the fundamental misconceptions it claims to eradicate. As Heidegger put the same point, albeit for very different purposes, "the reversal of a metaphysical statement remains a metaphysical statement" (LH 208).

Philosophy's only proper task is to dismantle itself. By detailed, case by case exercises, Wittgenstein hoped to untangle those "knots of thought" found in traditional philosophical quandaries that are generated largely by the misuse and misunderstanding of what are ordinary and even prosaic features of language. Primarily, then, philosophy finds itself concerned with language: "Philosophy is a battle against the bewitchment of our intelligence by means of language."[1]

What one must be cured of, Wittgenstein argues, is the continuing hope for there to emerge some decisive philosophical method, discovery, or conclusion; what remains, in contrast, is a struggle to domesticate the impulse to philosophize.[2]

> The real discovery is the one that makes me capable of stopping doing philosophy when I want to.—The one that gives philosophy peace, so that it is no longer tormented by questions which bring *itself* in question.—Instead, we now demonstrate a method, by examples; and the series of examples can be broken off. Problems are solved (difficulties eliminated), not a *single* problem.
>
> There is not *a* philosophical method, though there are indeed methods, like different therapies.[3]

In notes to Chapters 1 and 2 there were some suggestive links between Wittgenstein's aphoristic insights and certain themes in Husserl and Heidegger. These links did not, however, go much beyond a shared dissatisfaction with traditional philosophy and a demand for some radically new direction, a new direction quite distinct among the three. Similarly, in this chapter, I am beginning with these reflections about the notion of how to conceive philosophy coming to an end not to treat the two thinkers discussed here as Wittgensteinians. They were not significantly influenced by him. But the suspicion about philosophy expressed in the above quotes, especially Wittgenstein's attacks on systematic philosophy, serves as an introduction to the idea of escaping both the demands and authority of philosophy that I believe now dominates the continental approach and has in effect displaced the idea, with which the book began, of there being an autonomous philosophical subject matter.

Michel Foucault and Jacques Derrida emerged from similar intellectual backgrounds. Both careers began in philosophy during the immediate postwar period when phenomenology and existentialism, as interpreted by Sartre and Merleau-Ponty, reigned with virtually undisputed orthodoxy within French intellectual life. Within this orthodoxy, both began as its critics, repeating, for the most part, Heidegger's criticism of Sartre discussed in Chapter 2. In particular, both took seriously Heidegger's project of the destruction of the history of philosophy and his suspicions concerning "humanism." Finally, both came to subsume the study of philosophy, in somewhat different ways, within a broad conception of literary studies.

In using the term "sophist" in my title I am not being insulting. Both Derrida and Foucault have argued in their writings on philosophy and culture that ancient sophism was a more significant critical strategy against Platonism, the hidden core in both of their views for philosophy's suspect impulses, than traditional academics fully appreciate. But, more important, each makes an appeal to sophistic strategies in his own writings.

In his 1970 inaugural lecture at the Collège de France, Foucault outlines the main themes of his research indicating, among others, a study of truth in its function to exclude certain viewpoints from consideration, that is, a sociological rather than formal study of truth. He immediately connects this theme to his understanding of ancient philosophy. "A division emerged between Hesiod and Plato, separating true discourse from false; it was a new division for, henceforth, true discourse was no longer considered precious and desirable, since it had ceased to be discourse linked to the exercise of power. And so the Sophists were routed" (AK 218). In a very similar way, Derrida's study of Plato treats the Platonic opposition to sophism as a deeply compromised assault: "The argumentation against writing in the *Phaedrus* is able to borrow all its resources from Isocrates or Alcidamas at the moment it turns their own weapons, 'transposing' them, against the sophists."[4]

In respect to contemporary philosophy, both exploit rhetorical over argumentative strategies, they deploy paradoxical formulations as a device for dislodging philosophical assumptions, they deny that philosophy constitutes an autonomous or distinct type of inquiry into epistemological or ontological problems, and they deploy relativist and skeptical arguments against both science and philosophy as such. Thus their aim is also to block those who respond to philosophy's repeated failures by defending the sciences. For all of these reasons I have decided to call this recent reaction sophistic.

Michel Foucault's death at the age of fifty-eight came at the peak of a career marked both by restless reconceptions of his work and compulsive returns to the same topic. His studies, which often are as difficult to clearly identify as to critically assess, consist of intellectual histories, specifically histories of science (broadly understood), and a quasi-philosophical book (the point of this qualifier will be clearer as the exposition proceeds) reflecting upon the possibility of such histories.

Though trained as a philosopher, with a second advanced degree in pathological physiology, Foucault often referred to himself as a historian. But even within that discipline, Foucault's work is hardly orthodox and often seems philosophy by other means. His histories, such as they are, consist largely of interpretative expositions of a wide range of topics, everything from minor philosophical works to textbooks and diaries, in which he locates or teases out various assumptions or even an entire conceptual framework whose influence and effects upon other political, economic, and cultural structures he traces, largely by speculation and reliance on literary devices.

Though Foucault often contrasts the patient collection of empirical evidence with tiresome philosophical speculation, his historical works are actually little involved in either the normal problems of documentation or in resolving historical controversies. He writes as though the evidence unearthed in these documents, or archives, as he prefers to call his sources, directly and rather simply overturns a range of traditional historical and philosophical theses. The evidence he speaks of is supposed to involve epistemological or ontological assumptions within those protoscientific or prescientific disciplines Foucault found so fascinating and whose impact he thought vastly understated. This thematic emphasis on what Ian Hacking calls "the immature sciences"[5] includes Foucault's attention to those idiosyncratic and obscure (the more obscure the better) documents in which a mass of speculations concerning medical treatment, madness, or the nature of sexuality proliferated in the eighteenth and nineteenth centuries. It was a fertile ground, in his view, for understanding in general how knowledge comes to be invented, secured, defended, and then promoted.

Foucault claims to document how objects of study within these protosciences were constructed from the various conceptual schemes that haunted these historical periods and whose shape can only now be barely discerned in the documents cited above; it is an anonymous type of construction, however, whose features and nature Foucault never fully discusses and the evidence for which he never seriously defends. This construction, at any rate, makes possible the surface phenomena of thinking, hypothesizing, and experimenting upon which historians normally and thus incorrectly concentrate, historians Foucault dismisses without ever naming.

Foucault's historical work, in this way, expanded into a broad discussion of the underlying epistemology and ontology of the "European sciences," as Husserl had called them, but without Husserl's intent of either reconstructing or justifying these assumptions. Foucault's aim is largely to debunk the objectivity and realism of the sciences. In claiming to find within these disciplines an unintended, quasi-sociological function for their implicit background assumptions as well as the various philosophies that then emerged around them, Foucault conceives of himself as both demystifying and disarming the mutually supporting authority of science and philosophy, though this strategy is somewhat inconsistent since at times Foucault appears to appeal to a scientific conception of history, namely, structuralism, as shall be seen.

My focus will be on three of his works. Foucault's *The Archaeology of Knowledge,* which I called a quasi-philosophical essay, reflects upon his own earlier writings in terms of their significance for a new conception of the theory of knowledge replacing both traditional philosophy as well as reforms such as phenomenology. Foucault's *The Order of Things,* easily the most ambitious of his historical works, seems equal parts history and philosophy of the social sciences. These two books constitute his core assessment of contemporary philosophy. However, since Foucault's assessments of philosophy are wholly intertwined with his approach to history, I begin with *The Birth of the Clinic* as an example of his historical writing.

Clumsy Butchers

Though written in a frustratingly distant and elusive style requiring a reader already familiar with the history of medicine, Michel Foucault's *The Birth of the Clinic* focuses on what the history of medicine contributes to answering the following question: Are the categories by which medical phenomena are investigated imposed upon or discovered in the world? For Foucault, the answer revealed in the history of medicine is that these categories are invented, though not by individual thinkers, and thus he organizes his narrative of medicine and various theories of disease around conceptual changes in the nineteenth century that he claims made "our present conception" possible.

Foucault's central theme turns on a response to Plato's attack on sophism. In the *Phaedrus* Socrates is presented as requiring that "we . . . divide into forms, following the objective articulation; we are not to attempt to hack off parts like a clumsy butcher."[6] The image of the "clumsy butcher" is used against the sophists, for whom categories are, as they are for Foucault, fundamentally arbitrary, conventional, and at the whim of various social purposes or interests. The possibility of "objective articulations," in what Foucault dismisses as Plato's "reassuring dialectic," is the kind of metaphysical realism that Socrates asserts against sophism and that Foucault seeks to dismantle. To fully understand this debate between realist and nominalist accounts of classification, I briefly turn to some contemporary language concerning the notion of a natural kind.

John Stuart Mill, reflecting upon Hume's empiricist attack on the same kind of Platonic realism, coined the term "natural kinds" for whatever categories limn reality rather than impose an arbitrary classification.[7] Mill's concept of natural kinds concerns the objective articulations guiding Plato's supposed skilled butchers. Natural kinds link classification and the generation of knowledge, because they pick out properties that can be projected as lawlike regularities of the natural world.

Water, for example, is a Millian natural kind, since it is a way in which a set of properties, distinct from one another, cohere in a manner open to empirical inquiry and yet replicated in every sample of water. The coexistence of properties that characterize a kind does not consist of what might strike investigators as a useful arrangement or simply how studies of the world have been traditionally ordered; it marks a coexistence independent of whatever are the assumptions researchers bring to their task of determining the structure of the world's stuff.

In contrast, "all yellow things," to use another example from Mill, does not constitute a natural kind. It is a provisional, perhaps temporarily useful ordering. But it fails to project any regularity other than the specific task for which it was invented. The aim of science is the discovery of natural kinds, not the proliferation of arbitrary groupings.

Hilary Putnam further developed the concept of a natural kind in recent writings by making a distinction between a kind's "stereotype" and its "extension."[8] A natural kind is fixed by its extension, the underlying, microphysical structure, for example, that, given whatever are the laws of nature, establishes that those parts of the world necessarily cohere in such and such a way. This extension, which is the object of scientific inquiry, contrasts then with the diverse stereotypes available at the macro level for identifying and locating kinds within prescientific experience and when access to the extension of a kind is not available.

Some kinds, such as water, predate the scientific theories that attempt to determine their extensions. The stereotype for water, "liquid flowing in lakes, rivers, and streams," provided a guide to this fixed aspect of the world long before an underlying microstructure for water was even conceivable, let alone discovered. But, in that way, a stereotype will always be trumped by the determination of its extension. If it should turn out, however, that there is no extension for some stereotype, then that stereotype would either remain as a mere convention or disappear as a prescientific confusion (e.g., phlogiston, caloric, the four elements).

Whether something is or is not water is settled by its underlying structure, not by simply consulting the stereotype. Stereotypes are in that fashion dispensable, whereas kinds are permanent and immune to the vagaries of whatever human preferences there are for the design and function of classificatory schemes. If there were a domain, however, that admitted of only stereotypes (only those conventional groupings or definitions, in other words), then there would be no natural kinds within that domain and thus no science of it would be possible.

The notion of a natural kind has, however, always had a questionable status in philosophy and has often been the object of devastating attacks; such criticisms, especially those of Hume, were Mill's topic when he posed the problem as he did. In contemporary philosophy the concept of a natural kind has been criticized in terms of the ontological and epistemological assumptions that back it up. If the concept of a natural kind is, however, the key to the very possibility of objectivity and lawlikeness (the pride of modern science), then questioning its background assumptions may reveal that indeed the whole of science is "rotten to the core."[9]

Foucault smells this rot. The central theme of his work on the history of medicine is to investigate what fixes medical classification, given his assumption that disease is not a natural kind; and perhaps this assumption rests on an even deeper one that there are no natural kinds at all. To confirm his suspicion that the sophists were right and Plato wrong about the impossibility of a realist taxonomy of the world, Foucault claims to find historical evidence, in this one case, of deep modifications and shift in what he calls *epistemes*, the conceptual schemes making classification and even evidence possible. Such a story of deep conceptual change, not guided by evidence, leads him in this example to an antitraditional history of medicine that, among its other tasks, challenges the traditional narrative of the history of medicine in which enlightenment triumphs over superstition.[10]

Prior to *The Birth of the Clinic*, Foucault had argued in his first book that mental illness was not a disease and therefore the medical treatment of the insane was somehow politically motivated and morally illicit.[11] The treatment of persons as "patients" was only justified, he argued, in cases of genuine disease. With regard to mental illness, the concept of disease was playing only an ideological role for the nefarious purpose of extending institutional and political control over a dispersed population of poor vagrants.

Foucault lacked in that first book a clear distinction between the state of "being diseased" and that of having a mental illness. All he offered in defense of his thesis was historical evidence of the errors and prejudices that marked past theories and treatments of mental illness. But such historical evidence could not constitute the difference between mental illness and cases of genuine disease, since similar historical errors, confusions, and speculation are found with regard to nonmental medical disorders. Such historical facts are consistent, in other words, with the disorders in question turning out to be genuine diseases.

Foucault objects to the medical conception of mental illness because it treats as physiological what he views as cultural or even aesthetic differences.[12] Foucault is correct that, were mental illness not a disease, then treatment (especially if involuntary) would be morally objectionable. The key step in the argument is establishing the antecedent condition, namely, that mental illness is not a disease. But Foucault does not argue for this step at all beyond reminding his reader that such mental conditions were once viewed differently, as "divine disturbances." Would one be convinced that epilepsy is not a physiological disorder by being reminded that it was once viewed as a divine punishment?

The Birth of the Clinic takes up the topic of disease again so as to block the above objection. Foucault pursues a broader thesis than denying that madness is a disease. He declares the entire concept of disease a conventional act of classification. One can see the rationale for this strategy since, as I pointed out above, the condition of being diseased has much the same history of conceptual confusion and speculation as Foucault discovered concerning mental illness.

Before I discuss this thesis, it should be noted that it weakens rather than strengthens the original argument concerning madness. If Foucault were able to demonstrate that disease as a whole, not just in the case of mental illness, is a mere conventional definition (a classification like "all yellow things" rather than like "water"), then the point of his argument that extending the medical model to mental illness was illicit would be blunted. I will return to this problem with his strategy below.

In what follows I largely ignore the ethical subargument above. My focus is on the defense of the central metaphysical claim that disease is not a fixed feature of the natural world. Foucault begins by declaring that "our" current understanding of how disease invades the body and is observed by trained specialists is only one model among many. "But this order of the solid, visible body is only one way–in all likelihood neither the first, nor the most fundamental–in which one spatializes disease. There have been, and will be, other distributions of illness" (BC 3). The book claims to demonstrate this relativization of our current understanding by marshaling evidence of how different medicine was before the transition to our current conception and by studying how that transition occurred by way of studies of medical textbooks and treatises. The crucial point of the book is the emergence of the model of nineteenth-century medicine, which Foucault calls the "anatomical-clinical" model, from the "medicine of species," which he claims dominated the eighteenth century and resulted in both a different conception and practice of medicine.

The reason these changes are not responsive to matters of evidence is that what changes is the very nature of observation. Foucault speaks of how *le regard* ("the gaze") of clinical experience was invented or made possible by our current *episteme*. Before assessing Foucault's antirealism concerning epistemology, I want to discuss the book's thesis.

> The exact superposition of the "body" of the disease and the body of the sick man is no more than a historical, temporary datum. Their encounter is self-evident only for us, or, rather, we are only just beginning to detach ourselves from it. The space of *configuration* of the disease and the space of *localization* of the illness in the body have been superimposed, in medical experience, for only a relatively short period of time—the period that coincides with nineteenth-century medicine and the privileges accorded to pathological anatomy. This is the period that marks the suzerainty of the gaze, since in the same perceptual field, following the same continuities or the same breaks, experience reads at a glance the visible lesions of the organism and the coherence of pathological forms; the illness is articulated exactly on the body, and its logical distribution is carried out at once in terms of anatomical masses. The "glance" has simply to exercise its right of origin over truth. (BC 3–4)

Since this passage's central idea is rather elusive, a paraphrase and then a recent interpretation of it may prove helpful. Today, apparently, "we" take it as self-evident (wrongly) that diseases are such that they have always acted upon human bodies in the same ways. We believe diseases are natural phenomena. We believe, therefore, that before there was the modern conceptual scheme that allows us to conceive and identify viruses, there were viral illnesses. This assumption, Foucault argues, is a mere prejudice and its self-evidence is weakening; "we" are beginning to doubt it. Under the cover of this repeated pronoun, Foucault conceals an argumentative sleight of hand, that is, that the current view *is* a dogma and that there *are* widespread doubts about it.

What Foucault contrasts with the now eroding self-evident conception is a "historical" conception of disease, in which the relationship between diseases and bodies is a "historical, temporary datum." To say it is "historical and temporary" would mean that this relationship between a body and a disease changes in a very special manner. The change in question cannot be naturalistically temporal; it is not simply that symptoms are gradually manifested as the disease progresses in the body or that diseases are biologically adaptive and thus change over time. Foucault suggests that the kind of change that occurs with regard to disease is the kind of change that occurs with regard to cultural artifacts or the conception of legality, for instance, over time. What is transitory, then, is the meaning of disease, not the contingency of its physical features. Being diseased is not a matter of nature, it is a matter of our conventions.

Foucault also asserts that the self-evident view of disease he is resisting is built from a certain theory of experience in which the truth manifests itself to a "disinterested eye," as he will later characterize the clinical observer. Thus what is eroding and leading us to doubt the naturalistic view of disease, if that is the right characterization of the "self-evident" view, is the simultaneous erosion of a theory of knowledge concerning the access to truth by way of purifying the act of perception. Foucault, in this way, ties the claimed natural-kind status of disease to a version of empiricism. I will ignore this part of his argument for now, since the metaphysical question of whether the being of the world includes natural kinds is separate from the epistemological question of whether there is access to these kinds by way of unaided perception.

François Delaporte recently has interpreted Foucault's argument as one in which Foucault denies the very existence of disease: "'Disease' does not exist. It is therefore illusory to think that one can 'develop beliefs' about it or 'respond' to it. What does exist is not disease but practices."[13] When Foucault concludes his book by saying that "there are no longer either essential diseases or essences of diseases" (BC 189), Delaporte takes him to be claiming that diseases are not "things," but a kind of shorthand for these larger social "practices." In this reading, Delaporte puts the emphasis on Foucault's nominalism, or what could be called, using a current philosophical term, Foucault's "eliminativism," with regard to socially constructed entities.

For Delaporte, as I understand him, Foucault's account of medicine raises this question: If the history of medicine is a history of such diverse classificatory accounts lacking any common reference, what accounts for conceptual change in medical theory? Foucault offers, largely in passing, two answers to this question. First, alterations in the concept of disease are due to formal, "syntactic changes" in the various conceptual systems that blink on and off in the history of medicine and make classification as well as treatment possible. Second, changes in the conceptual systems themselves are brought about by various social and economic pressures selecting those medical theories, treatments, and classifications whose functional effects are beneficial to the social system.[14] Both of these answers, in Delaporte's account, deny the existence of the entities referred to by these so-called scientific theories of medicine.

But the context in which Foucault states "there are no longer . . . essences of disease" suggests he could simply mean that disease is not a natural kind and thus must admit of the above types of explanation. But it is a mere naturalistic prejudice, after all, to go on to add that whatever admits of only those transitory historical classifications does not exist. Thus in denying that diseases are a natural kind, Foucault could be read as saying that whereas diseases exist and thus "being diseased" is not illusory, it is not a purely natural phenomenon, but additionally a socially "contested" one in which various interests and social powers collide and collude. If diseases are not essential features of the world, then being diseased is, as another critic of such medical naturalism recently put it, "deciding what sort of people we ought to be."[15] Such a position can be critical of naturalism without also arguing that the phenomena in question are illusory.

If Foucault is understood as mounting an epistemological challenge to the natural-kind status of disease, then it is only the essential nature, not the existence of diseases, that is at issue. If the emphasis is placed on an ontological challenge to self-evident naturalism, then Foucault's austere nominalism or eliminativism with regard to disease entities tends to dominate in accounts of his views.

This tangle of questions about precisely what are the implications of Foucault's dramatic claim can be ignored, however, since the book fails to establish what is presupposed by either the ontological or epistemological version of its thesis, namely, that disease is not a natural kind. The book only offers historical evidence, by way of the interpretation of textbooks and treatises in medicine, that the conception of disease and treatment has changed since the 1700s. But that set of facts, even if Foucault has established them, does not entail, without further argument, that diseases are transitory, cultural classifications constructed anonymously by way of social structures and practices.

A naturalist, one who considers disease a fixed feature of the natural world, need not disagree with Foucault that the history of medicine is characterized by this type of massive conceptual change or that it exhibits bias, prejudice, and faulty assumptions, including in its efforts at self-criticism. Nor need a naturalist disagree with Foucault concerning the problems with treating perception as a reliable guide to the underlying nature of such kinds or purifying perception of its theoretical biases.

What Foucault has documented, from the view of the naturalist, are changes in the available stereotypes concerning disease and the epistemological difficulties faced in determining the underlying nature of disease. But such facts alone are not sufficient to demonstrate that there is no such underlying extension or that diseases are inventions any more than similar historical facts about physics, chemistry, or biology are sufficient to establish the absence of natural kinds in those fields. I am not denying that there are arguments against the entire idea of a natural kind; the influence of such arguments was cited above. I am denying that mere historical documentation of the sort Foucault provides could establish a conclusion concerning whether or not there is some fixed feature of the natural world.

Foucault's plausible history of changes in disease stereotypes and the gradual emergence of the modern concept of disease may have persuaded him that disease has no common underlying structure and thus is not a fixed feature of the natural world. Perhaps he is correct. But if he is correct on this aspect of the natural world, it is not on the basis of those historical facts he cites about the theory or practice of medicine. However interesting may be Foucault's catalog of what he unearthed in medical archives, these results cannot mutate, as if by rhetorical magic, into the much stronger conceptual support his conclusion requires.

If we already knew disease was not a fixed feature or had reason to doubt the very concept of a natural kind, then such historical evidence would be just what we would expect. But, as Putnam's account shows, the concept of a natural kind includes the idea that stereotypes historically fail to capture a kind's extension. Thus, even assuming there are natural kinds, historical evidence of deep conceptual change is still what we would expect.

Historians who remind us of how past errors were once taken as obvious truths perform the valuable function of encouraging fallibilism about our current accounts, but Foucault seeks a stronger result.

> The access of the medical gaze into the sick body was not the continuation of a movement of approach that had been developing in a more or less regular fashion since the day when the first doctor cast his somewhat unskilled gaze from afar on the body of the first patient; it was the result of a recasting at the level of epistemic knowledge *(savoir)* itself, and not at the level of accumulated, refined, deepened, adjusted knowledge *(connaissances)*. (BC 137)

The above passage is counseling neither fallibilism nor skepticism. Foucault ambitiously claims evidence for an epistemological distinction between *savoir* and *connaissance* (a distinction without an adequate English equivalent). He claims evidence of a structure of knowledge *(savoir)* that makes possible the accumulation of evidence and thereby the practical or theoretical discoveries normally associated with knowledge *(connaissances)*. This distinction supports Foucault's notion that disputes about evidence are not central to the structure of medical knowledge. Observation *(connaissance)* shifts after and as a result of shifts in the conceptual scheme *(savoir)*. Contrary to traditional histories, then, empirical evidence could not have led physicians to abandon their prejudices.

However, if the only argument for such a claim concerning underlying conceptual schemes and the relativity of observation are historical matters of fact themselves, supposedly uncovered by Foucault "reading" (in an unprejudiced manner?) historical documents, the conclusion exceeds Foucault's support of it. He seems aware of the gap between the book's reach and its grasp, since he calls it a mere "experiment" in using a method for a "confused, under-structured, and ill-structured domain of the history of ideas."

> Its historical support is limited since it deals, on the whole, with the development and methods of medical observation over less than a half a century. Yet it concerns one of those periods that mark an ineradicable chronological threshold; the period in which illness, counter-nature, and death, in short, the whole dark underside of disease came to light, at the same time illuminating and eliminating itself like night, in the deep, visible, solid, enclosed, but accessible space of the human body. What was fundamentally invisible is suddenly offered to the brightness of the gaze, in a movement of appearance so simple, so immediate that it seems to be the natural consequence of a more highly developed experience. It is as if for the first time for thousands of years, doctors, free at last of theories and chimeras, agreed to approach the object of their experience with the purity of an unprejudiced gaze. But the analysis must be turned around: it is the forms of visibility that have changed; the new medical spirit to which Bichat is no doubt the first to bear witness in an absolutely coherent way cannot be ascribed to an act of psychological and epistemological purification; it is nothing more than a syntactical reorganization of disease in which the limits of the visible and invisible follow a new pattern. (BC 195)

This passage leaves a number of unanswered questions. First, what method is Foucault alluding to as his book's experimental guide? How would extending the study to other periods and other domains of medicine, that is, providing more of the same kind of historical evidence, strengthen the underlying conceptual argument? Is the formation of medical knowledge, which appears to be the book's object of study, merely described or critically assessed in the book? If the aim of the book is only descriptive, then how is such an aim consistent with the argument against the possibility of a disinterested, descriptive "gaze"? If the aim of the book is then critical, on the basis of what standard or criteria (given that traditional epistemology and all present-centered standards are dismissed by him) does the book adjudicate claims about the history of medicine?

The evocative language in the above quote, characteristic of Foucault's style, both asserts and yet leaves unclarified two strategies. First, there is an epistemological criticism of both traditional medical inquiry and history of medicine. Foucault pictures both the practice and history of medicine, though that distinction is often left vague, as dominated by a rather simplistic Baconian theory of knowledge, cited above, in which truth reveals itself immediately and directly once a mind is cleansed of theoretical prejudices, the kind of obstacles to enlightenment Bacon called "idols of the mind."

Second, there is the enigmatic appeal to "nothing more than a syntactical reorganization of disease in which the limits of the visible and invisible follow a new pattern" as a prototype of an explanation, if that is the right word, for these changes in knowledge. Syntactic reorganization, whatever Foucault precisely means by that phrase, is contrasted with either psychological accounts of scientific change (as in biographical accounts of individual scientists) or the epistemological analyses of the traditional philosophy of science. But "nothing more than a syntactic reorganization of disease" is not thereby magically freed of epistemological or ontological assumptions and does not in that way allow Foucault to somehow escape the entire business of philosophical debate concerning these claims.

The above account sketches enough of Foucault's historical work to profit turning now to his defense of and theoretical reflection upon this new brand of the history of ideas. Before proceeding with stating Foucault's position about it and my criticisms, I need to defend my approach against a complaint that Foucault often raises in his own defense.

First, I am treating him as though he were primarily a philosopher and he has repeatedly objected to that label. I will return to that point in a moment. Second, and related, Foucault objects to those who comment on his work and yet ignore the bulk of it, that is, those lengthy passages of detailed exposition concerning largely unknown texts or writers ranging widely in intellectual history and specifically within the protoscientific disciplines he lovingly cultivated. His critics insist, Foucault complains, on focusing instead on whatever passages he writes, no matter how fleeting, on a Kant, a Descartes, or a Hume, while nothing is said about his more substantial discussions of a Cuvier, a Boop, or a Bichat.

I agree that his comments on classic figures in the history of philosophy are, for the most part, too brief and sketchy to sustain any deep examination; and I am not discussing any of those passages here.[16] But Foucault does engage in philosophical disputes concerning epistemological or ontological matters and adopts and defends distinct philosophical positions. These philosophical topics (I do not know what else to call them) are a central focus in much of his writing; and they remain philosophical topics even when he aims to show that such disputes are idle or confused. Whether he should be called a philosopher or historian is a separate issue. As he says, "Leave it to our bureaucrats and our police to see that our papers are in order" (AK 17). The main point concerns what kind of issues he raises.

There is, in addition, another reason for ignoring the expository passages I agree form the bulk of his writing. Though Foucault can ask to be judged on these historical expositions, it is simply not the case that these expository passages he cites provide an opportunity for a critical discussion. The reason they do not can be appreciated by very briefly using his discussion of David Ricardo's political economy in *The Order of Things* as an example.

Foucault's comments on Ricardo's political economy in that book range from the plausible, namely, that Ricardo and Marx shared economic concepts that are more important than their obvious political differences, to the quite mysterious, namely, Foucault's gloss upon the phrase *homo economicus* as a "finite being" who "wastes his life in evading the imminence of death." Even if one were to decide to critically discuss these passages on Ricardo by way of a lengthy discussion of Ricardo's economic writings and their various interpretations, it would be fruitless. Foucault provides the reader with no indication of what in the writings of Ricardo has led him to these various conclusions. He cites no specific passages, no facts about Ricardo's career; nor does he analyze concepts in political economy or the various controversies, both practical and theoretical, that either shaped Ricardo or in which Ricardo was involved (nor does he provide such material on Marx). Thus a critical discussion (or at least a criticism that amounts to more than paraphrase and synopsis) of his views and these expositions is not possible.

In *The Archaeology of Knowledge* Foucault regrets that he used names, such as Ricardo and Boop; it suggests, he confesses, a misconception of his own work. But my point is not to demand biographical information, if he thinks that is irrelevant, or to insist on treating Ricardo's *oeuvre* in whatever way Foucault considers naive. Whatever this system of concepts that is called, perhaps incorrectly, "Ricardo's political economy" consists of, it must be possible to identify it independently of Foucault's discussion of it. If it cannot be identified independently of Foucault's account, then there can be no critical discussion of his summary of it.

What is required is at least the following: What is Foucault discussing? Second, by what criteria of assessment does Foucault analyze "Ricardo's political economy," and are those criteria defensible? The first requirement will be discussed in the next section, but the second point concerns those many philosophical asides that litter his writings. I agree that his discus-

sions of specific philosophers do not provide that material, but these epistemological and ontological digressions effectively guide his work.

The Encoded Eye

Foucault's answers to the kind of questions I raised above concerning *The
Birth of the Clinic* are explored in two later works. Building on the above,
Foucault undertook an even more ambitious study he subtitled "an archaeology of the human sciences." *The Order of Things* documents deep conceptual change in the topics of life, labor, and language, topics Foucault
identifies as the "human sciences," from roughly the sixteenth to the twentieth centuries. Though he warns against those who would understand this
periodization as summarizing anything like the "spirit of the age," and his
characterization of the work is to call it a "regional study," the book neatly
divides itself into three traditional historical periods: the Renaissance, the
Classical Age, and Modernism. Like Heidegger, Foucault appears to enjoy
warning his reader not to reach a conclusion he makes every effort to
prompt.

The resulting book is an intoxicating mixture of philosophical speculations, expositions of economics, biology, and linguistics in that impressionistic manner mentioned above, and prophetic Nietzschean pronouncements
concerning the "death of man" and the "naked experience of order."
Within each period, there are similarities at the deep level of the *episteme,*
making it possible for these topics to be recognized as belonging to the human sciences. The book's heated, literary style and its symphonic conception found a receptive audience and won for Foucault intellectual and even
celebrity status, however momentary such finally proves to be in Paris.

The book begins with a literary allusion.[17] The problem of classification
is again raised and this book is thus directly linked with his two earlier histories on medicine and insanity. Foucault says the book arose "out of the
laughter that shattered . . . all familiar landmarks of my thought" in reading a short story by the Argentinean writer Jorge Luis Borges that "quotes a
'certain Chinese encyclopedia' in which it is written that 'animals are divided into: (a) belonging to the Emperor, (b) embalmed, (c) tame, (d) suck-
ling pigs, (e) sirens, (f) fabulous, (j) innumerable, (k) drawn with a very fine
camelhair brush, (l) *et cetera*, (m) having just broken the water pitcher, (n)
that from a long way off look like flies'" (OT xv).

Foucault makes the interesting point that what strikes "our thought, the
thought that bears the stamp of our age and our geography" about this fan-
ciful classification is its impossibility. Not that the beings described within
it are impossible or that the mere fact of their classification is. The impossibility resides in the absence of any conceivable "ground" or "framework"
within which such an ordering would be either obvious or meaningful to

us. "What transgresses the boundaries of all imagination, of all possible thought, is simply the alphabetical series (a, b, c, d) which links each of those categories to all the others" (OT xvi).

Though his discussion quickly exhibits something of a "tin ear" on his part for what is after all Borges's lampoon of the alien as alluring, Foucault reports that his laughter gave way to an uneasiness about the passage; it reminded him, he confesses, of those aphasics whose "language has been destroyed." Curiously treating Borges's literary conceit as a factual report about Chinese culture, Foucault views the passage as evidence of the impossibility of a rationale for classification. "There would appear to be, then, at the other extremity of the earth we inhabit, a culture entirely devoted to the ordering of space, but one of that does not distribute the multiplicity of existing things into any of the categories that make it possible for us to name, speak, and think" (OT xix).

Without pressing this introduction for more than it can give, there are two points Foucault appears to derive from this literary tale that guide him throughout the book. First, the present, embracing the "obviousness" of our current thought and its orderings, ought not to serve as the yardstick against which the history of thought is measured. Foucault treats Borges's story as challenging our "naturalistic" prejudice against even the possibility of a radically alternative order of knowledge. History of ideas, Foucault asserts, must no longer be in the service of a defunct philosophy of history, namely, a story in which history is made to teleologically support our present conception.

Foucault's concern here is not, however, unique. For example, Herbert Butterfield's *The Whig Conception of History* made a case against this type of prejudice. Butterfield understood it as a way in which our present certainties and deeply embedded assumptions guide historical narratives. He anticipates thereby both Foucault's analysis and criticism.

> It is part and parcel of the whig interpretation of history that it studies the past with reference to the present; and though there may be a sense in which this is unobjectionable if its implications are carefully considered, and there may be a sense in which it is inescapable, it has often been an obstruction to historical understanding because it has been taken to mean the study of the past with direct and perpetual reference to the present. Through this system of immediate reference to the present-day, historical personages can easily and irresistibly be classed into the men who furthered progress and the men who tried to hinder it; so that a handy rule of thumb exists by which the historian can select and reject, and can make his points of emphasis. On this system the historian is bound to construe his function as demanding him to be vigilant for likenesses between past and present, instead of being vigilant for unlikenesses; so that he will find it easy to say that he has seen the present in the past, he will imagine that he has discovered a "root" or an "anticipation" of the 20th century, when

in reality he is in a world of different connotations altogether, and he has merely tumbled upon what could be shown to be a misleading analogy.[18]

Though Butterfield emphasizes the role of values and political aims in historical reconstruction and, more carefully than Foucault, notes that "there may be a sense in which it is inescapable," he also extended this fallacy of "whiggism" from the purely evaluative prejudices of historians to epistemological ones, as Foucault claims to do. In Butterfield's *The Origins of Modern Science: 1300–1800,* he warns that "little progress can be made if we think of the older studies as merely a case of bad science" and states the following aim.

> It is not sufficient to read Galileo with the eyes of the twentieth century or to interpret him in modern terms—we can only understand his work if we know something of the system which he was attacking, and we must know something of that system apart from the things which were said about it by its enemies. In any case, it is necessary not merely to describe and expound discoveries, but to probe more deeply into historical processes and to learn something of the interconnectedness of events, as well as to exert all our endeavours for understanding of men who were like-minded with ourselves.[19]

It is not that Butterfield objects to "our" making the judgment that Galileo was closer than the Aristotelians to the truth as we presently understand it; rather, Butterfield objects to restricting the historian to confirming or documenting that judgment. The historical facts of the matter about those past scientific debates are simply independent of our present understanding, and there is an immanent structure of the theoretical and conceptual controversies involved that the historian ought to study. If done properly, the historian's reading of such a debate in the history of science would remain untouched by even the possibility, at least in some cases, that the present assessment of who were the past's "winners" and "losers" may dramatically alter.

But Foucault intends an even stronger claim against epistemological whiggism than Butterfield's. I am not convinced that Foucault's stronger objection to whiggism is defensible as an error of historical knowledge at all; nor am I convinced that even Foucault succeeds in escaping it. Foucault's concern is not only with the influence of our present values; he does not even defend the kind of autonomy of the historical facts from present theoretical assumptions that Butterfield appears to defend. In fact, Foucault argues against such an autonomy for historical facts. Foucault's case against the "authority of the historian's present" is that our current conceptual scheme, as well as classifications it sustains and makes meaningful, ought not to provide the organizing principles for any retrospective history of ideas.

How, it might be asked, would such a history even begin if something as fundamental as the current underlying conceptual scheme were to be bracketed along with other specific scientific results? This question does not have to be answered, since it turns out that Foucault does not follow his own recommendation. He begins his book, after all, by simply taking for granted the divisions between the human sciences as they are currently conceived; that is, that there are separate fields called biology, economics, linguistics. Furthermore, he repeats at the end of the book, discussed below, how his own study was made possible by *current* changes in the human sciences. Though Foucault stresses that he always appeals to criticisms of our current conceptual scheme, such a point hardly consists of abandoning the "whig conception," as presented above. A bias is not removed by its opposite or, as Butterfield puts it, "by merely adding the speech of the prosecution to the speech for the defense."

The second point Foucault derives from the Borges passage that guides his book is a reiterated ban on using the philosophical discipline of epistemology to guide the history of ideas. The challenge to our thinking generated by confronting *outré* classification systems is not met by such traditional philosophical devices as natural kinds, justified true belief, or the logic of evidential justification.

This second point brings me to a crucial passage in which Foucault distinguishes his aims from those of the traditional theory of knowledge, on the one hand, and the sciences themselves, on the other. There is an "intermediary realm," as Foucault calls it, in which the investigation of conceptual change is possible outside of theories of knowledge. Foucault speaks of the problems that concern him as involving that which makes possible identities, similarities, resemblances, or analogies (what he calls "a study of coherence"). Although this formulation may remind one of Husserl's distinction between conceptual and empirical inquiry, Foucault immediately distinguishes his project from that of those who investigate what is "a priori and necessary" as against what is "immediately perceptible."

> The fundamental codes of a culture—those governing its language, its schemas of perception, its exchanges, its techniques, its values, the hierarchy of its practices—establish for every man, from the very first, the empirical orders with which he will be dealing and within which he will be at home. At the other extremity of thought, there are the scientific theories or the philosophical interpretations which explain why order exists in general, what universal laws it obeys, what principle can account for it, and why this particular order has been established and not some other. But between these two regions, so distant from one another, lies a domain which, even though its role is mainly an intermediary one, is nonetheless fundamental: it is more confused, more obscure, and probably less easy to analyze. It is here that a culture imperceptibly deviat-

ing from the empirical orders prescribed for it by its primary codes, instituting an initial separation from them, causes them to lose their original transparency, relinquishes its immediate and invisible powers, frees itself sufficiently to discover that these orders are perhaps not the only possible ones or the best ones; this culture then finds itself faced with the stark fact that there exists, below the level of its spontaneous orders, things that are in themselves capable of being ordered, that belong to a certain unspoken order; the fact, in short, that order exists. As though emancipating itself to some extent from its linguistic, perceptual and practical grids, the culture superimposed on them another kind of grid which neutralized them, which by this superimposition both revealed and excluded them at the same time, so that the culture, by this very process, came face to face with order in its primary state. It is on the basis of this newly perceived order that the codes of language, perception, and practice are criticized and rendered partially invalid. It is on the basis of this order, taken as a firm foundation, that general theories as to the ordering of things, and the interpretation that such an ordering involves, will be constructed. Thus between the already "encoded" eye and reflective knowledge there is a middle region which liberates order itself; it is here that it appears, according to the culture and the age in question, continuous and graded or discontinuous and piecemeal. . . . This middle region, then, in so far as it makes manifest the modes of being of order, can be posited as the most fundamental of all; anterior to words, perceptions, and gestures, which are then taken to be more or less exact, more or less happy, expressions of it (which is why this experience of order in its massive and primary being *[en son être massif et premier]* always plays a critical role); more solid, more archaic, less dubious, more "true" than the theories that attempt to give those expressions explicit form, exhaustive application, or philosophical foundation. Thus, in every culture, between the use of what one might call the ordering codes and reflections upon order itself, there is the naked experience of order *[l'expérience nue de l'ordre]* and of its modes of being. (OT xx-xxi)[20]

This passage trumpets Heideggerianism. There is an appeal to some primary form of ontological disclosure and a contrast of a pretheoretical, ordinary encountering of the world with efforts at explanation and theorizing. Foucault pictures two opposed ends of a continuum of knowledge. At one end, there is theorizing about the world that encompasses scientific explanations and philosophical systems and, at the other end, the mundane, active involvement with the world from which observing and measuring emerge; like theorizing, however, encountering the world in this mundane manner is made possible by a conceptual scheme, "fore-structure," or "cultural code," as Foucault prefers it.

Between these two ends of possible knowledge is a "middle region" of critical possibilities. This middle region reflects upon how a simple act of observation is possible. It makes "manifest the modes of being of order." Before words, gestures, theories, or observations there is "the naked experience of order and of its modes of being." Thus this midpoint of analysis can raise questions about the code or schema, not merely operate within it as its mere possibility. The intermediary domain allows for questions about the scheme itself, rather than simply "internal questions" concerning, for instance, whether or not some given entity exists, as presupposed within a scheme. The traditional intellectual histories Foucault rejects fail because they do not distinguish critical from coded analyses.

The positing of such an experience somehow outside the "encoded experiences" provides for some sort of critical reflection in Foucault's view upon those fundamental assumptions, normally undetected, that are both historically mutable and yet not able to be suspended or bracketed. At certain moments, mysteriously enough, there occurs "this experience of order in its massive and primary being."

The above passage defends, then, the second constraint upon the history of ideas, as discussed above. The second constraint excluded epistemological guidelines from such histories. Foucault groups such guidelines within the kind of theoretical elaboration made possible by conceptual codes. He seems to think, furthermore, that any such epistemological inquiry is then dependent on this "primary experience."

But serious reservations arise with regard to this strategy. First, Foucault ought to give the reader some reason for preferring his approach to the traditional epistemological defense. Merely appealing to the "naked experience of order" is hardly such a defense. Second, Foucault's aim is a philosophical one, after all. He wants to establish whether or not criticism is possible concerning basic and fundamental ontological or epistemological assumptions. To put his point differently: Are the different encoded schemas capable of being judged true or false? Are the classifications made possible by them right or wrong? Even concluding, as Foucault apparently does, that matters of truth and falsity do not apply to conceptual schemes and that a "correct ordering" is a metaphysically disreputable notion is, likewise, a philosophical conclusion. It is also a conclusion to which others have arrived before Foucault; for example, Rudolf Carnap's attack on metaphysics as discussed in Chapters 1 and 2 reaches similar antirealist conclusions.

Third, the possibility of some mysterious direct experience of order and being is simply another traditional and to a great extent exhausted philosophical strategy, an appeal to some form of perceptual realism. In addition, the possibility of such experience stands in stark opposition to the otherwise nominalist and antirealist arguments permeating Foucault's criticisms. If being could disclose itself in this way, to use the Heideggerian phrasing Foucault evokes, then both the conventionalist and relativist challenges to ontology and epistemology, to which Foucault repeatedly appeals in his critical analyses, would collapse.

Foucault has been arguing in this book that "our current conceptions" of life, labor, and language fail to fully understand the Classical and Renaissance conceptions that preceded them. We distort this past by imposing upon these studies our own unexamined classifications and assumptions. The book ends, therefore, with a clarification of what he means by "our current conception." He makes the plausible case that the human sciences are grouped as a related body of sciences because they study human beings. But there remains a deeper assumption, he argues. "Man" is both the entity studied and the epistemological foundation of these sciences. He claims this foundation has emerged very recently in intellectual history, and he seeks to dismantle its authority, in part by dismantling the authority of any epistemological foundation whatsoever. Only at the very end of the book does Foucault reveal that it is Husserl's transcendental subject that he has had in mind all along and it is Husserl's philosophy in which subjectivity is improperly both an epistemological foundation and an empirical object. Husserl is "our current conception."

> If man is indeed, in the world, the locus of an empirico-transcendental doublet, if he is that paradoxical figure in which the empirical contents of knowledge necessarily release, of themselves, the conditions that have made them possible, then man cannot posit himself in the immediate and sovereign transparency of a *cogito*; nor, on the other hand, can he inhabit the objective inertia of something that, by rights, does not and never can lead to self-consciousness. ... Because he is an empirico-transcendental doublet, man is also the locus of misunderstanding—of misunderstanding that constantly exposes his thought to the risk of being swamped by his own being, and also enables him to recover his integrity on the basis of what eludes him. This is why transcendental reflection in its modern form does not, as in Kant, find its fundamental necessity in the existence of a science of nature ... , but in the existence ... of that *not-known* from which man is perpetually summoned towards self-knowledge. (OT 322–323)

Though he does not mention the name, Foucault's subsequent criticisms of such views are tailor-made for Husserl. For instance, Foucault proceeds, after the above, to criticize those who seek to separate philosophical from empirical, scientific inquiry. He claims that all modern theories of knowledge, because they are required to serve the above function, cannot "avoid reviving the theme of the *cogito*." The modern *cogito* does not find truth in a simple insight, however, but through some laborious methodological discipline. "In this form, the *cogito* will not therefore be the sudden and illuminating discovery that all thought is thought, but the constantly renewed interrogation as to how thought can reside elsewhere than here, and yet so very close to itself; how it can *be* in the forms of non-thinking" (OT 324).

Foucault's phrase "the forms of non-thinking" refers to those aspects of the ego as a natural, worldly object that Husserl conceptually distinguished from reflective subjectivity. Thus, in spite of Foucault's dismissal of Sartre at this stage in his career, these passages repeat the very same criticism of Husserl raised by Sartre's early essay attacking the transcendental ego. As Foucault continues:

> This is why phenomenology—even though it was first suggested by way of anti-psychologism, or, rather, precisely in so far as, in opposition to anti-psychologism, it revived the problem of the *a priori* and the transcendental motif—has never been able to exorcise its insidious kinship, its simultaneously promising and threatening proximity, to empirical analyses of man; it is also why, though it was inaugurated by a reduction of the cogito, it has already been led to questions, to *the* question of ontology. The phenomenological project continually resolves itself, before our eyes, into a description—empirical despite itself—of actual experience, and into an ontology of the unthought that automatically short-circuits the primacy of the "I think." (OT 325–326)

This criticism of Husserl's analysis as "empirical despite itself" and in a "threatening proximity to empirical analyses of man" assumes either that the phenomenological reduction fails to prevent such contamination by the empirical or that the a priori/a posteriori distinction collapses. Though Foucault does not argue for either assumption, I assume he rejects the reduction, since Foucault himself appeals to the concept of the a priori.

Foucault's attack on our current conception—"the empirical-transcendental doublet"—is, however, not finally pursued as a philosophical objection at all, in spite of the above account of Husserl. In his conclusion, he embraces contemporary theories of anthropology and psychoanalysis that have reconceived themselves as scientific studies, but not studies of "man"; rather, they investigate formal, syntactic-like structures. These transformed disciplines, which are no longer concerned with consciousness as traditionally understood, make it possible to dispense with the "fiction" of an empirical-transcendental "doublet." Foucault identifies these new sciences as "structural" and it seems to partly explain his earlier appeal to "syntactic reorganization" as the aim of the "ill-defined" intellectual histories he hoped to clarify.

But even if these sciences are as Foucault describes them, namely, studies of what had been previously called "human beings" through the elimination of postulated mental states, subjectivity, or consciousness, the mere fact of their existence would not constitute a refutation of either phenomenology or the epistemological and ontological debates he wishes to steer around. Eliminativism, as Foucault promotes it in his defense of the new structural anthropology and psychoanalysis, is a philosophical, not a scientific, position. As such the position either wins or loses by argument, not by merely being assumed as scientific.

Foucault finally holds that philosophical issues are wholly idle or mere "shadows" of the practice of the sciences of their day, contrary to Husserl's original strategy. Thus his attack on philosophy seems naturalistic in the end (in the sense of collapsing philosophy into the sciences or treating it as a mere ideology) and, what is worse for his own restrictions, a "present-centered" form of scientific naturalism. The conclusion of the book thus seems in tension with one of the guiding directives of the book, that "present-centered" standards not be the yardstick of intellectual history.

Foucault's often cited announcement at the end of the book concerning the "end of man" is neither as pertinent to this issue nor as radical as it first sounds. The "death of man" is the death of the above "current conception," specifically the conception of the human being as conscious in the dual sense of an empirical object and a transcendental foundation for the possibility of inquiry. If what has ended, then, is another conceptual scheme, it does not imply, on Foucault's own terms, that such *epistemic* change says anything definitive about what is in fact true, real, foundational, or even scientific. There is nothing outside the scheme, given Foucault's nominalist drumbeat in the book, and thus nothing could dramatically "cease to exist" or thereby prove or disprove the scientific status of this or that form of inquiry. After all, the modes of representation his works claim to document are not tethered to "objective articulations."

The Fabric of Sentences

The Archaeology of Knowledge is Foucault's only sustained attempt at careful philosophical discussion, though it aims of course to dismiss philosophy. I suggested above that such an antiphilosophical strategy was implicit in Foucault, since he treats ontological and epistemological assumptions as both transitory and idle. *The Archaeology of Knowledge* does, however, mark a change in Foucault's conception of what his intellectual histories had achieved, and he attempts to answer certain criticisms.

The book tries to clarify Foucault's own historical work, work he thought representative of a larger movement in historical research.[21] He proceeds, oddly enough, in a Husserlian manner. He questions the "self-evident unities" involved in historical studies and announces that he will not take for granted any fundamental concepts. Specifically, he seeks to suspend what "our thinking" takes as obvious or natural. In pursuing this end, the book outlines a good deal of terminology he claims avoids metaphysically contentious issues, the traditional concepts of the philosophy of history, and any confusions occasioned by misleading comparisons of his work with that of others. Whether Foucault achieves these aims is in question, but the sober-minded and critical attitude in the work is a welcome change of pace.

It may be best to begin where the book ends and work back to the terminology that even Foucault describes as "a whole apparatus, whose sheer

weight and no doubt somewhat bizarre machinery are a source of embarrassment" (AK 135). This apparatus captures what Foucault was doing, often without realizing it, and outlines future investigations. Foucault speaks
hopefully here of determining laws, correlations, regularities, and functions
where there had been previously only those impressionistic and uncritical
summaries. I will return to the quasi-scientific language he uses in defense
of his work below.

The two connected notions in this reconception of intellectual history are
"archaeology" and "discursive formation." Archaeology refers to a kind of
history, unlike the traditional history of ideas of course, that Foucault
claims was the prose he spoke without realizing it. What an archaeology in-
vestigates is a discursive formation. A discursive formation is not a group
of thoughts, representations, images, or themes; rather, it is a "kind of regularity" that makes possible objects, concepts, statements, theoretical
choices, discoveries, and even the sciences themselves. Discursive practices
are, therefore, broader than sciences, but also not just a cumbersome way
to talk about the old tired themes of mind, rationality, or culture.

> This group of elements, formed in a regular manner by a discursive practice,
> and which are indispensable to the constitution of a science, although they
> are not necessarily destined to give rise to one, can be called *knowledge*.
> Knowledge is that of which one can speak in a discursive practice, and which
> is specified by that fact: the domain constituted by the different objects that
> will or will not acquire scientific status . . . ; knowledge is also the space in
> which the subject may take up a position and speak of the object with which
> he deals in his discourse . . . ; knowledge is also the field of coordination and
> subordination of statements in which concepts appear . . . ; lastly, knowledge
> is defined by the possibilities of use and appropriation offered by dis-
> course. . . . These are bodies of knowledge that are independent of the sci-
> ences (which are neither their historical prototypes, nor their practical by-
> products), but there is no knowledge without a particular discursive practice;
> and any discursive practice may be defined by the knowledge that it forms.
> (AK 182–183)

I noted that Foucault, in spite of his criticism of philosophy in general
and Husserl in particular, continues to use the notion of the a priori. He
specifically introduces the "historical a priori," which he then calls a "bar-
barous term," as a recurrent feature of his research.

> Juxtaposed these two words produce a rather startling effect; but what I mean
> by the term is an *a priori* that is not a condition of validity for judgements, but
> a condition of reality for statements. It is not a question of rediscovering what
> might legitimize an assertion, but of freeing the conditions of emergence of
> statements, the law of their coexistence with others, the specific form of their
> mode of being, the principles according to which they survive, become trans-
> formed, and disappear. An *a priori* not of truth that might never be said, or re-

ally given to experience; but the *a priori* of a history that is given, since it is that of things actually said. (AK 127)

The contrast in the above discussion between a "condition of validity," which would appear to be the traditional conception (the one held by Husserl, for example), and the "condition of reality for statements," which Foucault identifies as his conception of a priori, is supposed to explicate how the a priori can also be historical and thus transient. Foucault concludes that "this *a priori* . . . is defined by the group of rules that characterize a discursive practice."

Since Foucault defines these terms by way of each other, as seen in the definition of the historical a priori, a critical assessment of his terminology requires breaking free of these tiny circles of exposition. One way to do so is to ask about the "statement" that constitutes in his language the smallest unit of a "discursive formation."[22]

Foucault begins the book, strikingly enough, by stating his aim as one of questioning both the book and the *oeuvre* as "unities." But, as he proceeds, it becomes apparent that he has abandoned the ambitious radicalism of *The Order of Things*. He admits that these unquestioned unities must be the starting point for such histories, yet they can still be critically examined.

> I shall take as my starting-point whatever unities are already given (such as psychopathology, medicine, or political economy); but I shall not place myself inside these dubious unities in order to study their internal configuration or their secret contradictions. I shall make use of them just long enough to ask myself what unities they form; by what right they can claim a field that specifies them in space and a continuity that individualizes them in time; according to what laws they are formed; against the background of which discursive events they stand out; and whether they are not, in their accepted and quasi-institutional individuality, ultimately the surface-effect of more firmly grounded unities. (AK 26)

As a way to defend the "more firmly grounded unities" that produce books and *oeuvres* as their "surface-effects," Foucault considers three candidates for what would be the smallest unit of a discursive formation sustaining "surface-effects." The three candidates are the concept, the proposition, and the grammatical sentence. To simplify my task I will ignore the third possibility, though Foucault uses it as an opportunity to discuss and criticize his earlier structuralist flirtation with the notion of a syntactic level of analysis.

Before introducing Foucault's objections to the other two candidates, namely, the proposition and the concept, I want to briefly motivate the issue. The historian of ideas, who has now become critical and self-reflective in the fashion Foucault recommends, is asking: What groups "ideas" to-

gether into distinct disciplines? What concerning these groupings is properly an object of historical study? If Foucault is correct that the historian
ought to focus on discursive formations and their statements, then in part
he must show what is wrong with focusing on the more familiar grouping
by propositions or concepts.

The propositional and conceptual answers to the above questions present
a contrast. The propositional approach offers a kind of "content analysis"
and the conceptualist approach a kind of "thematics" of intellectual history. In the first case, the historian analyzes texts in search of the actual
content buried beneath the vagaries of the way in which the text has been
written. For example, the historian of science may distinguish factual from
presuppositional contents and in extracting and reformulating them assess
whether the intellectual work in question defended an assumption, described an empirical result, or posed a theoretical problem.

The thematic approach, in contrast, denies, for instance, that historians
can clearly distinguish factual and presuppositional content or clearly reformulate the wording of historical documents in such a way that the reasoning of the historical text can be assessed in the somewhat formal fashion
suggested above. Rather, the conceptualists hold, the historian is guided by
a looser picture of how interdependent structures of assumptions, images,
concepts, and various different types of evidence form the topics of intellectual history, but one whose architecture its historical authors neither were
fully aware of nor had under control.

The conceptualist account of intellectual history is the nearest cousin to
Foucault's own account, and he treats such a view as his central challenge.
For instance, E. A. Burtt, an early defender of such a thematic approach,
speaks of studying "the ultimate picture which an age forms of the nature
of its world" and notes:

> We inevitably see our limited problem in terms of inherited notions which
> ought themselves to form part of a larger problem. The continued uncritical
> use in the writings of these men of traditional ideas like that of "the external
> world," the dichotomy assumed between the world of the physicist and the
> world of sense, the physiological and psychological postulates taken for
> granted, as, for example the distinction between sensation and the act of sens-
> ing, are a few illustrations of what is meant. Our questions must go deeper,
> and bring into clear focus a more fundamental and more popularly significant
> problem than any of these men are glimpsing.[23]

The following account of how conceptual schemes function in such a
task similarly defends a new conception of the history of the science.

> The history of science is cluttered with the relics of conceptual schemes that
> were once fervently believed and that have since been replaced by incompati-
> ble theories. There is no way of proving that a conceptual scheme is final. But,

rash or not, this commitment to a conceptual scheme is a common phenomenon in the sciences, and it seems an indispensable one, because it endows conceptual schemes with one new and all-important function. Conceptual schemes are comprehensive; their consequences are not limited to what is already known. Therefore, ... the theory will transcend the known, becoming first and foremost, a powerful tool for predicting and exploring the unknown. It will affect the future of science as well as its past.[24]

Foucault was likely influenced by the above arguments, especially Thomas Kuhn's emphasis on conceptual change in the history of science. But, by the time of *The Archaeology of Knowledge,* he had come to doubt both the function of conceptual schemes as well as the opposition between continuity and discontinuity in these sorts of histories of knowledge.

Foucault hopes in contrast to demonstrate that statements—the units of a discursive formation—are not sentences, propositions, or these bits of "conceptual architecture." Since the sentence model has been set aside, I now focus on why a statement is neither a proposition nor a concept. A way to state the issue is to ask whether what links statements together is what links propositions together. If it is not, then propositional analysis will not be robust enough for this new history of ideas.

> Nor should the relation between a statement and what it states be confused with the relation between a proposition and its referent. We know that logicians say that a proposition like "The golden mountain is in California" cannot be verified because it has no referent: its negation is therefore neither more nor less true than its affirmation. Should we say similarly that a statement refers to nothing if the proposition, to which it lends existence, has no referent? Rather, the reverse. We should say not that the absence of a referent brings with it the absence of a correlate for the statement, but that it is the correlate of the statement—that to which it refers, not only what is said, but also what it speaks of, its "theme"—which makes it possible to say whether or not the proposition has a referent: ... "The present king of France is bald" lacks a referent only if one supposes that the statement refers to the world of contemporary historical information. The relation of the proposition to the referent cannot serve as a model or a law for the relation of the statement to what it states. The latter relation not only does not belong to the same level as the former, but it is anterior to it. (AK 89–90)

This discussion is very confusing. I'll set aside for the moment, but return to it, Foucault's introduction of "referent" and "verification." The aim is to draw a distinction between statements and propositions by taking a certain example that Foucault considers a problem for the propositional approach. The example turns on how a propositional analysis would handle the sentence "The golden mountain is in California." Would such an approach conclude, as Foucault claims it does, that "its negation is therefore neither more nor less true than its affirmation"? If Foucault were correct, propositional analysis would shipwreck over those cases in which a statement and its negation are both "neither more nor less true." Such a possibility effectively blocks the use of propositional analysis, much as Burtt had claimed it would when he defended the conceptual approach. Since Foucault thinks that will be the case for much of the study of the history of ideas, the propositional approach will fail.

But Foucault has misunderstood, apparently, both the technique and the example. Propositional analysis distinguishes propositions from their surface grammatical structure by way of a formal notation system. In this fashion it can show how the surface structure of grammar misleads concerning deep logical structure. Avoiding the complication of introducing formal notation here, the propositional reformulation of the first statement would read: "There is exactly one golden mountain, and that golden mountain is in California." This example exhibits what Bertrand Russell famously called a "definite description." (Foucault makes quite clear in these passages that he has Russell's work in mind.) A "definite description" exemplifies how logical structure is concealed within the grammatical garb of two referring expressions linked by the "is" of identity.

But Russell's analysis shows that only when confusion is caused by the surface grammar will it seem that in such a case "its negation is therefore neither more nor less true than its affirmation." The negation of the original statement, as reformulated, could either be "There is *not* exactly one golden mountain" or "There is exactly one golden mountain, and this golden mountain is *not* in California." The first possibility is the "proper" negation and affirms, truly as it turns out, that there is no such thing as a golden mountain. Thus Foucault's claim that in this case the negation is neither true nor false is false.

The second reformulation ("There is exactly one golden mountain, and this golden mountain is *not* in California") is not a proper negation like the one above. It is the kind of claim that produced confusion to begin with, since it appears that in denying some property of the "golden mountain" one is forced to assume its existence. But once clarified by being reformulated this phrase turns out to be a description that, like the description that the golden mountain *is* in California, is also false.

Hence, propositional analysis precludes the tantalizing leap into paradox that Foucault seems all too willing to take and thereby aids in understanding. Therefore, the example Foucault has chosen does not show the limits of propositional analysis—precisely the opposite. In separating the rhetorical and logical aspects of a text, propositional analysis can claim to benefit the intellectual historian by revealing the basic units the intellectual historian studies.

Now I turn to the problem of reference. "Should we say similarly that a statement refers to nothing if the proposition, to which it lends existence, has no referent?" First, Foucault is not using the notion of "reference" carefully, because he is discussing simultaneously, apparently, the practice of logical analysis and the practice of historians who would use this technique in their work. It is important in logic, however, to be attentive to the point that both statements and those who use statements can refer. Thus Foucault, at the very least, is muddying the waters by having the logician conclude that "the golden mountain" refers to nothing. The logical notation was introduced, as shown above, for the precise purpose of escaping such a paradoxical way of expressing the content of the statement. The expression was not, when reformulated, a referring expression.

Furthermore, the logician is not properly, as logician, concerned with verification; the formal level is all the logician requires. At such a formal level there would be no point in seeking empirical verification. Foucault is likely correct that a historian using the device of propositional analysis could not simply remain at the formal level and would need to consider what those using such statements were referring to; and that is why, I suppose, he introduces this talk about reference and verification.

The purpose of propositional analysis was as a tool for clarifying the content of documents prior to and independent of having evidence concerning what those using these statements were referring to or whether or not the statements in question could be verified. Foucault's point about reference, additionally, makes the unfortunate assumption that the concepts of verification and meaning coincide. But such a contentious position ought not to be introduced as an unexamined assumption of his argument against propositional analysis.

Although I agree with Foucault that propositional analysis is not a promising candidate for reforming the study of intellectual history, I am not simply scoring points on what may have been a lapse into carelessness.[25] The above types of confusion are not, unfortunately, isolated cases in the book and suggest two concerns about how he proceeds. First, Foucault's efforts to disentangle and clarify both how he is using these special terms he has introduced and why he thinks he needs to introduce this new vocabulary are in part dependent on his claims that the more familiar approaches, those of logical, linguistic, and content analysis (and perhaps others), are inadequate. But if he is confused about how these other techniques are used and what implications they have, then the claim that they are inadequate to his purposes may be mistaken, whether or not he can defend an alternative approach.

Second, Foucault's concerns are much wider than that of the right methodology. He seeks to elucidate, for example, such basic notions as reference, realism, truth, concept, and object, issues he thinks precede and make possible formal and methodological devices. Furthermore, like Frege and Husserl, he distinguishes his effort at clarifying these matters from the study of the psychological processes of thinking.

But if we isolate . . . the occurrence of the statement/event, it is not in order to spread over everything a dust of facts. It is in order to be sure that this occurrence is not linked with synthesizing operations of a purely psychological kind (the intention of the author, the form of his mind, the rigour of his thought, the themes that obsess him, the project that traverses his existence and gives it meaning) and to be able to grasp other forms of regularity, other types of relations. (AK 28–29)

But that is just to say, once again, that these are properly philosophical questions, questions Foucault simultaneously raises and yet suggests will somehow dissolve, misleadingly I think, once some new, quasi-scientific discipline concerning the study of discursive formations replaces traditional disputes. His approach-avoidance attitude toward the philosophical problems that litter these discussions leads, as seen above, to deeper confusions rather than the clarity and precision toward which Foucault, to his credit, strives.

But to return to the discussion again, Foucault's central debate is with the conceptual-scheme approach. For instance, Foucault often explains what he means by the term "statement" by saying what a statement is not. The following quotations stress Foucault's partial agreement with conceptualists like Kuhn.

A statement is not confronted (face to face, as it were) by a *correlate*—or the absence of a *correlate*—as a proposition has (or has not) a referent, or a proper noun designates someone (or no one). It is linked to a "referential" that is made up not of "things," "facts," "realities," or "being," but laws of possibility, rules of existence for the objects that are named, designated, or described within it, and for the relations that are affirmed or denied in it. (AK 91)

In the descriptions for which I have attempted to provide a theory, there can be no question of interpreting discourse with a view to writing a history of the referent. In the examples chosen, we are not trying to find out who was mad at a particular period, or in what his madness consisted, or whether his disturbances were identical with those known to us today. . . . What, in short, we wish to do is to dispense with "things." To "depresentify" them. . . . To substitute for the enigmatic treasure of "things" anterior to discourse, the regular formation of objects that emerge only in discourse. (AK 47)

The statement, then, is not an elementary unity that can be added to the unities described by grammar or logic. It cannot be isolated like a sentence, a proposition, or an act of formulation. (AK 108)

Why are the units of statements not simply concepts? First, Foucault agrees that on either approach what groups together ideas into a discipline is not reference to the same object. Foucault is not a realist, though he dismisses realism rather too quickly. But then his antirealism does not distinguish discursive formations from conceptual schemes, because Kuhn, for example, is also an antirealist. The closest Foucault comes to a face-to-face argument is the following:

I do not wish to take as an object of analysis the conceptual architecture of an isolated text, an individual *oeuvre*, or a science at a particular moment in time. One stands back in relation to this manifest set of concepts; and one tries to determine according to what schemata (of series, simultaneous groupings, linear or reciprocal modification) the statements may be linked to one another in a type of discourse; one tries in this way to discover how the recurrent elements of statements can reappear, dissociate, recompose, gain in extension or determination, be taken up into new logical structure, acquire, on the other hand, new semantic contents, and constitute partial organizations among themselves. These schemata make it possible to describe—not the laws of the internal construction of concepts, nor their progressive and individual genesis in the mind of man—but their anonymous dispersion through texts, books, and *oeuvres*. . . . Such an analysis, then, concerns a kind of preconceptual level, the field in which concepts can coexist and the rules to which this field is subjected. (AK 60)

The central objection, then, is that the statements that make up a discursive formation are a "preconceptual field" concerning whatever makes the "heterogeneous multiplicity of concepts" possible and in that fashion replaces the "profusion of themes, beliefs, and representations with which one usually deals when one is writing the history of ideas" (AK 63).

This contrast is, however, not satisfying for two reasons. In calling it "preconceptual," that is, that which makes possible beliefs or representations, Foucault is focusing on an equivocation about the term "concept." The same point is being made by the conceptual-scheme approach to intellectual history, as summarized in Kuhn's quote about the history of science. That approach distinguishes between a concept, such as inertia, and the conceptual scheme that makes that concept possible. Thus the best that can be said about Foucault's objection is that it involves a narrow terminological dispute.

But, more important, Foucault's objection rests on an ambiguity about the phrase "make possible." There are two possible meanings. It could mean "causally make possible," as in revealing the causal mechanism, whether social or natural, by which "surface-effects," as he calls them, are produced. Or it could mean "conceptually make possible," as in the traditional philosophical account of epistemological justification.

If it is obvious that Foucault dismisses the second sense, a point he repeats throughout his work, it is not at all obvious that he embraces the first. *The Archaeology of Knowledge*, for all its comments about correlations, dispersions, and lawlike regularities, is devoid of any discussion of causal mechanisms, whether natural or social. In fact, as noted above, the book proceeds as though Foucault were bracketing scientific claims of that type. Having in this way left the phrase "make possible" unclear, Foucault's defense of this terminological machinery against the criticism that it merely imitates the study of conceptual schemes either reduces to a terminological squabble or is seriously ambiguous.

Foucault's promissory note concerning these studies of regularities, correlations, laws, series, dispersions, and so on, is only as good as the claim that these future studies are not guided by the very "pre-given unities" dismissed as mere "surface-effects." If it were the case that the apparatus Foucault has mounted is parasitical on and thus surreptitiously guided by the discredited concepts of the book, *oeuvre*, author, or theme (the long list of notions he wishes to replace), then the "machinery" would indeed be "embarrassing."

A discursive formation, which needs to be defined more precisely than telling us what it is not, must be shown to provide an object of study for historians distinct from concepts, propositions, and sentences. If, on the other hand, Foucault merely draws attention to a claim that there are assumptions "built into" the everyday language of the "book" or the "author," and yet treats these assumptions as neither capable of being replaced nor analyzed any further, then his argument amounts to a "plague" on all these vocabularies.

The newly introduced discursive formation, statement, archive, and archaeological method would likewise share, by this argument, questionable and indeed indefensible presuppositions. This vocabulary would not only offer no improvement over the tools of everyday life, but it would lack even the gift of familiarity. My point is that carrying out these archaeological studies of discursive formations remains, for all these arguments, parasitical on the prearchaeological, self-evident concepts of the book, theme, author, *oeuvre*, or discipline; and this point is strikingly obvious in Foucault's own historical studies in which the radical chest beating often leads to rather tame and somewhat familiar results. Foucault has not determined a "more firmly grounded" level that replaces the mere "surface-effects." Furthermore, lacking a firmly grounded history of ideas in some quasi-scientific manner, Foucault's announcement of having killed philosophy is greatly exaggerated.[26]

Destruction

Like Gadamer's, Jacques Derrida's arguments and analyses, such as they are, are detailed commentaries or interpretations of other philosophical and literary texts. Since there is often not space enough for discussing both Derrida's points and the views he is analyzing, assessments of Derrida regularly reduce to a sterile standoff between the true believers and angry debunkers; at least that has been the pattern in my view.

There may be an alternative, however, at least for my purposes. Derrida's *Speech and Phenomena* is a collection of essays on Husserl's *Logical Inves-*

tigations. Since Husserl's thought has been covered in some detail, these essays will allow me to examine Derrida's now widely imitated approach to philosophy closely and critically, specifically by examining both his summaries and criticisms of Husserl's work. Also, this approach will have the satisfying and perhaps comforting result of ending this book where it began—a Derridean effect if there ever was one.[27]

Though Derrida can hardly be identified with a specific philosophical position, except for his embrace of Heidegger's project of fundamental ontology, many of Derrida's enthusiasts point to general conclusions about the ineliminable nature of ambiguity and the indeterminacy of the meaning of written texts as consisting of a Derridean "creed." But these quasi-skeptical conclusions need careful discussion and assessment before we agree either that they are Derrida's conclusions or that they say what they are popularly understood to say. My question is initially a much narrower one. What are precisely Derrida's criticisms of Husserl's account of meaning and signification? Only then can we ask: How do those criticisms support wider, albeit negative, conclusions concerning any theory of meaning at all?

As is common in the continental tradition, Derrida mixes together his expositions and criticisms of Husserl, making it difficult to appreciate either. I will try to sharpen that distinction by explicating Husserl, focusing on those passages in Husserl Derrida "reads," before turning to his critical assessment.

Husserl speaks of how "astonishing" he finds it that immanent mental life can represent objects external to mental phenomena, an astonishment not lessened in the least, in his view, by causal explanations of how representation might "work." Husserl proposes a theory of meaning in response to this wonder. Such a theory would account for representation and the systematic relationship between thought contents. It connects, using Husserl's favored expression, the immanent and transcendent worlds; it directs us "inward" toward conceptual content as well as "outward" toward the world.

Husserl begins by holding that meaning ought not to be restricted to only linguistic meaning; he takes it as a general account of mental acts. In *Ideas* he makes this point explicitly:

> We shall restrict our regard exclusively to "signifying" and "signification." Originally, those words concerned only the linguistic sphere, that of "expressing." But one can scarcely avoid and, at the same time, take an important cognitive step, extending the signification of those words and suitably modifying them so that they can find application of a certain kind to the whole noetic-noematic sphere; thus application to all acts, be they now combined with expressive acts or not. (Ideas 294)

This extension of the concept of meaning is presented above in *Ideas* as something "one can scarcely avoid" and "an important cognitive step."

When Husserl first discussed these points in *Logical Investigations,* he noted the confusions in everyday usage. For example, even purely physical events can have an "expression" or can function as a sign; for example, smoke is said to be a sign of fire. Husserl thus suggests an initial distinction between "indication" and "expression" with respect to what a sign stands for. ("Every sign is a sign for something, but not every sign has 'meaning,' a 'sense' that the sign 'expresses'" [LI 269].)

When a sign stands for something other than itself, but without involving a meaningful content, Husserl calls it an "indication." Smoke indicates fire, or, similarly, a facial expression indicates an emotion. Thus it is only the case of a sign's *expressing* a meaning or sense that Husserl wishes to generalize beyond linguistic phenomena (to perception, for instance). Indication, furthermore, is a contingent feature of the world, whereas expression involves a conceptual necessity with respect to any experience whatsoever. "While what is intimated [indicated] consists in inner experiences, what we assert in the judgement involves nothing subjective. My act of judging is a transient experience: it arises and passes away. But what my assertion asserts, the content . . . neither arises nor passes away" (LI 285).

Husserl therefore defends doing "violence to usage."

> We shall lay down, for provisional intelligibility, that each instance or part of *speech,* as also each sign that is essentially of the same sort, shall count as an expression, whether or not such speech is uttered, or addressed with communicative intent to any persons or not. Such a definition excludes facial expression and the various gestures which involuntarily accompany speech without communicative intent, or those in which a man's mental states achieve understandable "expression" for his environment, without the added help of speech. Such "utterances" are not expressions in the sense in which a case of speech is an expression, they are not phenomenally one with the experiences made manifest in them in the consciousness of the man who manifests them, as is the case with speech. In such manifestations one man communicates nothing to another: their utterance involves no intent to put certain "thoughts" on record expressively, whether for the man himself, in his solitary state, or for others. Such "expressions," in short, have properly speaking, *no meaning.* (LI 275)

Derrida will focus almost exclusively on the above passage and on the way in which Husserl's concept of expression excludes the following. First, Husserl excludes gestures and facial expressions from meaning as expression, even though such contextual facts make understanding possible. Specifically Derrida will focus on Husserl's example of "speaking" as a case in which the understanding of meaning can occur in abstraction from any contextual features of indication.

Second, Husserl excludes indications of a speaker's mental state, translated as "intimations" above, because these are matters of psychological or even physiological fact, on a par with smoke indicating fire, irrelevant to the philosophical study of meaning.

Indication of mental states is relevant solely for the purpose of communicative success. Such features may allow a hearer, for instance, to "gain uptake" on meaning (to borrow an expression from J. L. Austin). Thus, to "gain uptake" in communication sometimes involves simply seeing the speaker as a speaker. As Husserl puts it: "When I listen to someone I perceive him as a speaker, I hear him recounting, demonstrating, doubting, wishing, etc. The hearer perceives the intimation in the same sense in which he perceives the intimating person" (LI 277–278). But these are practical matters of communication, and again Husserl sets them aside.

Husserl defends this approach and his basic distinction by convincing the reader that expressions have meaning even in the absence of their functioning indicatively. Meaning is independent of communication, and Husserl calls this autonomy of meaning its "ideality." A soliloquy, then, is an example wherein indication is necessarily absent, whereas meaning is necessarily present. In a soliloquy the meaning of one's thoughts or self-expression does not require gaining uptake because speaking to oneself does not require bringing oneself to see oneself as intending such and such.

Thus meaning as expression is essential, whereas indication as intimation is contingent. All communicative speech is necessarily meaningful speech, but not all meaningful speech is necessarily communicative speech.

> One of course speaks, in certain sense, even in soliloquy, and it is certainly possible to think of oneself as speaking, and even as speaking to oneself, as e.g., when someone says to himself: "You have gone wrong, you can't go on like that." But in the genuine sense of communication, there is no speech in such cases, nor does one tell oneself anything: one merely conceives of oneself as speaking and communicating. In a monologue words can perform no function of indicating the existence of mental acts, since such indication would there be quite purposeless. For the acts in question are themselves experienced by us at the very moment. (LI 279–280)

Meaning is, then, neither a private nor a subjective phenomenon. In a soliloquy one does not invent the meanings of one's thoughts any more than one literally speaks to oneself. Meaning for Husserl is not an inner mental experience at all; it, unlike acts of thinking and speaking, "neither arises nor passes away."

The above summary sketches Husserl's first steps in *Logical Investigations*. Derrida claims, however, that these tentative steps already introduce a surreptitious metaphysics making possible but also undermining the phenomenological project of philosophical reform.

> We have thus a prescription for the most general form of our question: do not phenomenological necessity, the rigor and subtlety of Husserl's analysis, the

exigencies to which it responds and which we must first recognize, nonetheless conceal a metaphysical presupposition? Do they not harbor a dogmatic or speculative commitment which, to be sure, would not keep the phenomenological critique from being realized, would not be a residue of unperceived naïveté, but would *constitute* phenomenology from within, in its project of criticism and in the instructive value of its own premises? This would be done precisely in what soon comes to be recognized as the source and guarantee of all value, the "principle of principles": i.e., the original self-giving evidence, the *present* or *presence* of sense to a full and primordial intuition. In other words, we shall not be asking whether such and such metaphysical heritage has been able, here and there, to restrict the vigilance of the phenomenologist, but whether the phenomenological form of this vigilance is not already controlled by metaphysics itself. . . . What is at issue . . . is to see the phenomenological critique of metaphysics betray itself as a moment within the history of metaphysical assurance. (SP 4–5)

Before examining how Husserl betrays himself, the force of Derrida's critical strategy needs to be clarified.[28] The metaphysical presupposition Derrida claims to locate in Husserl cannot be a mere matter of carelessness or inattention. Derrida claims to have identified a dogmatic assumption undermining even the subsequent phenomenological method of Husserl's later writings, and thus it is an assumption presupposed by, rather than detected by, this method. The assumption manifests itself in the obscurities and confusions concerning these first steps that Derrida draws to his readers' attention by his various paraphrases and some additional vocabulary (I will return to a discussion of this critical strategy below). For Derrida, then, phenomenology exemplifies, against its reformist agenda, "the classic metaphysics of presence," "the tradition of voluntaristic metaphysics," and the "adherence of phenomenology to classic ontology" (SP 23–25).

What metaphysical assumption makes phenomenology possible and thereby subverts it? Derrida locates it in the soliloquy passage: "The move which justifies this exclusion should teach us a great deal about the metaphysical tenor of this phenomenology. The themes which will arise therein will never again be re-examined by Husserl; on the contrary, they will be repeatedly confirmed. They will lead us to think that in the final analysis what separates expression from indication could be called the immediate nonself-presence of the living present"(SP 37).

In isolating Husserl's central "move," Derrida draws attention to two features of the soliloquy example. Meaning is pictured by Husserl as immediately and faultlessly accessible to self-reflection by way of pure intuition. Second, Husserl models the soliloquy on the act of "speaking." Husserl characterizes speech as uttering words with the intent to put certain "thoughts on record expressively, whether for the man himself, in his solitary state, or for others." It should be recalled, however, that Husserl adds in the passage quoted above that "there is no speech in such cases [soliloquies], nor does one tell oneself anything: one merely conceives of oneself as speaking and communicating." When I turn to Derrida's point about the role of speaking in this passage, Husserl's qualification will be relevant.

Derrida does not directly debate these issues with Husserl, given the type of analysis he favors. Rather, Husserl is to be shown dismantling his own example and distinctions. Derrida's claimed role of the "innocent bystander" before phenomenology's internal collapse is somewhat disingenuous, given how extensively he paraphrases Husserl so as to locate the assumption concerning, in Derrida's words, the "being of the sign." "Pure expression will be the pure active intention (spirit, *psychē*, life, will) of an act of meaning *(bedeuten)* that animates a speech whose content *(Bedeutung)* is present. It is present not in nature, since only indication takes place in nature and across space, but in consciousness. Thus it is present to an 'inner' intuition or perception" (SP 40).

Therefore this paraphrase, if I understand Derrida's strategy, means to capture the ontological assumption in words Husserl did not use, and it is an assumption Husserl did not realize he had made, but it is revealed, nevertheless, upon careful examination of the soliloquy example. Thus Derrida's paraphrase ought not to be taken as introducing the assumption contentiously.

> The notion of *presence* is the core of this demonstration. If communication or intimation *(Kundgabe)* is essentially indicative, this is because we have no primordial intuition of the presence of the other's lived experience. Whenever the immediate and full presence of the signified is concealed, the signifier will be of an indicative nature. (This is why *Kundgabe* . . . does not manifest, indeed, renders nothing manifest, if by manifest we mean evident, open, and presented "in person." The *Kundgabe* announces and at the same time conceals that which it is to inform us about.) (SP 40)

> The reduction of the monologue is really a putting of empirical worldly existence between brackets. In "solitary mental life" we no longer use *real (wirklich)* words, but only imagined *(vorgestellt)* words. And lived experience . . . does not have to be so indicated because it is immediately certain and present to itself. . . . When expression is *full*, nonexistent signs *show* significations *(Bedeutungen)* that are ideal (and thus nonexistent) and certain (for they are presented to intuition). (SP 43)

Derrida's criticism concerns Husserl's distinction of meaning from matters of fact, including matters of linguistic fact. Derrida holds in addition that Husserl's doctrine of intuition, the doctrine that "they [meanings] are presented to intuition" and "we have no primordial intuition of the presence of the other's lived experience," is an ontological doctrine, consonant with the previously defined ontological assumption, and resting upon an implicit and illicit identification of what is real with what is "immediately present" in experience. Before returning to these claims about Husserl below, I want to recall two points from Chapter 1. First, Husserl repeatedly objects to those who understand the theory of intuition as making any ontological claim whatsoever, and specifically the claim that the object of pure intuition (namely, the intentional object) is identical with a real object is explicitly and repeatedly denied by Husserl, as I discussed at some length. Second, Husserl was widely criticized, within and outside the continental tradition, for introducing the doctrine of "pure intuitions" and for failing to suspend all ontological assumptions. I argued in Chapters 1 and 2 that these criticisms are often less persuasive upon closer examination. Whether Derrida's version is more effective remains to be seen.

To begin the closer examination, there is a perplexing confusion in Derrida's paraphrase of Husserl. I call it perplexing, because Derrida seems aware he is introducing it. Throughout his study of Husserl, Derrida freely uses the vocabulary of Saussure, specifically the terms "signified" and "signifier," as though Saussure's terms were interchangeable with Husserl's concepts of *Sinn*, *Bedeutung*, and *Gegenstand*. This violates Derrida's announced approach to Husserl's writings (to work immanently to Husserl's concepts and arguments and not introduce contentious paraphrases) as well as Derrida's expressed reservation about such an identification.[29]

Saussure's "signified," discussed in Chapter 3, separated the content of a "signifier" (word or sound) from its referent. Structural linguistics, for Saussure, concerns the systematic connections between the concept (signified) and the word (signifier) only, and the referent of language can be set aside as an extralinguistic issue. My objection to Derrida's use of Saussure's terminology does not concern the various problems with Saussure's approach briefly mentioned in Chapter 3, but Derrida's surreptitious introduction of contested assumptions and problems into his paraphrasing when Husserl was unaware of Saussure's work and when there is no evidence (or at least Derrida offers no evidence) that Husserl agrees with that way of distinguishing meaning and reference.

For example, Derrida's sentence, "Whenever the immediate and full presence of the signified is concealed, the signifier will be of an indicative nature," distorts the passage it claims to paraphrase. Husserl does not defend the distinction between expression and indication by holding that whenever meaning is "concealed," then a sign functions indicatively. The indicative function of a sign is not a matter of meaning at all in Husserl's account, and thus he rests his case on making a conceptual distinction at this point, a point independent of whether meaningful content is concealed or not (again assuming that the term "signified" would translate Husserl's *Sinn* and *Bedeutung*). Derrida's account, then, is contentious, and it is the paraphrase, not Husserl, that supports Derrida's critical strategy. At least on this one point Husserl does not indict himself.

Ignoring this unnecessary confusion, Derrida's strategy is to drive a wedge between Husserl's distinction between indication and expression and Husserl's notions of "ideal meaning" and "pure intuition." If Derrida can show that these two positions are at odds with one another, Husserl will have, in some sense, betrayed his own project by a suppressed presupposition. Derrida proceeds to direct his readers' attention, again by contentious paraphrasing in my view, to how "ideal meaning" and "pure intuition" are improperly defended by Husserl through a factual feature of communication, namely, speaking, or what Derrida claims is a traditional philosophical dogma concerning the transparency of speech versus writing. Derrida's version of this improper defense is: "When I speak, it belongs to the phenomenological essence of this operation that *I hear myself [je m'entende] at the same time* that I speak. The signifier . . . is in absolute proximity to me" (SP 77).

Setting aside the term "signifier," Derrida presents Husserl as having made the assumption that a physical, contingent connection between speaking and hearing is a priori necessary and thereby illicitly supporting both the autonomy of meaning (its "ideality" in Husserl's conception) and the subsequent distinction between expression and indication at the beginning of *Logical Investigations*. When Husserl pictures meaning as, ideally, immediately present to the mind, he has illicitly introduced a dogma concerning speaking. But then he either rests his distinction on a matter of fact about communication, forbidden to Husserl, or upon a traditional but unexamined philosophical dogma. Hence, the necessity that makes possible Husserl's project of pure philosophical inquiry and distinguishes it from empirical inquiry turns out to be dependent on either an empirical fact or a piece of traditional metaphysics. "Between the phonic element (in the phenomenological sense and not that of a real sound) and expression, taken as a logical character of the signifier that is *animated* in view of the ideal presence of a *Bedeutung* (itself related to an object), there must be a necessary bond" (SP 76).

But I am suspicious of this strategy. As reviewed in Chapter 1, Husserl does think there is a necessary, a priori, pure relation between a sense and its intentional object (it is a conceptual truth for Husserl that any experience is directed toward an object). Husserl does not, however, claim that there is conceptual necessity between meaning and the real object of expression (for him the only necessity possible in that relation is contingent, causal, lawlike necessity). I grant that if Derrida were to show Husserl making such a blunder (namely, confusing conceptual and causal relations), he would weaken our confidence in much of Husserl's analyses. However, I have already raised a warning about the contentious paraphrasing, and the burden falls to Derrida given that Husserl repeatedly points out the "absurdities" arising from precisely this type of error.

Derrida's critical strategy then with regard to Husserl's phenomenology, though unnecessarily convoluted and coy, is at base very simple. The way to undermine Husserl's central project is to undermine the very idea of pure, conceptual truths. One way to undermine that idea is to demonstrate that some analysis of a pure conceptual connection in Husserl rests either upon a contingent matter of fact or, worse, upon a past philosophical dogma. It should be noted, however, before asking whether Derrida shows this, that such a case by case criticism of Husserl's conceptual analysis is not very effective. If Husserl improperly relied on some received historical philosophical doctrine or some contingent matter of fact, that alone would not show the effort to purge such considerations from philosophy is itself illicit; on the contrary, it might support the aim of reform by providing a lesson in how difficult it is to carry out these analyses properly. Derrida still requires a stronger argument to indict phenomenology itself.

Derrida's passage, however, blunts his limited critical strategy, because the passage describes the "necessary connection" in question (the connection Derrida must challenge) as "between the phonic element (in the phenomenological sense and not that of a real sound) and expression." If Derrida's parenthetical remark is noted, and if Derrida is following Husserl's terminology, then the "sense of the phonic element" is an intentional correlate, rather than any feature of the world. Husserlian senses are necessarily distinct from real objects of thought or expression. But then the necessary connection in question only concerns the intentional, adverbial object of analysis.[30]

Derrida's strategy then concerns indicting Husserl for illicitly appealing to the transparent nature of speech as a matter of fact concerning the relationship between speaking and hearing, a relation improperly treated as necessary and pure. The above paraphrase with the parenthetical remark noted does not indicate Husserl making that mistake. Whatever other weaknesses there are in Husserl's project, Husserl consistently distinguishes intentional and real objects of expressions; thus Derrida's objection to this case of conceptual analysis as failing on Husserl's own terms does not succeed.

I want to make clear that I am not declaring Husserl invulnerable to criticism. The fundamental aspects of his theory of meaning have been under attack for much of the twentieth century, ever since Gilbert Ryle raised this line of criticism in his essays on phenomenology. I indicated in previous chapters that I find more value in Husserl's account than others do, though I would not begrudge Derrida joining with the majority.[31] Also, Husserl's attempt to exclude ontological commitment from philosophy, as Husserl himself admitted, has proven more difficult and complex. Granting the force of these criticisms of Husserl, not just any version of them is effective. At minimum, philosophical criticism must be directed to a version of the doctrine that the critic can charitably attribute to the passage in question and then defend. Simply noting weaknesses in Husserl's theory of meaning, for instance, is not enough; one must show that the weaknesses are fatal or in principle not correctable.

In contrast, Derrida often fails to fully capture Husserl's view and proceeds as though with the mere suggestion of a possible inconsistency his work is done. For example, Husserl does not deny that there are contingent features of communication and language use; nor would he deny that meaning is sometimes ambiguous. These concessions are consistent with his project. Although Derrida realizes that the idea of ideal or pure meaning is parasitical on a family of other distinctions going back finally to the a priori/a posteriori distinction, he gives his readers no reasons, other than the questionable paraphrases, for thinking all these distinctions collapse.

I said in Chapter 1 that this family of distinctions has been under attack in recent philosophy and Quine, the source of many of these attacks, holds, in an approach implicit within Derrida's discussion, that "analyticity" involves a "circle of terms" each failing to clarify "analyticity" or parasitical upon it.[32] If Quine were correct, then doctrines of meaning as essence and pure intuition would be defeated in principle. I believe Derrida aims at this type of criticism. Even Quine characterizes this challenge as involving a dogma of the history of philosophy: "Meaning is what essence becomes when it is divorced from the object of reference and wedded to the word."[33]

In the end, however, Derrida provides no reason for abandoning these distinctions and the claim that they fall apart or are dismantled within Husserl's own discussion depends entirely on Derrida's paraphrasing. For example, whether in these paraphrases the term "speech" refers to the factual feature of communication or the so-called philosophical dogma Derrida claims to find throughout the history of philosophy is rarely clear. Rather than proceeding within Husserl, as he advertises his approach, Derrida's case relies on a debatable speculation concerning the history of philosophy, an illicit introduction of terminology unknown to Husserl, and a special use of the term "speech" not found in Husserl.

Even if the history of philosophy were characterized, as Derrida claims it is, by a general and illicit distinction between speech and writing, and even if it could be shown more clearly how that traditional distinction illicitly supports Husserl's concept of meaning, the distinctions in question are not illicit merely by being traditional. Nor is a special use of the term "speech," as some kind of ideology of "the ontology of presence," sufficient to convince us that Husserl's efforts to purge ontological commitment necessarily fail.

Derrida offers his readers a criticism of Husserl but not an interpretation of Husserl. Readers are told that rather than arguing against him, it is the suspect's own words that will incriminate him; Derrida merely asks questions and displays Husserl's answers. Extensive knowledge of Husserl, however, is hardly needed to be suspicious that the self-impeachment supposedly evidenced in these passages is a confession extracted under torture. Derrida's writing style is playful and baroque, containing many Heideggerian traps or pitfalls for the unwary. It would take a true "textual innocent," to coin a phrase, to blindly accept Derrida's rhetorical stance of unobtrusive and attentive commentator. It is hardly by chance that this stance diverts attention from what is contentious, embedded, and at minimum debatable within Derrida's account. It is disingenuous for some of Derrida's enthusiasts then to treat any debate of Derrida's philosophical criticism as necessarily involving a misunderstanding of it or to insist that his account of Husserl is simply beyond reproach.[34]

I said at the start of this section that after discussing Derrida's objections to Husserl I would proceed to consider what larger claims follow from this approach. These larger claims, rightly or wrongly attributed to Derrida, are what have brought about the massive attention he currently enjoys within the academic world and, as seems to be the French fashion, popular culture as well. But to examine these larger claims associated with Derrida's work I am forced to take considerable liberties. Derrida has been viewed by some commentators, for example, by Christopher Norris cited above, as reaching general conclusions concerning philosophy and even metaphysics on the basis of analyses such as the one I have just reviewed. It is difficult to determine whether Norris, whom I will use as my example, is correct about this point, because Derrida's writings raise the art of being coy and evasive about such matters to the level of a science. Efforts to settle such questions would take me beyond the limits of this book, and I only wish to consider whether, if Norris is correct about what Derrida concludes, Derrida would be justified in such conclusions.

There are two general conclusions. First, the meaning of any sufficiently complex system of signs is indeterminate. Second, traditional philosophical disputes should not be resolved, but reconceived as a new form of literature. The second conclusion leads to the view that once the lines between the genres of literature and philosophy have been sufficiently blurred, philosophy is freed from (or deprived of, depending on how one views the matter) such questionable distinctions as those between logic and rhetoric, fact and fiction, or truth and falsity. Philosophy is itself neither reformed nor dismissed, nor does it literally come to an end; it is submerged under a wider study of "textuality" and thereby takes its place within the theory and practice of literary criticism.

The first conclusion appears to be a skeptical one. To conclude that meaning is indeterminate, if the type of indeterminacy in question is specified, would limit the possibility of knowledge, including philosophical knowledge, and it would limit knowledge in principle, not just in fact. Thus Derrida should be understood as not concluding that meaning is indeterminate in a case in which information is scant or corrupt. That conclusion would be neither skeptical nor shocking, though some commentaries on Derrida use contingent examples of indeterminacy in the mistaken belief that they support the stronger, principled conclusion.

This skeptical conclusion then constitutes for Derrida doubts about the very possibility of philosophy. This conclusion, however, would not shock epistemological naturalists of twentieth-century philosophy who would embrace it and who dismiss philosophical projects concerning the foundation of knowledge. For these philosophers, however, this conclusion does not entail skepticism in general or paradoxical beliefs in particular; there are ways to stop philosophizing when needed, as Wittgenstein put it. Thus I find Norris unpersuasive on his claim that Derrida's views about meaning are unique as a challenge to contemporary philosophy.

But there is an additional confusion with regard to attributing this conclusion to Derrida. It is not clear at all, even if we were to grant the generalized skepticism, that Derrida supports it by his deconstructive analyses, such as the one on Husserl. If Derrida were correct about Husserl's theory of meaning, and philosophers who agreed with nothing else here might agree that the theory is wrong, a possible response would consider other theories of meaning. For example, there are theories that reject the notion of ideality, the direct presence of meanings to the mind, or the very concept of intentionality; or perhaps the entire concept of meaning should be abandoned, as Quine recommends. If the analysis of Husserl is taken as a model, Derrida's general skepticism about the determinacy of meanings is not a direct consequence of the specific weaknesses he finds there, especially if such an internal criticism of Husserl were then intended to block any possible theory of meaning.

Derrida's second attributed position concerns escaping philosophy by a larger study of texts. As Norris states it: "Indeed, one of Derrida's chief concerns is to break down the rigid demarcation of realms which holds that 'philosophy' is an autonomous discipline, a pursuit of timeless self-validating truths, having nothing to do with politics and everyday experience."[35] Though attacking the autonomy of philosophy is hardly unique to Derrida, escaping philosophical argument in the fashion Norris attributes to Derrida turns out to be problematic.

Norris's idea is that since philosophy is not a subject matter about which agreement is possible (and thus about which there are any conclusions), then it ought to be studied as poetry or any other literary text. Norris again: "Crucially, it was the intensive reading of Husserl that led him [Derrida] to perceive certain problems in the way of phenomenological enquiry, problems which had to do with writing, inscription and what might be called the 'literary' aspects of philosophy." But this conclusion generalized requires a Zen-like silence. The conclusion, once stated, is open to the very philosophical argument it disdains concerning, for instance, the assumed difference between literary and nonliterary statements or the criteria upon which the distinction rests. Nor can this questioning be avoided by simply denying any difference at all between literary and nonliterary statements (or denying there are any such criteria). Such a strategy would defeat itself since the general case against philosophical claims presupposes this apparently empty distinction.

But suppose the reply is much larger still: Studying the "literary aspects" of philosophy involves no longer pursuing the traditional themes of epistemology and ontology, but introducing wholly new themes and problems. Norris agrees with this version, since he objects to those who take deconstruction as "antiphilosophical." Nothing much can be said against such an effort, just as nothing much can be said against such efforts with regard to any subject matter, not just philosophy. It would certainly be beyond the scope of this book to predict or preempt studies of philosophy that proceed in wholly new and unimaginable ways, at least new and unimaginable to me. Such studies, however, either do or do not bear on traditional philosophy. If they do not bear on philosophy, then there is hardly a reason for philosophical debate about them, nor are their conclusions philosophically significant or shocking; they would be irrelevant, however interesting otherwise. If the results do bear on the philosophical tradition, as Christopher Norris argues they do, then the philosophical implication of Derrida's thesis about meaning must be shown in a manner itself open to criticism, rather than only rhetorically proclaimed. Or, if Norris insists, there must be a defense of the claim that no distinction can be made between what is "rhetorically" and "demonstratively" proclaimed, and that defense must itself be open to criticism (assuming the whole strategy is not one of an infinite regress). Such steps are necessary even were the aim to destroy or undermine traditional philosophical concepts and distinctions. Also, as noted in the above discussion of skepticism, the effort to undermine philosophy is widely entertained by contemporary thinkers anyway, contrary to Norris's belief. Therefore, judged as philosophical criticism, scrutiny of arguments against or about philosophy (no matter how fashionable) cannot be dismissed by a mere turn of phrase (no matter how fashionable).

Notes

1. Ludwig Wittgenstein, *Philosophical Investigations*, trans. G. E. M. Anscombe (New York: Macmillan, 1953), p. 47.

2. "The philosopher is the man who has to cure himself of the many sicknesses of the understanding before he can arrive at the notions of the sound human understanding." Ludwig Wittgenstein, *Remarks on the Foundation of Mathematics*, ed.

G. H. von Wright, R. Rhees, and G. E. M. Anscombe, trans. G. E. M. Anscombe (Cambridge, Mass.: MIT Press, 1967), p. 157.

3. Wittgenstein, *Philosophical Investigations*, p. 51.

4. Jacques Derrida, *Dissemination*, trans. Barbara Johnson (Chicago: University of Chicago Press, 1981), p. 112.

5. Ian Hacking, "Michel Foucault's Immature Sciences," *Nous* 13, no. 1 (March 1979), pp. 39–51.

6. Plato, *The Collected Dialogues of Plato*, ed. Edith Hamilton and Huntington Cairns (New York: Pantheon Books, 1969), p. 511.

7. John Stuart Mill, *A System of Logic*, 8th ed. (New York: Harper and Brothers, 1874), pp. 415f.

8. Hilary Putnam, "Is Semantics Possible?" in *Mind, Language and Reality, Philosophical Papers*, vol. 2 (New York: Cambridge University Press, 1975), pp. 139–152.

9. "From a scientific point of view . . . the notion of a kind, or similarity, is . . . disreputable. Yet some such notion, some similarity sense, was seen to be crucial to all learning, and central in particular to the processes of inductive generalization and prediction which are the very life of science. It appears that science is rotten to the core. Yet there may be claimed for this rot a certain undeniable fecundity." W. V. O. Quine, *Ontological Relativity and Other Essays* (New York: Columbia University Press, 1969), p. 138. There are also Goodman's influential criticisms concerning the notion of "projecting" the properties of kinds. Nelson Goodman, *Fact, Fiction and Forecast* (Indianapolis, Ind.: Bobbs-Merrill, 1965).

10. In his chapter "Open Up a Few Corpses," Foucault attacks those who reconstruct the birth of pathological anatomy and dissection in this fashion: "The same explanation had been repeated: medicine could gain access to that which founded it scientifically only by circumventing, slowly and prudently, one major obstacle, the opposition of religion, morality, and stubborn prejudice to the opening up of corpses" (BC 124). The history of these various "prohibitions" limiting medicine is "historically false," he claims, and a "retrospective justification" of the picture in which "old beliefs" in medicine functioned like Baconian idols. Foucault's alternative picture is not a clash between science and a mass of stubborn prejudices, but a clash between different "types of knowledge."

11. Michel Foucault, *Madness and Civilization*, trans. Richard Howard (London: Tavistock, 1967).

12. Foucault perhaps had in mind Plato's *Phaedrus*, in which it is stated that "there are two kinds of madness, one resulting from human ailments, the other from a divine disturbance of our conventions of conduct." Plato, *Collected Dialogues*, 265b. In Foucault's history of madness, the physiological account of madness as an "ailment" entirely displaces the "divine disturbance of our conventions of conduct" by the late eighteenth century, supporting, thereby, regimes of enforced treatment.

13. François Delaporte, *Civilization and Disease*, trans. Arthur Goldhammer (Cambridge, Mass.: MIT Press, 1986), p. 6.

14. For example, the "syntactic" approach can be found in Foucault's "nominalist reduction" of disease: "In relation to the individual, concrete being, disease is merely a name; in relation to the isolated elements of which it is made up, it has all

the rigorous architecture of a verbal designation. . . . Disease, like a word, is deprived of being, but, like the word, is endowed with a configuration. The nominalist reduction of existence frees a constant truth" (BC 119). The contrasting sociological or functional approach is normally how he introduces various ethical and political themes. "In a regime of economic freedom, the hospital had found a way of interesting the rich; the clinic constitutes the progressive reversal of the other contractual part; it is the *interest* paid by the poor on the capital that the rich have consented to invest in the hospital; and interest that must be understood in its heavy surcharge, since it is a compensation that is of the order of *objective interest* for science and of *vital interest* for the rich. The hospital became viable for private initiative from the moment that sickness, which had come to seek a cure, was turned into a spectacle" (BC 85). Functional explanations involve appealing to how, in terms of their causal effects, conventional classifications, for instance, promote the stability and reproduction of the social structure. Hence, although Delaporte stresses that diseases are not real, he emphasizes the reality of those medical "practices" and their causal effects.

15. Lawrie Reznek, *The Nature of Disease* (New York: Routledge, 1987), p. 166. Lester King has similarly argued: "Health and disease are value judgements based on something more than the study of reactions. . . . All medical science studies facets of behavior under a wide variation in conditions. Many of these variations we call disease. But the grounds for calling them disease are not any essential part of the studies. Disease is an arbitrary designation." Lester King, "What Is Disease?" *Philosophy of Science* 12 (1954), pp. 193–203. He later softened his view somewhat by granting that the imposition of social values "does not convert pregnancy into a disease, but it does show the influence of social pressures on problems of health." *Medical Thinking: A Historical Preface* (Princeton: Princeton University Press, 1982), p. 144.

16. Robert D'Amico, "*Sed Amentes Sunt Isti*: Against Michel Foucault's Account of Cartesian Skepticism," *Philosophical Forum* 26, no. 1 (Fall 1994), pp. 33–48.

17. There is a second quasi-preface in the form of a lengthy commentary on the painting *Las Meninas* by Velázquez that precedes the historical account of the book. If Foucault's reading of *Las Meninas* is that it contains a "representational paradox," then this reading is likely based on a misunderstanding of that painting. Foucault's account is defended by John Searle in "*Las Meninas* and the Paradoxes of Pictorial Representation," *Critical Inquiry* 6, no. 3 (Spring 1980), pp. 477–488. A reply to both Searle and Foucault making a persuasive case against the idea of there being any "representational paradox" in the painting is found in Joel Snyder and Ted Cohen, "Reflections on *Las Meninas*: Paradox Lost," *Critical Inquiry* 7, no. 2 (Winter 1980), pp. 429–447. I also ignore the "Foreword to the English Edition," since Foucault repeats there, in brief, the conclusions of *The Archaeology of Knowledge*.

18. Herbert Butterfield, *The Whig Conception of History* (New York: Norton, 1965), pp. 11–12.

19. Herbert Butterfield, *The Origins of Modern Science: 1300–1800* (New York: Macmillan, 1959), p. ix.

20. The English translator's decision to translate both *nue* and *massif* as "pure" in those places in the above quote where I insert the French is misleading, because

"pure" is used in philosophy to refer to that which is a priori and conceptual, not that which is "primitive" or pretheoretical.

21. Traian Stoianovich, *French Historical Method: The Annales Paradigm* (Ithaca: Cornell University Press, 1976).

22. "Statement" is a translation of *l'énoncé* and is somewhat misleading because of the use of "statement" in Anglo-American philosophy of language and logic. But the literal translation "enunciation" hardly seems much better, and thus I simply follow the translator's alternation between "statement" and "enunciation" where syntactically appropriate.

23. Edward Arthur Burtt, *The Metaphysical Foundations of Modern Physical Science* (London: Routledge & Kegan Paul, 1950), p. 15.

24. Thomas Kuhn, *The Copernican Revolution* (Cambridge, Mass.: Harvard University Press, 1957), pp. 39–40.

25. In an earlier passage, for example, Foucault more accurately states the aim of such logical analysis when he explicitly discusses Bertrand Russell's example, "The present king of France is bald," and concludes: "It can be analyzed from a logical point of view only if one accepts, in the form of a single statement, two distinct propositions, each of which may be true or false" (AK 81).

26. "On ne tue pas l'histoire mais l'histoire des philosophes, ça, qui, je veux la tuer [It's not history, but the history of philosophers that I wish to kill]," *La Quinzaine Littéraire*, no. 40 (March 15, 1968).

27. If another reason for proceeding in this way is needed, these essays have a special significance for Derrida: "*Speech and Phenomena* is the essay I value most." *Positions*, trans. Alan Bass (Chicago: University of Chicago Press, 1981), p. 13.

28. "The movements of deconstruction do not destroy structure from the outside. They are not possible and effective, nor can they take aim, except by inhabiting these structures. Inhabiting them *in a certain way*, because one always inhabits, all the more when one does not suspect it. Operating necessarily from the inside, borrowing all the strategies and economic resources of subversion from the old structure . . . deconstruction always in a certain way falls prey to its own work." Jacques Derrida, *Of Grammatology*, trans. Gayatri Chakravorty Spivak (Baltimore: Johns Hopkins University Press, 1974), p. 24.

29. The distinction between "signifier" and "signified" originated with the linguist Ferdinand de Saussure, whose writings exercised an enormous influence among French philosophers and literary critics during the 1960s and 1970s, as I discussed in Chapter 3. Derrida says of this vocabulary: "The equivalence signifier/expression and signified/*Bedeutung* could be posited were not the *bedeuten*/*Bedeutung*/sense/object structure much more complex for Husserl than for Saussure" (SP 46, n. 5). In view of this comment, it is then perplexing, at least to me, why Derrida proceeds with this equivalence in his various paraphrases.

30. I discuss these issues in Chapters 1 and 2. David Bell distinguishes in his account of Husserl's *Logical Investigations* between a "genuinely or fully relational theory of intentionality" and an "adverbial theory." Bell argues that Husserl held only to the adverbial theory, and Bell criticizes Husserl for failing to then clarify the relation between the intentional object and the corresponding real object. But there is no reason to suggest, as Derrida does, that Husserl would have assumed it was a

pure, a priori relation. Such a position would be wildly inconsistent with the rest of Husserl. See Bell, *Husserl* (New York: Routledge, 1990), pp. 133f.

31. A recent criticism of "meaning rationalism," attacking doctrines such as Husserl's and focusing on the illusion of a self-reflective, transparent mind can be found in Ruth Garrett Millikan, *White Queen Psychology and Other Essays for Alice* (Cambridge, Mass.: MIT Press, 1993), pp. 286–296. "The various different forms of meaning rationalism . . . hold that all aspects of thought lie within and directly before the mind. I conclude that meaning rationalism is untenable, that there are no (a priori known) logical possibilities" (p. 287).

32. For a penetrating summary and criticism of this position in philosophy, see Laurence BonJour, *In Defense of Pure Reason: A Rationalist Account of A Priori Justification* (New York: Cambridge University Press, 1998).

33. W. V. O. Quine, *From a Logical Point of View* (New York: Harper Torchbooks, 1961), p. 22.

34. "His [Derrida's] own early texts on Husserl are evidence enough of Derrida's close and productive engagement with phenomenological thought." Christopher Norris, *Derrida* (Cambridge, Mass.: Harvard University Press, 1987), p. 234. Norris also adopts what is becoming a characteristic defensive strategy. He speaks of Derrida's "vigilant skepticism" against confused critics and how Derrida "shrewdly" blocks such criticism in advance by rejecting the naive critic's very notions of the book, the theme, and the author. "The conceptual operation that extracts 'themes' from writing has its counterpart in the notion that *books* exist as self-enclosed systems of meaning and reference, their signifiers all pointing back toward some 'transcendental signifier' or source of authentic and unitary truth. The traditional idea of the book is of a writing held within bounds by the author's sovereign presence; a writing whose integrity of purpose and theme comes from its acceptance of these proper, self-regulating limits" (*Derrida*, p. 63). I might very well agree (assuming I can follow Norris's jargon) that books are not "self-enclosed systems of meaning and reference," that there is no "transcendental signifier," and that an author is not a "sovereign presence" and yet not agree that Derrida's books are not books, his theses not theses, his positions not positions, though I agree such a defense makes Derrida bulletproof.

35. Norris, *Derrida*, p. 12. The second quotation from Norris in the following paragraph is from this same page.

Suggested Readings

Both figures in this chapter have occasioned a remarkable amount of commentary in recent years extending beyond philosophy to such new domains as postmodernism, poststructuralism, feminism, and cultural criticism, where they are virtually omnipresent. However, for the most part, the issues I have focused upon are ignored or treated uncritically, since commentators often aim at either imitation or manifesting an allegiance.

What I would recommend as an introduction, however, are three recent biographies of Foucault. Likely due to his death from AIDS rather than the normal amount of attention paid to the life of a philosopher these days, these three studies cover similar ground concerning French intellectual life: Didier Eribon, *Michel Fou-*

cault, trans. Betsy Wing (Cambridge, Mass.: Harvard University Press, 1991); James Miller, *The Passion of Michel Foucault* (New York: Simon and Schuster, 1993); David Macey, *The Lives of Michel Foucault* (London: Hutchinson, 1993). Miller pictures Foucault, ironically given the latter's stated opposition to such ideas, as an "existential hero," basing this claim on his private life. Macey and Eribon are, in comparison, fairly sober studies of the significant intellectual movements, debates, themes, and politics of Foucault's time. A useful summary of Foucault's main works can be found in Hubert L. Dreyfus and Paul Rabinow, *Michel Foucault: Beyond Structuralism and Hermeneutics* (Chicago: University of Chicago Press, 1982).

The situation with regard to Derrida is, if such can be imagined, even worse, and the discussion of him grows daily in both range and antagonism. In this chapter I restrict myself to two secondary works by Christopher Norris, *Derrida* (Cambridge, Mass.: Harvard University Press, 1987) and *The Deconstructive Turn: Essays in the Rhetoric of Philosophy* (New York: Methuen, 1983). A critical account accusing Derrida of massive and even malicious misinterpretations of Husserl specifically and the history of philosophy generally can be found in J. Claude Evans, *Strategies of Deconstruction: Derrida and the Myth of the Voice* (Minneapolis: University of Minnesota Press, 1991).

Bibliography

AK: Foucault, M. *The Archaeology of Knowledge.* Translated by A. M. Sheridan Smith. New York: Pantheon Books, 1972.

BC: Foucault, M. *The Birth of the Clinic: An Archaeology of Medical Perception.* Translated by A. M. Sheridan Smith. New York: Pantheon Books, 1973.

Ideas: Husserl, E. *Ideas Pertaining to a Pure Phenomenology and to a Phenomenological Philosophy.* First Book. Translated by Fred Kersten. Boston: Kluwer Academic Publishers, 1982.

Intro: Derrida, J. *Edmund Husserl's "Origin of Geometry": An Introduction.* Translated by John P. Leavey, Jr. Lincoln: University of Nebraska Press, 1989.

LI: Husserl, E. *Logical Investigations.* Translated by J. N. Findlay. London: Routledge & Kegan Paul, 1973.

OT: Foucault, M. *The Order of Things: An Archaeology of the Human Sciences.* New York: Vintage Books, 1973.

SP: Derrida, J. *Speech and Phenomena.* Translated by David B. Allison. Evanston, Ill.: Northwestern University Press, 1973.

CONCLUSION

What is the core of the continental philosophical tradition, how does it compare with analytic philosophy, and is there a future for continental philosophy as a distinct and separate philosophical tradition? In asking the last of these questions, I grant that books about the figures and topics discussed here continue to appear. Also I agree, as should now be obvious, that there are fruitful or interesting issues, analyses, and approaches within this tradition. But there is a difference between studying thinkers and issues as specimens in the history of ideas and viewing them as part of a continuing philosophical project or tradition. Has the latter come to an end?

I intend to paint, in the broadest strokes, the basic impulse for this tradition as I understand it. My aim is to raise criticisms of this philosophical impulse as well as to contrast where it all began, in Husserl and the early Heidegger, with the "good-bye to all that" tone of Foucault and Derrida, for example.

Husserl thought that there were real philosophical problems and that philosophy's "inextinguishable" and cultural task was to answer them. He considered it a cultural crisis that this task had been abandoned. Relativism and irrationalism were symptoms of such a crisis, but he remained convinced that its root was the replacement of philosophical inquiry by empirical science. Nevertheless, Husserl, like his contemporary Bertrand Russell, thought philosophy could become systematic and rigorous inquiry, not in the manner of empirical science, but a science nonetheless.[1]

Finally, philosophy must be distinct from sophistry. Husserl found much of the philosophical debate he knew confused and inconclusive. Rather than merely chastise his fellow philosophers for a collective lack of rigor, he strove for a methodical reform that would serve to filter out and neutralize the surreptitious assumptions and contentious vocabulary that had reduced such debates to rhetoric and assertion.

Did the reform succeed? A method's value lies finally in its results, either in clarifying disputes or guiding us toward answers. Husserl thought he had discovered necessary conditions for experience. Second, he claimed that fears about skepticism were mostly idle or confused.[2] Finally, Husserl defended the view that our thoughts refer to the "real world," not merely the contents of our minds. These three results are examples of how Husserl might be pictured as responding to perennial philosophical problems.

My criticisms of Husserl with regard to the above conclusions are at two levels. First, it is not clear that the above results require, let alone actually emerge from, Husserl's method. Other philosophers have reached similar conclusions through mundane and far less perplexing analyses of what is conceptually presupposed by the notions of knowledge, belief, evidence, or representation.[3] Of course, it is interesting that similar conclusions emerge among theorists, but Husserl's method neither establishes nor defends such conclusions any more securely than does ordinary, pedestrian conceptual analysis. In many cases, on the contrary, Husserl's analyses read as though the process were reversed. Husserl often seems to have grasped the conceptual necessities involved first, only then claiming that unidentified phenomenological exercises support the result. Often the claim about the proposed necessities is easier to defend, on its own terms, than the cumbersome methodological vocabulary, details, and qualifications he struggled with and continually revised.

Second, Husserl makes the above results depend on an act of recognition or "seeing," albeit in an abstract sense, rather than on argumentative reasoning (even taking argument and reasoning, as I am, very broadly). As I quoted earlier, Husserl speaks in *Crisis* of how in the phenomenological method the a priori necessities of intentionality are "exhibited rather than argumentatively constructed or conceived through mythical thinking" (Crisis 181). He seems to take it that since the necessities are in this way "exhibited," one is thereby absolved of any further defense or argument.

But philosophical debate can hardly be resolved in this fashion, assuming with Husserl that it is a serious form of debate. The resolution of even perennial philosophical debates must include some larger account of why one "must," the word being used in a sense of a priori that has been clarified and is neutral with regard to the debate in question, understand experience in such and such a way. To think it is a matter of simply "seeing" that it is so underestimates the resources of one's philosophical opponent.

The appeal to "seeing" and "intuition" becomes deeply misleading, therefore. To "see" a conclusion as inconsistent or a claim as incoherent is to grasp the reasoning involved. It is only a well-worn metaphor that uses the verb "to see" in such a context. As Husserl correctly understood elsewhere, normally perception cannot be challenged on grounds of consistency or coherence; that is simply how something appears. It is only in going beyond what is in this way given to experience that the fundamental disputes and issues arise; even if the debate is properly a matter of critically examining what "given in experience" means, that is not a matter literally of "seeing" that it means such and such.

Precisely at these points Husserl blurs matters. He speaks, properly enough, of the intuitions to which one is directed for purposes of philosophical debate as self-evident or pure. By such terms he means that pure intuitions are independent of physical or psychological contingencies. But that appeal to self-evidence illicitly transfers, without discussion, to Husserl's philosophical views, specifically to the way he then systematizes these intuitions. This mimicry of those contemporaries he began by criticizing has the unfortunate consequence of exacerbating persistent misreadings of Husserl and his idealism. Intuitions are, as Husserl says, "exhibited"; they are not themselves matters for argument. That is why they properly function as evidence within philosophical dispute. But the inextinguishable task of philosophy only begins there. Such evidence could no more directly resolve philosophical debates than observational data could directly resolve matters in the empirical sciences. There must also be, roughly stated, the systematic or theoretical discussions of a philosophical position, systematizations subject to further argument, modification, and clarification by appeal to pure intuitions. Properly understood, phenomenological analyses direct thought to the kind of evidence appropriate for philosophical knowledge. Husserl's idealism, to summarize, requires a defense and does not automatically follow from an appeal to pure intuitions, as he clarified that notion and cleansed it of philosophical presuppositions.

I now turn to the even more difficult task of capturing Heidegger's contribution to or modification of this philosophical project. I begin with Heidegger's criticisms of Husserl. The weaknesses of Husserl's epistemological project of pure inquiry and his commitment to idealism were, as I have already said above, the central points to challenge, and Heidegger's criticisms are examples of how a philosophical tradition evolves through such critical reflection. Yet for a philosophical tradition to continue, such criticisms must remain part of some continuing philosophical project. In the case of Heidegger, for at least the early part of his career, the study of ontology was understood to subsume problems of epistemology and effectively dissolve the traditional debates between realism (materialism) and idealism.

Heidegger's defense of the philosophical study of ontology against the contribution of the sciences is an important and worthwhile philosophical point. Whether one agrees with Heidegger's subsequent analyses, he contributed to reviving metaphysics and ontology against the widely held assumption that such efforts were futile exercises in "armchair" science. Although Heidegger also held that such inquiry had been misunderstood in traditional philosophy, he claimed that those misunderstandings were at the root of the dogma of scientific naturalism and the efforts to abandon philosophical inquiry. Even more speculatively, Heidegger claimed that such a form of naturalism had already been present in ancient philosophy, specifically in Plato. Only in the fragments of the pre-Socratics, he mused, could philosophy be glimpsed as undertaken outside of these assumptions.

Whether he was correct about these historical claims, Heidegger was quite justified in challenging those contemporaries, for instance, who thought the techniques of advanced formal logic would transform any metaphysical or ontological dispute into some simple syntactic confusion. Thus, as I argued in Chapter 2, the distinction between ontic and ontological questions does a great deal of work in opening up a space for autonomous philosophical inquiry into the world that is distinct from naturalistic inquiry, whether scientific or commonsensical. Thus he was able to preserve the central aim of Husserl to reinvigorate a philosophy freed from either scientific or popular opinion, even while rejecting much of Husserl's project.

Any inquiry, however, requires constraints. Others must be able to arrive, then, at the same conclusions on these topics in such a way that those conclusions follow, in some fashion yet to be specified, from either defended or broadly uncontroversial assumptions; at least these conditions are necessary if there is to be a tradition and not a single thinker's personal vision.[4]

In those terms Heidegger's alternative to Husserl's project is vastly underargued, but in a manner quite distinct from my previous criticism of Husserl. Though some commentators continue to think that Heidegger's Dasein-analysis, for instance, remains a significant philosophical result, even supporters remain perplexed about how Heidegger arrived at those conclusions, what exactly this analysis contributes to the "question of being," as Heidegger announced it, and what philosophical conclusions are meant to follow from it.[5] If even defenders of Heidegger are led to speak of much of the literature on him as "fawning gibberish," then perhaps the fault lies in the nature of the project rather than the personal failings of his followers.[6]

A philosophical tradition requires an open horizon of issues, problems, and possible clarifications. It cannot consist of only the "founding" texts. It must also be clear how to go on and do what the "founding" texts did. I think the study of ontology is possible and that such a topic need not reduce to either pure formalism or scientism.[7] I do not see how a tradition of such study could proceed, however, from Heidegger's directions, nor do I believe even he thought it possible; his turning away from philosophy and toward private, poetic insights seems evidence of that doubt to me. Whether I am correct in characterizing his career in this way and whether the turning away from philosophy was more profound than I am able to see, a philosophical tradition it did not and does not make.

After World War II, philosophers began to reflect on the fact that contemporary philosophy seemed to divide into these two separate traditions and naturally sought to compare them. At first the comparison was taken up by analytic philosophers, especially in England, who claimed that the analytic and continental traditions dovetailed.[8] Recently, the debate has changed and more often consists of defenders of the continental tradition criticizing the limitations and aridity of analytic philosophy. The relatively pedestrian and old-fashioned concerns of analytic philosophy are treated as eclipsed by a diverse and rich panoply of relativistic, historicist, and sociological projects that are thought now to properly belong within a broad conception of continental philosophy.[9] I have nothing much to contribute to this second stage of the debate, except to agree that some current fascination with the continental tradition is not an interest in philosophy at all; it seems motivated primarily by political and literary agendas. Furthermore, where the two traditions may have been thought to dovetail, the matter is now largely moot, since ongoing philosophy work that could be treated as distinct from the mundane, pedestrian philosophy the above critics reject as passÈ has utterly disappeared.

There are many surface differences between these traditions that I am setting aside. The nature of the writing in the two traditions, which I often mentioned in my own account, and the state of the secondary literature are important aspects of this difference, but finally even they are not central. I often find Husserl's approach very frustrating, and he became even more rigid, jargonistic, and often needlessly obscure as he aged. I also often sense that Heidegger's bent to produce a quirky literary effect actually smothers any possible critical debate about what he is attempting and how he is attempting it. But, as Dallas Willard suggests in note 9, passages in Wittgenstein are equally enigmatic and frustrating, and therefore it could not be the kind of difference to focus upon in understanding a division in how philosophy came to be studied in the twentieth century.

My conclusion is that the central difference is that analytic philosophy remained, even given large and contentious debates about its core ideas, a philosophical movement, whereas the continental tradition has largely ceased to be one; whether continental philosophy is, on the contrary, some postmodern literary phenomenon, as some would apparently have it, is thankfully not my concern. I can imagine some readers objecting that both logical positivism and the ordinary language movements in analytic philosophy, since I am accepting the broadest conception of the term "analytic philosophy," also claimed to abandon traditional philosophy. Why do I ignore these efforts in my claim that analytic philosophy remains a philosophical tradition? But these strategies within analytic philosophy were widely debated, have been dismissed or greatly modified from their original form in what continues to be called analytic philosophy, and even when put forward were accompanied by different philosophical tasks substituting for the discredited efforts of the past; thus these criticisms were more in the spirit of Husserl than Foucault.

In contrast, the continental tradition has reached in effect a curious consensus among its recent proponents (though "consensus" is not quite the right word) in which, if I may put it crudely, epistemological naturalism has effectively triumphed (using the phrase in Husserl's sense). Whether it is Foucault abandoning philosophy for history, or Derrida proclaiming, in so many, many words, that it is impossible to distinguish between what is a priori and a posteriori, the intent is to be against the possibility of philosophy; I agree that these thinkers remain critical of the sciences, but naturalism for Husserl was a larger position than that of the sciences. The point is that to be freed from this meddlesome discipline is taken by these figures, just as it was for the original positivists, as liberating; it is for these postmodernists and poststructuralists the freedom from the constraints of necessity, generality, and universality, which, once discredited, allow a thousand flowers to bloom.

When I say, therefore, that the continental tradition has come to an end, I do not mean, as I hope is apparent, that Foucault or Derrida, for example, actually mount a decisive case against Husserl or in defense of their broad attack on the possibility of philosophical reflection. What I do mean is that the core tasks of the tradition are not being carried on or even criticized any longer as philosophical tasks; if mentioned at all, they are taken as rhetorical or literary matters. Setting aside the seemingly endless supply of summaries of Husserl and Heidegger (let alone of Foucault and Derrida), there is now simply a deafening silence on the continental side of the philosophical divide. Whether philosophers ought to have carried on the work of this tradition is a proper, but separate, question. If it were to be undertaken once again, it would find itself within and against a culture (and an academy) in a trenchantly antiphilosophical mood, postmodernism only being its most recent and perhaps shallowest expression. In recalling, as this century comes to an end, Husserl's effort to take philosophy seriously once again at the turn of the last century, against an earlier but reminiscent cultural and intellectual mood, it does seem "The more things change . . ."

Notes

1. "Apart from one or two brief flirtations, British thinkers have showed no inclination to assimilate philosophical to scientific enquiries; and a fortiori no inclination to puff philosophy up into the Science of sciences. Conceptual enquiries differ from scientific enquiries not in hierarchical rank but in type . . . they are not on the same ladder. . . . Husserl wrote as if he had never met a scientist-or a joke." Gilbert Ryle, *Collected Papers*, vol. 1 (London: Hutchinson, 1971), p. 181.

2. Husserl's way of dismissing the problem of skepticism weakens his case against naturalistic epistemology. Why are "reliabilist" accounts of knowledge, for instance, countersensical or inadequate, given that the threat of skepticism is otiose?

Husserl's arguments against epistemological naturalism, then, turn on his appeal to the largely unclarified notion of the a priori.

3. For example, Paul Grice, "The Causal Theory of Perception," in *Studies in the Way of Words* (Cambridge, Mass.: Harvard University Press, 1989), pp. 224-247. Not only do Grice and Husserl share reasons for rejecting other philosophical accounts, such as sense-datum theories, but Grice's central thesis, that the causal theory of perception is "a necessary rather than a contingent truth," echoes Husserl's approach to the problem. I realize, in the comments that follow, that some analytic philosophers have raised challenges concerning the possibility of conceptual analysis and its results. But these challenges would also count against Husserl. For a recent exchange over conceptual analysis, see Frank Jackson, "Armchair Metaphysics," and Gilbert Harman, "Doubts About Conceptual Analysis," in *Philosophy in Mind: The Place of Philosophy in the Study of Mind*, ed. Michaelis Michael and John O'Leary-Hawthorne (Boston: Kluwer, 1994), pp. 23-48.

4. "Nearly all philosophers seek answers to such questions as the nature of substance, mind, intelligence, consciousness, sensation, perception, knowledge, wisdom, truth, identity, infinity, divinity, time, explanation, causation, freedom, purpose, goodness, duty, the virtues, love, life, happiness, and so forth. When we think of the sort of things that would qualify as answers to questions of this sort, three features stand out-universality, generality, and necessity." George Bealer, "On the Possibility of Philosophical Knowledge," *Philosophical Perspectives* 10 (1996), pp. 2-3.

5. "The rich and detailed ontology of Dasein is a remedy against superficial reductionisms and eliminative materialisms which abound in the modern philosophical tradition." Herman Philipse, "Heidegger's *Question of Being*: A Critical Interpretation," in *European Philosophy and the American Academy*, ed. Barry Smith (La Salle, Ind.: Monist Library of Philosophy, 1994), p. 106. Though Philipse argues against what he calls Heidegger's "anti-naturalist thesis" that "human existence is ontologically more fundamental than nature as science understands it," he does not make his case against any of Heidegger's statements or defenses of this "anti-naturalist thesis." One looks in vain for such a defense in Heidegger's writings.

6. David E. Cooper, *Heidegger: Thinkers of Our Time* (London: Claridge, 1996), p. 89.

7. Two recent studies of fundamental ontology of this opinion are: Peter van Inwagen, *Material Beings* (Ithaca: Cornell University Press, 1990) and John Searle, *The Construction of Social Reality* (New York: Free Press, 1995). An attempt to rescue Husserl's approach can be found in Barry Smith, "Logic and Formal Ontology," in *Husserl's Phenomenology: A Textbook*, ed. J. N. Mohanty and W. McKenna (Washington, D.C.: University Press of America, 1989), pp. 29-67.

8. *Linguistic Analysis and Phenomenology*, ed. Wolfe Mays (Lewisburg, Penn.: Bucknell University Press, 1972). This book is a record of a conference titled "Philosophers into Europe" held at the University of Southhampton in 1969. For the authors and discussants at the conference, the central figures of the philosophical detente between Britain and the continent were J. N. Findlay, A. J. Ayer (who commented on Merleau-Ponty's work), and Gilbert Ryle.

9. Dallas Willard, in strong language, has recently argued that the recent fascination with continental thought in academic departments beyond philosophy is spurred by the recent fashion in skeptical, antagonistic, and idiosyncratic stances.

"What this all really comes down to, I think, is that 'deconstruction' is not a *method* of thought. It is at best a set of *claims about* thought and discourse and their meanings. . . . You will not find a sound argument, or even anything put forward as such, for Derrida's earth-shaking conclusion. . . . Derrida is a brilliant and fascinating individual who has been able to make a personal style look like cognitive substance in a professional context where knowledge in the traditional sense has already been socially displaced." Dallas Willard, "The Unhinging of the American Mind," *European Philosophy and the American Academy,* ed. Barry Smith (La Salle, Ind.: Monist Library of Philosophy, 1994), pp. 17-18. Willard, not to be taken as partisan, draws a parallel then with the lionization of Wittgenstein within enclaves of the analytic tradition similarly sustained by a "personal style." A recent study of Husserl makes Willard's point, since it ends on a note of "postmodernist" triumph. "[Husserl] thus came to recognize that the phenomenological method was a powerful instrument for achieving progress in truth by regressive clarification of the historicity of philosophy itself. . . . Philosophy's role is ever to seek alternatives, and to criticize comfortable conclusions. Hence, there can be no totalizing syntheses." Richard Cobb-Stevens, *Husserl and Analytic Philosophy* (Boston: Kluwer, 1990), p. 200.

INDEX